Virtue Ethics

A Pluralistic View

CHRISTINE SWANTON

OXFORD
UNIVERSITY PRESS

OXFORD

UNIVERSITY PRESS

Great Clarendon Street, Oxford ox2 6DP

Oxford University Press is a department of the University of Oxford
It furthers the University's objective of excellence in research, scholarship,
and education by publishing worldwide in

Oxford New York

Auckland Cape Town Dar es Salaam Hong Kong Karachi
Kuala Lumpur Madrid Melbourne Mexico City Nairobi
New Delhi Shanghai Taipei Toronto

with offices in

Argentina Austria Brazil Chile Czech Republic France Greece
Guatemala Hungary Italy Japan South Korea Poland Portugal
Singapore Switzerland Thailand Turkey Ukraine Vietnam

Published in the United States
by Oxford University Press Inc., New York

© Christine Swanton 2003

The moral rights of the author have been asserted
Database right Oxford University Press (maker)

First published 2003
First published in paperback 2005

British Library Cataloguing in Publication Data

Data available

Library of Congress Cataloging in Publication Data
Swanton, Christine, 1947–
Virtue ethics : a pluralistic view / Christine Swanton.
p. cm.
1. Virtue. 2. Ethics. I. Title.
BJ1531 .S93 2003   179′.9—dc21   2002070156
ISBN 0–19–925388–9
ISBN 0-19–927847–4 9780199278473 (pbk.)

1 3 5 7 9 10 8 6 4 2

Printed in Great Britain
on acid-free paper by
Biddles Ltd., King's Lynn, Norfolk

To All My Family

ACKNOWLEDGEMENTS

My academic debts are many. My greatest, by far, is to my friend and colleague Rosalind Hursthouse, with whom I have over a long period of time discussed virtue ethics and Aristotle. I benefited greatly from her comments on an earlier draft of the manuscript. For the development of my views on what Nietzsche (and continental philosophy in general) can offer virtue ethics, I am indebted to Michael Slote, Robert Solomon, Kathy Higgins, and Julian Young. I owe to Marcia Baron a better understanding of Kant than I would otherwise possess and my thanks to her for critical comment. To members of the Hume Society, especially Rachel Cohon, Jacqueline Taylor, and Geoffrey Sayre McCord, I owe thanks for a better understanding of Hume's ethics. For discussion, my gratitude also to Neera Badhwar, Jonathan Dancy, Walter Sinnott-Armstrong, Linda Zagzebski, Maria Merritt, Julia Driver, and, especially, to Viviane Robinson for our collaboration and discussion of the application of theory to practice. For discussion of Christian ethics, I thank my son, Julian, and John Bishop.

I am grateful to the following for permission to reprint material previously published elsewhere.

A section of Chapter 1 is reprinted from 'Virtue Ethics', *International Encyclopedia of Social and Behavioral Science*, 16218–24, © Elsevier Science 2001. Reprinted with permission from Elsevier Science.

Chapter 2 is reprinted with minor modifications from 'Virtue Ethics, Value-Centredness, and Consequentialism', *Utilitas* 13 (2001), 212–235, © Edinburgh University Press 2001. By permission of the editor of *Utilitas* and the publishers.

Chapter 6, section iv is based on 'The Supposed Tension between "Strength" and "Gentleness" Conceptions of the Virtues', *Australasian Journal of Philosophy*, 75 (1997), 497–510. Reproduced by permission of Oxford University Press.

Chapter 11 is reprinted with minor modifications from 'A Virtue Ethical Account of Right Action', *Ethics* 112 (2001), 32–52, © The University of Chicago. All rights reserved.

CONTENTS

x   CONTENTS

Introduction

The academic context of virtue ethics in its modern incarnation has largely been its opposition to the two kinds of moral theory that have dominated moral philosophy in recent times. These are consequentialism and Kantianism. The need for contrast has precipitated a corresponding need to define virtue ethics 'as such'. There has been pressure to distil features which all virtue ethics supposedly share. As a result, there has been a tendency to define the genus 'virtue ethics' in terms of its dominant species, neo-Aristotelianism. It is true that neo-Aristotelianism has been salient in the understanding of virtue ethics. Its distinctive conception of right action as action that would be chosen by a virtuous agent, and its eudaimonistic conception of virtue status, have satisfied a desire for a relatively tidy and assimilable contrast with consequentialism and Kantianism. However, the moral philosophical climate is changing. Virtue ethics is becoming more familiar, and it is time now for the articulation of more varied understandings of the theory. As a genus, virtue ethics should be thought of as analogous to consequentialism, as opposed to, say, hedonistic utilitarianism. This book contributes to the varied understandings of virtue ethics by outlining a theory which is pluralistic, and which differs from neo-Aristotelianism. The pluralism embraces both the conception of virtue, and the view of rightness of action based on that conception.

The basis of my pluralistic virtue ethics lies in my conception of virtue. A virtue is defined in Chapter 1 as a disposition to respond to or acknowledge, in an excellent (or good enough) way, items in the field of a virtue (whether those items are people, objects, situations, inner states, or actions). This conception leads to a pluralistic virtue ethics on the assumption that some or all of the following are true:

(1) The fundamental *bases* of responsiveness to items in the fields of the virtues are plural.

(2) The fundamental *modes* or forms of responsiveness to items in the fields of the virtues are plural.

(3) What *makes* traits of character virtues is not just one feature (such as the promotion of good states of affairs or benefiting the agent), but several features.

(4) The standard of what makes responsiveness to items in the field(s) of a virtue *excellent* or *good enough* is not something single, such as the responsiveness of a fully healthy or excellent specimen of a human being.

(5) The conception of rightness of action involves a pluralistic account of the right.

My virtue ethics is pluralistic in all the above ways. In this introduction, let me briefly explain these features. First, I possess a pluralistic view of the bases of moral responsiveness or acknowledgement. A basis of moral responsiveness is a morally significant feature of the item responded to or acknowledged, and which at least partially grounds or rationalizes the form or mode of acknowledgement. For consequentialists, the basis of moral responsiveness to things or states of affairs is their value, and for consequentialists, that value grounds a requirement to *promote* it (maximally or satisfactorily). For Nietzsche on some readings, the basis of moral responsiveness is also value (e.g. the 'life-affirming' values which sweep away the creeping sickness and ugliness of mediocrity), but that value grounds not simply a requirement to promote it, but rather a requirement to promote it *through* those acts of creativity which express fine motives of strength. For Kantians, the basis of moral acknowledgement of things is their status (such as status as an individual having dignity or intrinsic worth), and this morally significant feature justifies a requirement to treat with respect. For relationship ethics, the fundamental basis of moral acknowledgement of things is the bonds of relationship between them, and those bonds ground primarily the mode of responsiveness of love or at least receptivity. Various forms of love or receptivity range from care and agape to the various forms of partialistic love: parental love, the affection of friendship, the love/caring/concern of therapist, teacher, doctor, or nurse. On my view there is some truth in all these ethical views, and this truth needs to be preserved in a pluralistic virtue ethics.

Second, I possess a pluralistic conception of what I call the fundamental *modes* of moral responsiveness or acknowledgement, modes such as love, respect, creativity, and promotion. We not only promote value or good, but also respect individuals in virtue of various kinds of status, show bonds of love, appreciate things, create things of high quality, are receptive to the value in things, and so on.[1] What I call the *profile* of a virtue is that constellation of modes of moral responsiveness or acknowledgement which comprise the virtuous disposition. I shall argue that virtues standardly have a complex profile, that is, they require of an agent that she respond to items in their fields through several different modes. Furthermore, I share the standard virtue-ethical view that all virtue expresses fine inner states of the agent, and that therefore each mode of moral acknowledgement, insofar as it is part of the profiles of the virtues, expresses such states. Part II discusses those modes of moral acknowledgement that are central to all virtue.

Third, the plurality of bases and modes of moral acknowledgement precludes, on my view, a monistic conception of what makes a trait of character a virtue. On my view, what makes a trait of character a virtue is that it is a disposition of sufficiently good responsiveness to items in their fields, and the modes of responsiveness are plural. This view effectively rules out not only virtue consequentialism, but also monistic forms of relationship ethics of love or care and a version of eudaimonism according to which *the* rationale of *all* the virtues is their being needed for the flourishing (good) of the agent.

Fourth, on my view, virtue is a threshold concept. This implies that the requirements for virtue are not set by one standard, for example, that attainable by the ideally healthy or splendid human specimen (see Chapter 3). The standards for virtue should reflect the fact that the world is marred by the difficulty of attaining (full) virtue, and the all too frequent occurrence of catastrophe, scarcity, evil, and conflict. The standards for meeting thresholds of virtue are thus plural, in the sense of contextual, and what is salient and important for behaviour to count as displaying virtue will vary. Importantly, the standards are to some extent relative to the individual's own capacities (understood in a dynamic sense). This view has implications for a virtue-ethical understanding of the demandingness of ethics (see Chapter 9).

---

[1] I use the terms 'mode of response' or 'acknowledgement' in a sense much broader than they are sometimes used, as in Steven Tudor's exploration of compassion and remorse as modes of moral acknowledgement of the 'Other'. See his *Compassion and Remorse: Acknowledging the Suffering Other* (Leuven: Peeters, 2001).

Fifth and finally, my virtue ethics has a pluralistic conception of right-ness of action. I shall claim (Chapter 11) that virtuous action is action which hits the target of a virtue, and right action is overall virtuous. Since the profiles of the virtues are complex, there is a corresponding com-plexity and plurality in the requirements for virtuous action and thereby right action. For example, a right act may be a generous act or a benevo-lent act, but a benevolent or generous act may (variously) be one that pro-motes good, promotes value, shows love for certain individuals, expresses an 'overflowing' sense of a need to expend, respects a person's status as deserving of benefit. For example, we (at times) withhold the label 'benevolent' in our description of an act which promotes good but expresses a stingy misanthropy; which promotes good but fails to display love towards beneficiaries; which promotes good but fails to respect sta-tus as unworthy to receive such benefit, or which callously or negligently disregards the superior claims of more deserving candidates; which pro-motes good but fails to respect status as autonomous or independent; which promotes good but is completely unappreciative of the qualities of the beneficiary; which promotes the good of strangers but egregious-ly fails to express bonds of love to near and dear.

Although it is time for alternative possibilities within virtue ethics to be presented, and although my book is a contribution to that end, we should not lose sight of the fact that the similarities between species of virtue ethics are more important than their differences. It still should be recognized that virtue ethics as a genus has a distinctive way of concep-tualizing the moral universe. To be taken seriously as a separate kind of moral theory, virtue ethics must offer its own virtue-centred conceptions of fundamental moral ideas: the modes and bases of moral response (as they feature in virtue), objectivity, the demandingness of ethics, practice, rightness of actions, 'maximizing' or 'satisficing' conceptions of ethics. In this book I spend considerably more time in this endeavour than in arguing for the superiority of virtue ethics over its rivals. Accordingly, I do not offer knock-down arguments which at any rate in the realm of moral theory have little or no chance of total success. It is much more important for virtue ethics to rise to its own challenges, for example, to remedy the neglect of the problem of demandingness (see Part III) and to provide an adequate epistemology (see Part IV). However, for virtue ethics to be taken seriously and then thrive, a certain amount of ground must be cleared. The ground with the toughest thickets, in my view, is consequentialism. Accordingly, I devote some time to reducing the vigour of the apparent truisms that make consequentialist theory retain its power over our thought (see Chapter 2). (This is not the same project as providing knock-down arguments.) By contrast, the differences between virtue ethics and Kantianism have I think been overdrawn. Rosalind Hursthouse in *On Virtue Ethics*[2] has done much to rehabilitate reason and 'dutiful' motivations as central in the virtuous agent, and to lessen the contrasts between Aristotle and Kant on the distinctions between *enkrateia* or continence and virtue. Recent interpretations of the Categorical Imperative by Christine Korsgaard and Barbara Herman, and the recent attention to Kant's *Metaphysics of Morals* by, for example, Marcia Baron and Onora O'Neill have done much to establish Kant's emphasis on relationship, humanity, emotions, love, respect, and virtue.

Although I prefer to get on with the job of developing a virtue ethics than in tarrying over questions of definition, the issue of definition of virtue ethics cannot be ignored. Taking heed of Julia Driver's distinction between virtue theory and virtue ethics,[3] one might ask: why should I take myself to be offering a variety of virtue ethics as opposed to virtue theory? All the major moral theories including Kantianism and utilitarianism can offer a theory of virtue, that is, a theory of the nature of virtue, but what makes a theory virtue ethics? 'Virtue ethics' resists precise definition, and rightly so. For as I mentioned, it is frequently observed that virtue ethics in its modern development is still in its infancy. It should not therefore be shackled by preconceived ideas about its progeniture and nature. However, this much at least can be said. In virtue ethics, the notion of virtue is central in the sense that conceptions of rightness, conceptions of the good life, conceptions of 'the moral point of view' and the appropriate demandingness of morality, cannot be understood without a conception of relevant virtues. This book displays the pivotal role of virtue in all these central issues of normative ethical theory.

The claim that virtue is central in virtue ethics is not the claim that other important moral concepts, such as status, bonds, good, value, are not employed in virtue ethics. Virtues are, after all, dispositions of responsiveness to items in the world, and these items have morally significant features (such as status, value, or a good) which shape the requirements for appropriateness of response. The claim that virtue is central in virtue ethics is not therefore opposed to Bernard Williams's defence of pluralism:

---

2 Oxford: Oxford University Press, 1999.
3 In 'The Virtues and Human Nature', in Roger Crisp (ed.), *How Should One Live? Essays on the Virtues* (Oxford: Clarendon Press, 1996), 111–29.

If there is such a thing as the truth about the subject matter of ethics—the truth, we might say, about the ethical—why is there any expectation that it should be simple? In particular, why should it be conceptually simple, using only one or two ethical concepts, such as *duty* or *good state of affairs*, rather than many?[4]

A focus on the primary task of developing a virtue ethics will shift attention away from common objections to 'virtue ethics' as such. There are two reasons for a relative lack of explicit attention to these objections except insofar as they help develop the positive account. First, some common objections have already been dealt with in an excellent way. In his 'Internal Objections to Virtue Ethics',[5] David Solomon has persuasively addressed what he calls 'the self-centredness objection', 'the action-guidingness objection', and 'the contingency objection'. Some of these objections have also been discussed in detail in books; for example, Julia Annas discusses the first in relation to Greek ethics[6] and Rosalind Hursthouse the second.[7] Second, some of these objections derive their apparent power from simplistic skeletal understandings of 'virtue ethics'. The best way to combat them is to develop virtue-ethical theories to replace these skeletal understandings, and then it may turn out the objections fail to get a purchase. Not only is it the case that the self-centredness objection stems from faulty understandings of eudaimonism (see Chapter 4), but not all virtue ethics need be eudaimonistic. Secondly, it is arguable that even monological versions of virtue ethics, where a virtuous agent is compared to a wine taster relying on her own discernment, can avoid the objection that virtue ethics is insufficiently action-guiding.[8] Furthermore, not all virtue ethics need be monological. Mine is not (see Chapter 12).

Though a virtue ethics ideally needs to provide a full account of its distinctive views of fundamental moral ideas, the task of providing anything like a complete pluralistic virtue ethics is large indeed. The immensity of the task is due to two major features. Given that I share the standard virtue-ethical belief that virtues express fine inner states, the delineation of virtue needs to be informed by psychological theories of character which give a sufficiently deep account of those states. Such

---

[4] *Ethics and the Limits of Philosophy* (London: Fontana/Collins, 1985), 17.

[5] Reprinted in Daniel Statman (ed.), *Virtue Ethics: A Critical Reader* (Edinburgh: Edinburgh University Press, 1997), 165–79.

[6] See *The Morality of Happiness* (Oxford: Oxford University Press, 1993).

[7] See *On Virtue Ethics*.

[8] See Solomon, 'Internal Objections to Virtue Ethics', esp. 176.

theories enable us to distinguish between, for example, virtuous and vicious (or non-virtuous) forms of aggression, love, politeness, obedience, ambition, compassion, productivity, and creativity. Thus one needs, for example, distinctions such as benign and malignant aggression;[9] respectful politeness and compliance with legitimate rules, requests, and commands on the one hand, and weak complaisance or submissiveness on the other;[10] 'genuine' love and passive-dependent love; productive, valuable, or high-quality creativity and grandiose creativity; altruism expressive of strength and altruism expressive of weakness; sublimation and shrinking withdrawal/resignation; self-protection and selfishness; a proper sense of one's limitations and place in the world, and self-effacing, cringing humility; toleration and acceptance, and blind charity. Theories offering accounts of these distinctions are complex and to varying degrees controversial, and in the course of this book I have space to touch on just some of them. My main concern is to show the importance of this kind of theory for such virtue-ethical concerns as the integration of modes of moral acknowledgement in the profiles of the virtues, the importance of self-love for understanding such virtues as benevolence and caring, and the development of a virtue-ethical conception of objectivity in ethics and of demandingness in ethics.

A second reason for the immensity of the task of providing a fully detailed pluralistic virtue ethics lies in the multiple aspects of the pluralism. A full development of a pluralistic virtue ethics requires an account of the several features which comprise the pluralism, such as all the bases and modes of moral acknowledgement and their manifestation in virtue.

Given that I cannot provide a theory that is both complete in scope and very detailed, I could have concentrated more or less entirely on one or two of its central features: for example, the relation between virtue, the evaluation of action, and practice; the problems of demandingness and objectivity in ethics; the relation between virtue, the good life, and the moral; the modes of moral responsiveness and acknowledgement

9 See Erich Fromm, *The Anatomy of Human Destructiveness* (London: Penguin Books, 1977; first published 1973).
10 It interested me that several times taking classes in New Zealand, and reading papers in Australia, the idea that politeness is a virtue was treated with derision, even shock. It was sad that politeness was identified by many in that part of the world with complaisance, submissiveness, and even deference for the sake of gain.

constituting the profiles of the virtues. For each of these general topics deserves a book-length treatment. However, in the current moral philosophical climate there is a need for virtue ethics not only to display the variety of possibilities within it but to explicate its distinctive way of understanding the moral universe as a whole. It is important therefore to show how the various concepts in various types of virtue ethics relate to each other, and to provide thereby fresh understanding of the central problems of ethics. I have therefore chosen to cover all the topics mentioned above, in four different parts which I summarize at the end of this Introduction. For reasons of space, there is a need for selectivity and a less detailed treatment than separate treatments would have made possible.

The virtue ethics developed in this book is inspired primarily by both Aristotle and Nietzsche. From Aristotle I take the conception of virtue itself as a disposition in which both reason and emotion are well ordered. In a state of virtue the agent has (at least standardly) practical wisdom, right ends which are both expressed in and promoted by her actions, and correct affective states. I also take from Aristotle the idea that virtue is a state of appropriate responsiveness to, or acknowledgement of, what I call 'the demands of the world', where the criteria of 'appropriateness' of that acknowledgement are shaped, at least in part, by a correct conception of human flourishing. What is missing from Aristotle, I feel, is a sufficiently satisfying conception of the relation between the demands of the world and the flourishing of the possessor of the virtues. The reason for this is the lack of a sufficiently deep account of flourishing in Aristotle. I share the view of Martha Nussbaum that Aristotle saw the task of normative ethical theory as rendering coherent the *endoxa*—the beliefs of the many or the wise.[11] We might say, to use Rawls's term, that Aristotle provides a reflective equilibrium. But it turns out that the equilibrium achieved is somewhat narrow by comparison with that which Norman Daniels described as a *wide* reflective equilibrium.[12] In a narrow equilibrium, one renders coherent conflicting moral intuitions, 'considered judgements', or *endoxa* concerning the topic under discussion, but one does this without providing or supposing background theories

---

[11] See *The Fragility of Goodness: Luck and Ethics in Greek Tragedy and Philosophy* (Cambridge: Cambridge University Press, 1986).

[12] See 'Wide Reflective Equilibrium and Theory Acceptance in Ethics', *Journal of Philosophy* 76 (1979), 256–82.

which help resolve conflicts amongst the *endoxa*. In naturalistic ethical theory, these background theories are theories about human nature.

It may seem that a background theory of human nature has been provided by Aristotle. It is a theory of human flourishing which plays the role of justifying claims about virtue. However, as has been frequently noted, we do not, in Aristotle, understand virtues via an account of flourishing—we understand flourishing via an account of the virtues. That is the basic reason for the somewhat narrow base of the resulting equilibrium. Peter Simpson puts the point this way:

If [Aristotle] does not derive the virtues from the notion of flourishing, whence does he derive them? What other justification does he give in their defence? To the question of whence he derives the virtues, there seems to be a very simple answer. From common opinion.[13]

Unlike some, I do not go so far as to claim that the 'common opinion' underpinning Aristotle's equilibrium is the prejudice of the gentlemanly elite. However, the equilibrium could be wider. And it would be wider if a richer account of human flourishing, sufficiently independent of 'common opinion' as to function as a background theory, were to be given or presupposed.

Virtue ethics in modern form has gone some way towards meeting this need. It has been rightly praised for taking seriously the richness and complexity of the moral domain, for its sensitivity to context and situation, and for its scepticism about the codifiability of ethics. The importance of the situational appreciation of a virtuous agent of practical wisdom and fine sensibilities is a feature of virtue ethics owed to Aristotle.[14] But on my view, virtue ethics has not yet gone far enough in connecting ethics to concrete phenomena. It tends to think that the complexity of the characterizations of virtue and vice in act evaluation lies in the complexities of *situations*. The conception of virtue itself is by comparison seen to be relatively straightforward. For example, we may feel we have a pretty good idea of the nature of generosity as a virtue, but it is just frequently difficult to know in a concrete case what the wise, generous act would be. However, if we take seriously the incorporation of background theory into virtue ethics we see that the delineation of virtue itself is extremely complicated. Uncodifiability is not just founded in the

13 'Contemporary Virtue Ethics and Aristotle', repr. in Daniel Statman (ed.), *Virtue Ethics*, 245–59, at 248.
14 The precise role of this feature in virtue theory may be exaggerated: see Chapter 12.

intricacies of practical wisdom; it is sourced in the extreme difficulty of knowing how to distinguish virtue itself from (very closely allied) vice. Karen Horney puts this point as follows:

We are inclined to put too great an emphasis on the actual situation, and to think that it determines our reactions, we are inclined, for instance, to regard it as 'natural' for a person to react with *shame* if he is caught in a lie. But then the next fellow does not feel that way at all; instead he feels *humiliated* by the one who found him out and turns against him. Our reactions are thus determined not merely by the situation but even more by our own neurotic needs.[15]

Inasmuch as theories of 'neurotic needs' shape (at least in part) our conception of virtue and vice, the task of delineating virtue inherits the complexities of the task of understanding psychic health. For example, given that 'neurotic pride' must be distinguished from 'a solid sense of self-confidence', we need some kind of background theory of neurotic pride. Apparent virtues sourced in neurotic pride, as opposed to solid self-confidence, become vices rather than virtues. Horney gives a list of vices sourced in neurotic pride whose superficial features look like virtues:

inconsistency turns into unlimited freedom, blind rebellion against an existing code of morals into being above common prejudice, a taboo on doing anything for oneself into saintly unselfishness, a need to appease into sheer goodness, dependency into love, exploiting others into astuteness. A capacity to assert egocentric claims appears as strength, vindictiveness as justice, frustrating techniques as a most intelligent weapon, aversion to work as 'successfully resisting the deadly habit of work', and so on.[16]

It hardly needs emphasizing that distinguishing genuine from apparent virtue in the light of background theory is no easy matter. The difficulty of distinguishing virtue from closely allied vice is compounded by the fact that we are not simply a 'self' but a self existing 'within a matrix of concentric fields extending from the intra-psychic through the interpersonal to the larger culture in which we are all immersed'.[17] As a result, distinctions such as that between 'vicious' or 'neurotic' ambition and a healthy ambition or pursuit of success rely on a sensitivity to, and informed critique of, cultures in which ambition or relative lack of ambi-

---

[15] *Neurosis and Human Growth: The Struggle Toward Self Realization* (New York: Norton, 1970; first published 1950), 97.

[16] Ibid. 94.

[17] Ibid. 5.

tion are salient. For example, in her denigration of neurotic drivenness to success, Horney claims that 'since we live in a competitive culture these remarks [a criticism of certain forms of competitiveness] may seem strange or unworldly'. However, she nails her colours to the mast: 'the fact that compulsive drives for success will arise only in a competitive culture does not make them any less neurotic. Even in a competitive culture there are many people for whom other values—such as, in particular, that of growth as a human being—are more important than competitive excelling over others.'[18] But, we may want to ask, is drivenness necessarily competitive excelling over others, and are we necessarily to deplore the artistic passion of, say, Howard Roark in Ayn Rand's *Fountainhead*?[19] Once we see the moral universe through the prism of the language of virtue and vice, we see that uncodifiability is not just due to the complexity of situations. It is due to the complexity of virtue and vice itself, and ultimately to the complexity (and opacity) of human nature.

My appropriation of Nietzsche and Nietzsche-inspired psychology is in the service of shedding some light on this complexity and opacity. Virtue ethics, with its emphasis on the inner, needs to take seriously the spirit of Nietzsche's remarks about the importance of depth psychology.[20] The debt to Nietzsche is most obvious in my account of self-love—a crucial depth-psychological component of virtue. It is an account of the nature and role of self-love in the virtues which enables us to gain insight into the important distinctions alluded to above between virtue and closely allied vices—self-confidence and the neurotic pride of vindictive triumphalism, vanity, ostentation; strong and weak altruism; virtuous and non-virtuous or vicious perfectionism. It is self-love which provides the cornerstone of my account of objectivity as an aspect of virtue opposed to hyperobjective and hypersubjective vice in Chapter 8, and which underpins the account of perfectionistic virtue and vice in Chapter 9.

Self-love as an aspect of virtue features as follows. Chapter 6 introduces a Nietzschean account of self-love as expressing strength in undistorted ways, which incorporates respect for self and other, but which is not reducible to respect-based accounts of self-love. That chapter

[18] Ibid. 26.
[19] New York: Signet, 1952.
[20] See e.g. Friedrich Nietzsche, *Beyond Good and Evil*, trans. R. J. Hollingdale (London: Penguin, 1973), sect. 32, p. 63.

elaborates the idea of expression as an aspect of the profiles of the virtues, and there I show how the account of self-love can be applied to the distinction between virtuous altruism and the non-virtuous or vicious altruism expressive of resentment and grandiosity. In Chapter 8, I further elaborate the account of self-love in its application to an analysis of objectivity as an aspect of virtue.

Central to my use of Nietzsche for the development of my virtue ethics, and for a conception of self-love in particular, is the distinction between distorted and undistorted manifestations of what Nietzsche calls variously 'will to power' and 'discharging strength', and what I call expressing strength. Surprisingly, given the frequently admitted connection between 'will to power' and health in Nietzsche, the distinction is not generally emphasized. For example, Robert C. Welshon identifies both health and 'will to power' in Nietzsche as 'augmenting influence' but, as I shall argue particularly in Chapter 8, not all 'augmenting influence'[21] manifests undistorted, healthy forms of will to power. Again, in Stephen D. Hales's consequentialist interpretation of Nietzsche,[22] the distinction between will to power generally, and unhealthy, distorted will to power is not drawn. For Hales, the value Nietzsche wants promoted is power as such, whether or not it expresses or promotes distorted forms: 'It appears that [Nietzsche's] consequentialism ultimately aims at the maximization of power.'[23] Nietzsche's distinction between 'life affirming' and 'life denying' will to power, a distinction giving some content to the idea of distorted versus undistorted will to power, is ignored in much philosophical writing on Nietzsche,[24] in contrast to psychology, where, for example, Erich Fromm distinguishes between 'malignant' and 'benign' forms of aggression.[25] Finally, R. Kevin Hill claims that for Nietzsche, the fundamental human motive is 'will to power' understood as 'successful pursuit of power'.[26] However, not only is it the case that expressing or 'discharging' strength is more general than augmenting

[21] 'Nietzsche's Peculiar Virtues and the Health of the Soul', *International Studies in Philosophy* 24 (1992), 73–89.

[22] 'Was Nietzsche a Consequentialist?', *International Studies in Philosophy* 27 (1995), 25–34.

[23] Ibid. 32.

[24] Exceptions include Walter Kaufmann, *Nietzsche: Philosopher, Psychologist, Antichrist*, 4th edn. (Princeton, N.J.: Princeton University Press, 1974), and John Richardson, *Nietzsche's System* (New York: Oxford University Press, 1996).

[25] *The Anatomy of Human Destructiveness.*

[26] 'MacIntyre's Nietzsche', *International Studies in Philosophy* 24 (1992), 3–12.

influence or *pursuing* power, not all pursuit of power is a form of healthy or undistorted will to power. In short, the distinction between distorted and undistorted will to power allows for an analysis of self-love in terms of 'expressing strength well', which need have nothing to do with augmenting influence, pursuing power, or having power over others, let alone doing these things in cruel, vindictive, or triumphalist ways.

It is important to appreciate the role of background theory in the virtue ethics to be propounded in this book. Such theory is not to be understood as formed from a value-free 'empirical' standpoint which renders it 'neutral' and thereby privileged. On the contrary, the psychology constituting such theory is itself deeply philosophical, and is actively informed by the thinking of philosophers such as Aristotle, Nietzsche, and Kierkegaard. What then is the point of employing such theory when one could just stop with the insights and speculations of the philosopher-psychologists (as opposed to the psychologist-philosophers)? Its point is simply to strengthen the network into which our virtue ethics is tied. Such theory can be seen as extensions of the thought of Aristotle, Nietzsche, and others, but extensions which are closer to the 'coal face' of human nature. The writings of 'self-realizationist' psychologists who emphasize the importance of personality and character, such as Karen Horney, Erich Fromm, and Abraham Maslow, are informed by a training and a clinical experience unavailable to the philosopher as such. That is why they enrich and are useful, even if they are not a touchstone. Aspects of such theory serve the overall package which constitutes a virtue ethics, sharing its presuppositions. These are that personality and character are a central feature of human nature and human ethics, that human nature is to be understood in a holistic way, and that human beings should be understood via a psychology which recognizes their nature as beings who grow and mature.

Aristotle, too, sees human beings as essentially growing, maturing agents, whose development can be more or less healthy, more or less subject to interferences, blockages, and vicissitudes. The fundamental insight of Aristotle is to see the relevance of this to virtue and to ethics. It is just that in Aristotle, not surprisingly, there is no developed view of healthy human growth and of the vicissitudes which interfere with it of the kind we see in post-Nietzschean psychology. It is such theories that broaden the kind of equilibrium achieved by Aristotle.

Though, I argue, the background theory to be discussed can meet certain objections, it is not intended to be definitive or complete. Psychology is a large and controversial field, though I am more impressed with the confluences in psychological thought than with its differences. Appealing to such thought enriches our understanding of virtue and moral theory generally.

One final important point about the nature of my theory. It is not a species of ideal world theory. This fact has important implications for the nature of my virtue ethics, and my conception of virtue. Though I have enormous sympathy for the following Platonic view about the nature of virtue, it is not one I can adopt, for it is suitable for ideal world theory only. That view, as adumbrated by John M. Cooper,[27] has two aspects. First, virtue 'has to be understood as standing in for whatever turns out to be the basis in human psychology, once that is developed to perfection, for leading the best life'.[28] Second, 'there is a single, unified condition constituting its basis'.[29] It might be thought that self-love plays this role in my theory, for it certainly provides a psychological basis for distinguishing between virtues and closely allied vices (for example, perfectionistic vice, altruistic vice, and hyperobjective and hypersubjective vice). However, given the following three points, and the fact that my theory is intended to be applicable to this very imperfect world, I cannot adopt the above Platonic conception of virtue. These points are:

(1) The point or rationale of the virtues is meeting appropriately 'the demands of the world'. This includes self-realization, but is not exhausted by self-realization.
(2) Given the vicissitudes most of us face in our development, the chances of most of us developing to perfection the psychological basis for leading the best life are vanishingly small.
(3) Given, too, the urgency of the demands of the world, due to evil, catastrophe, and vulnerability, strategies for attaining the goals of personal self-realization and meeting the demands of the world cannot be assumed to coincide.

Though I sympathize with the view that there is a deep underlying psychological basis or *condition* of virtue, it does not follow that the *rationale* of all virtue is to realize that condition. Given that the rationale of virtue is to meet the demands of the world, it is natural to divide and delineate the virtues according to a pluralistic taxonomy of 'fields' of virtue such

---

[27] 'The Unity of Virtue', *Social Philosophy and Policy* 15 (1998), 233–74.
[28] Ibid. 234.
[29] Ibid.

as Aristotle's. Virtues are thus delineated according to their spheres of concern, as dictated by the varied nature of those demands. Hence there is conceptual scope for pluralism, indeed disunity, in the virtues. Potential for disunity is heightened given the above three points and the adoption of a threshold conception of virtue.

Certainly, this I grant. *If* we standardly developed to *perfection* the psychological basis for leading the best life, it may well be true that virtuously meeting the demands of the world, including those of our children, ourselves, near and dear, society, and the natural environment, would coincide exactly with the pursuit and attainment of personal psychological perfection. Then virtue would be unified, and the goals of self-realization and meeting the demands of the world would coincide. I also grant that the pursuit of a goal of psychological improvement (if not perfection) is extremely important in the life of virtue and the good life. That is why great importance is placed in this book on the psychological components of virtue.

The book is divided into four parts. Part I, 'Virtue', explains the nature of virtue, and its connection with the flourishing and moral life. Chapters 1 and 2 are ground-laying chapters explicating the components of virtue and justifying key aspects of virtue pluralism, namely, pluralism in the modes and bases of virtuous moral response. Chapters 3 and 4 explore the connections between the virtuous life, the flourishing life, and the moral life. I concur with a standard virtue-ethical view that the virtuous and the flourishing life are rather closely connected, and argue for this primarily via the 'Constraint on Virtue' (the claim that what counts as a virtue is constrained by an adequate theory of healthy human growth and development) and via arguments for a broad construal of what counts as a 'moral' virtue. Though the tension between the flourishing and the moral life is not as great as might be supposed, I do not close the gap between the flourishing and the moral life in the way proposed by eudaimonism: the virtue-ethical view that a virtue characteristically conduces to, or at least partly constitutes the flourishing of the agent. The Constraint on Virtue does not entail eudaimonism, and in Chapter 4 I argue against that view. Part I closes with my own pluralistic account of what makes a trait of character a virtue.

Part II, 'Profiles of the Virtues', discusses the central modes of moral acknowledgement constituting the profiles of the virtues. I concentrate primarily on love, respect, and creativity. The aim is to show the complexity of our virtuous responsiveness to items in the fields of the virtues, and to show how they are related and integrated in virtuous response to those items. Expression is also discussed, since excellence in the modes requires the expression of fine inner states. The idea of expression allows for the integration of different modes of moral acknowledgement within the virtues. For example, I argue that virtuous altruism (generosity and so forth) is not just a matter of promoting the good of others, or caring for or loving others, but involves also the expression of fine inner states such as love of self. Furthermore, the mode of respect allows us to understand that benevolence and other virtues aimed at the good of others are constrained by respect for status (as e.g. client, patient, student, friend), and their profiles will reflect this complexity.

Part III, 'Shape of the Virtues', is concerned with a virtue-ethical treatment of topics traditionally described as 'the limits of morality'. To adequately describe a virtue, it is not enough simply to give an account of its profile. We also have to describe its limits—what I call its shape. Insofar as a virtue calls for us to promote good, or to love our neighbour, we need to know the demands such a virtue makes on us. What are the limits of such love, and such promotion of good? In Chapter 8, I give an account of the objective perspective as an aspect of virtue, contrasting objectivity with 'hyperobjective' and 'hypersubjective' vice. On my view, objective forms of meeting the demands of the world are determined by highly complex characterological requirements suitable to human beings. Chapter 9 discusses perfectionistic vice and virtue, and anti-perfectionistic vice and virtue, in the context of the demandingness of ethics. I finally (in Chapter 10) consider constraints (or agent-centred restrictions) and their relation to virtue.

Part IV, 'Virtue and Action', explores the relation between virtue and action. Chapter 11 outlines my virtue-ethical notion of the right. Chapter 12, 'Virtues of Practice', presents a dialogical picture of the task of ethics, and shows how a virtuous agent should approach problem-solving. That discussion raises the spectre of the 'action-guidingness objection' to virtue ethics—the objection that the indeterminacy licensed by virtue ethics renders it impotent in the field of applied ethics. I answer this objection in Chapter 13.

Part I

VIRTUE

1

The Anatomy of Virtue

(i) The Nature of Virtue

This chapter introduces the basic elements of my pluralistic virtue ethics. Section (i) outlines the components of my account of virtue: my pluralistic conception of the *modes* of moral acknowledgement, the idea that these modes must *express fine inner states* if they are to manifest a state of virtue, the 'limits' of virtue (what I call the shape of the virtues), my pluralistic account of the *bases* of moral acknowledgement, and the concept of the target of a virtue and its connection with right action. Section (ii) further elaborates the nature of virtue by considering the 'deflationary challenge'[1] of situationist personality psychology, which threatens to undermine virtue ethics by casting doubt on the very idea of character.

(a) The Definition of Virtue

I begin with a definition of virtue that, I shall claim, is shared not only by forms of virtue ethics that differ from my own (including eudaimonism) but by those virtue theorists who are not virtue ethicists.

> A *virtue* is a good quality of character, more specifically a disposition to respond to, or acknowledge, items within its field or fields in an excellent or good enough way.

This definition of virtue is intended to be neutral with respect to a variety of virtue theories and virtue ethics: pluralistic and monistic, eudaimonistic and non-eudaimonistic. According to eudaimonism, though a virtue is a disposition to respond in an excellent or good enough way to items within its field or fields, it is at least a necessary condition of a trait being a virtue that it characteristically be good for the possessor of the virtue. Non-eudaimonistic views can also accept my definition of virtue.

---

[1] See Maria Merritt, 'Virtue Ethics and Situationist Personality Psychology', *Ethical Theory and Moral Practice* 3 (2000), 365–83.

According to Michael Slote's 'agent-based' virtue ethics, a virtue is a trait that is admirable, and its admirability need not be based on its tendencies to promote further value or good, such as the good of the agent. Thus, again, though a virtue is a disposition to respond well to items within its field, it is a necessary (and sufficient) condition of a trait being a virtue that it be an admirable trait of character. On my own view, it is possible for a trait to be a virtue even where it has tendencies to be bad for the possessor in non-utopian universes such as our actual world (see further Chapter 4). I also admit the existence of virtues such as charm or tact which do not reach the somewhat lofty status of admirability, but which, in Hume's terms, are socially useful and agreeable (see further Chapter 3).

The definition of virtue raises two broad questions about the nature of virtue. We need to know what *kinds* of response to items in a virtue's field constitute virtuous responses, and what are the *standards* for a response to count as *good enough* to be virtuous. Consider now the former issue.

(b) The Field of a Virtue

In order to discuss the first issue, we need to specify the notion of a virtue's field. The *field* of a virtue consists of those items which are the sphere(s) of concern of the virtue, and to which the agent should respond in line with the virtue's demands. These items may be within the agent, for example, the bodily pleasures which are the focus of temperance, or outside the agent, for example, human beings, property, money, or honours. They may be situations, for example, the dangerous situations which are the concern of courage; abstract items such as knowledge or beauty; physical objects such as one's children, friends, sentient beings in general, art works or cultural icons, or the natural objects which are the concern of the environmental virtues.

In the analysis of Greek texts there is intricate debate about the relation between fields of the virtues and the individuation of the virtues.[2] It is beyond the scope of this book to investigate this territory, but it is worth pointing out that considerable indeterminacy and scope for debate exists. For example in her 'A False Doctrine of the Mean',[3] Rosalind Hursthouse claims that an unjust appropriation of rations on a campaign 'in pursuit of physical pleasure' is a failure in *temperance*, where-

---

[2] See, for example, Cooper, 'The Unity of Virtues'.
[3] *Proceedings of the Aristotelian Society* 81 (1980–1), 57–72, at 64.

as one might be inclined to say simply that it is a failure in *justice*. Insofar as the failure in justice is due to excessive appetite for pleasure, I would be inclined to say that it is a failure in both virtues; insofar as the unjust behaviour is due to a desire for revenge, it is not a failure in *temperance* but a failure in both justice and those virtues associated with the regulation of anger.

Items in a virtue's field make demands on us. As I shall put it, a virtue is a disposition to respond well to the 'demands of the world'. Because the fields of virtues are broad-ranging, I use the phrase 'demands of the world' in a broad sense to include the demands on our virtue not only of items which are in a position to make claims on us, but also of items which are not, such as inanimate objects. The demands of the world in the above broad sense include those of oneself: on Kant's view, for example, there is a moral duty of self-perfection arising from the treatment of oneself as a moral end. This Kantian view is reflected in those virtues which are at least in part self-regarding, for example, those of self-love, temperance, and the creative virtues necessary for developing one's talents.

(c) Modes and Bases of Moral Responsiveness

Let us turn now to the idea of *kinds of responsiveness* to items in a virtue's field. I shall argue in Chapter 2 that responding well to items in the field of a virtue may take several forms.[4] These forms I shall call *modes* of moral responsiveness (or acknowledgement). They include not only promoting or bringing about benefit or value, but also honouring value[5] (roughly, not dirtying one's hands with respect to a value, e.g. by not being unjust in promoting justice), honouring things such as (appropriate) rules, producing, appreciating, loving, respecting, creating, being receptive or open to, using or handling appropriate things in appropriate ways. One may respect an individual in virtue of her status as an elder or one's boss; promote or enhance value; promote the good of a stranger or friend; appreciate the value of an art work, nature, or the efforts of a colleague; create a valuable work of art, creatively solve a moral problem; love an individual in ways appropriate to various types of bonds; be open

---

[4] For another perspective on pluralism in responsiveness, see Elizabeth Anderson, *Value in Ethics and Economics* (Cambridge, Mass.: Harvard University Press, 1993).

[5] The term 'honouring value' was introduced by Philip Pettit. See his 'Consequentialism', in Peter Singer (ed.), *A Companion to Ethics* (Oxford: Blackwell, 1991), 230–40.

or receptive to situations and individuals; use money or natural objects. In Part II, I shall discuss several of these modes, particularly love, respect, and creativity, and in Part III, I discuss the controversial idea of honouring value in relation to constraints or agent-centred restrictions.

The modes of moral acknowledgement of items are richly displayed in the virtues. The virtue of justice is primarily concerned with the honouring of rules of justice by adhering to those rules oneself, and with respect for the status of individuals. The virtues of connoisseurship are concerned not with the promoting of, for instance, art (by giving money to art foundations, say), but with the appreciation of valuable items such as works of art. Thrift is a virtue concerned with use of money; temperance a virtue concerned with handling of and pursuit of pleasure; consideration, politeness, appropriate deference are virtues concerned with respect for others and their status. Many virtues, such as that of friendship, exhibit many modes of moral acknowledgement. A good friend does not merely promote the good of her friend: she appreciates her friend, respects, cares for, and even loves her friend. Caring as a virtue involves receptivity, perhaps love in some sense, and to a large extent promotion of good.

It might be thought odd that appreciation is an aspect of a virtue of character: in reply two points should be made. On my view, a disposition to appreciate is as much a part of virtue as wisdom, and is in fact integral to wisdom. For it involves a habit of fine discrimination, 'delicate sentiment' as Hume puts it. Second, it is just as much a matter of character that one is appreciative of, for example, the wonders of nature, or dismissive and careless of it, as are benevolence or callousness towards people.

The question arises: how are the modes of moral responsiveness integrated within virtue? On this question one can believe that the modes are relatively unified or disunified. On my own view, a relatively general unified account is to some extent forthcoming (see especially Chapter 5, section i), though the application of this view to concrete cases is highly resistant to general formulae.

What I shall call the *profile* of a virtue is that constellation of modes of moral responsiveness which comprises the virtuous disposition. I claim not only that the virtues exhibit many modes of moral acknowledgement, but that a single virtue, such as benevolence, friendship, or justice, may require that we acknowledge items in its field through several different modes. This does not imply that in the profiles of the virtues modes of moral acknowledgement are not to some extent at least integrated.

Though the modes of moral acknowledgement are conceptually distinct, in the profiles of the *virtues* they are connected in rich ways. Indeed, in their best manifestations some are incorporated into others. For example, in its most austere and 'utilitarian' form, benevolence simply involves promoting the good of others. As a virtue, however, it is arguable that benevolence requires the promotion of good with love in various manifestations, ranging from parental love to humane concern. Now love as a mode of acknowledgement forming part of the profiles of various virtues, incorporates other modes. As I argue in Chapter 5, love as a form of 'coming close' must be tempered by respect as a form of 'keeping one's distance'. Furthermore, love involves receptivity, or a kind of openness to the other—receptivity which allows for appreciation. Virtuous using of and handling of (for example) natural resources requires at least appreciation of and respect for the resources used. Receptivity has also been described as a precursor to creativity.

An important aspect of virtue-ethical pluralism, then, is that the modes of moral responsiveness to items in the fields of the virtues are plural. This conception of virtue acknowledges the complexity of *human* responsiveness to the world. The virtues, with their complex profiles, recognize that we are beings who are not only agents of change in the attempt to promote good, but also agents of change in the attempt to produce and to create. As I shall claim below, the standards for success in creativity are not the same as those for success in (merely) promoting value. They also recognize that we are not only agents who are active in changing the world by promoting good (often at the expense of causing harm), but also agents who love and respect (often at the expense of maximizing good). Finally, they accept that we are not only active beings hell-bent on change, but are also passive in a sense: in our openness to, receptivity to, and appreciation of value and things. Not all ethics is 'task-oriented'. In short, attention to the profiles of the virtues reminds us of the complexity of our human nature and our modes of moral response.

(d) Bases of Moral Responsiveness

A second reason for the variety of types of response acknowledged in the virtues lies not in the nature of the responder but in the nature of the items responded to. Different types of response are warranted by the different types of morally significant features in the items constituting the fields of the virtues. Call such a feature *a basis* of moral acknowledgement. I discuss four such bases: value, status, good (or benefit), and bonds. For example, various virtues will call for the value of objects to be promoted or honoured, or for objects containing such value to be created or loved in some way. Bonds between an agent and items within the field of a virtue may call for such items to be loved in ways appropriate to those bonds, as exhibited in virtues such as compassion, parental love, friendship. The good of items will call for the promotion of that good, as exhibited in virtues such as benevolence and generosity. The status of items will be the concern of virtues primarily calling for respect of individuals in ways befitting their status: virtues of deference, respect for authority, non-maleficence, or respect for physical, psychological, or aesthetic integrity.

I have no argument for the claim that the itemized modes and bases of moral acknowledgement are a complete list. My purpose is rather to motivate a conception of virtue which allows a virtue ethics to accommodate the views of a wide variety of moral theories on what is morally significant. These include a Kantian emphasis on respect for status, the consequentialist view that what is valuable should be promoted, the insights of an ethics of creativity which claims that, as Abraham Maslow, Sigmund Freud, Karen Horney, and other psychologists emphasize, healthy well-functioning human beings are creative human beings. They include also the recognition by Nel Noddings, Max Scheler, and many Asian philosophical traditions of the moral significance of receptivity. Noddings incorporates receptivity as integral to a relationship bond-centred ethics of care, and Scheler's value-centred ethics regards as central 'attention' and the 'emotional intuition' of value. The task of accommodating these insights within an ethics of virtue is endless, and I can but make a beginning in this work.

More needs to be said about both the modes and bases of moral acknowledgement. Section (iii) of this chapter defends my view that the fundamental modes are plural by arguing against the consequentialist thesis of 'The hegemony of promotion' as the fundamental mode of moral acknowledgement. In section (ii) of this chapter I discuss the bases of moral acknowledgement.

(e) Virtue as Threshold Concept

The second major feature of virtue and the second broad issue to be discussed is that a virtue sets a *standard* for responsiveness to items in a virtue's field: such responsiveness has to be excellent or good enough if it is to be virtuous. Discussion of this standard involves several issues. First one needs to consider whether virtue is, or is not, a threshold concept. The definition of virtue itself is neutral between perfectionistic or idealized conceptions of virtue and threshold conceptions of virtue. One may think of virtue as an ideal state towards the realization of which one may progress, but which it is difficult or impossible to attain. Alternatively, one may think of virtue as something to be admired, as something to be praised, or as something which is very useful for the well-functioning of the agent and/or the wider community. On that conception, in a world characterized by considerable evil, neediness, and frequent catastrophe, less than ideal states may count as virtuous. It does not follow from such a conception, however, that *all* admirable, useful, and praiseworthy states of the agent are to count as virtuous, for one may wish to distinguish virtue from other states which in certain contexts are useful and praiseworthy, such as self-control. On the threshold view of virtue, especially a threshold view in which the standards for virtue are relative to context, it would be a mistake, however, to think that such distinctions are always clear-cut. In the course of this book, I shall defend a threshold concept of virtue.

(f) Virtue and the Limits of Morality

A second aspect of a standard of 'good enough' responsiveness to items in a virtue's field concerns the limits of morality. That is, the standards of 'good enough' responsiveness to items in a virtue's field set limits to moral demands of various sorts. The problem of the limits of morality has a virtue-ethical variant, which I have called the problem of the *shape* of the virtues. Assume that certain virtues are centrally concerned with the promotion of value, others with respecting individuals, others with creativity, and yet others with expressing bonds. Now, we can promote a value maximally or satisfactorily; we can respect someone or something more or less assiduously or strictly; we can love in more or less demanding ways; we can create in ways more or less draining of our energy and more or less painfully and obsessively. Inasmuch as virtue demands that we transcend various personal desires, attachments, feelings, and emotions in our responses to the demands of the world, we want to know just what is the nature and extent of that demand. The specification of that demand determines the shape of a virtue. A virtue requires that we respond to the world in ways that manifest a more or less 'objective' point of view, or are more or less demanding. I understand the problem of demandingness in terms of virtues of perfectionism contrasted with related vices of exceeding the limits of one's strength and underperforming in relation to those limits; objectivity is contrasted with vices of hyperobjectivity and hypersubjectivity. More accurately, both objectivity and appropriate demandingness are part of the anatomy of the individual virtues; objectivity, for example, is an aspect of, say, benevolence, determining its shape (see Chapters 8 and 9).

Another aspect of the shape of the virtues is the 'problem' of constraints or agent-centred restrictions. In Chapter 10, I show that the profiles of the virtues have constraints built in: it is a task of that chapter to show just how various modes of moral responsiveness featuring in the profiles of the virtues function as constraints.

(g) Expression of Fine Inner States

There is a third aspect to the broad issue of what counts as excellent or good enough responsiveness to or acknowledgement of items within a virtue's field or fields. A central distinguishing feature of a *virtue-ethical* account of virtue lies in its conception of what counts as acknowledgement of an item which is good enough to count as manifesting a state of virtue, as opposed to self-control or otherwise flawed states. For the virtue ethicist, in order for virtue to be displayed, such acknowledgement must *express inner states* that are sufficiently fine. Note that this requirement is not entailed by the definition of virtue (p. 19); not all accounts of virtue are part of a virtue ethics. In my own virtue ethics, expressing fine inner states is an aspect of the profile of the virtues, for each mode of moral acknowledgement comprising that profile, be it promoting value or respecting individuals, must express those states. For example, parental virtue involves love of one's children, but that form of moral acknowledgement must not be suffocating or expressive of one's own pathological needs if it is to display virtue. Insofar as promotion of good is a central feature of benevolence, for the virtue ethicist that promotion must at least be well motivated if virtue is to be displayed, and on Aristotelian views it must also display practical wisdom and express a firm disposition of relevant fine feelings and emotions. Again, virtues of respect (e.g. respect for authority, human beings as such, elders) must exhibit more than the mere outward signs of respectful keeping of one's distance (e.g. the absence of inappropriate touching, insult, or other forms of invasive approach).

What it is to *express* a fine inner state requires some elucidation. Indeed, the idea of expression as an aspect of the profiles of the virtues is of sufficient importance and interest to warrant a separate chapter (Chapter 6). However one understands the idea of expression, the general requirement that virtue express fine inner states distinguishes a virtue-ethical view of virtue from a consequentialist view like Julia

Driver's. For her, a moral virtue is simply 'a character trait (a disposition or cluster of dispositions) which, generally speaking, produces good consequences for others.'[6] Virtuous moral acknowledgement for Driver neither requires good intentions nor good motives if it is to manifest a state of virtue.[7] My conception of virtue, by contrast, recognizes not only a plurality of modes of moral acknowledgement, but also a requirement that each mode express fine inner states of some form if it is to be part of the profile of a *virtue*.

I say 'some form' of inner state advisedly. We should be careful not to assume too readily that certain internal states are necessary conditions for any trait to count as a virtue in virtue ethics. For Aristotle, practical wisdom is necessary for all virtue, and I certainly hold that this feature is characteristically important, and indeed crucial both in areas of policy making and in quotidian ethics. The 'bungling do-gooder' objection, so often directed at virtue ethics, is puzzling, because it forgets that Aristotle (rightly) regards practical wisdom as the glue which not only integrates the components of the profiles of the individual virtues, but also unites those virtues one to another. However, as will be revealed in Chapter 7 on creativity, Nietzsche's downplaying of practical wisdom as a necessary feature of *all* virtue has force. Following Nietzsche, Robert Solomon makes an eloquent plea for the centrality of passion, rather than wisdom in one kind of virtuous life.[8] Though passion is important, however, its importance is contextual: passion without the cautionary effects of wisdom will not be a virtue in a parent bringing up a child, an administrator, a policy maker, and the professional life.

A full study of the connection between virtue and practical wisdom involves the study of three issues, not always clearly separated. These are:

(i) Are there virtues *requiring* ignorance such as possibly modesty and blind charity?[9]

---

[6] 'The Virtues and Human Nature', 122. Notice that for Driver, a virtuous agent need not always *aim* at promoting good consequences.

[7] Ibid. 116–22.

[8] The Virtues of a Passionate Life: Erotic Love and "The Will to Power"', *Social Philosophy and Policy* 15 (1998), 91–118.

[9] See Julia Driver, 'The Virtues of Ignorance', *Journal of Philosophy* 86 (1989), 373–84; G. F. Schueler , 'Why Modesty is a Virtue', *Ethics* 107 (1997), 467–85; Julia Driver, 'Modesty and Ignorance', *Ethics* 109 (1999), 827–34; G. F. Schueler, 'Why IS Modesty a Virtue?', *Ethics* 109 (1999), 835–41.

28 VIRTUE

(ii) Does action from virtue require not merely practical wisdom but also a degree of reliability in securing the ends of virtue, which may transcend the wisdom of agents? (See further Chapter 11.)

(iii) Is there a tension between the passional requirements of some modes of moral acknowledgement (notably creativity and love) such that the profiles of those virtues requiring these modes do not (or cannot) require a high degree of practical wisdom? (See further Chapter 7.)[10]

The view that virtue expresses fine inner states is important for the virtue-ethical claim that the gap between the virtuous life and the good life is not as wide as often thought (see Chapter 3, section ii). It is also a feature which distinguishes virtue ethicists from virtue theorists who are not virtue ethicists. For a virtue ethicist, a virtue is not simply a disposition to perform right acts with respect to items in the field of a virtue. For an action to be *from* a state of virtue, that is, for an action to be expressive of virtue, it must be expressive of fine inner states. It will be claimed, however, that some versions of consequentialism and Kantian ethics also require that virtue express fine inner states. The question arises then whether virtue ethics can be distinguished from these other theories by having a distinctive view of the *nature* of the fine inner states expressed in virtue. I believe that it can be so distinguished. Virtue ethics differs from trait consequentialism, 'objective', 'indirect', or 'sophisticated' act consequentialism, and Kantianism in its account of what constitutes excellence in what Peter Railton calls 'standing commitments'. For a virtue ethicist, a virtuous agent has a standing commitment to act from virtue.[11] This contrasts with that of the 'sophisticated consequentialist' agent who, according to Railton, 'is someone who has a standing commitment

---

[10] In his 'The Virtues of a Passionate Life', Solomon claims in a footnote: 'We may well insist that love is a virtue even when it is foolish or destructive, however, just as we insist on calling justice a virtue even when the results are disastrous' (96). However, (ii) and (iii) above must be distinguished: disastrous consequences may not betray lack of practical wisdom, whereas foolish and destructive love does. Whether such love can be part of virtue depends on one's views about virtuous passion and its link with wisdom.

[11] According to Robert Audi, this claim is a distinguishing feature of virtue ethics. He claims that according to virtue ethics, 'the basic normative aims of moral agents are aretaically determined ... by the requirements of acting from virtue as opposed, say, to being dictated by a commitment to following certain deontic rules.' *Moral Knowledge and Ethical Character* (New York: Oxford University Press, 1997), 186.

to leading an objectively consequentialist life, but who need not set special stock in any particular form of decision making and therefore does not necessarily seek to lead a subjectively consequentialist life'.[12]

It also differs from sophisticated Kantianism, which demands that the Kantian moral agent has a standing commitment to perform her duty. Notice, however, that virtue ethics is not to be distinguished from sophisticated consequentialism or sophisticated Kantianism in its account of appropriate foreground motivation. Virtue ethicists share with sophisticated consequentialists and Kantians the view that a virtuous agent possesses as foreground motivations such things as desires to help a friend or spouse for the friend's or spouse's sake, desires suffused by love and concern rather than dutiful or instrumental motivations. The foreground desire to help a friend for her own sake is not of course identical with a background desire to be virtuous for its own sake (including the desire to be a good (virtuous) friend), and it is in their conception of fine background motivation that virtue ethicists differ from other theorists. Virtue *ethicists*, in short, claim that moral responsiveness expressive of virtue must express fine inner states, and amongst those states will be a background motivation of acting from virtue.

(b) The Target of a Virtue and Rightness

There is one more aspect of the standards of good responsiveness to consider: what counts as *rightness of action* on a virtue-ethical view. On my account, elaborated in Chapter 11, a right act is an excellent realization or attainment of the target or end of a virtue. According to Robert Audi, one 'dimension' of virtue is 'the characteristic *targets* it aims at, such as the well-being of others in the case of beneficence and the control of fear in the case of courage'.[13] As Audi suggests, the target of a virtue may be external or internal to the agent, though in the case of internal targets it is necessary to distinguish a target of a virtue, as opposed to a target of self-control.

The idea of the target of a virtue and its connection with right action is explicated in Chapter 11. Suffice to say here that an act may hit the target of a virtue—realizing its end—without the act being an act *from a state of* virtue. As Aristotle puts it, a right (virtuous) act need not be performed

---

12 'Alienation, Consequentialism and Morality', *Philosophy and Public Affairs* 13 (1984), 134–71, at 153.

13 *Moral Knowledge and Ethical Character*, 180.

in the way a virtuous person would perform it. This distinction of Aristotle's, and its importance for a virtue-ethical account of rightness, is discussed in Chapter 11.

(ii) The Situationist Critique

One of the most interesting recent criticisms of virtue ethics derives from the social sciences, specifically 'situationist' personality psychology.[14] According to some philosophers who make use of this psychology, virtue ethics is inadequate because based on characterological psychology that is empirically inadequate. According to situationist psychology:

> Behavioral variation across a population owes more to situational differences than dispositional differences among persons. Individual dispositional differences are not as strongly behaviorally individuating as we might have supposed.[15]

The claim that experiments such as Milgram's study of obedience[16] demonstrate the empirical inadequacy of virtue ethics, because there is a lack of cross-situational consistency in *behaviour*, betrays a lack of understanding of the virtue ethicist's concept of virtue. For a virtue ethicist, a virtue is not simply a disposition to perform acts of a certain type (e.g. beneficent acts). The possession of virtue requires also the possession of fine inner states. Admittedly, the Milgram experiments show that a remarkable number of subjects, responding to experimenters' instructions, are prepared to administer electric shocks of considerable severity. The tendency to perform *beneficent acts* is arguably not as robust as one might hope. However, there was considerable variation in the mental states of those prepared to administer such shocks, and these differences may point to character traits of, for example, compassion, benevolence, respect for authority and commitments, which manifest themselves in various ways in dilemmatic situations. According to Milgram, the subjects differed markedly in their emotional reactions to increasingly pressuring requests to administer shocks. Milgram claims that an

---

[14] See esp. L. Ross and R. E. Nisbett, *The Person and the Situation: Perspectives of Social Psychology* (Philadelphia, Pa.: Temple University Press, 1991).

[15] John M. Doris, 'Persons, Situations, and Virtue Ethics', *Nous* 32 (1998), 504–30, at 507.

[16] Stanley Milgram, 'Behavioral Study of Obedience', *Journal of Abnormal and Social Psychology* 67 (1963), 371–8.

unanticipated effect 'was the extraordinary tension generated by the procedures'. He says:

One might suppose that a subject would simply break off or continue as his conscience dictated. Yet this is far from what happened. There were striking reactions of tension and emotional strain. While some subjects reported and manifested intense strain and anguish, however, 'some subjects [who had administered maximum shocks] had remained calm throughout the experiment, and displayed only minimal signs of tension from beginning to end.[17]

For the virtue ethicist, emotional reactions are crucial for the attribution of virtue and vice, and the mark of the virtuous is the propensity to violate a 'virtue rule' such as 'Be benevolent' only with reluctance, anguish, distress. The degree to which these emotions are present will vary according to the circumstances. Furthermore, it is clear from Milgram's account that the anguished saw themselves as operating under a rather severe virtue dilemma. A benevolent agent may also possess the virtues of respect for authority, trust, honouring commitments (fidelity), and appreciation of (the value of) knowledge. All of these virtues were in play during the experiment. Subjects rightfully assessed the experimental situation as warranting trust, the honouring of a commitment, and as promoting a worthy objective. Now where virtues such as trust and fidelity appeared to conflict acutely with another—non-maleficence—many subjects gave insufficient weight to the latter. But virtue ethicists are not committed to the view that many actual agents are capable of resolving such dilemmas correctly when under severe stress. The degree of virtue in agents can, however, be determined by their emotional reactions to their admittedly faulty resolutions of dilemma (e.g. reactions of anguish or indifference). And those differences were evident. It is open to the virtue ethicist to argue that while trust was not misplaced, and though (proper) obedience to authority is a virtue, in this case subjects erred on the side of excess. Arguably this failure hindered the exercise of the virtue of non-maleficence present in those who suffered anguish.

The above reply to the situationist critique gives rise to a more radical criticism of the idea of virtue as understood in virtue ethics. Virtue ethics supposedly subscribes to what Maria Merritt calls the thesis of motivational self-sufficiency of character.[18] This thesis may rescue the idea of

[17] Ibid. 376.
[18] Merritt, 'Virtue Ethics and Situationist Personality Psychology'.

individual character from the situationist critique, by assuming that a virtuous agent has a robust disposition to be on guard against the various perturbations which undermine virtuous behaviour, and is well motivated to overcome them. Furthermore, these dispositions of fine motivation explain our normal tendencies to good behaviour. However, situationist psychology casts doubt on the motivational self-sufficiency of character by claiming that our behaviour is better explained by factors outside the agent—by what Merritt calls the 'sustaining social contribution'.

Merritt defends virtue ethics from this charge by denying that all virtue ethics needs to be committed to the thesis of motivational self-sufficiency. She claims:

What situationist psychology makes problematic is not as such the recommendation to have the virtues, but the normative ideal of the virtues as qualities that must be possessed in a strongly self-sufficient form.[19]

A defender of virtue ethics need not be committed to a particular psychological account of character and what sustains it. The debate now is not whether there is such a thing as character, but how we are to understand it in psychological terms. A plausible account has it that upbringing can solidify what may be called virtues as prototypes (see further below, Chapter 13), but that the manifestations of these prototypes in non-core areas can be sustained (or fairly readily undermined) by the institutions in which the agent manifests (or fails to manifest) those virtues. Merritt puts the point this way:

Suppose you are well-brought-up, in that you have developed such things as the capacity for empathetic feeling, the ability to take a reasonably detached view of your own wants when they conflict with other people's legitimate claims, the capacity to form deep affective attachments, and the ability to control your impulses. So far, so good. But situationist personality psychology requires us to recognize that this good upbringing does not suffice to endow you, forever after, with the full motivational structure you will need, in order to display the specific virtues in every situation that calls for them: e.g., compassion, kindness, generosity; fairness, justice, fidelity to trust; loyalty, open-heartedness, consideration, or other excellences of friendship and love; confident self-possession with respect to aggressive feelings, physical and social fears, and sexual desires.[20]

---

[19] Ibid. 375.
[20] Ibid. 376.

Here is an example. As a result of an upbringing in which honesty and striving for excellence is emphasized, an academic has a rather solid foundation of basic integrity. However, she works in an institution in which the reward structures tend to undermine that virtue at the fringes—in its role manifestations. For example, student evaluations which measure consumer satisfaction and popularity, instead of solid academic values, reward the elimination of difficult material, and the provision of many handouts, eliminating the need for note-taking, and discouraging thinking for oneself. Furthermore, promotions and research grants reward quantity rather than quality of publications, undermining the tendency to produce the best work possible. She increases her publication rate, searching for lower calibre journals.

It is quite consistent with virtue ethics in general that it require social institutions to serve the worthwhile ends for which they are (or ought to be) designed, and to foster role virtues. It need not suppose that such virtue is sufficiently entrenched in the agent in all departments, that it remains forever wholly intact in systematically corrupt institutions.

Situationist personality psychology has much to offer a psychologically realistic account of the nature of character. It has not removed virtue ethics from the moral-theoretic landscape.

2

Normative Dimensions of Virtue

(i) Bases of Moral Acknowledgement

A discussion of the nature of virtue is incomplete without an account of its normative components. The normative demands of a virtue derive from two sources, the kinds of moral responses appropriate to *human* beings, and the nature of the items in the field of a virtue for which these responses are fitting. This section focuses on the second of these sources, which I have called the bases of moral acknowledgement. The discussion focuses on two problems. The first is the putative independence of the bases of moral acknowledgement from virtue. The second is the question whether virtue is a matter of being responsive to things entirely according to their degree of value. With respect to the first problem I shall discuss and reject what I shall call the Thesis of Non-Aretaic Value.

(1) The Thesis of Non-Aretaic Value

Virtues and vices are understood derivatively as forms of responsiveness to, or as instrumental in the promotion of (or minimization of respectively) 'base-level' goods or evils, or intrinsic values or disvalues, understood non-aretaically.

With respect to the second problem, I shall discuss and reject what I shall call the Thesis of Value-Centred Monism.

(2) The Thesis of Value-Centred Monism

The only 'rightness relevant respects' which serve to make one option better than another are the degree or strength of the values which inhere in those options.[1]

---

[1] This is a formulation derived from Philip Pettit. See his 'The Consequentialist Perspective', in Marcia W. Baron, Philip Pettit, and Michael Slote, *Three Methods of Ethics: A Debate* (Oxford: Blackwell, 1997), 92–174, at 107.

We now discuss in turn these two theses. The Thesis of Non-Aretaic Value is a standard view about the relation between virtue and the bases of moral acknowledgement. According to that thesis, virtues are to be understood derivatively, for they require for their specification a set of values or goods (which may include status, benefit, or bond-related features) understood non-aretaically. The thesis has two components.

First it claims that we can present a robust list of non-aretaic values of the kind presented in 'list theories'. Depending on the theorist, these include as values such things as achievements, knowledge, pleasure, friendship, and play, and as disvalues pain, false belief, and failure.[2] Second, it claims that in relation to these values, certain actions and attitudes are required, permitted, or intrinsically good; and these actions and attitudes are not themselves virtue-based notions. For example, according to Thomas Hurka, if pleasure is intrinsically good, desiring, pursuing, or taking pleasure in it for itself is also intrinsically good. Furthermore, instantiating the good in one's own life is permitted or required (on deontological views) and (on classic consequentialist views), promoting the most good possible is morally required. The ideas of promoting, instantiating, desiring, pursuing, are not understood as virtue-based notions.

Let us now consider the first component of the Thesis of Non-Aretaic Value. Why would one think that the specification of a robust list of non-aretaic goods and evils is necessary in moral theory? Part of the answer lies in a certain kind of view about the field of a virtue, a view which entails that an account of the virtues requires the prior specification of a 'base-level' set of non-aretaic goods and evils (or values and disvalues).

If one thinks, as does Hurka, that the field of a virtue is a good (or goods) or an evil (or evils), then one is in a bind if one wishes to reject the Thesis of Non-Aretaic Value. For one cannot define a virtue as an attitude of loving a good, for example, unless one assumes the existence of goods, which are the fields of certain virtues, understood independently of virtue.[3] However, if one rejects the idea that the field of a virtue is a good or evil, one escapes this bind. On Aristotelian virtue-ethical views,

2 For examples of theorists who assume the existence of 'objective lists' of values (and disvalues), see John Finnis, *Natural Law and Natural Rights* (Oxford: Oxford University Press, 1980), James Griffin, *Well-Being* (Oxford: Oxford University Press, 1986), and Thomas Hurka, *Perfectionism* (Oxford: Oxford University Press, 1993).

3 See Thomas Hurka, 'Virtue as Loving the Good', *Social Philosophy and Policy* 9 (1992), 149–68.

the fields of virtues are a heterogeneous array of things such as pleasure (rather than the good of pleasure), friends (rather than the good of friendship), small details (rather than the good or evil of small details), failures (rather than the evil of failures), threatening situations (rather than the evil of threatening situations), and so on. A virtue is understood as being well disposed (in respect of reason, emotion, desires, motives, and actions)[4] in regard to these things. This allows for the possibility that pleasure, friendship, and failure, for example, are neither good nor evil in themselves. What is good, for example, is pleasure and friendship, handled *well*—that is, virtuously, where 'handling' covers behaviour, motivation, and emotional response.[5]

Certainly, such things as failure, even if handled *well*, would not unequivocally be called 'good', but other normatively positive descriptions such as 'honourable' or 'worthy' may well be ascribed to the failure, precluding the attribution 'evil'. Let me illustrate. Consider the supposed intrinsic evil of failure with the example of Prada's failure in the America's Cup in February to March 2000. Prada, the Italian syndicate, lost the America's Cup match in Auckland, New Zealand, 0–5. A spectacular failure on the surface—they were beaten by a better crew and a faster boat. But in what way was their failure intrinsically evil? One cannot separate the failure from the surrounding context, its history, and its manner. The *context* includes their defeat by a vastly more experienced match-racing crew and shore team with the home advantage in some of the most difficult sailing conditions in the world. The *history* must take account of the nature of the Prada campaign—their years of hard work mastering conditions on the Hauraki Gulf and boat and sail testing. The *manner* included the style, graciousness in victory and defeat, impeccable conduct of the Prada team, and the skipper in particular, throughout their incredibly tough five-month campaign in the Louis Vuitton challenger series and the match itself. Their conduct made the team stunningly popular in Auckland and New Zealand generally, so much so that they took part in the ticker-tape parade—normally a victor's parade—where they received cheers almost as loud as those given Team New Zealand. Failure suffused with so much virtue and tinged with so little vice is not intrinsically evil in my view. It should also be noted that Prada's

---

[4] See Hursthouse, *On Virtue Ethics.*

[5] See Aristotle, *Nicomachean Ethics*, trans. J. A. K. Thomson, revised Hugh Tredennick (Harmondsworth: Penguin, 1976), 1104b20–1105a9.

failure is inseparably connected with Team New Zealand's success. But if Prada had taken the America's Cup to the Mediterranean, would Team New Zealand's failure, after a sterling campaign, have been regarded as an intrinsic evil? I think not.

I am not saying that failure, met with virtuously, would be an end of a virtuous person. Francesco de Angelis, Prada's skipper, certainly did not take pleasure in his failure. Indeed it is something he avoided, in an intense way. 'So it must have been at least prima facie intrinsically evil', one may claim. No, I think different language is required here—language more at home in virtue ethics. The failure was honourable.

Consider, too, knowledge as a supposed intrinsic value. On the view of Thomas Hurka and others, assuming that knowledge is an intrinsic value, the existence of knowledge as such always contributes positively to the value of a state of affairs. This I think is false. If Team New Zealand had revealed unintentionally the knowledge that it tried to keep closely guarded, that would have contributed negatively to overall value. Part of the point and mystique of America's Cup racing is the zealous guarding of knowledge of syndicates' equipment, boat appendages, special sails, crew competencies, and so forth. That is why they have strict rules about spying.

The Thesis of Non-Aretaic Value also has counterintuitive consequences in its treatment of attitudes towards sadistic pleasure. According to Hurka, a virtuous agent should love more intensely a good or value, the greater it is. Insofar as the goodness of pleasure is independent of its virtue, the pleasure in sadistic pleasure is an intrinsically valuable component of the sadistic state. So a virtuous agent should love more intensely the more intense pleasure of the sadist, even if the sadist's more intense pleasure is produced by acts of even greater cruelty.[6] I find this very

---

[6] Hurka recognizes this difficulty for his view in 'How Great a Good is Virtue', *Journal of Philosophy* 95 (1998), 181–203. In this article, Hurka considers and rejects two opposing views, namely that (a) only pleasures with good objects are good and (b) pleasures with neutral intentional objects can't be good. The first view Hurka regards as counterintuitive because it denies that 'nonintentional pleasures, such as those of suntanning or eating icecream are good' (197). The second implies that a sports fan's pleasure at his team's winning a championship isn't good. However, the view that pleasure suffused with vice (or sufficient vice, or certain kinds of vice) can't be good, does not have these unwanted implications. Hurka tries to capture such a view in a hypothesized revised account of the base-level goods: pleasure is good except when directed at pain, false belief, and failure. He then argues that this view has difficulties. But the revised account is still wedded to the Thesis of Non-Aretaic Value: on a virtue-ethical account, pleasure at certain kinds of failure and pain may not be vicious in certain contexts, and at any rate, failure, false belief, and so forth need not themselves be intrinsically evil.

counterintuitive, even though on Hurka's view a virtuous agent, while loving the *pleasure* of the sadist, should hate the sadism. My own view is that, just as lemon juice is no longer a good thing in a liquid when cyanide is added to it, because it is contaminated, so the pleasure of the sadist is contaminated, and should not be loved. When pleasure, a normally good thing, is sufficiently contaminated by vice, it ceases to be even prima facie good, and is not desired, enjoyed, or pursued by a virtuous person. For such a person, such pleasure is distasteful, even repugnant. It is not a matter of it being outweighed by greater goods.[7]

Notice that I say 'sufficiently' contaminated by vice. Given that virtue is on my view a threshold concept, I do not claim that pleasure or welfare admixed with any vice is worthless. Even assuming that a desperate mother who steals fruit or bread to feed her starving children from those much better situated, would find another way if she were perfectly wise and had considerable energy, we would not say that she is pursuing a worthless end.

It should also be noted that a virtue ethicist should allow that there are some things that are valuable independent of virtue, such as natural objects, human infants, and animals. Their value does not depend on their being virtuous themselves, their being virtuously created, their being virtuously loved, or their being handled virtuously. To say they are valuable is to say that, depending on the kind of objects they are, the context of activity, and the role and position of the agent, they are worth bringing into being, protecting, conserving, maintaining, restoring, pursuing, desiring, and so forth. But the story does not end there, and does not end without a conception of *virtuous* conservation and so forth. These valuable objects are worth pursuing, loving, conserving, and so on, *well*, that is, virtuously.

Consideration of this point brings us to the rejection of the second component of the Thesis of Non-Aretaic Value. The second component is this. Having specified a list of non-aretaic values (and disvalues), the theorist is to understand moral requirements in terms of actions (e.g. pursuing, promoting, instantiating) which are themselves understood non-aretaically. However, if a human being, for example, is worth pursuing, she is worth pursuing *well*, and it is extremely context-dependent

---

[7] For an example of an explicit virtue-ethical rejection of the idea that pleasure (and other so-called goods) are valuable or good independently of virtue, see Michael Slote, 'The Virtue in Self-Interest', *Social Philosophy and Policy* 14 (1997), 264–85.

what counts as pursuing well. Some forms of pursuit are invasive, unjust, or offensive, in other words, manifest vice. At least some valuable objects are worthy of love, but some forms of love are passive-dependent or morbidly dependent,[8] abusive, sadistic. Many valuable objects are worthy of conservation, but some forms of conservation are tasteless, insensitive, inauthentic, or obsessive. Some forms of bringing valuable things into being are unjust, profligate, or uncaring. Again, there are forms of desiring which are obsessive and in a variety of ways lack virtue. It is true that some value-centred theorists such as Hurka accommodate obsessive or over-intense desiring via ideas of proportionality, an account of which does not depend on prior notions of virtue. But this quantitative approach does not begin to capture the rich terrain of appropriateness and inappropriateness captured in virtue and vice language.

It may be replied to this charge that both bonds and status may be recognized in the Thesis of Non-Aretaic Value, in the following way. The bonds of friendship, for example, may be included as a value to which virtues are responsive. Status may be recognized by the inclusion of, for example, knowledge or legitimate authority (understood non-aretaically) in the list of values, and virtues understood to involve loving or promoting these things, or honouring or instantiating these things in one's own life.

However, it is my point that the connection between bonds and virtue and status and virtue (as well as between value and virtue) is not to be understood through the Thesis of Non-Aretaic Value. For example, since friendship is not good without qualification, the bonds of friendship are not good without qualification. T. D. C. Chappell thinks, by contrast, that the chain of justification for an action such as renewing a friendship comes to an end with the statement, 'It's good to renew friendships',[9] because friendship is a basic good. But the chain does not end there, because some friendships may be bad or bad for one, renewal may be bad because one has far too many obligations already, the friendship may have been for a variety of good reasons terminated some time earlier, and so forth. In short, the virtue of friendship involves being well disposed with respect to its field (friends), and that in turn requires virtuous handling, sustenance, and even termination of the bond of

---

8 See Horney, *Neurosis and Human Growth*.

9 *Understanding Human Goods: A Theory of Ethics* (Edinburgh: Edinburgh University Press, 1998), 34.

friendship. The bond must display and express fine inner states including practical wisdom and fine motivational states.

Finally, just how status is to be respected cannot be understood independently of virtue. It is not the case that X's having status is necessarily good without qualification, and it is not the case that *virtuous* acknowledgement of that status can be understood in terms of respect, or some analogous idea, understood non-aretaically. X's status as Y may be compromised: X himself may handle his status viciously, or the status properties may be embedded in vicious institutions. Certainly, obedience as a *virtue*, for example, involves being well disposed with respect to its field (legitimate authority), and that in turn requires virtuous acknowledgement of the status of the authority. However, obedience as a virtue is not *blind* obedience. On occasion, practical wisdom may demand a *questioning* or even disobeying of orders from that authority, where the virtuous agent nonetheless recognizes (as appropriate) her fallibility, her role as just one member of the organization, and the authority of the agent giving orders.

Let me summarize my view on the relation between a virtue and the bases of moral acknowledgement (such as value and bonds). A virtue is a disposition of good responsiveness to items in its field. Though that involves responsiveness appropriate to morally significant features, such as the value of items in a virtue's field or the bonds between those items and the agent, it is not the case that these features are in general set up as good or evil independent of virtue, and that a virtue is standardly a form of responsiveness to these goods. In brief, a virtue is a disposition of being well disposed towards items, and virtuous handling of those items may *make* those items good. Positive evaluation of items in the fields of virtues falls under several categories.

(1) The items may be of a sort that have value independent of virtuous handling, such as (at least many) natural objects, including human infants, animals, large rocks, rock formations, rivers.

(2) The items may be such that their goodness is dependent on virtue, and they may be sought by a virtuous agent. The effect of virtue on these for their goodness is of two types. Though virtue is necessary to make goods of the first type good without qualification, their goodness does not lie simply in their being instruments or fields for the operation of virtue. Goods of this kind include pleasure, wealth, friendship, and honours.

Goods of the second type are goods simply because they are instrumental for the operation of virtue, as a lump of clay is good for the creativity expressed in a fine statue.

(3) Some items have aretaic value, though they are not 'goods', and thus not of either type identified above. They may, however, be fields for the operation of virtue, and may even be instrumentally good in strengthening an agent towards virtue. They would not, however, constitute aims of the virtuous individual. Items of this kind having aretaic value would be failure borne honourably and sickness borne patiently, courageously, or cheerfully.

Let us turn now to the second important thesis related to the bases of moral acknowledgement or responsiveness to be discussed in this section. This is the thesis of Value-Centred Monism.

I have said that to claim that something has value is to claim that it is worth (in varying kinds of context) bringing into existence, nurturing, sustaining, protecting, respecting, loving, pursuing, conserving, preserving, maintaining, protecting, and so forth, well, that is, virtuously. According to Value-Centred Monism, the rightness of moral responsiveness is determined entirely by degree or strength of value. Now I grant that we may speak of items as being more or less valuable, in various ways, according to the degree to which they possess a variety of different features, such as merits (of various sorts), utility (of various sorts), beauty, rationality, creative excellence, sublimity, and so on. Thus we say, for example, that this person is more valuable (to the company, to the team, as a citizen, as a teacher) than that person, this painting is more valuable than that one, this ecosystem or historic building is more valuable (more worthy of preservation) than that one. Certainly, not all things which are valuable are worth bringing into the world or conserving on all possible occasions, in any type of manner, at any cost. It may be thought therefore that the appropriateness of our moral response towards these objects is a function entirely of their degree of value—the claim of the Thesis of Value-Centred Monism.

I shall argue, on the contrary, that just how things are to be pursued, nurtured, respected, loved, preserved, protected, and so forth may often depend on further general features of those things, and their relations to other things, particularly the moral agent. In particular, I shall claim, just how valuable objects are to be respected, nurtured, pursued, and so forth may depend on their good (if they have a good), their status, and the bonds between those things and agents. Degree of value is not necessarily commensurate with other morally relevant bases of moral responsiveness, such as degree of status and strength of bond. In the remainder of this section I argue for the rejection of Value-Centred Monism by considering the role of status and bonds in a range of virtues.

Mary Midgley is one philosopher who rejects Value-Centred Monism. In her *Animals and Why They Matter*, she claims:

> Now there are broadly speaking two things which can make a preference reasonable, namely value and bonding.[10]

On my view, these do not necessarily exhaust the field of bases of moral responsiveness, but let us begin with bonds. The *reason* for the fundamental importance of bonds is explained in *Valuing Emotions* by Michael Stocker and Elizabeth Hegeman, who claim that the virtuousness of response is not always determined by amount or strength of value. According to them:

> various emotions which are absolutely basic and central to our life and to our values are sensitive to self and other, and distance and closeness, not just value and amount of value. This goes a long way toward showing that at least some of our basic values and evaluative structures are to be understood in terms of self and other, and distance and closeness, not just value and amount of value.[11]

Why self and other and distance and closeness are morally relevant has to do with nature and strength of bonds. Consider one of Stocker and Hegeman's own examples, grief. The appropriateness of grief as a virtuous moral response is not characteristically dependent on the degree of value of the item grieved for, but on the bonds between the person grieving and the person grieved for. It may be, of course, that the bonding has lacked virtue, and indeed there has been interesting discussion on whether, for example, the bonds occasioning much of the grief for Princess Diana were phoney or pathological.

There are virtues such as loyalty and perseverance which focus on demands of bonding to institutions and projects, as well as people. For example, perseverance is a virtue requiring one to stick with and bond with one's projects. The rationale of that requirement does not seem entirely to pertain to the value of the projects pursued. Consider a student who begins her university studies doing philosophy. In her second

10 Harmondsworth: Penguin, 1983, 103.
11 Cambridge: Cambridge University Press, 1996, 320.

year she decides that though she enjoys philosophy a great deal she would do more good in the world being a lawyer. So she switches to a law degree. After two years there, she realizes that being a doctor is even more useful. She enrols in Medical School. There she discovers that she is better at the pure sciences than she had thought and realizes that if she works hard she would do more good in the world as a research biochemist. She changes to a Bachelor of Science degree. Let us say that each of these value judgements is absolutely correct. Yet we feel there is something wrong, especially if failure to stick with projects is a form of escape characteristic of lack of self-love. There is a lack of bonding with her own projects that should see her through those projects in a way that survives recognition that there is something she could be doing that is even more useful to the world than the course on which she is currently engaged. The point is that perseverance is a virtue of bonding rather than merely a virtue responding to the demands of value.

Not all virtues of bonding should be seen as involving the responses of respect or love, as opposed to proper use or handling. Respect or love is apt for people, some or all kinds of living things, and perhaps all kinds of natural objects. However, one's bonding with one's money should be weaker than this. Miserliness is the vice of being too strongly bonded with one's money; thrift the virtue of being appropriately bonded with it. In profligacy, the bonds are too weak—money is frittered away in a 'here today, gone tomorrow' attitude. The same applies to other material things such as one's possessions. Carelessness and 'throw-away' consumerism are vices related to inadequate bonding; in the latter vice one is greedy for more and more things without being attached to a modicum of possessions. By contrast, there is a vice of excessive sentimentality where one is unable to give away, sell, or throw away relics of one's childhood.

Relationship ethics emphasizes bonding as a basis of moral response; other ethical systems emphasize status. As Geoffrey Cupit argues in his *Justice as Fittingness*,[12] acknowledgement of status is a distinctive basis of moral acknowledgement which can vary according to type and degree of status. A person can have higher or lower authority, higher or lower rank, higher or lower prestige, higher or lower standing in relation to deferential treatments, worship, or other respectful behaviours. However, variation in status is not always associated with differential degree of status.

12 New York: Oxford University Press, 1996.

Though status properties such as marital status may be associated with a status hierarchy, they need not be. Indeed, various liberation movements are best understood as removing from status hierarchies properties such as social class membership, sexual status, race, and ethnicity. However, some agents with higher status may have legitimate intellectual, cultural, moral, or legal or quasi-legal authority, and failure to acknowledge this may indicate the existence of vices of authority complex, excessive pride, resentment, arrogance, or self-importance.

Types and degrees of status are virtuously recognized and acknowledged by various modes of respect, ranging from forms of deference and worship, acceding to authority, politeness, taking notice, taking seriously, not harming or offending or violating, not deceiving or manipulating, and the various kinds of demeanour which acknowledge status as an elder, woman, married, parent, confidant, and so on. In short, status morality is basically a respect morality, and is characterized by a variety of behaviours which signify and acknowledge status of various sorts. For example, virtues associated with *recognition of* and *respect for* the aged are status-centred as opposed to virtues *of* the aged which focus on what is good for them. (For example, certain sorts of dispositions to act and feel like young people may be a vice in the aged.)

Because of the great variety of status-giving properties, even those virtues which are not specifically role-dependent need to be interpreted in very heterogeneous ways, according to the relevant status of the virtuous agent and the object to whom treatments of various kinds are accorded. Benevolence will take different forms—permitting and prohibiting various kinds of promotion of good, displays of affection, and so on—depending on whether the agent is a spouse, friend, parent, teacher, or therapist.

Answers to the question what counts as status-conferring properties, in given areas and contexts, and why, are controversial. For example, is age a status-conferring property, and do we owe the aged veneration by virtue of that status?[13] And if we owe the aged veneration by virtue of their status as aged, what is it about age that warrants that status? Answers to these questions will determine whether or not (distinctive) respect for the aged is a virtue, and what the nature of that virtue will be. If the high status is warranted by a presumption of greater wisdom

---

[13] See Geoffrey Cupit, 'Justice, Age, and Veneration', *Ethics* 108 (1998), 702–18, for a discussion of this issue.

borne of experience, then the habit of respect will take the form of a certain form of deference to their opinion. If (as Geoffrey Cupit suggests)[14] the status-making property is simply their 'size' in the sense of longevity—the sense that we 'enlarge' with age—the respect will be more akin to the awe or veneration that we accord large mountains or old buildings. On my view, the virtue of veneration or respect for the aged[15] rests on it being decent to mark the fact that they have had (by and large) a long period of productivity (work, raising children, creative endeavours) and that it is therefore indecent to slight or insult them by failing to respect their seniority in various ways by rushing them into retirement, by treating their medical conditions as less worthy of concern than the medical conditions of the younger, and so on. Where an aged person has, however, been a (known) wastrel all of his or her life, a respectful veneration for that person will shade into a compassionate kindness appropriate to her aged condition. The basis of the latter virtue will centre more on bond than on status.

In neo-Kantian ethical theory, the 'problem of status' is conceived as the problem of establishing the scope of universal practical or moral principles.[16] The problem is seen as the problem of the 'ethical standing or status'[17] of, for example, infants, 'barbarians', criminals, 'heretics'; and that is the problem of inclusion or exclusion from the scope of universal principles. Onora O'Neill claims that this problem is 'surprisingly difficult'.[18] In virtue ethics, issues of status are formulated and conceptualized in a distinctive way. If one sees the moral domain through the prism of the virtues, the problem of status is more tractable, because it breaks down into many different problems, identified by the fields of the virtues, and the contexts of their manifestation. Instead of asking whether rocks, rivers, plants, foetuses, children, or art works all have ethical standing, moral status, or are 'morally considerable' in a highly general way, one filters the problems through the various virtues as they

---

14 Ibid.

15 People may think this is too specific to be a virtue of character. But just as the general virtue of benevolence has specific forms of concern, promotion of good etc. according to differing status and bonds, so the general virtue of respectfulness takes specific forms according to those differing features.

16 See, for example, Onora O'Neill, *Towards Justice and Virtue* (Cambridge: Cambridge University Press, 1996), ch. 5.

17 Ibid. 91.

18 Ibid.

operate in different contexts. Art works by comparison with kitsch, trivial dabblings, or jokes have status as cultural icons, and the relevant virtues indicate that a virtuous (moral) agent treats them accordingly, via appropriate appreciativeness, use, handling (including display and conservation), and receptivity. Similarly, inanimate natural objects such as rock formations or beaches have status as natural objects (as opposed to e.g. artificial rocks and beaches), and the relevant environmental virtues indicate how the moral agent regards and treats them (both emotionally and through action) through appropriate appreciativeness, use, handling, and so forth. Again, living non-sentient objects have status not only as natural, but as having a good, and that may call for a somewhat different set of virtues prescribing somewhat different responses. The virtues of friendship recognize status as a friend (rather than just human being). The institutional role virtues recognize status as parent, chief executive of a corporation, lawyer, and so forth. And such virtues concern, variously, how the occupier of a role behaves, feels, and so on, and how non-occupiers of that role behave towards the occupier. In brief, there is not just one difficult problem of moral status. There are innumerable such problems. All these problems will be difficult but not 'surprisingly' so, and the difficulties are tractable because less general.

Many forms of moral acknowledgement based on status are heavily determined by convention. There are legitimate cultural variations in the forms of deference and other kinds of respect owed to individuals by virtue of for example, their age, role, or tribal position. As Sarah Buss argues in a fine discussion,[19] the virtue of courtesy—a virtue 'essential to good manners', which in turn is essential to the respecting of status—has significant cultural and class variations. However, as she also argues, legitimate variation has limits. 'Ritualized humiliations and insults'[20] in caste systems cannot be classed as a mark of virtuous acknowledgement of status position, since the system requiring such behaviour is itself morally flawed. Though certain kinds of familiarity can properly be seen as a vice in relation to *legitimate* hierarchies, as Buss points out, the disposition to humiliate, ritualized or not, cannot be seen as a status-centred virtue acknowledging hierarchy. For no legitimate hierarchy rationalizes a disposition to humiliate.

---

[19] 'Appearing Respectful: The Moral Significance of Manners', *Ethics* 109 (1999), 795–826.
[20] Ibid. 810.

Status-centred virtues may legitimize procedural limits to individual moral autonomy in one's dealings with superior authority. Given that the authority of the moral agent is limited in this way, it is a mark of virtue and practical wisdom in an agent that she knows these limits.[21] As a result, the authoritativeness of status may preclude behaviour which is proportional to degree of value. Assume that the managing director of a company is of less value to that company than an astute, more capable underling. The underling, while properly acknowledging his own greater value, will nonetheless still need to acknowledge in a variety of ways the superior authority of his managing director. If he consistently fails to do so, he may well possess a vice of authority complex.

We turn to a fourth basis of moral acknowledgement, the 'good for'. The good for an individual, or what constitutes its flourishing or well-being or is to its benefit or advantage, is a basis for moral acknowledgement different from value, status, or bond. For some moral philosophers, the 'good for' exhausts the domain of bases of moral acknowledgement. According to Soran Reader:

All moral action, and only moral action, is action that seeks the good of its patients. It is action in other words, that aims to see to it that the needs of the patient are met.[22]

There are the following problems with Reader's monism. It is clear that this kind of monism excludes from the moral domain those status-centred considerations concerned with forms of respect which not only are unconnected with a person's needs, but which constrain their satisfaction. Secondly, not *all* aspects of bond-centred virtues, such as friendship, focus on a patient's good, and some responses expressive of bonds of friendship may even to an extent militate against that good.[23] Thirdly, not all environmental virtue focuses on good. As is well documented, not all things having 'moral considerability' have a good. Though they have no needs, they may have value, in the sense of being worthy of conservation or preservation. Fourthly, response to value-centred considerations such as merits of various kinds is not reducible to response to a patient's good or needs, and certain virtues focus on that kind of

21 See further, Conrad Johnson, 'The Authority of the Moral Agent', in Samuel Scheffler (ed.), *Consequentialism and Its Critics* (Oxford: Oxford University Press, 1988), 261–87.

22 'Principle Ethics, Particularism, and Another Possibility', *Philosophy* 72 (1997), 269–96, at 284.

23 See my 'Profiles of the Virtues', *Pacific Philosophical Quarterly* 76 (1995), 47–72.

response. They are dispositions to recognize, deploy, and not be threatened by people's merits, and to be creative in ways that are not driven by people's needs or good. Finally, we are not morally required to promote or seek the good of all kinds of 'patients'. What about various kinds of harmful bacilli?

(ii) Modes of Moral Acknowledgement and the Hegemony of Promotion

A pluralistic ethics will flourish only if the lush monoculture of consequentialist thought is lessened in vigour. That will happen only if the fertilizer is removed; namely, the pervasive belief in a set of apparent truisms which sustain that thought. These 'truisms' are the tendrils from which we need to extricate ourselves. The last section dispatched two of these: the Thesis of Non-Aretaic Value and the Thesis of Value-Centred Monism. There is a third which has encircled a considerable body of moral theory. This is the Hegemony of Promotion Thesis: the thesis that the only right-making mode of moral acknowledgement is promotion (of value). This section is devoted to undermining that thesis, by challenging the truisms which sustain the Hegemony of Promotion Thesis. The first truism, however, is one I accept, but it may be confused with another thesis which I shall reject. Here is the thesis I accept:

(3) The Value-Relatedness Thesis

> What is right is reckoned in relation to what is actually valuable or good (or disvaluable or bad).

A central attractive feature of consequentialism lies in the following. How can we accept (3) which is so plausible, and avoid consequentialism? Stephen Darwall thinks that this is virtually impossible. He claims:

(i) If the fundamental truths of ethics concern what is intrinsically valuable and worthy of existence for its own sake, then it will seem unavoidable that what one ought to do must be reckoned, in some way, in relation to such value.[24]

(ii) On a value-based approach, a consequentialist theory of the right will seem almost inevitable.[25]

---

[24] 'Rational Agent, Rational Act', *Philosophical Topics* 14 (1986), 35–57, at 41.
[25] Ibid.

However there are a number of moves which must be made if acceptance of (i) is legitimately to lead to acceptance of consequentialism. The two major moves are these. First there is the move from the Value-Relatedness Thesis to what I have called Value-Centred Monism, which, it will be recalled, states that the only 'rightness relevant respects' which serve to make one option better than another are the degree or strength of the values which inhere in those options. Darwall's term 'value-based' is ambiguous between (3) and the stronger thesis of Value-Centred Monism. The move from Value-Relatedness to Value-Centred Monism is discussed below.

The second major move in the acceptance of consequentialism is the move from Value-Centred Monism to consequentialism. That move is made possible by the assumption that promotion is the only fundamental mode of moral acknowledgement. This assumption is the central issue of the present section. But first we need to address the following issue.

I claimed in section (i) that morally appropriate response is not always determined by amount or strength of value, because it can be determined by the recognition of bond, status, or the 'good for' as bases of moral acknowledgement. It seemed that the fundamental bases of moral acknowledgement are plural and that Value-Centred Monism is therefore false. But if the Value-Relatedness Thesis is true how can we avoid Value-Centred Monism? And surely, one may claim, Value-Relatedness is true because the appropriateness of our moral responses—whether the expression of bonds or the respecting of status—requires a prior sorting of items in the world into value categories. And this can be granted, as we shall see, even by those who reject the Thesis of Non-Aretaic Value. I grant that the way the different bases of moral responsiveness or relatedness operate requires a prior sorting of things in the world according to their value status. Think of the difference that would be made were we to think of the world in the manner depicted in the satire 'Report on Resistentialism'.[26] If 'les choses sont contre nous' and my body is a 'chose-en-soi' which I cannot control and a 'Hostile-Thing-to-the-Other', then perhaps we should adopt a view which 'formalizes hatred both in the cosmological and in the psychological sphere'.[27] If all objects were disvaluable, in the ways described, then hatred would be formalized

---

[26] In Paul Jennings, *The Jenguin Pennings* (Harmondsworth: Penguin, 1963), 196–206.
[27] Ibid. 206.

in the non-promotion of good, the non-expression of bonds, and the non-accordance of respect.

The Value-Relatedness Thesis is true, in a sense which does not entail the Thesis of Non-Aretaic Value, because one needs to know which items are worthy of (virtuously) bringing into existence, protecting, nurturing, conserving, loving, desiring, pursuing, and so forth, and which items are not. Such judgements will affect the nature of our bonds, and our acknowledgement of status, and benefit. If hateful or evil things have high status on grounds of power, authority, religious status, ancestry, or whatever, our moral acknowledgement of them may be a (virtuously) propitiatory or pro forma keeping of one's distance, rather than a respectful keeping of one's distance. Again, one will not promote the good of the anthrax bacillus if it is thought to be disvaluable, but one will *ceteris paribus* promote the good of all human beings given that they are 'worthy of existence for [their] own sake'.[28] However, the Value-Relatedness Thesis does not entail that other bases of moral acknowledgement are not superimposed on our prior conceptualizations of items in the world in terms of good or bad or evil, and valuable or disvaluable. The modes of moral acknowledgement may not be entirely determined by strength, degree, or amount of value, for good or benefit, status, or bond may also determine them. In short, (3) Value-Relatedness does not entail (2) Value-Centred Monism. I conclude: though the Value-Relatedness Thesis is true, Value-Centred Monism is false.

Let us turn now to the Hegemony of Promotion Thesis. Even if Value-Centred Monism is accepted, does consequentialism become almost inevitable, as Darwall thinks? I want now to undermine that assumption, whose force depends on the hegemony of promotion as a form of moral response. That is, if one's ethics is value-centred, it is quite standardly assumed that one ought to promote as much value as one is able, or at least, promote a satisfactory amount of value.

Why is the move from Value-Centred Monism to consequentialism so apparently easy to make? The answer lies in the acceptance of:

(4) The Hegemony of Promotion Thesis

The only right-making relation is that of promotion.

Though love, respect, and so forth may feature in the virtues, the consequentialist will claim, *promoting* value is the only relation that determines

---

[28] Darwall, 'Rational Agent, Rational Act', 41.

rightness of acts. Let us now diagnose the appeal of (4), and show why the apparent truisms which support (4) are far from truistic. There is no better place to begin than with Philippa Foot's 'rather simple thought' which she thinks makes utilitarianism (psychologically) compelling.

(5) The Simple Thought

It can never be right to prefer a worse state of affairs to a better.[29]

For the sake of argument, I shall accept the Simple Thought. What I shall argue is objectionable is the progressive strengthening of that thought towards consequentialism.

Here is the next coil of the consequentialist embrace. Once the Simple Thought is granted, we tend to accept as a truism:

(6) The More is Better Thesis

We regard as better a state of affairs in which there is more value rather than less value.

Since more net value may have been produced by an action sufficiently bad that (on certain views) the state of affairs is rendered worse than before, (5) does not entail (6). Despite the fact, however, that the acceptance of (6) makes consequentialism more compelling not even (6) entails (4), the Hegemony of Promotion Thesis. Even if we are glad that there is more value rather than less, why should we see ourselves as beholden to a standard of moral assessment of action as right if and only if value is *promoted* by us? Two steps are required to get from the More is Better Thesis to the Hegemony of Promotion Thesis. Stephen Darwall gives us a clue about the first step in his diagnosis of the appeal of consequentialism:

We begin by thinking of actions as the initiating of changes in the world; actions have consequences.[30]

From this fundamental idea it is but a short step to think of the ethical significance of action, its rationale, as lying in the initiation of change in the direction of the good. Call this view:

---

[29] 'Utilitarianism and the Virtues', *Mind* 94 (1985), 196–209, at 198.
[30] 'Agent-Centred Restrictions from the Inside Out', *Philosophical Studies* 50 (1986), 291–319, at 292.

(7) The Point of Action is to Initiate Change (in the direction of the good).

However, this task-oriented conception of action is itself controversial. For as the responses of appreciation and receptivity or openness indicate, much of our activity reflects our nature as rather more passive. And other responses such as love may incorporate receptivity as a more important response than the initiation of change. This thesis also trivializes the importance of honouring as a response to value, and drives the rejection of the acts and omissions doctrine. If we think that the point of action is to initiate change (in the direction of the good), we downgrade the significance of ways of failing to initiate change, namely those ways which involve a contamination of the agent, a dirtying of her hands.

The task-oriented conception of both action and morality is of central concern to Iris Murdoch in 'The Idea of Perfection',[31] where she criticizes the view that 'actions are, roughly, instances of moving things about in the public world' and nothing counts as an act unless it is 'a bringing about of a recognisable change in the world'.[32] Combine this view of action with the view that morality begins at the point of action, and you get the task-oriented view of morality. Yet the stuff of morality, on Murdoch's view, involves 'attention' or appreciation with a loving gaze. To use Murdoch's own example, when through greater wisdom and love you see someone in a new light, thinking of her as 'gay', 'refreshingly simple', 'spontaneous', 'delightfully youthful', rather than 'bumptious', 'vulgar', 'undignified', and 'tiresomely juvenile', you are 'acting' morally. On my view, appreciation and love are important aspects of the profiles of a wide range of virtues.

The task-oriented conception of action and ethics is not the only assumption made in the implicit identification of the More is Better Thesis with the Hegemony of Promotion Thesis. Even if (7) is accepted, there is a further assumption that promotion is the ethically significant *vehicle of change*. However, change can be wrought by love and creativity, as well as by 'bringing it about', with which love and creativity as vehicles of change should be contrasted. I can bring it about that my child do something by a variety of means, some of which are through love but some of which are the antithesis of love; I can bring it about that art works be created by giving money to art foundations, but this of course is not to

31 In *The Sovereignty of Good* (London: Routledge, 1970), 1–45.
32 Ibid. 5.

create or produce art works myself. But though change is wrought by love, love is not a form of promotion or bringing about, and though creation is (perhaps) a form of 'bringing about', it is not of the same ilk as 'mere' bringing about. So (6) plus (7) are not enough to get us to the Hegemony of Promotion Thesis. We also need:

> (8) The only right-determining method of 'initiating change' is acting so as to bring about or promote (maximal or satisfactory) net value or good.

Thesis (8) as it stands appears innocuous until it is realized that creation is a way of bringing about change which could result in the promotion of net disvalue. And yet if creation is regarded as an independent right-making activity appropriate to human virtuous agents, we might be prepared to claim that such acts of creation in certain circumstances are right, given the satisfaction of distinctive normative standards associated with creation as a form of moral acknowledgement emphasized as central to humans by thinkers such as Nietzsche. Though creation initiates change and has consequences, it would be odd to understand the overall success of creativity in terms of the ideals associated with the *promotion* of value. When assessed as doing well or the best she can when creating an art work, the artist is assessed on the basis of standards and requirements quite other than those emphasized by consequentialists—standards internal to the practices of artistic endeavour where the idea of high *quality* is not reducible to that of 'conducive to the production of a high degree of value'. Only where consequences are sufficiently hideous does overall assessment of the creative act on the basis of value *promoted* kick in: the relation of promotion (of value) constrains that of creation (of items of high quality) only to a certain (though highly controversial and indeterminate) degree. By contrast, the standard of success associated with the promotion of value is that specified in standard definitions of consequentialism. In such definitions, it is assumed that betterness of states of affairs is understood in terms of amount of net value (compare the More is Better Thesis).

Again, doing well or the best we can in changing things through love will preclude change which exhibits or displays the antithesis of love— for example, maximizing the good via the ruthless or callous infliction of harm, as opposed to harm or damage caused by 'tough love'. A philosophy based on love of individuals has a different conception of the virtue of benevolence than that of consequentialism.

In summary, I suspect that a deep-seated source of the error that right

responses always *realize* value is the view that the point of action is to initiate change, and a deep-seated source of the error that right action
which realizes value must *promote* value in a standard consequentialist
sense is that the standards of success for those various kinds of response
which realize value are thought to be reducible to those which constitute
success in promoting value. It is only by a study of human character and
of distinctively human responses to the world that we can gain a full
appreciation of right-making responses to items in the fields of the
virtues. An appreciation of morally correct ways of going on is not to be
gained by appeal to a set of truisms or 'platitudes' which supposedly flow
from the nature of value alone. It is not the nature of value alone which
yields the More is Better Thesis, the Hegemony of Promotion Thesis, or
the Point of Action is to Initiate Change Thesis. An adequate view about
how morally to go on must be derived rather from an appreciation of
human relations to objects in the world, and that appreciation derives not
just from the nature of those objects but from a study of human nature.
Once we focus on that, we see that the apparent truisms about moral
action flowing from 'truisms' about *value* turn out to be very controversial.
Once we appreciate there are a variety of human ways of relating to items
in the fields of the virtues, it becomes highly controversial which of these
types of relations should dominate, if any. Those views depend not on
truisms about value, but on extremely controversial views or *Welt-
anschaungen* about *human* relations to the world.

The consequentialist may make the following replies to the foregoing
arguments. Here is the first. Though *the virtues* are constituted by a plurality of modes of moral acknowledgement in their profiles, these modes
may be instrumentally valuable as ways of promoting value.[33] Such a
reply would have virtues understood as instrumental goods which serve
a basket of values specifiable independent of virtue. However, I have
already questioned the assumption that values such as love, friendship,
and pleasure are independent of virtue. For these are valuable only insofar as they are pursued, expressed, and so on, excellently (or well enough).
The second reply invokes a distinction between acting well and acting
rightly. To act well is to act from a fully virtuous disposition, but to act
rightly is simply to promote best consequences. However, once pluralism
in the profiles of the virtues is accepted within a consequentialist theory

---

[33] See Julia Driver, 'Introduction', *Character and Consequentialism. Utilitas* 13 (2001), 136–51,
at 147.

of the right, the distinction between acting rightly and acting well is not just a matter of the former being more austere in its requirements than the latter. It is not merely the case that acting well involves fineness of inner states, whereas acting rightly does not involve fineness of inner states. Rather, there is arguably a serious dissonance between acting well and acting rightly, since, once pluralism in the profiles of the virtues is accepted, fineness of inner states cannot be understood in terms simply of being motivated, as a matter of disposition, to produce the best possible outcomes. For such fineness must be constituted not merely by motivations to promote good and value, but also by motivations to express bonds through love, respect status, and so forth.

In my response to the two consequentialist replies I do not aim to add to the literature on moral schizophrenia and the difficulties of indirect versions of consequentialism. The point of this section is to remove the motivation for consequentialist thought. In realizing this aim I focused attention on the various faces of value-centredness: the thesis of Non-Aretaic Value and the Thesis of Value-Centred Monism, as well as the Thesis of the Hegemony of Promotion (and its supporting supposed 'truisms'). Once the struts supporting these theses are removed, we can study the moral terrain afresh and accept pluralism in the modes and bases of moral acknowledgement not just within the virtues, but within the broad compass of moral theory.

3

Virtue and the Good Life

(i) Introduction

In *The Hitch Hiker's Guide to the Galaxy*,[1] we know the Answer to the Ultimate Question, but we don't understand the Ultimate Question. In a sense this is true of ethics. At a mundane enough level, we know what counts as being morally decent. There is pretty solid agreement on many of its features: treating people with respect and consideration, being loyal to friends and colleagues, being charitable, showing appropriate care and affection. But what is the question to which these are answers?

Even for virtue ethicists, this is not obvious. For some in the eudai-monist tradition, the Ultimate Question is 'What is it to live well?'[2] That is, given a standard reading of 'living well', ethics begins with a conception of the good life. However, according to the definition of virtue given in Chapter 1, virtues are qualities which enable their possessors to respond well to the 'demands of the world', as a matter of disposition. Such dispositions make a person good, but do they make for a good *life*? As Charles Guignon notes, 'asking about the good life for humans is not the same—or is not obviously the same—as asking what it is to be a good human'.[3] So maybe, for virtue ethics, the Ultimate Question is 'What makes a person good?'

It remains unclear then, what is the Ultimate Question for a virtue ethics. On my account, virtue by definition makes for goodness in human beings, and the Ultimate Question is what constitutes this goodness. Eudaimonism shares this view, but argues for a connection between

---

[1] Douglas Adams, *The Hitch Hiker's Guide to the Galaxy: A Trilogy in Four Parts* (London: Pan Books, 1979).

[2] See Rosalind Hursthouse, 'Aristotle, Nicomachean Ethics', in *Philosophers Ancient and Modern*, Royal Institute of Philosophy Lecture Series 20 (suppl. to *Philosophy*) (Cambridge: Cambridge University Press, 1985), 35–53, at 35.

[3] Introduction to Charles Guignon (ed.), *The Good Life* (Indianapolis: Hackett, 1999), p. vii.

goodness in humans and a good *life* for a human which is so intimate that for eudaimonism, the Ultimate Question of ethics is what it is for a human being to have a good life.

It is the task of this and the next chapter to explore the connection between the possession and exercise of virtue as a disposition of excellent (or good enough) responsiveness to the demands of the world, and the living of a good life. I argue in this and the next chapters that there are deep connections, but that they are not as tight as is claimed by eudaimonism. To explore these connections, we need a basic concept of the good life. Unfortunately, what is the basic concept of the good life and how it differs from the concept of what it is to be a good human are questions not easy to answer, for there are several basic concepts of the good life in the current literature. Here is the first:

(1) A good life is a flourishing or thriving life.

According to Guignon:

The question of the good life aims at identifying the most fulfilling, meaningful, and satisfying life possible for humans, a life which may be described as thriving, flourishing, and (to use a still older vocabulary) 'blessed'.[4]

This is the basic concept of the good life employed in standard eudaimonistic virtue ethics. Such an ethics claims that a virtue is not merely a good quality in a human being (i.e. something that makes for goodness in humans), but is also needed for a thriving or flourishing life. That is, a virtue is characteristically beneficial to a human being. Eudaimonistic virtue ethics, then, makes a rather tight connection between the good life and goodness in humans. The precise nature of this connection and the credentials of eudaimonistic virtue ethics is the topic of the next chapter.

Another concept of the good life makes moral meritoriousness an essential component of the good life, explicitly, and by definition. So we have:

(2) A good life is both morally meritorious and personally satisfying (thriving, personally successful).

A view such as this is held by John Kekes:

A life will be called ... 'good' only if it is both personally satisfying and morally meritorious. Either component alone would not be sufficient to make life good.

---

[4] Ibid.

For personal satisfaction may be obtained at the cost of causing much evil, and the price of moral merit may be the frequent frustration of reasonable desires, and neither evil nor frustrated lives should be supposed to be good.[5]

Kekes's account of the good life, however, does not effect a conceptual tie between the good human and the good human life, since it is at least conceptually possible for a human to lead a morally meritorious life, but lack elements of a good life which are necessary to, or further enhance, her personal satisfaction.

A third account of the good life is the following:

    (3) A good life is a life in which personal goods dominate.[6]

On this concept, personal goods are contrasted with moral goods, and on standard views are assumed to come into conflict to some extent with the living of a moral life. Concept (3) of the good life is not equivalent to either concept (1) or (2), since the notion of enjoying personal goods is not equivalent to that of flourishing, thriving, and personal satisfaction. There is a further problem in understanding how the good life and the moral life on concept (3) are related. It would be odd to class the appreciation of nature, love of individuals, and the products and results of creativity as (mere) personal goods like the enjoyment of tennis or eating. So are they moral goods? Not obviously, for on dominant current conceptions of morality in the analytic tradition, to class all of these as *moral* goods would be to espouse a problematically broad conception of morality. It is unclear then how to classify aspects of the profiles of virtues—such as creativity, love, and appreciation—in terms of the distinction between 'personal' and 'moral' goods. Here as elsewhere, the interests of virtue ethics are not well served by current classifications which arise within alternative traditions and systems.

How then can the problem of the relation between virtue and the good life be conceived in virtue-centred terms? Given that a person who consistently responds appropriately to the demands of the world is good (even if not fully excellent if they do not do so from a state of virtue), the following problem arises for the good life. How severe is the tension between so-called 'prudential' components of the good life, such as per-

---

  [5] *The Morality of Pluralism* (Princeton, N.J.: Princeton University Press, 1993), 9.

  [6] This is the notion of the good life adopted by Brian Leiter in 'Nietzsche and the Morality Critics', *Ethics* 107 (1997), 250–85, at 260. See also Thomas Nagel, *The View from Nowhere* (New York: Oxford University Press, 1986), 193 ff.

sonal satisfaction and thriving, and (consistent) appropriate responsiveness to the demands of the world?

For the sake of terminological convenience, I shall assume that a good life has both prudential components (personal satisfaction, thriving, and so on), and a component of moral meritoriousness, that is, consistent appropriate responsiveness to the demands of the world. In terms of this terminological assumption, we can understand the central, substantive claim of this chapter as follows. A *virtuous* life, that is, one in which virtue is possessed and exercised consistently, reduces the potential tension between these two broad components of the good life in two main ways. First, we can show a certain sort of connection between the thriving, flourishing life of personal satisfaction and the life of *virtuous* responsiveness to the demands of the world. Second, we can show that *virtuous* responsiveness to the demands of the world should not be understood in terms of the narrow understandings of the moral, and moral virtue, currently popular in much philosophy, and that as a result, the gap between the good and the moral life is reduced. The first way of reducing the tension between the two broad components of the good life in the assumed sense is the topic of section ii below, 'Virtue and Flourishing', and the second way is the topic of section iii, 'Virtue and the Demands of the World'.

A claim that virtue integrates the two broad components of the good life has both a stronger and a weaker reading, which I shall call the 'optimistic' and the 'less optimistic' views. Though virtue ethics in general rejects the common presupposition of severe tension between the components of the good life, species of virtue ethics can be distinguished according to their relative optimism or pessimism about the potential for tension between these components. On the optimistic view, the components of the good life are not only broadly integrated, but the virtues central to the moral meritoriousness of a life are also characteristically good *for* the agent. When possessing and exercising the virtues does not lead to the benefit of the agent, that is due to ill luck rather than to a tendency of the virtue itself. On the less optimistic view, it is possible for a virtue to have tendencies to reduce personal satisfaction by causing harm and unhappiness to the agent. Such harm and unhappiness cannot be laid at the door of ill luck. Though the optimistic view is most closely associated with virtue ethics, I shall reject it in Chapter 4, and defend a version of the second, less optimistic view.

In short, I aim to show how a virtue-centred ethics can reduce the gap between the potentially conflicting components of the good life, but, I shall claim, the gap cannot be closed completely. Having brought the components together in this chapter, I pull them apart somewhat in the next, arguing against the eudaimonistic claim that a virtue should be understood not merely as a trait that makes humans good, but as a trait that characteristically benefits its possessor.

Let us turn now to the first of the two prongs of my virtue-ethical argument for a claim that virtue is central to the good life.

(ii) Virtue and Agent-Flourishing

I consider here the first of the two main ways my virtue-ethical theory integrates the two components of the good life: namely the connection between virtue and the flourishing of the agent. The theory shares the following standard feature of virtue ethics. A conception of the virtues is partly shaped by a conception of the flourishing of the kind of being who possesses them. Human beings are creatures who develop or mature: they grow both psychologically and physically. On this conception of virtue, any theory of virtue must have a conception of excellence of character (partly) shaped by a conception of healthy human growth. If this is so, then a full theory of virtue is parasitic on a 'background' theory of human psychology and development. An adequate theory of the virtues would then be answerable to a constraint, which I shall call the Constraint on Virtue:

A correct conception of the virtues must be at least partly shaped by a correct conception of healthy growth and development which in part constitute our flourishing.[7]

In Chapter 1, I defined a virtue as a disposition of acknowledging items in the fields of the virtue in an excellent or good enough way. The Constraint on Virtue is not entailed by this definition, but is part of a substantive virtue ethics, which aims to be naturalistic, at least in a weak sense. Note that it is not thereby committed to a stronger naturalism espoused by Rosalind Hursthouse (discussed in Chapter 4, section v). Note, too, that the constraint does not claim that the point of a virtue is to maximize or even conduce to the health or flourishing of the possessor of the virtues, but it does suggest that our conceptions of virtuous

---

[7] I say in part, because I share Aristotle's view that external factors such as lack of resources and very bad fortune can prevent human flourishing.

modes of moral acknowledgement should be appropriate to both human development and to ideals of human health. This has two general implications. First, virtue may be relative to phases of development (so that there may be virtues of childhood that are not virtues of adulthood and there may be virtues of old age that are not virtues of those in their prime).[8] Second, the characterization of the profiles of the virtues is at least influenced by conceptions of human psychic and physical health.

A conception of virtue partly shaped by the Constraint on Virtue allows for a close connection between virtuous, morally meritorious lives, healthy growth and development, and personal satisfaction and flourishing. The connection between virtue and the flourishing of the agent is confirmed by psychological findings. For example, as Daniel Goleman points out,[9] chronic anger and hostility form the basis not only of much vice, but also of human ill health: ill health that can be averted by the cultivation of virtue:

The antidote to hostility is to develop a more trusting heart. All it takes is the right motivation. When people see that their hostility can lead to an early grave they are ready to try.[10]

Furthermore there is a connection between chronic hostility and vice. As Goleman puts it,

hostility becomes so constant as to define an antagonistic personal style, one marked by repeated feelings of mistrust and cynicism and the propensity to snide comments and put downs, as well as more obvious bouts of temper and rage.[11]

On the positive side, a conception of virtue subject to the Constraint on Virtue provides an understanding of psychological health as a state necessitating the living of lives that are virtuous in (at least) many respects. Karen Horney puts the point this way:

Apparently, [a human being] cannot . . . develop his full human potentialities unless he is truthful to himself; unless he is active and productive; unless he relates himself to others in a spirit of mutuality. Apparently he cannot grow if he

---

[8] For a defence of this view, see ch. 1 of Michael Slote, *Goods and Virtues* (Oxford: Clarendon Press, 1983).

[9] In *Emotional Intelligence: Why it can Matter more than IQ* (London: Bloomsbury, 1996).

[10] Ibid. 172.

[11] Ibid. 173.

indulges in a 'dark idolatry of self' (Shelley) and consistently attributes all his own shortcomings to the deficiencies of others.[12]

Finally, mature, healthy agents characteristically derive personal satisfaction from morally meritorious behaviour which springs from virtuous character. This is not to say that they are self-righteous or self-congratulatory: rather, as Aristotle notes, for such agents virtuous behaviour is standardly pleasurable,[13] or at least not irksome. In brief, then, the first main way in which virtue is central to the good life by integrating its two components is through the Constraint on Virtue.

However, this claim needs some explication and qualification. A number of difficulties stand in the way of a correct understanding of the Constraint on Virtue, and its ability to integrate the two major components of the good life. First, does it follow from the fact that a correct conception of the virtues is (partly) shaped by a correct conception of human development, growth, and flourishing, that living a life in accordance with the virtues is necessarily good for the agent, barring ill luck? Second, does it follow from the fact that a correct conception of the virtues is (partly) shaped by a correct conception of human flourishing that the specification of the virtues is entirely determined by the qualities of a fully flourishing human agent? And if virtues are so determined, but it is rare for us fully to flourish, how can virtues be central to the good life for most of us?

My discussion of these questions will reveal my understanding of the Constraint on Virtue, and the nature of its ability to integrate the two components of the good life. It will reveal the character of my virtue ethics as the 'less optimistic' variety identified above. The first question concerns the issue of whether a virtue ethics which accepts the Constraint on Virtue should be eudaimonistic in character. This issue is so complex, and so central to the modern conception of virtue ethics, that it deserves a separate chapter. Acceptance of the Constraint on Virtue does not entail eudaimonism; indeed, I shall reject eudaimonism.

The second question is whether it is the fully healthy individual who sets the standards for virtue. We should not understand the Constraint on Virtue to entail that all virtues are traits which only fully healthy,

[12] *Neurosis and Human Growth*, 15.

[13] Though not necessarily always: see Rosalind Hursthouse's discussion of virtue and self-control in 'Virtue Ethics and the Emotions', in D. Statman (ed.), *Virtue Ethics: A Critical Reader* (Edinburgh: Edinburgh University Press, 1997), 99–117.

mature agents possess. For as has been noted (by e.g. Linda Zagzebski), 'to have a virtue it is not necessary that one be perfect'.[14] This permissiveness about virtue has two aspects, one of which is noted by Zagzebski. She claims that a virtuous agent, virtuous in respect *x*, need not display *x* on *every* occasion in which displaying *x* is the appropriate behaviour. 'It is sufficient if one is reliably virtuous in sensitivity and behaviour.'[15]

Furthermore, the standards of what counts as displaying a virtue need not be set by the perfectly healthy person. One reason for this is that 'virtue' is a threshold concept. A person can be virtuous while another can be even more virtuous. Even if only the perfectly psychologically strong and healthy person can be perfectly virtuous because, for example, only such a person is entirely free of those vices associated with hostility, fear, anxiety, and lack of self-love, the standards for virtue *tout court* should be less lofty. For our standards for virtue *tout court* should be responsive to the state of the world relative to the costs borne by individuals in achieving utopian or perfect virtue. It may be the case, for example, that the demands the world places on us are seen by some as calling for considerable self-sacrifice. But maybe only the strongest, healthiest agents can bear such sacrifice with complete virtue. On my view, defended in later chapters, altruism that exhibits less than the full profile of relevant virtues (such as generosity, compassion, or benevolence), or exhibits them in a less than excellent way, can be regarded as manifesting virtue in certain circumstances, even though the altruism is expressive of states not fully psychologically healthy (see Chapters 4, 6, and 9).

The above point is particularly important given the real possibility that, as Nietzsche says, sickness caused by factors obstructing health, is a standard condition and difficult to ameliorate. This is how Nietzsche puts it:

For man is more sick, more uncertain, more mutable, less defined, than any other animal ... he is *the* sick animal.[16]

He is ... the most endangered, the most chronically and deeply sick of all sick animals.[17]

[14] Linda Trinkhaus Zagzebski, *Virtues of the Mind: An Inquiry into the Nature of Virtue and the Ethical Foundations of Knowledge* (Cambridge: Cambridge University Press, 1996), 156.

[15] Ibid.

[16] *On the Geneaology of Morals*, trans. Douglas Smith (Oxford: Oxford University Press, 1996), 3rd Essay, sect. 13, p. 100.   [17] Ibid.

The question arises: do we want to confine virtue in general to 'mankind's *strokes of luck*'?[18] Why not reserve for them a special type of virtue, analogous to Aristotle's heroic virtues? Let us leave open the possibility of a conception of virtue which permits us lesser mortals to display virtue in relation to the demands of the world and ourselves.

Nietzsche's pessimism is echoed by later psychoanalytic theory influenced by Nietzsche's thought, and by subsequent neurophysiological study. In his *Understanding Human Nature*,[19] Alfred Adler points out the variety of vicissitudes to which we are standardly subject, and which cause our natural striving for growth to be in various ways stunted and inhibited. This view is confirmed by neurophysiological studies, as Daniel Goleman claims:

Le Doux turns to the role of the amygdala in childhood to support what has long been a basic tenet of psychoanalytic thought: that the interactions of life's earliest years lay down a set of emotional lessons based on the attunements and upsets in the contacts between infants and caretakers. These emotional lessons are so potent and yet so difficult to understand from the vantage point of adult life because, believes Le Doux, they are stored in the amygdala as rough, wordless blueprints for emotional life.[20]

Add to this the fact that these attunements and interactions are all too frequently negative and damaging, leading to fear and anger as forms of 'blueprints' (see further Chapter 8), and you have Nietzsche's 'imperilled' status of human beings. If the views of Nietzsche and post-Nietzscheans on human nature are correct, it is vital that we form a conception of virtue that is appropriate for what Nietzsche has called 'the convalescent'. Such a conception is open, indeterminate. There are two broad possibilities. We could lower our sights, tempering the extent of our benevolence, caring, perseverance, or courage, and call these virtues. Or we could directly emulate and cultivate the virtues of the strong, 'being virtuous beyond our strength', and call that virtue. This, however, is a risky manoeuvre, possibly resulting not just in harm to the agent but in, for example, damaging, misguided altruism, which is based more on resentment than on genuine love for fellow human beings (see further Chapter 6). Or it may result in apparently strong, ruthless leaders, who

---

18 Ibid. 3rd Essay, sect. 14, p. 100.

19 Trans. Walter Bevan Wolfe (London: Allen & Unwin, 1932).

20 Goleman, *Emotional Intelligence*, 22.

are convinced that they are doing good, but are really motivated by greed or power needs reflecting a weak psyche.

Whether or not less than ideal virtue reaches the threshold for virtue is a matter of judgement, involving assessments about the degree to which the exercise of such putative virtue meets the demands of the world in its various forms. Since the demands of the world which it is the point of the virtues to acknowledge include not just the demands of the agent (to e.g. realize herself), and insofar as some pessimism about the capacities of agents to attain full strength and health is warranted, I am led to reject a strong version of 'an ethics of self-realization'. According to Karen Horney, we should espouse what she calls a 'morality of evolution', 'in which the criterion of what we cultivate or reject in ourselves lies in the question: is a particular attitude or drive inductive or obstructive to my human growth?'[21] The combination of a suitably pessimistic view about the possibilities for full health, and the fact that personal growth is but one value which makes demands on us, leads me to adopt a conception of virtue which is constrained by views on human health and growth, but virtues are not actually defined as 'dispositions conducive to personal growth'.

My warnings against strong versions of a connection between virtue and health allow me to escape the following objection of Gary Watson:

our conception of morality resists the analogy with health, the reduction of evil to defect.[22]

My view avoids this rather familiar objection to virtue ethics. A virtue, as a good quality of character in a human, is a disposition to acknowledge the 'demands of the world' in ways suitably constrained by *human* nature. However, this constraint is not to reduce virtue to health. The constraint entails only that, although there are many possible ways of meeting the demands of the world, some of these ways are not excellences in *humans*.

In summary, the Constraint on Virtue allows for a connection between morality and the flourishing of the individual agent, and thereby a closing of the putative gap between so-called prudential and moral components of the good life. However I have claimed that the connection is not tight for two basic reasons. As I shall argue in the next chapter,

---

21 *Neurosis and Human Growth*, 15.

22 See Gary Watson, 'On the Primacy of Character', in D. Flanagan and A. O. Rorty (eds.), *Identity, Character, and Morality* (Cambridge, Mass.: MIT Press, 1990), 449–83, at 462.

the constraint does not entail eudaimonism (the view that all virtues—barring ill luck—benefit their possessors). Secondly in imperfect worlds, the standards for virtue should not be set by the fully strong, healthy, flourishing individual, though according to the constraint, they are influenced by their qualities.

The Constraint on Virtue is implicated in another aspect of a lessening of the contrast between 'self-interest' and morality, namely a certain virtue-ethical conception of the place of the 'subjective' and 'self-interest' in the objective requirements of morality. Through the concepts of objectivity, impartiality, and demandingness or stringency, morality is conceived as an enterprise in which we to an extent transcend the lower, base, or 'juvenile' aspects of our nature in responding to the demands of the world. The idea of virtue is friendly to the possibility of personal satisfaction in the moral life because the notions of objectivity and stringency are understood through the idea of human virtue rather than through abstract idealizations inimical to human nature. On my view, explicated in Part III, objectivity and demandingness or stringency should be virtue-centred notions, and in this way the ideas of appropriate personal satisfaction and moral meritoriousness are integrated through what I have called the 'shape' of the virtues. If the shape of a virtue is too demanding, because, for example, the requirements of objectivity are set at too transcendent a level, success in integrating the moral meritoriousness of a life and the personal satisfaction of that life will be elusive. The more transcendent is the shape of a virtue the more disconnected will be the moral life and the good life. It will be my purpose in Part III to bring together the ideas of the moral and good life through a suitable conception of the shape of a virtue, and a virtue-centred conception of objectivity and demandingness.

We turn now to the final way in which virtue closes the gap between the components of the good life, via a connection between virtue and the flourishing of the agent. This has to do with the nature of virtue itself as an excellence of *character* in which the agent's affective, motivational, and rational dispositions are all in good order. Only if one's character conforms to standards of moral merit will personal satisfaction and flourishing coincide with moral merit. For only if such coincidence flows from character will one's inclinations, emotions, and reasons meet moral standards as a matter of disposition. Mere knowledge of moral demands does not motivate in a frictionless way unless desire to respond to them is built into the fabric of one's emotional disposition. This feature is also necessary for the good life as a social being. For rules (with sanctions) alone do not make for a good society. Not only do rules have to be made and interpreted by agents, but where there is no desire to obey them appropriately as a matter of disposition, socially necessary rules will too often be circumvented, interpreted in self-serving ways, interpreted inhumanely or excessively rigidly, or interpreted loosely in ways that display weakness and cowardice. The social importance of the 'inner' life of virtue is expressed powerfully by C. S. Lewis:

> What is the good of telling . . . ships how to steer so as to avoid collisions if, in fact, they are such crazy old tubs that they cannot be steered at all? What is the good of drawing up, on paper, rules for social behaviour, if we know that, in fact, our greed, cowardice, ill temper, and self-conceit are going to prevent us from keeping them? I do not mean for a moment that we ought not to think, and think hard, about improvements in our social and economic system. What I do mean is that all that thinking will be mere moonshine unless we realize that nothing but the courage and unselfishness of individuals is ever going to make any system work properly. It is easy enough to remove the particular kinds of graft or bullying that go on under the present system: but as long as men are twisters or bullies they will find some new way of carrying on the old game under the new system. You cannot make men good by law: and without good men you cannot have a good society. That is why we must go on to think . . . of morality inside the individual.[23]

Lewis focuses on the integrative function of virtue in the good life: on virtue as a property of human beings in which their 'inner' lives are in order, and in harmony with and expressed by, their 'outer' actions.

Understanding the distinction between the harmony of virtue and the relative disharmony of self-control, and understanding the relationship between these distinctions and the fully excellent and moral life, are not without problems. Two issues deserve (and have received) attention. First, the facts that a virtuous agent's *choices* are in line with virtue, and that such an agent finds non-virtuous choices repugnant or distasteful, does not entail that she necessarily exercises those choices gladly and with pleasure, and ought to do so. There are two kinds of difficult cases. Some virtuous actions are (and ought to be) unpleasant for virtuous agents. Such cases are the bearing of very painful news to friends and relatives.[24] And Aristotle himself speaks of a virtuous agent's sacrificing himself

---

[23] *Mere Christianity* (London: Fontana, 1955), 68–9.

[24] Karen Stohr's example in 'Harmony, Continence, and Virtuous Agency', unpublished paper read to the American Philosophical Association (Pacific Division), Albuquerque, N. Mex., April 2000.

courageously as something not done with enjoyment.[25] Another kind of case is discussed by Hursthouse.[26] A virtuous agent, being a human being, is often overcome, quite properly, with strong emotions such as grief, and may be in straitened circumstances. Such emotions and circumstances may impede the performance of virtuous actions. Of course, it is controversial just what virtue requires in these kinds of case. Poverty should not tempt a virtuous agent to steal for the sake of possessing designer clothes; but temptation to steal in these circumstances for the sake of feeding one's severely malnourished children is another matter.

To emphasize the harmony of outer and inner in the life of virtue is not therefore to say that the moral life is always easy for the virtuous agent. Furthermore, even in normal circumstances, the attunement of emotion so that it is, as a matter of disposition, appropriately responsive to the complexities of the situation is not easy. Though the work of Rosalind Hursthouse, Nancy Sherman, Michael Stocker, Robert Solomon, and others has eloquently advocated the return of the emotions to centre stage in ethics, and deplored the suspicion with which emotion has been treated, virtue ethics *is* suspicious of *inappropriate* emotion. As Goleman claims:

Our passions, when well exercised, have wisdom; they guide our thinking, our values, our survival. But they can easily go awry, and do so all too often. As Aristotle saw, the problem is not with emotionality, but with the appropriateness of emotion and its expression. The question is, how can we bring intelligence to our emotions—and civility to our streets and caring to our communal life?[27]

And as Aristotle says:

Anyone can become angry—that is easy. But to be angry with the right person, to the right degree, at the right time, for the right purpose, and in the right way— this is not easy.[28]

(iii) Virtue and the 'Demands of the World'

We turn now to the second main way in which virtue integrates the two major components of the good life. I wish to show how a virtue-centred

---

[25] *Nicomachean Ethics*, 1117b10.   [26] 'Virtue Ethics and the Emotions'.

[27] *Emotional Intelligence*, p. xiv.

[28] *Nicomachean Ethics*, cited by Goleman, *Emotional Intelligence*, p. ix.

conception of morality renders problematic certain narrow conceptions of 'morality' which tend to drive the concepts of the good life and the moral life apart. Since the distinction between the moral and the non-moral, the distinction between moral and personal goods, and the distinction between the prudential and the moral are not well suited to virtue ethics, it is difficult to find non-tendentious language to express this argument. I shall argue for the 'pervasiveness of the moral' in a virtue-ethical sense, through the following claims.

(i) Virtue is pervasive in the sense that character is expressed in the warp and woof of daily life, and such expression should be seen as important.

(ii) To the reply that *moral* virtue is not pervasive, I argue that a distinction between a narrow set of 'moral' virtues (the cardinal virtues) and other so-called 'non-moral' virtues such as tact and charm is arbitrary.

(iii) Even those virtues seen as paradigmatically moral have a complex profile, constituted not merely by modes of moral response acknowledged in the dominant consequentialist and deontological traditions (namely, respectively, promotion of value, and respect for individuals in virtue of status). Their profile is also constituted by receptivity, appreciation, love, and creativity—forms of moral acknowledgement which, though clearly not merely in the domain of personal goods and the prudential, are not always recognized as clearly 'moral' either.

Given (i), (ii), and (iii), virtue (and vice) seep into every nook and cranny of life. Let me now consider my first claim—that character is pervasive and important. For a virtue ethicist, ethics is quotidian in two ways. First, morality is not just about one central feature of human life–justice and the regulation of conflict.[29] The 'warp and woof' of life in its various facets— the expression of culture or heritage, central activities such as bringing up children, work, or leisure—are part of the stuff of morality. Second, morality is quotidian in the sense that character is expressed in,

---

[29] See e.g. David Wong, for whom morality is a system of rules whose rationale is to resolve 'internal conflicts of requirements . . . that affect others and . . . interpersonal conflicts of interests in general': *Moral Relativity* (Berkeley: University of California Press, 1984), 1.

and either enhances or blights, all those activities. Let me illustrate these claims with an example.

One may imagine that nothing can be further removed from the heady, not to mention heavy domain of 'morality' than the world of 'talk sport' radio in a far-flung Pacific nation. Perhaps some moral rules apply: don't be racist or sexist, don't blaspheme, don't be obscene. (The last two in mild incarnations are not taken very seriously in all countries like the author's.) But my example does not bear on any of these traditional 'moral rules'. Here is the case. It applies to New Zealand, a tiny country of little more than three and a half million people, where sport is almost a religion, and for a great number of people substitutes for culture and for what Heidegger calls 'heritage'. Sport gives many New Zealanders a vicarious sense of importance through national success. Talk sport radio is very popular. Especially during the period before and after the rugby football World Cup, 1999, callers often vented their spleen against Auckland, New Zealand's largest city (now four contiguous cities), containing one-third of New Zealand's population. Callers denigrated Auckland players and attitudes, claimed that X, Y, and Z not from Auckland should replace Aucklanders in national sports teams, and demanded that the Auckland-based national rugby coach should be replaced. What is the relevance of this for a virtue-ethical conception of morality? One may argue that these callers were exhibiting resentment as a vice, which in this case manifested itself in hostility towards a (relatively) large and rich city. Such a vice blights a wide range of activities. In the area illustrated, Aucklanders who would otherwise enjoy talk sport radio turned off their radios in irritation, and resentment-filled individuals have booed Auckland players playing in national sides, whom they thought should be replaced by locals.[30] But resentment-filled, angry individuals may manifest this vice in more serious forms: in racism, abuse against children and women, murder, and genocide.

Let us now consider my second claim—the arbitrariness of a narrow understanding of *moral* virtue. Even if it is agreed that character is expressed in a wide range of activities constituting the good (or not so good) life, many of these traits are thought not to be *moral* virtues. There is a tendency to fixate on the 'cardinal' virtues as truly moral virtues,

---

[30] Here is another everyday example. It may be said that choosing an apple or a pear for lunch is paradigmatically a 'non-moral' choice. But either choice may be temperate (and thereby virtuous) when the agent could have eaten three doughnuts instead.

whereas other virtues, though important for the good life, have nothing to do with morality. This would not be so serious if a tendency to identify the 'moral' with the important or the overriding did not also exist. This tendency downplays the significance of those virtues relegated to the 'non-moral', for example, the quotidian, the 'merely' practical, or those such as solid self-confidence which are thought to be relevant to psychological health rather than 'morality'.

My view that moral virtues are legion (and not just limited to so-called 'cardinal' virtues) is disputed not just by dominant neo-Kantian traditions in contemporary American moral philosophy, but also by some sympathetic to virtue ethics. For example, Julia Annas takes Aristotle to task for failing to make a sharp distinction between the 'moral' and 'non-moral' virtues, citing magnificence and tact as non-moral virtues which Aristotle wrongly places in the category of the moral.[31] Arguing against Aristotle's view that magnificence is a (moral) virtue because it aims at the fine (*kalon*) rather than at *mere* display of wealth, Annas makes two points. Magnificence is not a moral virtue because it is limited to the rich, and the corresponding failures are mere lapses of taste involving issues of rather trivial convention rather than morality. I disagree with both of these claims. First, not all moral virtue need be universal. Certain virtues may be relative to role (e.g. that of parent, business executive, doctor), to circumstance, and even to abilities. (As I shall claim below, certain creative virtues may not be virtues in the totally talentless.) The fact that Aristotle considered magnificence to be a (moral) virtue showed that he had a substantive moral position with respect to one aspect of a very important field, namely, the spending of money. He believed that with respect to this one field the nature of virtue is relative to amount of disposable income: to be merely thrifty and just when one has large resources is to fail to be virtuous. Individuals with large resources are required to display their resources in splendid ways. Whether or not we agree with this position, it is clear that we are not talking of *conventions*: we have here a substantive ethical position concerning splendour and magnificence that Aristotle appears to share with Hume. The point can also be applied to civic and corporate spending—issues of considerable importance by comparison to mere matters of taste. If a corporation in a tiny country

31 See 'Aristotle and Kant on Morality and Practical Reasoning', in Stephen Engstrom and Jennifer Whiting (eds.), *Aristotle, Kant, and the Stoics: Rethinking Happiness and Duty* (Cambridge: Cambridge University Press, 1996), 237–58.

builds a tower in its largest city, a tower heralded as the tallest in the southern hemisphere, do we praise the corporation for its magnificence, or do we accuse it of a puerile grandiosity borne of the psychological failings of its managers? When a city spends lavishly on an annual fireworks display, not celebratory of any national day, justice may feature as part of the analysis of the morality of that expenditure, but even where there is poverty in the city, we may justify the expenditure in terms directly connected with the display of magnificence. We may say that the magnificence is expressive of a city's vibrancy, its delight in having its citizens come together to witness an event of splendour, its celebration of being situated alongside a magnificent harbour where the display takes place. None of these magnificence-connected justifications is exhausted by issues pertaining to 'cardinal' virtues of justice or temperance.

Annas believes also that Aristotle's conversational virtues such as tact are not moral. On my view tact is an important virtue relating to daily interactions. The issues of when tact becomes a dialogical vice of failure to disclose, or of when frank disclosure shades into a vice of absence of tact, are subtle and important (see further Chapter 12). Why are issues of tact not seen as moral? Lack of tact can hurt, harm relationships, destroy diplomacy, be expressive of hostility. 'Excessive' tact can be expressive of cowardice, but need not be. It too harms relationships through a failure to confront problems, to disclose concerns, to communicate. If anything is part of the domain of the moral, it is the quality of relationships.

In answer to those who cannot contemplate the idea that wit is a moral virtue,[32] let me content myself simply with a quote from Aristotle showing the importance of (proper) wit in conversation and the good life, and the avoidance of correlative vice:

---

[32] In his 'Interpersonal Virtues: Whose Interests do they Serve?', *American Catholic Philosophical Quarterly* 71 (1997), 31–60, J. L. A. Garcia asks, rhetorically, 'why should anyone today count charm or wit—let alone being "great-souled"—as a moral virtue?' (39). Well, I do (provided charm and wit are understood as 'proper' charm and wit): Garcia's point is much too dismissive. It is odd that Garcia holds such a view, since he regards virtues as features of character involving responses to value. The quote from Aristotle in the text immediately below pinpoints the value of (proper) wit in conversation (and the value of conversation in a good life). Maybe Garcia thinks that wit cannot be a character trait. But wit, too, involves a disposition of choice 'in a mean': a disposition to avoid showing off, vulgarity, sourness. Maybe some people cannot cultivate wit, and for this reason (proper) wit can't be a virtue. But just as some excellences of character are relative to circumstances which may be beyond one's control, so some may be relative to ability. Not all moral virtues need be universal. At any rate, even if one's capacity for wit is slight, it is an achievement to avoid correlative vices of mocking banter, cynical cleverness, and so on, especially when one's own culture is steeped in such vice.

Since one part of life is relaxation, and one aspect of this is entertaining conversation, it is considered that here too there is a kind of social conduct that is in good taste: that there are things that it is right to say, and a right way of saying them; and similarly with listening. And it will be an advantage if those in whose presence we talk and to whom we listen accept such standards. Clearly in this field too it is possible to exceed or fall short of the mean.

Those who go too far in being funny are regarded as buffoons and vulgar persons who exert themselves to be funny at all costs and who are more set upon raising a laugh than upon decency of expression and consideration for their victim's feelings. Those who both refuse to say anything funny themselves and take exception to the jokes of other people are regarded as boorish and sour; but those who exercise their humour with good taste are called witty, as one might say 'nimble-witted'.[33]

The moral domain of virtue ethics is particularly rich, detailed, and broad-ranging, and attention to this richness contributes also to a recognition of the artificiality of the moral/non-moral distinction in much contemporary ethics. This detail and broad range is reflected in the subtle vocabulary of virtues (and vices). However, that vocabulary is not the standard fare of philosophical ethics: for that, one needs to turn to psychologists and novelists. For example, in 'What We Know about Leadership', Robert Hogan, Gordon J. Curphy, and Joyce Hogan use a large array of virtue and vice terms in evaluating leadership and leadership potential.[34] 'Surgency' includes readiness to make decisions, activity and energy, extraversion, sociability; 'conscientiousness' includes responsibility, industriousness, initiative, honesty; 'agreeableness' includes concern for social appropriateness, sensitivity to social cues, ability to control expressive behaviour, warmth, friendliness; 'emotional stability' includes resistance to stress, tolerance of uncertainty, self-confidence, independence, and ability to adjust. A similar array of vices of leaders is also discussed, including arrogance, hostility, boastfulness, passive aggressiveness, and dictatorialness. Not only are virtue and vice terms rich, but their nuances and areas of applicability may vary according to different roles, all of which are important in the moral and good life. Leadership is but one facet of the good and moral life, yet an extremely rich virtue and vice vocabulary reveals its anatomy. Virtue ethics not only reveals the multifacetedness of our lives, but evaluates it

---

[33] *Nicomachean Ethics*, 1127b27–1128a11.
[34] *American Psychologist* 49 (1994), 493–504.

richly. For example, Hogan and his co-authors note the importance of leadership to the good and moral life: 'reactions to inept leadership include turnover, insubordination, industrial sabotage, and malingering'.[35] They may also have mentioned the bad effects of the stress that is brought home at night. And 'organizational climate studies from the mid-1950s to the present routinely show that 60% to 75% of the employees in any organization . . . report that the worst or most stressful aspect of their job is their immediate supervisor'.

An objection to a broad conception of morality is that such a conception would undermine the status of morality as important. To say that morality is important is not, however, to say that each action that is to be evaluated morally is important. The failure to return a small favour is squarely within the domain of the moral, but is not itself of great moral significance. Secondly, habits or patterns of small failures may be considerably important.[36] Regular failures of tact, ignoring of favours and good turns, resentful dealings with individuals of certain types, habitual unhelpfulness, are all important in a failure to lead a moral life.

Another objection is that some of the virtues recognized above, and others recognized by Hume (such as charm), do not involve choice of the good or fine, but are mere 'personality' traits. However, traits such as charm, tact, 'surgency', and cheerfulness can involve choice and be cultivated as virtues. Charm, for example, can be aimed at the good and the fine, or misaimed at the evil or sleazy, quite deliberately. It can be misemployed to seduce, and can disguise lack of talent in the acquiring of jobs. On the other hand, it can be employed to make difficult and taxing social occasions pleasant and even delightful. A person who makes efforts (and succeeds) in being charming in these situations is to be admired, as opposed to one who is surly or withdrawn, leaving others to make the effort. Robert Audi claims that 'charming personality can go hand in hand with execrable character'.[37] This is true. But this does not show (as Audi thinks) that there is an interesting philosophical distinction between a narrow set of 'moral' character traits and a broad set of personality traits. A charming person of execrable character possesses charm as a vice, and has an execrable personality.

[35] Ibid. 494.

[36] See Marcia Baron, *Kantian Ethics Almost Without Apology* (Ithaca, N.Y.: Cornell University Press, 1995).

[37] *Moral Knowledge and Ethical Character*, 160.

The same applies to cheerfulness, a 'personality' trait. Like charm, cheerfulness can lapse into vice—cheerfulness may be a front disguising problems that need to be confronted, or may persistently disguise sadness that needs at times to be expressed. The recognition of (proper) cheerfulness as a virtue underscores the artificiality of thinking that optimism and pessimism for example are 'mere' personality traits rather than virtues or vices. Excessive pessimism is a vice insofar as, in a myriad of small ways, the agent chooses to behave (and reinforces emotions) in ways that are inappropriately negative and cheerless, complains excessively, sees the glass as half empty rather than half full, and so forth. Excessive optimism is a vice insofar as the agent, through his choices or lack of effort, persistently fails to recognize difficulties or bad consequences of certain actions, calls people who understand these things 'negative', is too ready to embark on grand but costly schemes. The idea that these traits are not vices suggests that the agent is in no sense to be blamed for failures to ameliorate or attempt to ameliorate these tendencies, or is in no sense to take responsibility for inappropriate behaviour associated with them.

We turn now to the third aspect of the pervasiveness of the moral in my pluralistic virtue ethics. As we have seen, my virtue ethics recognizes a *wide range* of what I have called the fundamental *modes* of moral acknowledgements of items (whether things, activities, emotions, or feelings) within a virtue's sphere of concern (its field). These modes are forms of responsiveness to the different types of morally salient features of the world (which I have called *bases* of moral acknowledgement). Because of the wide range of modes of moral acknowledgement or responsiveness recognized by the various virtues, a morality in which *virtue* is central has more of a chance of integrating moral meritoriousness and personal satisfaction than does a narrower conception of morality, such as a conception according to which morality is merely concerned with the *claims* of *others*.

For example, creativity is squarely within the domain of the moral, being essential for the realization of Kant's obligatory end of self-perfection. And other 'values' which John Kekes has labelled non-moral are also important for this Kantian end—appreciation of beauty, playfulness, career plans, adventure.[38] Others, such as friendship, Hume's charm, affability, or Aristotle's conversational virtues, are essential or at

[38] Kekes, *The Morality of Pluralism*, 11.

least significant for sociability—an important aspect of morality. Virtues focused on other people may be concerned with property relations, with relationships in general, with collegiality, with conversational interaction. All these virtues (and their corresponding vices) recognize our nature as social beings and may include anything from the virtue of justice to the vice of buffoonery. In regard to the field of art works or cultural icons, we may focus on creative or appreciative activity or (relatedly) that of preservation and public display. Virtues applicable to those activities recognize our nature as creative and cultural beings, and our need for a 'heritage'. Finally, as Susan Moller-Okin has recently emphasized, the morally essential task of raising happy, healthy children of good character throws into the spotlight family and parental virtues;[39] and Michael Stocker has recently drawn our attention to the moral significance of work and the work place, which highlights not just virtues of leadership, but virtues of collegiality.[40]

If one sees the moral domain through the prism of virtue, one will see it as a rich kaleidoscope, complex and multifaceted. One is less likely to ignore important features of our nature which yield rich sets of virtues: one is less likely to consign these features and those virtues to the lesser domain of the 'non-moral'. On my view, then, the moral swallows up an enormous amount of what has traditionally (in modern ethics) been consigned to the non-moral.

[39] See *Justice, Gender and the Family* (New York: Basic Books, 1989), and 'Feminism, Moral Development, and the Virtues', in Roger Crisp (ed.), *How Should One Live? Essays on the Virtues* (Oxford: Clarendon Press, 1996), 211–29.

[40] *Valuing Emotions.*

4

What Makes a Character Trait a Virtue

(i) The Nature of Eudaimonism

The Constraint on Virtue, discussed in the previous chapter, implies that a correct conception of virtue is constrained by a conception of flourishing. But it does not in itself yield a view of what makes a trait of character a virtue. In modern virtue ethics, which is largely inspired by Aristotle, the dominant account of what makes a trait a virtue is eudaimonism. In this chapter, I first define eudaimonism before defending it against a criticism. Nonetheless, I reject the view, instead favouring a pluralistic account of virtue status which is given in the final section.

In the words of Rosalind Hursthouse eudaimonism is the view that:

A virtue is a character trait that a human being needs for *eudaimonia*, to flourish or live well.[1]

This view comprises two theses. The first is:

> It is a necessary condition of her flourishing that a human being possess and exercise at least the core virtues (assuming that not all virtues (even for Aristotle) are universal, for some are relative to circumstances).

The above thesis is not at issue in this chapter. What is at issue is the second thesis: a eudaimonist thesis of virtue status, which I call (E).

> (E) It is a necessary condition of a trait being a virtue that it characteristically (partially) constitute (or contribute to) the flourishing of the possessor of the virtue.

---

[1] *On Virtue Ethics*, 167.

Thesis (E) is intended as an answer to a question of justification: 'What makes *this* trait (humility, temperance . . .) a *virtue*?' Or 'Why is *this* trait, humility, temperance . . . claimed to be a *virtue*?'

The claim that a trait cannot be a virtue unless it characteristically benefits the agent is consistent with a claim that exercise of a virtue does not guarantee agent-flourishing. As Aristotle emphasizes, the truths of ethics are truths for the most part.[2] This leaves room for the eudaimonist to concede that in responding appropriately to various values, bonds, and so on, there is no *guarantee* that an agent will lead a life that is good *for her*. On the views of both Aristotle and neo-Aristotelians, one might exercise virtues needed for one's flourishing, but be dealt such a severe blow of tragic ill fortune that one's life, when seen as a whole, cannot be described as happy.[3] Just as healthy living does not guarantee health, so being virtuous does not guarantee happiness. However, one should cultivate the virtues because that is 'the only reliable bet' for one's flourishing, 'though . . . I might be unlucky and, because of my virtue, wind up on the rack'.[4]

Because the answer to the question of justification provided by (E) is given in terms of the agent's own flourishing, eudaimonism has been thought fatally flawed as the lynchpin of a moral theory. According to Thomas Hurka, for instance, a view such as Hursthouse's contains the 'egoistic assumption' that all of an agent's reasons for action derive ultimately from his or her own flourishing.[5] On the face of it, this is a very puzzling claim, for as Aristotle states, the virtuous agent chooses actions for their own sake, and surely this does not mean ' for the sake of the agent'. It is not entirely clear, however, what 'choosing virtuous actions for their own sake' means, but a clear account is given by Hursthouse:

'The virtuous agent chooses virtuous actions "for their own sake"' means 'the virtuous agent chooses virtuous actions for at least one of certain type or range of reasons, X', where 'the type or range X' is typical of, and differs according to, whichever virtue is in question.[6]

The question now arises, however, of what reasons of 'type or range

[2] See further on Aristotelian views on the generalizations of ethics, Michael Thomson, 'The Representation of Life', in R. Hursthouse, G. Lawrence, and W. Quinn (eds.), *Virtues and Reasons* (Oxford: Clarendon Press, 1995), 247–96.

[3] See Aristotle's reference to Priam, *Nicomachean Ethics*, 1100b27–1101a20.

[4] Hursthouse, 'Aristotle, Nicomachean Ethics', 42. See also *Nicomachean Ethics*, 1553b17.

[5] *Virtue, Vice, and Value* (Oxford: Oxford University Press, 2001).

[6] *On Virtue Ethics*, 127–8.

X' amount to. According to Hurka, such reasons are 'foundationally ego-istic' precisely because, in *justifying* a claim that X is a virtue, one has to show that X is needed for the agent's own flourishing. Nonetheless, in defence of eudaimonism, one may claim that reasons of 'type or range X' pertain to the point of X as a virtue, and that in turn is constituted by the aim or target of X. So, for example, if X is the virtue of friendship, X-type reasons have to do with expressing friendship in acts of affection, promoting the good of the friend, and so on. No surreptitious or covert egoism seems lurking here. In short, reasons of type X derive from the target of X and are not themselves reasons for a claim that X is a virtue.

It is difficult to see, then, why (E) should be thought to entail that the virtuous agent's reasons are ultimately egoistic. However, the argument against (E) resurfaces in the form of a dilemma. Either (E) is egoistic or it is self-effacing, 'telling agents not to be motivated by or even to think of their claims about the source of their reasons'.[7]

However, as I have claimed, the source of an agent's reasons, ultimate or otherwise, is the target or aim of a relevant virtue. That target is not always or even characteristically the agent's own flourishing. Though (E) is therefore neither foundationally egoistic nor self-effacing, Hurka's dilemma does, however, point up a puzzling dissonance between the aims of a virtue and what makes a trait of character a virtue as under-stood by (E). Indeed, Julia Annas describes eudaimonism as a 'two-level' view of a kind,[8] though she denies that it suffers from the objectionable features that she believes beset two-level consequentialism. For, as I have claimed, the 'two levels' are not such as to make (E) self-effacing.

It may still be thought puzzling why there is a dissonance between rea-sons for action and reasons for a trait being a virtue. For the eudaimonist, the puzzle is resolved by the expedient of providing at the foundations of eudaimonism the integrating concept of goodness qua human being. A virtue by definition is partially constitutive of goodness qua human being, and to be (fully) good qua human being it is necessary to flourish. Hence the eudaimonistic idea that what makes a trait a virtue is in part a certain connection to agent-flourishing. But for the eudaimonist, to be good qua human being also involves a sensitivity to the goodness of human ends, and although these include personal flourishing, they are by no means egoistic.

It may be replied that for the eudaimonist, one aims at one's own goodness qua human being in acting, and even though that goodness is

<hr>

[7] Hurka, *Virtue, Vice, and Value*, 246   [8] In *The Morality of Happiness*.

not wholly egoistic, it does include personal flourishing. Hence a troubling egoism remains. Indeed Julia Annas appears to concede that in acting one aims at one's good, but denies that any troubling egoism is involved, for two reasons. First, concern for oneself is a concern 'for oneself as a rational agent aiming at the fine'.[9] This recalls Aristotle's claim that:

> In all praiseworthy matters [such as sacrificing oneself for a friend] then, the good person appears as assigning himself more of what is fine. This is the way, then, that one should be a lover of self.[10]

Second, concern for self in doing what is fine is not a motivation that is in the forefront of one's mind at the moment of action. One doesn't do what is fine *in order* to promote one's own good: rather concern for oneself is a concern that one's 'life as a whole expresses concern for [oneself] as a rational agent aiming at the fine'.[11] At the point of action, by contrast, one acts for reasons pertaining to the aim or target of the relevant virtue.

(ii) Some Counterexamples

I believe that eudaimonism can successfully negotiate the kind of challenge posed by Hurka, but it does not follow that it is true. I shall argue in this section that (E) is false.

Let us grant the following assumption of eudaimonism: to be (fully) good qua human being it is necessary to flourish. It does not follow that, even though virtue is partially constitutive of goodness qua human being (by definition), it is a necessary condition of a trait being a virtue that it is characteristically (partially) constitutive of (or contributes to) the flourishing of the agent. For it may well be the case that at least some virtues contribute to aspects of a human's goodness other than her personal flourishing. Indeed, it may be the case that at least some virtues are inimical to personal flourishing while making that contribution. I shall argue in this section that there are some such virtues. Certainly it would be odd if all or most virtues were damaging to personal flourishing though partially constitutive of goodness qua human being. But the intuition that this is odd can be preserved without adopting a view as strong as (E).

9   Ibid. 260.
10   *Nicomachean Ethics*, 1169a18–1169b2 (cited in Annas, *The Morality of Happiness*, 258).
11   Annas, *The Morality of Happiness*, 258.

On my own view, most virtues are not damaging to personal flourishing, because self-love is part of the profile of all virtue, and certain kinds of damaging self-sacrifice are thereby precluded. This view is developed in Chapter 6.

Let us now cast doubt on the eudaimonist thesis that it is a necessary condition of being a virtue that its exercise characteristically brings in its wake personal satisfaction and flourishing. We shall do this first by making some distinctions and then by considering some putative counter-examples to the eudaimonist thesis.

First, the eudaimonist thesis (E) should be distinguished from three further theses, the last of which is the topic of the next section. These are:

(i) It is a necessary condition of a trait being a virtue that it be admirable (worthy of admiration).

(ii) It is a necessary condition of a trait being a virtue that it be partially constitutive of (or contribute to) a successful life.

(iii) It is a necessary condition of a trait being a virtue that it be partially constitutive of (or contribute to) a life that is meaningful.

'Living well', used synonymously with 'flourishing' in the passage from Hursthouse quoted above, is a broader notion than flourishing, and is ambiguous between (at least) living a flourishing life, a life of worthwhile achievement, an admirable life, and a meaningful life. It seems to me a truism that a human being can lead a successful life (a life of worthwhile achievement) and not flourish (the life may not be good *for her*). It is also true that a human being can lead a life that is admirable, but neither successful nor flourishing. Inasmuch as the goals of many virtues may be connected with worthwhile achievement and admirability, then given the above, it is at least prima facie questionable whether the eudaimonist thesis is true. It may be true that a flourishing life is also a life of worthwhile achievement, but the crucial point is that a life of success may not be a flourishing life. As far as admirability is concerned, I suspect that a flourishing life need not be an admirable life; if this is so, then given that an admirable life need not be a flourishing life, a virtue ethics based on the notion of admirability may be quite seriously disjoint from one based on the idea of flourishing.

Let us now consider three kinds of lives, none of which seem to display traits which are 'reliable bets' for personal flourishing, but which at first blush display virtues, since they are lives characterized by habits of appropriate responses to value, bonds, benefits, and so on. The first is a life 'dominated by a commitment to improving the welfare of others or society as a whole'.[12] A woman works ceaselessly saving lives and relieving suffering in the jungle. She suffers repeatedly from bouts of malaria and dysentery, and is most of the time in great discomfort even when not ill. She is always exhausted. Though she is standardly strong-willed, she sometimes falters in her humanitarian purposes, questioning her calling. Her suffering is not mitigated by a religious or quasi-religious joy, often experienced by saints, and which makes the latter happy (as Robert Merrihew Adams points out).[13] Having seriously undermined her health, she succumbs to a virus, and dies prematurely of complications.

Though I agree with Susan Wolf that it may be an ideal of personal *well-being* that the so-called moral virtues 'do not crowd out' the non-moral virtues, and that from this point of view one should leave space in one's life for developing one's backhand or one's garden, for example, it does not follow that the life of the 'moral saint' is thereby disqualified as a 'compelling personal *ideal*'. Indeed, Wolf glosses her claim that moral sainthood is not an unequivocally compelling personal ideal as 'it does not constitute a model of personal *wellbeing* toward which it would be particularly rational or good or desirable for a human being to strive'.[14] It is precisely my point that it may be rational and good (though not required) for someone to adopt the life of moral sainthood as a compelling personal ideal, though, I agree, it is not compelling as a model of personal well-being. Not unless, that is, one is fortunate enough to experience religious or quasi-religious joy in such a life.

Consider now my second example. A number of great artists suffer from manic-depressive illness. Though the depressive phase of the cycle is not conducive to creativity, the manic phase is perceived to be one of such creative energy that many such artists (and others such as scientists) refuse medication to relieve their disorder.[15] Consider such an artist who struggles to realize her creative goals, constantly feels she has failed, and commits suicide having achieved no recognition. Nor, let us say, does she achieve recognition after her death. Nonetheless, though she is afflicted

---

[12] Susan Wolf, 'Moral Saints', *Journal of Philosophy* 79 (1982), 419–39, at 420.

[13] 'Saints', *Journal of Philosophy* 81 (1984), 392–401.

[14] 'Moral Saints', 419.

[15] In her *An Unquiet Mind: Memoir of Moods and Madness* (New York: Vintage Books, 1996), Kay Redfield Jamison describes her opposition to the increasingly popular term for manic depressive illness—bipolar disorder—and her early resistance to lithium on account of its effect on the creative energy of the manic phases. See also Danielle Steel, *His Bright Light: The Story of My Son Nick Traina* (London: Corgi, 1999).

at times with self-doubt, her creative drive is fuelled by a not unreasonable belief that she is talented enough to say something important. It would be odd, I think, to say that such a person has flourished. Nor is her lack of flourishing due to ill luck: relatively few artists achieve recognition, just as relatively few aspiring sportspeople or entrepreneurs achieve the goals they hope for. Given the suffering of our artist, a more reliable bet for flourishing would have been for her to have deflected or curbed the artistic passions which make her such a driven personality.

Third, consider a person who has a character trait of active devotion to causes in which he believes passionately. He is ahead of his time in foreseeing environmental disaster, which will not, however, occur in his lifetime. Although he has no children or nieces and nephews, he works tirelessly and persistently in efforts to persuade people of the danger. Despite his dire warnings and his interpersonal skill, he is not taken seriously. Unsurprisingly, this puts him under great stress. He dies, of a heart attack, in despair. Possessing and manifesting a trait of persistence in the face of relentless opposition is not a good bet for personal flourishing. Nonetheless, one might argue, it is not obvious that such a trait is not a virtue when habitually directed at a good cause. Where the issue is of sufficiently great importance, behaviour in line with a trait posing great risk to personal flourishing may be appropriate. Indeed, let us say, after the well-publicized death of our imagined zealot, a spark is ignited, a few people take notice, and finally, the danger is appreciated.

My intuitions tell me that none of the agents of my examples flourished. The life of the aid worker is, however, successful and admirable. The life of the artist is an admirable failure, as would also have been the life of the environmentalist had the danger not been appreciated. His life is successful in a sense (like that of many artists), given that his work is appreciated after his death. The lives described could also be described as meaningful. Nietzsche, in *On the Genealogy of Morals* (Essay 3, sect. 28), claims:

Man, the boldest animal and the one most accustomed to pain, does *not* repudiate suffering as such; he *desires* it, he even seeks it out, provided that he has been shown *meaning* for it, a *reason* for suffering. The meaninglessness of suffering, and *not* suffering as such, has been the curse which has hung over mankind up to now.

One might claim in defence of eudaimonism that a flourishing life is a meaningful life; meaningful suffering of the kind experienced by the manic depressive artist is compatible with flourishing. This reply is discussed in the next section.

In presenting my examples, I am not saying that anyone *should* respond in the ways of the agents of my examples. Nor am I saying that *anyone* should cultivate the traits that facilitated those responses. Artistic drivenness of the kind displayed in the second example is not a virtue in the totally talentless. Again, persons with no interpersonal skills should not waste their time trying to persuade people of things about which they are extremely resistant. Nor should they cultivate virtues of fierce engagement in important but unpopular causes if they cannot acquire those skills. And someone whose ability to work with people is so poor that she destroys the effectiveness of her co-workers should not nurture passions for large-scale good works which necessitate working within complex organizations.

Finally, I am not saying that the *agents* of my examples *should* live the way portrayed in the examples, or *should* have cultivated the virtues they in fact displayed. I am merely saying that it is reasonable to think that they lived virtuously, though not happily. But it was open to them to have lived differently, and for different virtues, such as those of good parenting, to have assumed salience in their lives.

In the next two sections, I consider two arguments, which aim to show that the counterexamples are apparent only. They turn on the idea that a trait cannot be a virtue unless it characteristically benefits the agent, for there are deep connections between the two components of the good life identified in Chapter 3, namely, being good (morally meritorious) and having a flourishing life of personal satisfaction. The first argument for a deep connection claims that personal satisfaction and flourishing connects with meaning, and meaning connects with the sense of a worthwhile life associated with moral meritoriousness. The second argument for a deep connection claims that insofar as personal satisfaction and flourishing are part of the *good* life, the personal satisfaction and flourishing must involve and be the result of virtuous activity. For pleasure without temperance, the possession of money without the relevant virtues of getting and spending, having friends without the virtue of friendship, are not goods, nor do they bring the deepest forms of personal satisfaction. These arguments will be considered in turn.

(iii) Happiness, Meaningfulness, and 'Being True to Oneself'

Here is the first argument. One might imagine that all the lives described in my examples are *eudaimon* and good *for* the agent insofar as each agent is doing that which is worthwhile and that which she *considers* to be worthwhile. The lives thus contain a sort of personal satisfaction. Each life has meaning for the agent, where this is understood as a life devoted to projects that the agent thinks are worthwhile. As Susan Wolf arrestingly puts it:

meaning arises in a person's life when subjective attraction meets objective attractiveness.[16]

Put like this, there is indeed a temptation to think that lives which are meaningful are also good for the agent, for they are associated with the right kind of personal satisfaction.

However, Wolf's claim in fact shows that the appeal to meaningfulness does not obviously rescue eudaimonism by impugning the status of my examples as counterexamples. A life meaningful because one *thinks* it worthwhile need not be *attractive* to one and thereby personally satisfying. Consider persons brought up to believe that we were put on this earth to give service to others, and who have internalized this belief. Lives conforming to this belief may take many forms. One may be the kind of moral saint of my first example. Or one may have been brought up to give service as a high-level administrator in a far flung corner of the British Empire. These people believe their lives to be worthwhile, but they do not necessarily find their vocations attractive. If the woman of my first example found her life meaningful and *therefore* attractive, there might be a temptation to think her life happy. But even this temptation perhaps should be resisted, as Wolf herself recognizes. Having claimed that 'meaning arises in a person's life when subjective attraction meets objective attractiveness', she finds room for the possibility that doing something meaningful in this way can also lead to unhappiness: 'much pain and sorrow'.[17] She concludes:

Having a reason to live, then, and a reason to care about the world in which one lives, is linked fundamentally not with happiness but with meaning.[18]

Inasmuch as this claim applies to all my examples, one might be tempted to claim that eudaimonism should be understood not in terms of happiness or flourishing, but in terms of meaning in Wolf's sense. Perhaps, then, the virtues are 'reliable bets', not for personal flourishing or happiness, but for personal meaning. But that idea too, provides an overly narrow base for virtue status. Let us see why. One of the tasks of parents is to instil worthwhile character traits in their children. Though

[16] 'Meaning and Morality', *Proceedings of the Aristotelian Society* 97 (1997), 299–315, at 305.
[17] Ibid. 303.   [18] Ibid.

we are 'by nature constituted to receive the virtues',[19] such receipt (where it takes place) is courtesy of our upbringing, as well as our own efforts later in life. Now imagine a parent who conceived of the virtues solely in terms of personal meaning, and strove to ensure that her child's future life was invested with meaning rather than happiness. Perhaps she is the kind of parent who exhorts her child to be extremely achievement- and task-oriented in attempting to become, for example, a great concert pianist, and who has little regard for the child's own future happiness in that capacity or attempt. However, in training her child to be virtuous, a good parent has her *child's* interests at heart: she is concerned not to engage in rearing strategies carrying great risk to the child's happiness, in the cause of her being good for the world at large. Of course, I am not suggesting that in bringing up the child in ways conducive to her happiness she does not show the child that a happy life is one with meaning. But a meaningful life at the cost of happiness is one for a mature agent autonomously to decide upon, or is one maybe that she naturally finds herself impelled towards. My point is that if worthwhile traits were conceived solely in terms of meaningfulness, we couldn't make room for the idea that a parent's job is not to be understood as training children into worthwhile traits characteristically inimical to personal happiness or flourishing.

Where perseverance in the face of relentless opposition, artistic passion, moral sainthood, the courage of a freedom fighter in apartheid South Africa are virtues, they are so because they are habits of relating appropriately to items in the fields of the virtues, in line with their value, status, good, and bonds. It does not follow that it is a virtue in someone qua parent to train her children into those virtues, though we are glad if some mature agents develop virtues inimical to personal flourishing for the great benefit of the world at large, or portions of that world.

I consider now a second objection to my counterexamples to eudaimonism based on the connection between virtue and meaningfulness. It has been argued that:

self interest depends on the nature of the self or character—the central dispositions of thought, emotion and action—constituted by a person's fundamental values.[20]

---

[19] Aristotle, *Nicomachean Ethics*, 1103a14–b1.

[20] Neera Kapur Badhwar, 'Altruism versus Self-Interest: Sometimes a False Dichotomy', *Social Philosophy and Psychology* 10 (1993), 90–117, at 104.

Specifically, one has an interest in 'self-affirmation', and given that one has, for example, a character of artistic passion or an altruistic character, one has an interest in affirming those altruistic or creative dispositions. Not to do so is to fail to be true to oneself, to betray oneself, to be unable to forgive oneself, to feel unfulfilled, and so forth.

I take this point, but it does not support eudaimonism. It supports the view that, assuming one's character is sufficiently worthwhile, one has an interest in being true to it. It does not support the view that whatever is the nature of one's character that one has an interest in being true to, it is a character reliably (though not necessarily invariably) leading to personal happiness. Certainly one has an interest in being true to one's character—a person's character is an essential part of his conception of himself. But as a view about virtue status, eudaimonism is trivialized if it is merely the theory that whatever worthwhile trait is cultivated, it is a trait that one has an interest in affirming.

(iv) Moralizing Happiness

The objection to my counterexamples to eudaimonism, discussed above, has, however, a stronger form. In being true to one's character, one rules out of consideration as reasons actions which are counter to it. In this way it is not merely the case that one has an interest in being true to one's (worthwhile) character, what one finds personally satisfying is itself defined by one's character. If one adds to this the idea that in order for something to be *genuinely* satisfying it must be fine and not, for example, shallow, overly austere, overly materialistic, too demanding on oneself, then what is *genuinely* satisfying is what is satisfying to the virtuous, as opposed to what is satisfying to the materialistic and shallow. Indeed many have claimed that for Aristotle, 'virtues are the way to understand eudaimonia, eudaimonia is not the way to understand the virtues'.[21]

Call this strategy 'moralizing happiness'. It works as a defence of eudaimonism by refusing to countenance the independence of virtue from happiness. On this view, it is not merely the case that pleasure, for example, is not good with qualification unless it is infused with suitable virtue. Pleasure is not even in one's self-interest (good for one) unless it is infused with suitable virtue.[22]

[21] See Simpson, 'Contemporary Virtue Ethics and Aristotle', 257 n. 11.
[22] For a defence of this view in relationship to pleasure (and some other goods), see Slote, 'The Virtue of Self Interest'.

In many cases, the view that goods are not good *for* one unless they are handled virtuously by the agent has plausibility. A multimillion lottery win is not a genuine good for the winner if she is incapable of handling those winnings magnificently, or at least with ease. If she cannot bear the thought of abandoning the lifestyle to which she is habituated as a check-out operator, but yet is debilitatingly oppressed by the thought that she no longer needs to continue in that job, the money is not good *for* her. Even friendship must have virtue built in if it is to be good for the agent. For example, a certain amount of self-sufficiency in friends is necessary for the friendship to be good for one. If one merely uses a friend as a locus of complaint and lamentations, the friendship arguably does harm to both friends, and the friendship is not genuinely satisfying, or not as satisfying as it could be. Again, if a person is so receptive to the needs of others that she has more friends than is compatible with having a life of her own, the friendships are not good for her. In short, one cannot understand personal flourishing simply in terms of having and exercising traits apt for the mere *production* of and *having* of goods such as friends, honours, pleasure, money.

I accept that many apparent goods are not good for one, unless they are infused with virtue. However, my counterexamples focus on the fact that an agent may fail to flourish because of factors virtuously *forgone*, such as physical and mental health, contentment, and lack of stress. Eudaimonism needs not just a connection between virtue and 'goods' being good *for* one, but also a connection between virtue and 'bads' not being bad *for* one, at least characteristically. Indeed, eudaimonism has been defended by making this very connection. It has been argued by eudaimonists that virtues are characteristically good *for* the agent because a virtuous agent's conception of happiness enables her to see things virtuously forgone as not being a loss to her.

This thesis appears to be favoured by John McDowell. According to him, a person of settled character has a distinctive way of seeing things, such that acting as (his conception of) virtue demands 'silences' competing considerations (such as that doing this will give me pleasure). Considerations 'silenced' and forgone are seen as no loss, for considerations silenced are considerations which one has no reason to pursue. 'And if one misses something which one has no reason to pursue that is no loss.'[23]

[23] John McDowell, 'The Role of Eudaimonia in Aristotle's Ethics', in Amelie Rorty (ed.), *Essays on Aristotle's Ethics* (Berkeley: University of California Press, 1980), 359–76, at 370.

There certainly seem to be cases which support McDowell's view of the virtuous agent. Putative goods forgone are not seen as a loss insofar as possession of such goods would be contaminated by vice. Consider: I have recently acquired a taste for oriental rugs, and am visiting a friend who has just purchased one I particularly like. I know she loves it, and would not dream of selling it. I know I can't acquire one identical to it, or even one very like it. Yet I am not tempted to acquire it by vicious means; indeed, I see my not having that rug as no loss *in the situation it is in*. (I might see it as a loss if it were sitting in a shop window and someone bought it just as I was about to go in and buy it myself.)

However, notwithstanding examples such as the above, this version of the moralizing happiness strategy seems to be false. Its appeal lies in a confusion between the virtuous agent seeing possible reasons as 'irrelevant' and her seeing no personal loss in her acting on them. Consider the example of the 'rescuers' discussed by Neera Badhwar:

all the evidence points to the fact that rescuers' normal hierarchy of interests was sharply reversed when they were confronted with the need to save innocent lives from a monstrous threat. When this happened, their interest in their own and their families' and friends' welfare was not only *subordinated* to their interest in saving innocent lives, it became irrelevant in arriving at the decision to help.[24]

Considerations of family safety and well-being may in the circumstances have been 'irrelevant', but this does not entail that loss of family well-being is not a loss to the rescuer. Even if the rescuer had paid attention to the possibilities of harm to loved ones, the overwhelming force of requirements of humanity meant that considerations of that harm did not have practical force. This does not mean that the harm, should it occur, would not be a genuine loss, and not be seen as such.[25] It seems that the view that the virtuous agent does not see things virtuously forgone as a personal loss, is false, so the view cannot be used to support eudaimonism.

One important argument for eudaimonism remains. According to this argument losses of the kind which mar flourishing are matters of ill luck; other deprivations such as those endured by the woman of my first example are endured at the highest level of virtue without loss of flourishing. In later chapters, I discuss universal and self-love, and strength, which in their best manifestations conduce not merely to the flourishing of others but to the flourishing of the agent. However, on a threshold conception of virtue, the standards set by the strongest heroes and saints are too high for normal virtue, as I argue primarily in Chapter 9 on demandingness. Hence, even if eudaimonism can be retained as a viable theory of the highest virtue, it should be rejected as a theory of normal virtue.

(v) What Makes a Trait of Character a Virtue?
A Pluralistic View

In her book *On Virtue Ethics*, Rosalind Hursthouse combines a belief in eudaimonism with a version of what she calls 'naturalism'—the view that what makes a trait of character a virtue is its being partially constitutive of non-defectiveness in human beings. For her, a virtue is a trait of character which makes a human good qua human; and what makes a human good qua human is non-defectiveness as a member of the species Homo sapiens, understood in naturalistic terms. The traits possessed by a non-defective member of the species are not merely those (partially) constitutive of her own flourishing, but are those which serve the flourishing of the species as a whole. If eudaimonism is to be rejected, maybe it should be replaced by 'naturalism'. I shall consider Hursthouse's naturalism, contrasting it with non-teleological justifications of the virtues. I finally argue for my own pluralistic view.

According to Hursthouse, a virtue is a disposition of being well endowed with respect to the agent's actions, desires, and emotions, and whether a human being *is* thus well endowed is determined by whether the character trait in question well serves various ends appropriate to a higher animal and to Homo sapiens in particular. A virtuous life, for a mature member of the species Homo sapiens, according to Hursthouse, is a life characteristic of a 'good sophisticated social animal', and such an animal has the following features. It is 'well fitted or endowed' with respect to (i) its parts, (ii) its operations and reactions, (iii) its actions, and (iv) its desires and emotions. In the case of a human being, whether it is thus well fitted or endowed is determined by whether these four aspects well serve four ends which are appropriate to human life. These are (1) a human's individual survival through its natural lifespan, (2) the continuance of the human species, (3) a human's characteristic enjoyments, and (4) the good functioning of the social group in the ways characteristic of the human species.[26] Call this view, following Hursthouse, (virtue-

---

[26] *On Virtue Ethics*, 198–201.

ethical) naturalism. Naturalism is theoretically separable from eudaimonism, and has the attractive feature of expanding the basis for virtue status by comparison with eudaimonism. For Hursthouse, eudaimonism is integrated with naturalism, but efforts at integration have met with difficulties, as witnessed by Philippa Foot's attempts to show how justice can be a virtue on eudaimonistic principles.[27]

Let us turn now to some qualms about Hursthouse's 'naturalism'. The question is: can the grounds of status of a trait as a *virtue* be reduced to Hursthouse's four ends, which determine the characteristic, non-defective functioning of the human species?

There are two main issues. First, inasmuch as the grounds for virtue status are anthropocentric, should those grounds be understood *solely* in terms of Hursthouse's four ends? Second, is the ground of *all* virtue anthropocentric? Consider the first question. I challenge the view that all forms of, say, respect for humans' status and expression of human bonds, characterizing certain forms of virtuous response, serve the ends of enjoyment, the good functioning of the social group, and so forth. Some virtuous forms of friendship, for example, may not serve these ends, in fact the functioning of the social group may go more smoothly without them. Perhaps such friendships serve another of the four ends, the end of characteristic human enjoyment. That friendship serves the end of enjoyment may be true of the lamer forms of friendship described by Aristotle as utility or pleasure friendships, but this need not be true of the finest forms of friendship. As far as respect for status is concerned, we may question whether all forms of status recognition serve the ends of enjoyment or freedom from pain, and/or the well-functioning of the social group. It may be, for example, that respect for the aged enhances the functioning of the social group; but one can imagine contexts where the aged do not have a premium on wisdom, are useless for reproductive ends, are something of a burden, and do not add sufficiently to overall enjoyment. Respect for them may be decent or noble rather than socially useful, and be based fundamentally on bonds or norms of status recognition.

It may be thought that if status recognition neither enhances the enjoyment of at least certain groups, nor is socially useful, it is to be criticized. However, as even Hume recognized in some areas of his writing,

---

27 Philippa Foot, 'Goodness and Choice', in her *Virtues and Vices* (Oxford: Blackwell, 1978), 132–47.

the basis of certain virtues may involve quite different kinds of norms: norms marked by vocabulary such as splendid, revered, honourable, honoured, noble,[28] magnificent, awesome, dignified, having dignity, historic, respected. This is a source of evaluation not reducible to utilities of various sorts, whether those of survival, enjoyments, or absence of pain of individuals, or broad social utility. This point is perfectly compatible with the claim that if some forms of respect for status, grounded on norms of splendour, magnificence, or reverence, are associated with sufficiently serious loss of value of the kinds identified by Hursthouse, then those forms are criticizable.

Now to the second qualm. It seems that some virtues do not serve the *human*-centred ends (1)–(4) of Hursthouse, for example, some environmental virtues. On the classic view of deep environmental ethics, the respect we should accord natural objects by virtue of their status as natural is not based on their serving the enjoyment or smooth social functioning of the human species. It is unclear how Hursthouse's view allows for this, or maybe she wants to reject it. One may also ask: is the status of respect for and benevolence towards animals as virtues, also grounded on serving the four human-centred ends?

It may be replied that all *good* forms of expression of bonds, respect for status, or enhancement of the good of non-humans are constitutive of characteristic good functioning of the *human* species. Perhaps what is wrong is simply that Hursthouse's list of what makes for virtue—aspects of goodness qua human—is just too short. And in particular, perhaps, those aspects should not just be understood in terms of serving human-centred ends.

I am happy with such a reply, but in itself it does not add to the basic account of virtue. A virtue by definition is an excellent or good feature of a human being: that is, it is partially constitutive of goodness qua human, or qua human-in-a-role. The substantive task is to elucidate those features which make for such excellence or goodness. The truth in Hursthouse's view is that a good many, indeed probably most, virtues are grounded in their serving the four ends of human flourishing. Some virtues, however, are so because they serve ends other than human flourishing; for example, the flourishing or integrity of natural objects and

---

[28] In his oration on the occasion of the funeral of Queen Elizabeth the Queen Mother (9 April 2002), the Archbishop of Canterbury referred to the idea that though another cannot control happiness in a marriage, the partners can determine its nobility.

systems, whether sentient, living, or non-living. Other virtues may be grounded in intuitions about splendour, nobility, or greatness, where these cannot be cashed out in terms of *serving* any ends. According to Hume, generally disutile traits can be understood as virtues if we approve of them having adopted a corrected (educated) sympathy. A generally disutile trait can be approved in virtue of its 'dazzling' qualities, or its ability to 'seize the heart' by 'its noble elevation' or 'engaging tenderness'. And the reason that 'excessive bravery' and 'resolute inflexibility' are approved is that we take pleasure in 'splendour and greatness of appearance'.[29]

Hume's account of certain virtues suggests that some virtues may be grounded in non-teleological considerations. A modern proponent of a non-teleological view is Michael Slote. According to his 'agent-based' virtue ethics, virtues are grounded in aretaic intuitions about 'admirability', and it need not be the case that their admirability is further grounded in their serving ends or promoting value, whether those ends or values be flourishing, integrity, truth, beauty, or whatever. Slote's virtue ethics does not therefore rely on a teleological account of virtue status, for a trait's status as a virtue is based simply on its quality of admirability.

My pluralistic view of virtue status contains both teleological and non-teleological elements. I shall now explicate that view before showing how it can overcome objections of 'intuitionism' and 'ungroundedness'. On my view, the features which make traits virtues are exactly the same features that determine the virtuousness of response to items in the field of a virtue. This yields the following principle of virtue status.

(T) What makes a trait a virtue is that it is a disposition to respond in an excellent (or good enough) way (through the modes of respecting, appreciating, creating, loving, promoting, and so on) to items in the fields of the virtue.

The principle (T) has the advantage of allowing for the possibility that the ultimate point of various virtues may be flourishing, admirability, success (worthwhile achievement), or meaningfulness. What is the ultimate point depends on how the virtue is targeted at the good for, bonds, value, status, and so on, with respect to items in their fields.

---

[29] David Hume, *Enquiries Concerning Human Understanding and Concerning the Principles of Morals*, ed. L. A. Selby-Bigge; 3rd edn. revised by P. H. Nidditch (Oxford: Oxford University Press, 1975), sect. 208.

Principle (T) has the further, related, advantage of overcoming both problems faced by naturalism. First, it allows for the possibility that some virtues are non-teleological. Intuitions about the virtuousness of traits grounded in their admirability (regardless of their tendencies to promote certain ends or values) can be accounted for by appeal to the idea of expressiveness. The ability of the heart to be 'seized by engaging tenderness' is an ability which is expressive of those flourishing individuals who are capable of the finest love: the ability of people to respond to 'dazzling splendour' is a kind of appreciation expressive of those flourishing individuals whose lives are the opposite of grey, mediocre, resentment-filled. So certain modes of moral acknowledgement (e.g. love or appreciation) may be fine because expressive of the fine motivations characterizing flourishing human beings. And that is what *makes* such modes part of virtue. Of course, it is not an easy task to distinguish such a virtue from a vice of, say, being prone, in a gullible manner, to being duped by the kinds of grand display manufactured by Hitler in Nazi Germany. Nonetheless, many virtues are so not because they *serve* the end of human flourishing but because they are *expressive* of human flourishing.

Second, (T) avoids the problems of anthroprocentrism. The environmental virtues can be understood as being virtues not just because they are dispositions to promote human-centred ends, but also the ends of the flourishing and integrity of ecosystems, species, and natural objects (sentient and non-sentient) for their own sakes. Furthermore, (T) allows for the environmental virtues to have a complex profile, consisting not just of promotion of good or value, but also of respect, love for, and appreciation of natural objects.

The essential difference between (T) and neo-Aristotelian virtue ethics is this. The latter is characterized by an attempt to combine eudaimonism and naturalism through the unifying idea of the perfection of our (rational) nature—its substantive understanding of excellence qua human being. The virtues (characteristically) benefit their possessor, for the perfection of our nature is a state in which we *flourish*, but they also serve the wider ends demanded by naturalism.

Now, as eudaimonists would agree, the *perfection* of our nature certainly requires not merely that we personally flourish but that we respond excellently to the demands of the world. However, if the latter feature is the fundamental requirement of virtue (as I believe), compromises with our personal flourishing or even the (maximal) flourishing of the human species may be in order in imperfect worlds. For that reason, I prefer to understand the rationale of virtue not primarily through the idea of the perfection of our nature, but through the idea of the multifaceted, pluralistically understood demands of the world, 'naturalized' via the Constraint on Virtue.

We turn finally to the charge that (T) does not adequately ground the virtues. To be sure, the rejection of the Thesis of Non-Aretaic Value in Chapter 2 entails that I do not have a foundationalist picture of the justification of the virtues. I cannot, for example, present a set of base-level values and use that list as foundation stones for the explication of the demands of the world—for the justification of claims that, for example, dispositions to form certain types of bonds are virtuous. Is my view therefore circular? No: more accurately, a theory of virtue justification will be incomplete and rich.[30] It will be incomplete as long as the psychological theories which at least in part elucidate our understanding of, for example, what it is to be well disposed in regard to bonds of friendship are incomplete. It will be incomplete as long as our political and sociological theories explaining the function of institutions in which status properties are embedded, are incomplete. For without a theory of the functions of institutions, we cannot have a full theory of role and status properties. And we cannot therefore have a full theory of status-centred virtues such as role virtues. The provision of full theories of these, as well as other kinds of virtues, therefore lies well beyond the domain of the philosopher. However, the theory of virtue justification will be richer the more detailed is our conception of excellence in, for example, expressing bonds of love, respecting status, promoting good, creativity, and appreciation, and the role of these forms of moral response in individual virtues.

---

[30] My theory as a whole presupposes the method of wide reflective equilibrium more fully described in my 'On the Essential Contestedness of Political Concepts', *Ethics* 95 (1985), 811–27. See also my *Freedom: A Coherence Theory* (Indianapolis: Hackett, 1992), esp. ch. 2.

Part II

PROFILES OF THE
VIRTUES

5

Love and Respect

(i) The Integrating Role of Love and Respect

The central aim of Part II is to focus on the basic modes of moral acknowledgement which feature in all the virtues. These are taken to be universal love and its necessary precursors, receptivity and appreciation; self-love; universal respect and self-respect; and creativity. I consider difficulties in the idea of universal love in particular, arguing for an expressivist understanding of both universal and self-love. I show how such loves must be delimited by respect if they are to feature in virtue. I also show how self-love, appropriately understood, is necessary if universal love, and indeed love in general, are not to be criticizable as weak and excessively self-sacrificing.

Creativity, as a separate mode of moral response, is central in those virtues connected with the development of one's talents. Such development is not simply a matter of greater *promotion* of good or value: one should also *create* items of quality and value. Creativity is also part of the profiles of all virtues insofar as all virtue involves creative aspects of practical wisdom. Some virtues, such as patience, may not see a large role for creativity, but benevolence certainly does. Even when exercised in the quotidian realm (such as meal preparation, where virtues of good parenting are exercised) creativity may be much called for. Creativity is discussed in Chapter 7, but let us turn now to love and respect, which have a pivotal integrating role in the profiles of the virtues.

We first show how love and respect play this role. We need to ask: how, if at all, are the various modes of moral acknowledgement integrated in the virtues? Is it possible to give some sort of unifying account of the plurality of modes? I think this is possible, and Kant shows the way in 'The Doctrine of Virtue' in *The Metaphysics of Morals*. In arguably one of the most profound passages in normative ethical theory, Kant makes the claim that morality comprises two great opposed forces, love and respect, which must be integrated if the moral realm is not to fall apart.

The challenge of understanding this passage I defer till section (ii). In this section, I wish to set the stage for Part II by showing how modes of moral response can be understood as unified, or unified to some extent, in the virtues.

If Kant is correct in his claim that love and respect (including self-love and self-respect) are the two great moral forces, they must come into equilibrium if they are to constitute aspects of the profiles of all the virtues. I shall understand the requirement of 'coming into equilibrium' as a requirement of love (the more demanding form of moral response) being delimited by respect. That love (so understood) features in all virtue is a prima facie counterintuitive claim when we consider virtues whose fields are not individual human or sentient beings. However, even if the field of a virtue is one's projects (such as perseverance), future possibilities (such as hope), or details which can be overlooked (such as conscientiousness or concentration), love and respect are indirectly involved. For example, perseverance as a virtue requires self-love if a healthy bonding with one's projects is to be possible, and love or respect of other is required if one's projects are to be worthwhile and prosecuted in a virtuous manner. Hope is stillborn or distorted if the future possibilities are perceived with a misanthropic outlook.[1] Laboratory technicians and other specialists are less likely to concentrate on examination of cervical smears if they fail to have the attitude 'there is a woman behind every smear' and an attitude of concern for those women. And there may be research abuses if there is inadequate respect.

There are two ways to think of the role of universal love and self-love (delimited by respect) as foundational in a virtue ethics. The first is to think of one or other of them as a separate and dominating virtue, which may come into conflict with other virtues. If self-love is at the top of the hierarchy, one may end up with an ethics which appears to downgrade relationship and the needs or claims of others. If universal love is at the top of the hierarchy, there is a danger of embracing an ethics which downplays the self, or the claims of near and dear.

The second way, my own view, is to think of self-love and universal love as part of the profiles of all virtue.[2] On this understanding, to be

---

[1] I am grateful to Barbara Nunn for discussion of hope as a virtue.

[2] Another philosopher who sees self-love as central in all virtue is Marcia Homiak. Homiak draws on Aristotle to stress the importance of self-love in virtue: 'The virtuous person as a true self-lover, has a kind of positive self-regard and self-confidence: He enjoys himself and his life and does not wish to be different'. Marcia L. Homiak, 'Aristotle on the Soul's Conflicts: Toward

developed throughout this and the next chapters, virtues, including the partialistic virtues, require both forms of love if they are to be truly virtues. (Note however that on a threshold conception of virtue, this love may be imperfect relative to the standards of supreme virtue.) It is not merely the case that such love is a 'bloom' which, like Aristotle's idea of the role of pleasure, completes a virtue. Rather, without such love, partialistic love of others will lapse into excesses where, for example, the love is excessively self-sacrificing, or the loyalty of friendship excludes the demands and needs of 'outsiders' of various kinds.

The second understanding of the role of universal and self-love in a virtue ethics avoids the problems of seeing one or other of them as separate virtues at the top of a hierarchy. This does not entail that no conflict between the claims of universal love and the claims of parental love, for example, will arise. However, on the second understanding, the question of whether a Western aid worker should subject her children to the rigours of life as a 'Servant' in Cambodia remains open, for it is not my view that universal love is a separate virtue which trumps all other virtues.

If love and respect are aspects of the profiles of all virtue, we might ask: how do these feature in the different kinds of virtue? A virtue ethics recognizes that love and respect, as the 'two great moral forces', have to be interpreted through the various virtues. Their nature, as displayed in the virtues, will be appropriately contoured by the following sources of variation:

(1) The different types of objects which constitute the fields of the virtues.
(2) The different aims of the virtues in relation to those fields.
(3) The different bases of moral response which are appropriate to the kinds of items in a virtue's field, and to the aims of that virtue.
(4) The way the virtue is manifested in the narrative structure of an agent's life.

For example, bonds of friendship may be more or less intense and vary

an Understanding of Virtue Ethics', in Andrew Reith, Barbara Herman, and Christine M. Korsgaard (eds.), *Reclaiming the History of Ethics: Essays for John Rawls* (Cambridge: Cambridge University Press 1997), 7–35, at 21. She claims that 'the source and object of self-love are the exercise of one's rational powers' (22), whereas I claim that the full exercise and enjoyment of such powers would be an effect of, and a reinforcer of, self-love rather than the source of self-love.

in nature. But our understanding of what constitutes the precise forms of coming close (and keeping distance) required by the virtue of friendship requires an appreciation of other bases of moral response. A friendship bond may be powerful and may tempt one to share a friend's immoral ends, but friendship as a virtue will not sanction this *precise form* of coming close.

Again, bond-based features of parental virtue may be very powerful morally speaking, but are also more or less constrained by considerations of status (as e.g. citizen) and general good, which may suggest a requirement to turn in one's child to the police. The literature on admirable immorality[3] attests to the consequent murkiness of moral demands in this area. I do not have space to discuss these issues in detail, but my virtue-ethical pluralism suggests that it is a mistake to think of cases of 'admirable immorality' as an opposition between morality and admirability: rather the moral demands based on varying modes and bases of moral response inherent in different virtues are unclear and controversial. In everyday ethics, too, we see how virtue is contoured by varying modes and bases of moral response. Where, for example, promotion of good is constrained by status considerations, further complications arise when the constraints involve more than one status. Friendship, a status-sensitive virtue, will itself be constrained in a status-sensitive way, if the friend is also, for example, one's boss, so certain partialisms of friendship will have to be forgone in the professional relationship. However, the love of friendship may permit and require other partialisms (such as friendly chats) which are not incommensurate with a professional relationship.

The way love and respect are virtuously manifested will also be appropriately contoured by the narrative structure and idiosyncratic features of an individual's life. There is some latitude in choice of those to whom you come close and from whom you keep your distance in various ways. In this particularistic area, what counts as commensurate with a good life is not without controversy. For example, how important in an individual's life is a requirement of narrative unity or integrity?[4] Discussion of this and related issues in narrative ethics, and of how such ethics integrates (or could integrate) with virtue ethics, is beyond the scope of the present book.

---

[3] See, for example, Slote, *Goods and Virtues*, ch. 4, and Marcia Baron's reply to Slote, 'On Admirable Immorality', *Ethics* 96 (1986), 557–66.

[4] For more on this issue see Chappell, *Understanding Human Goods*.

The fact that love and respect are contoured in the above ways does not vitiate my claim that love is basically a bond-based response. However, if these responses are to feature in virtue, they must satisfy standards of excellence. This entails their being appropriately sensitive to the nature of the good (or value) of items in the fields of the virtues, the aims of the virtues, the status of the agent and other relevant parties, and the circumstances of a person's life.

A central aspect of the contouring of love and respect in the virtues concerns the dimension of impartiality and partiality. The question arises: how do universal love and/or respect, and partialistic love and respect, feature in the virtues? It is commonly believed that virtue ethics is well equipped to recognize fully the partialistic aspects of ethics.[5] The inclusion of partialistic virtues such as friendship, parental virtues, collegial virtues, (proper) loyalty, and so on is standard. However, it is less clear that virtue ethics can handle the impartialistic aspects of ethics. Certainly it eschews the idea that a 'principle' of impartiality should be at the foundation of ethics (e.g. Peter Singer's Principle of Equal Consideration of Like Interests).[6] From the perspective of virtue ethics this is quite the wrong way of looking at the matter. Rather, the targets of some virtues (e.g. benevolence) are broadly based; the targets of others such as parental virtue are narrowly based. The profiles of various virtues, then, will shift along axes of various types of partiality and impartiality, and will shift in ways appropriate to the various kinds of items within the fields of the virtues, the relation of the agent to those items, and so on. However, a full specification of the excellences involved in the virtues requires more than the specification of their targets: broad-based benevolence needs to be constrained by partialistic responsibilities; narrow-based parental virtue is constrained (and enhanced) by universal love and respect.

It may be questioned whether being a good parent, or a good friend, requires a disposition of universal love. Haven't we heard of the Nazi who was a good father, a mafioso who is a great friend? It is true that if we have a threshold conception of virtue (as opposed to an ideal notion) one can be said to have the virtue of friendship, say, without scoring maximal points on universal love. But the claims that the Nazi can be a good

---

[5] See e.g. John Cottingham, 'Partiality and the Virtues', in Roger Crisp (ed.), *How Should One Live? Essays on the Virtues* (Oxford: Clarendon Press, 1996), 57–76.

[6] See Peter Singer, *Practical Ethics*, 2nd edn. (Cambridge: Cambridge University Press, 1993).

father, the mafioso a good friend, need to be treated with scepticism. What kind of emotions and beliefs about the 'impure' races is the Nazi expressing to his children? As Rosalind Hursthouse says, racist attitudes seep through in all kinds of everyday behaviour.[7] What kind of friend will the mafioso turn out to be when he is under orders from the family to destroy or ruin him? A virtue ethics need not see partialistic love as totally disjoint from universal love, but as something which universal love completes and perfects in the various virtues.

The coming into equilibrium of love and respect as two separate moral 'forces' is not the only aspect of the unification of modes of moral acknowledgement. Another important and fascinating issue concerns the integration of creativity and receptivity—and the integration of both these with love and respect. Discussion of this must be left to a later occasion. The issue, broadly, is this. Caring or loving seems to involve receptivity, drawing out what is already there, as in Japanese dry-stone gardening, and as emphasized in the notion of *sorgen* in Heidegger's later philosophy.[8] But how is this to be integrated with a Nietzschean emphasis on creativity, which appears to be an imposition of one's will?

(ii) Love as Coming Close and Respect as Keeping Distance

Let us turn now to the nature of love and respect as modes of moral response. I shall follow Kant in claiming that love and respect (whether in their partial or impartial forms)[9] are to be distinguished on the grounds that love in general involves a 'coming close[10] whereas respect in general involves a 'keeping one's distance'. In this section, I will defend

---

[7] *On Virtue Ethics*, ch. 5.

[8] See further Julian Young, *Heidegger's Later Philosophy* (Cambridge: Cambridge University Press, 2002), who claims that e.g. 'active caring-for earth' (for Heidegger) is 'letting it be', in a sense explicated by Schopenhauer: 'completing nature's only half-uttered words' (106–7).

[9] Kant himself distinguishes between partial forms of respect (respect that is owed to people by virtue of differential status) from the impartial form of respect owed to all humans by virtue of their inherent dignity.

[10] I am grateful to Julia Driver and to an anonymous referee for drawing my attention to cases which seem to be counterexamples to this view, namely those like that portrayed in the film *Stella Dallas*. Here love seems to be compatible with a desire to keep distance. But, first, 'coming close' is not equivalent to 'desire to come close'; second, there are many forms of 'coming close', some of which may be present in such cases; and third, such cases are not characteristic.

Kant's distinction between love and respect, arguing that they are distinct forms of moral acknowledgement featuring in the profiles of the virtues.

Here is the crucial passage where the distinction is made in terms of coming close and keeping one's distance:

In speaking of laws of duty (not laws of nature) and, among these, of laws for human beings' external relations with one another, we consider ourselves in a moral (intelligible) world where, by analogy with the physical world, *attraction* and *repulsion* bind together rational beings (on earth). The principle of *mutual love* admonishes them constantly to *come closer* to one another; that of the *respect* they owe one another, to keep themselves *at a distance* from one another; and should one of these great moral forces fail, 'then nothingness (immorality), with gaping throat, would drink up the whole kingdom of (moral) beings like a drop of water' (if I may use Haller's words, but in a different reference).[11]

This passage has recently been discussed by Marcia Baron,[12] and also by Robert Johnson commenting on her paper.[13] Both express forms of scepticism about Kant's distinction between love and respect, but I shall argue in this section that Kant has things exactly right. Kant claims that love and respect are opposed and pull in opposite directions, as do 'attraction' and 'repulsion'. Baron objects to Kant, 'Love would seem to be opposed to hate and also to indifference, but not to respect'.[14] I propose a more sympathetic reading of the passage. Love and respect are indeed 'opposed forces', analogous to attraction and repulsion in physics. The former tends to come close, the latter tends to keep at a distance. However, and here is the crucial point: in the standard physical universe the 'opposed' forces of attraction and repulsion have an equilibrium point of stability. Things neither totally merge nor fly into tiny fragments. One force 'swamps' another in relatively non-standard cases, for example, in black holes where attraction dominates. Similarly, in virtuous love and respect, there is an equilibrium point: one is neither excessively close nor excessively distant. Only where the force of 'repulsion' swamps that of 'attraction' is there hate or indifference; only where the force of 'attraction' swamps that of 'repulsion' is there, for example, invasive paternalism, or clinging love. But the existence of an equilibrium

11 *The Doctrine of Virtue: The Metaphysics of Morals,* trans and ed. Mary Gregor (Cambridge: Cambridge University Press, 1996), sect. 24, pp. 198–9.

12 'Love and respect in the "Doctrine of Virtue"', *Southern Journal of Philosophy* 36, suppl. (1997), 29–44.

13 'Love in Vain', *Southern Journal of Philosophy* 36, suppl. (1997), 45–50.

14 'Love and Respect', 29.

point in proper love or respect does not mean that they are not opposing forces. Similarly, the existence of an equilibrium in atoms which are not undergoing either fission or fusion does not mean that they are not subject to the opposing forces of repulsion and attraction. Indeed, Kant makes the point that it is the very fact that the forces are opposing which makes it possible for elements to 'bind'. Without each of the opposed forces there would be a 'nothingness with gaping throat', as Kant puts it.

However, is the Kantian analysis illuminating? Baron claims that 'respect requires, for example, that we not be contemptuous, yet *that* would not fit under the heading of keeping one's distance'.[15] In fact, on my view, contemptuous behaviour is a violation of respect precisely because it is a failure to keep one's distance. How so? Wounding another is a failure to keep one's distance; contemptuous behaviour is a form of psychological wounding. Both physical and psychological wounding are forms of invasiveness and thereby violations of respect. Mockery, dismissiveness, and insults are all forms of contemptuous psychological attack. Other forms of lack of respect, such as manipulativeness and exploitation are also forms of failure to keep one's distance, insofar as they interfere with a person's pursuit of her good as she sees it.

The real problem on the present defence of Kant's position is not the portrayal of love and respect as opposing forces of approaching and keeping one's distance, but the substantive problem of delineating the equilibrium point. When does benevolence shade into disrespectful paternalism? When does affectionate banter shade into disrespectful mockery?[16] When does romantic love shade into invasive possessiveness? When does loving parental concern for the well-being and safety of one's children turn into disrespectful interference with their lives? When does self-protection (based on self-love) become a selfish disregard for or indifference to the well-being of others? When does it become active exploitation and using? Should keeping one's counsel be called respecting a brother's autonomy or an unloving neglect of his well-being? When is punishment a mark of parental love, a teacher's caring, a judge's agape, and when is it a mark of abuse? Kant's analogy is brilliant precisely because it locates the real problem of integrating love and respect. They are opposing *forces*, but they should not be opposed *in re*. The location of

---

15 Ibid. 30.

16 See *The Doctrine of Virtue*, sect. 25, p. 212, for Kant's distinction between mockery and banter.

the equilibrium point gives us an account of how love and respect as modes of moral acknowledgement fit into the profiles of various virtues.

In section iv I shall discuss impartial or universal love. A prior question needs to be asked here: how can such love be distinguished from (practical) respect, especially given that such love for Kant is not a feeling?[17] Kant answers in this way:

> The duty of love for one's neighbour can, accordingly, also be expressed as the duty to make other *ends* my own (provided only that these are not immoral). The duty of respect for my neighbour is contained in the maxim not to degrade any other to a mere means to my ends (not to demand that another throw himself away in order to slave for my end).[18]

Although this view of benevolence does not seem very demanding because it does not necessitate 'feelings', the requirement that we not only respect but also love in Kant's sense, makes what is demanded of us by love more stringent on Kant's view than one might think. The remarkable thing about Sister Prejean in her campaign against the death penalty in the United States is not so much that she had feelings of some kind for Sonnier, to whom she was spiritual adviser,[19] but that she made his (non-immoral) ends her own and in particular his end of avoiding the kind of punishment argued to be incommensurate with the respect owed to all human beings. Most of us could not do this in the case of extremely repulsive and criminal types; we could not come close in this way. But apart from the more vengeful of us, we find it easy to keep our distance. We have no desire to degrade them for our ends. We just want to keep as far away as possible.

In defending Kant's position, I do not want to suggest that respect and love do not shade into each other. Contempt for another person includes lack of respect as a form of failure to keep one's distance: taunting, bullying, talking down, suppressing opinions by interruption, and cutting off. But it also involves a failure to come close in a minimal sense: a failure to express a weak form of agape. Such contempt (in this milder form) consists in ignoring the presence of another, being cold and indifferent.

Having defended Kant's distinction between respect as a form of keeping one's distance, and love as a form of coming close, it remains for

---

17 Johnson in 'Love in Vain' claims that practical love is just a form of respect.

18 *The Doctrine of Virtue*, sect. 25, p. 199.

19 Sister Helen Prejean, *Dead Man Walking* (New York: Vintage Books, 1993).

me to consider objections to the 'coming close' analysis of love. In his 'Love as a Moral Emotion', J. David Velleman appears to question the idea that love is essentially a form of coming close. He claims:

Love does not feel (to me, at least) like an urge or impulse or inclination toward anything; it feels rather like a state of attentive suspension, similar to wonder or amazement or awe.[20]

For this reason, Velleman rejects as 'fantasy' 'coming close' analyses of love according to which love involves desires to 'care and share' or to 'benefit and be with'. Velleman's analysis therefore suggests that my distinguishing love and appreciation as different modes of moral acknowledgement is mistaken. Love just is a form of appreciation of a particularly deep kind. In particular, for Velleman, the appreciation involved in love 'disarms our emotional defences; it makes us vulnerable to the other'.[21]

Velleman's defence of his position involves the method of counterexample: one can think of cases where love does not involve a desire to benefit, one can think of cases where one cannot stand to be with the beloved. Two points need to be made in defence of the 'coming close' analysis against this method of counterexample. First, as Aristotle claims, the truths of ethics are 'truths for the most part'.[22] Love *characteristically* involves forms of coming close; if it does not, we need not withdraw the claim that there is love, though we will probably argue that it is deficient in some way. If a parent has no inclination to hug or affectionately touch her child, if she has no inclination to share her child's successes, sorrows, and problems, if she involves herself in her child's activities in only a limited and grudging way, her love, if present at all, is seriously deficient. Of course, the forms of coming close characteristic of love will depend on kinds of context, role, and bond.

I agree that impartial love of human beings as such involves at least receptivity, but I shall argue that this is compatible with love as 'coming close'. However, Velleman cites with approval Iris Murdoch's account of attention as 'really looking' in a way that is 'impersonal' and 'an exercise of detachment'. It may seem then, that the 'attention' aspect of love is in tension with an analysis of love as forms of coming close, but there is no

---

[20] 'Love as a Moral Emotion', *Ethics* 109 (1999), 338–74.

[21] Ibid. 361.

[22] See *Nicomachean Ethics*, 1104a1–9, and for further discussion, Nancy Sherman, *Making a Necessity of Virtue: Aristotle and Kant on Virtue* (Cambridge: Cambridge University Press, 1997).

such tension. Murdoch's 'really looking' is in fact not detachment necessarily, but practical wisdom, which for her is a receptivity not marred by psychological distortions (see further below, section iii) .

However, Velleman alludes to another form of potential tension between the appreciativeness proper to love, and love as forms of coming close. He criticizes forms of 'coming close' analyses of love as derived from a faulty Freudian analysis of love as inhibited aim. On that analysis, love is thought at least to have an aim—an aim to get close to someone in some way. In opposition to this account, Velleman denies that love is an aim to bring about a result: 'I venture to suggest that love is essentially an attitude toward the beloved himself but not toward any result at all'.[23]

I agree, but 'coming close' analyses of love need not be aim- or result-oriented. In the next chapter, I give an account of expression which demonstrates why love as a form of coming close need not be result-oriented. As an aspect of *virtue,* love as coming close—for example, virtuous concern for the well-being of the beloved, virtuous desire to be with the beloved, to show affection for the beloved, to share with the beloved—are *expressive* of fine states of compassion, passion, parental love, agape. Such expressions need not be result-oriented at all, and if they are, not in self-serving or otherwise suspect ways. My affectionate rumpling of my son's hair need not be aimed at seeking his attention or making him show me that he loves me. My expressed desire to be with my beloved need not be aimed at getting him to be with me because I am chronically bored, lonely, and empty. My sharing my money with my beloved need not be aimed primarily at relieving me of the responsibility of looking after my own. Such aims would show that the forms of coming close manifested in those actions were not expressive of fine inner states. In such cases, virtues of parental love, sharing, companionship, or friendship would not display love in the appropriate way, and would therefore be imperfectly manifested. This is not to say of course that love should never be expressed in result-oriented behaviour. It would be odd indeed if a parent did not look out for the welfare of her child, or a spouse for the welfare of her partner. Love involves forms of coming close, but as an aspect of the profiles of the virtues it involves wise forms of coming close.

What counts as wisdom in the ways love (and respect) feature in the

---

23 'Love as a Moral Emotion', 534.

virtues depends on the ways they are contoured by the various features identified in section i. As we have seen, the kinds of distance and closeness required by respect and love will vary according to the virtue, permitting and prohibiting varying kinds and degrees of closeness and distance. In the case of punishment, justice (as a role virtue in judges, teachers, and parents) will prohibit abusive, cruel, and 'unusual' punishment as a failure of respect (not to mention love), but will permit violations of personal integrity which would be prohibited in other contexts as a failure of respect.[24] The role virtue of goodness as a psychotherapist arguably involves some form of love (as the psychologist Carl Rogers advocated), but that love must be tempered by some form of keeping one's distance (respect) in virtue of the patient's status as a human being, and not as a lover. The virtue of friendship enjoins both a *bond* of friendship (a form of coming close) and respect for status as a friend (as opposed to e.g. a lover) in forms of keeping a distance suitable to friendship. The virtue of benevolence arguably involves not only the promotion of the good of individuals, but promotion of good with love (in some sense), and respect for status of human beings in general as inviolable.[25]

(iii) Receptivity and Appreciation

In Part I, I identified receptivity and appreciation as modes of moral acknowledgement. Both are essential for excellence in the coming close of love. This section considers receptivity as understood through Iris Murdoch's notion of 'attention' and Nel Noddings's notion of 'engrossment'. Appreciation is also briefly discussed.

Although (Kantian) moral philosophy has highlighted respect, Murdoch claims that 'love is a central concept in morals'.[26] She claims this for one important reason. Love is a way of seeing the world, and if you do not see it with a loving eye, virtue is impossible. On the other hand, if you do see the world with a loving eye, respect will follow. Loving

---

[24] What counts as cruel and abusive will be a matter of great controversy in many areas: cf. recent debates (e.g. in New Zealand) about corporal punishment in schools, and the attitudes of social welfare officers to corporal punishment, putatively sanctioned by religious views, inflicted by parents on their children.

[25] For the view that human beings have a special status as inviolable, see F. M. Kamm, *Morality, Mortality*, vol. ii (New York: Oxford University Press, 1996).

[26] 'The Idea of Perfection', 1–2.

parents, as opposed to parents for whom children satisfy a need, will tend to give their children appropriate independence. They will 'keep their distance' appropriately. A caring employer will not be constantly breathing down the necks of her middle managers as a way of satisfying her need for power. I shall show how Murdoch's notion of attention (involving both receptivity and appreciation) relates to wisdom and love.

Murdoch illustrates the importance of (loving) attention with her well-known example of the daughter-in-law.

A mother, whom I shall call M, feels hostility to her daughter-in-law, whom I shall call D. M finds D quite a good-hearted girl, but while not exactly common yet certainly unpolished and lacking in dignity and refinement. D is inclined to be pert and familiar, insufficiently ceremonious, brusque, sometimes positively rude, always tiresomely juvenile. M does not like D's accent or the way D dresses. M feels that her son has married beneath him. Let us assume for the purposes of the example that the mother, who is a very 'correct' person, behaves beautifully to the girl throughout, not allowing her real opinion to appear in any way. We might underline this aspect of the example by supposing that the young couple have emigrated or that D is now dead: the point being to ensure that whatever is in question as *happening* happens entirely in M's mind.

Thus much for M's first thoughts about D. Time passes, and it could be that M settles down with a hardened sense of grievance and a fixed picture of D, imprisoned (if I may use a question-begging word) by the cliché: my poor son has married a silly vulgar girl. However, the M of the example is an intelligent well-intentioned person, capable of self-criticism, capable of giving careful and just *attention* to an object, which confronts her. M tells herself: 'I am old-fashioned and conventional. I may be prejudiced and narrow-minded. I may be snobbish. I am certainly jealous. Let me look again.'[27]

Two important issues arise from this example, namely:

(i) What is the relation between attention and love?
(ii) Can (loving) attention be distorting, and inaccurate to the facts?

In short, what is the relation between attention and wisdom?

Let us discuss each issue in turn. At first sight it seems that attention has little to do with love. It is a form of receptivity—a form of responsiveness which is well described by Nel Noddings. Noddings attributes to receptivity, which she calls 'engrossment', several features which I think are also properties of Murdoch's attention. These include a heightened awareness, an openness which is pre-analytical and involves feeling rather than thinking, a quietness, an ability to reduce the impact of extraneous noise and racket. It may look as if none of these features has anything to do with a *loving* receptivity. However, to think this is to fail to appreciate the importance of emotional attitude in attention and engrossment. First, emotional attitude renders certain features salient, and others invisible or unimportant. A hostile gaze will downplay or ignore important good features of a person, and that can unfairly cloud one's perception of her as unsuitable for a job, or a promotion, or a raise. A loving gaze will render salient useful or good qualities, will bring to attention abilities which a person is failing to expose or is hiding, and will motivate caring behaviour.

However, is a loving gaze just as distorting as a hostile one? Murdoch's example may invite the question: what if the daughter-in-law really is vulgar and juvenile? What if the redescriptions as 'refreshingly simple' and 'delightfully youthful' are the workings of blind charity motivated by a fear of conflict abhorred by a woman described by Murdoch as 'correct'? Indeed, is emotional take on a subject an entirely subjective or relative matter, where there is no possibility of standing back and assessing the truth?

It is clear that according to Murdoch, 'attention' allows for the possibility of truth, which can be missed through distorting emotions. She describes the daughter-in-law as 'certainly unpolished and lacking in dignity and refinement'.[28] The question remains, however: why should the loving gaze's account of 'unpolished' as 'refreshingly simple' be privileged over the hostile gaze's account of 'unpolished' as 'vulgar'? The answer to this question lies in our discussion of the second issue identified above: the role and nature of wisdom in attention.

Assessing whether a loving attention is required in virtue requires an analysis of what role wisdom plays in loving attention. At first sight, further inspection of the daughter-in-law will determine what wise attention amounts to. But we already have the novelist's apt descriptions of her—unpolished, unrefined, lacking in dignity. The issue is no longer what further observations of her need to be made, but what psychological and historical traits of her mother-in-law are distorting her emotional perceptions. The requirement is not further knowledge of the daughter-in-law, but self-knowledge. As Murdoch claims, 'The world is

---

28 Ibid.

aimless, chancy and huge, and we are blinded by self'.[29] The point made here is that because the world is 'chancy and huge' perception is necessarily highly selectiv,[30] but the selection must be free of psychological distortions. As she puts it, 'The difficulty is to keep the attention fixed upon the real situation and to prevent it from returning surreptitiously to the self with consolations of self-pity, resentment, fantasy, and despair'.[31] Receptivity is also inhibited by anxiety, according to Murdoch:

By opening our eyes we do not necessarily see what confronts us. We are anxiety-ridden animals. Our minds are continuously active, fabricating an anxious, usually self-preoccupied, often falsifying *veil* which partially conceals the world.[32]

Attention, required to gain an increased perception of detail in a huge, complex world, and a sense of the relevance of details to problems, cannot therefore be 'blinded by self' and 'the obscure devices of the psyche'.[33] For example, the insecure manager, whose 'attention' is hostile as a consequence of his own ego problems, will fail to recognize the strengths of his employees, let alone utilize those strengths in ways optimally beneficial to the company. We can now understand why the mother-in-law's later loving attention is wiser and less distorted than the earlier hostile perceptions. It is the later loving attention which is undistorted by the 'falsifying veil' of psychological defences, including 'narrow-mindedness', 'snobbishness', 'jealousy', and the lack of knowledge of self as overly conventional and old-fashioned. In short, attention is loving insofar as it is undistorted by the falsifying veil of hostility fed by the various vices of lack of self-love; vices such as resentment and jealousy, cowardice, aggression, greed at others' expense, or deceit serving one's own power needs. Attention does not entail blindness to others' faults; it demands that perception of those faults not reflect the distortions of one's own ego needs.

However, even if loving attention requires the elimination of distorting hostility-driven conceptualizations, it may lack other features necessary for wisdom. In particular, it seems to share features of Nel Noddings's receptivity or engrossment, themselves thought to be

---

[29] 'The Sovereignty of Good over Other Concepts', in *The Sovereignty of the Good* (London: Routledge, 1970), 77–104, at 100.

[30] See further Andy Clark, *Being There: Putting Brain, Body, and World Together Again* (Cambridge, Mass.: MIT Press, 1997), for an account of just how selective perception necessarily is.

[31] 'The Sovereignty of Good over Other Concepts', 91.

[32] Ibid. 84.   [33] Ibid.

opposed to wisdom. Let us now discuss those features, before claiming that wise attention (and love) requires receptivity followed by appreciation. Receptivity is not opposed to wisdom, but nor is it the whole of wisdom.

Murdoch's attention is a kind of openness to the world. For this openness to occur, as we have seen, she emphasizes eliminating the falsifying veil of narcissistic focus on self; Noddings emphasizes the importance of the pre-analytic, 'receptive-intuitive' mode.[34] This latter feature of attention may make it appear inimical to wisdom, traditionally understood to be a reason-receptive and reason-giving attribute. However, this appearance is mistaken. Noddings's receptivity does not (or need not) *replace* analysis; it is a receptive, intuitive precursor of it. As Noddings puts it, it is a heightened awareness rather than a degradation of consciousness, which allows ourselves to be put 'quietly in the presence of objects'.[35] It 'clears our minds',[36] reducing 'noise'. In Noddings's example of the mathematics teacher's advice to a stumbling student, the teacher strives to ensure receptivity in the student before the analytic phase of problem solving begins.[37]

If receptivity is a pre-analytic phase of openness to the world, the analytic phase enters with appreciation. Appreciation is most salient in virtues of connoisseurship, but in case there is a temptation to think of appreciation as of interest only in aesthetics, one should note that it is clearly of universal applicability to the world of nature at large, including human beings and their artefacts. The 'analytic phase' of appreciation is famously understood by Hume, who searched for a 'standard of taste':

It is natural for us to seek a *Standard of Taste*, a rule, by which the various sentiments of men may be reconciled: at least, a decision, afforded, confirming one sentiment, and condemning another.[38]

Of particular importance is the idea that 'mere' taste should not be contrasted sharply with ethics: appreciation and its standards enter into all areas, although of course connoisseurship of tea or coffee is of much less import to the good life than the appreciation of cultures and the

---

[34] *Caring: A Feminine Approach to Ethics and Moral Education* (Berkeley: University of California Press, 1984), 34.

[35] Ibid.   [36] Ibid.

[37] Ibid. 34–5.

[38] 'The Standard of Taste', *Collected Essays* (1777), repr. in *Enquiries Concerning Human Understanding and Concerning the Principles of Morals*, ed. L. A. Selby-Bigge, 3rd edn. revised P. H. Nidditch (Oxford: Oxford University Press, 1975), 229.

more significant aspects of nature. It is beyond the scope of this book to discuss in any detail possible standards of appreciation, though a promising place to start is the 'joint verdict' of 'true judges', who according to Hume have the ability to make fine discriminations, without prejudice, and who possess delicacy of sentiment, improved by practice and perfected by comparison.[39] This, of course, is highly reminiscent of virtue-ethical qualified agent criteria of rightness (see Chapter 11), but notice that I would understand the above standards to be standards (putatively) constituting excellence in appreciation as an aspect of the profiles of the virtues. It does not follow that judgements reached as a result of applying such standards are right on a target-centred virtue-ethical conception of rightness. (See further Chapter 11.)

Delicacy of taste as an aspect of excellence in appreciation is for Hume a matter of being refined, in the sense of being sensitive to more pleasures and displeasures.[40] This sense of delicacy is controversial as a criterion of excellence of appreciation in the area of vice: is it necessary, for example, to appreciate the virtue of individuals that one possess 'delicacy of taste' in, for example, the varieties of sadism?

It is also interesting to explore the relation between delicacy and the other criteria for excellence in appreciation. It is possible, for example, to have a refined sense of displeasure caused through study of various kinds of weta (an 'ugly'-looking and 'fearful' insect), a study informed by comparisons of different kinds, but the appreciation of them all as 'ugly' is itself informed by prejudice.

'Attention' as receptivity and appreciation is necessary for virtuous love, but as aspects of wisdom they do not entail detachment (as opposed to freedom from 'falsifying' psychological deficiency). Hence accepting receptivity and appreciation as necessary for (good) love does not preclude coming close analyses of love.

The next section concentrates on the problems of a 'coming close' analysis of universal love.

(iv) Universal Love

The importance of universal love as an aspect of the profiles of at least many virtues is suggested in this passage from Schopenhauer:

[39] Ibid. 241.
[40] See Theodore A. Gracyk, 'Rethinking Hume's Standard of Taste', *Journal of Aesthetics and Art Criticism* 52 (1994), 169–82.

Boundless compassion for all living beings is the firmest and surest guarantee of pure moral conduct, and needs no casuistry. Whoever is inspired with it will assuredly injure no one, will wrong no one, will encroach on no one's rights; on the contrary, he will be lenient and patient with everyone, will forgive everyone, will help everyone as much as he can, and all his actions will bear the stamp of justice, philanthropy, and loving kindness.[41]

Schopenhauer here suggests that loving concern is an important constituent of the profiles of a range of virtues. He mentions many of these, including justice, philanthropy, kindness, forgiveness, tolerance, patience, non-maleficence, and helpfulness. They may also include gentleness, unreadiness to carp and criticize, and non-proneness to anger and hostility. Because Schopenhauer does not limit love to virtues whose field is near and dear, such as friendship, but grounds a wider range of virtues on 'boundless compassion'—what I shall call universal love—an important task of this chapter is to understand how such love can be an aspect of the profile of those virtues with a broader field, even justice. For though justice as a virtue is primarily concerned with respecting status and honouring (legitimate) rules and procedures, rules and procedures have to be made and interpreted, and making and interpreting them with a loving eye will enhance or 'perfect' justice.[42] A judge may be procedurally just in dispensing justice in a rape case, but if he betrays his misogyny in his summing up, the virtue of justice has not been displayed to the highest degree.[43]

A central difficulty in the understanding of universal love as an aspect of the profiles of the virtues is the combining of such love with respect for self and others as individuals. For Schopenhauer himself valorized the capacity to break down the barriers between self and other and laud-

---

[41] Arthur Schopenhauer, *On the Basis of Morality*, trans. E. F. J. Payne (Providence, R.I.: Berghahn Books, 1995), 172.

[42] Some theorists distinguish those virtues which should express love from those which do not, e.g. justice (see discussion of Pufendorf in Jerome B. Schneewind, 'The Misfortunes of Virtue', in Roger Crisp and Michael Slote (eds.), *Virtue Ethics* (Oxford: Oxford University Press, 1997), 178–200, at 186. Pufendorf's view was, however, based in a natural-law understanding of justice as comprised entirely of highly determinate specific rules. This view would be rejected in a virtue ethics.

[43] In his 'The Justice of Caring', *Philosophy and Social Policy* 15 (1998), 171–94, Michael Slote understands the virtue of justice as a form of caring. On my view, justice has a complex profile, and the important truth in Slote's view which I would want to capture is that love (whether partial or impartial) is a mode of moral responsiveness which is part of (but not the whole of) the profile of justice.

ed those capable of the greatest love *on that basis*: 'the character that has reached the highest goodness and perfect magnanimity will sacrifice its well-being and its life completely for the well-being of many others'.[44] But in such beings the *principium individuationis* has broken down and the fate of others is treated exactly as one's own.

However, such love does not appear compatible with respect for self and others as separate individuals. How do we prevent the self being swallowed up in self-sacrifice, and how do we prevent the other being swallowed up in invasive compassion? My answer to these questions is revealed in this chapter and the next through a study of universal love and self-love, and the role of expression in such love.

I take universal love to have the following features which distinguishes it from other ideals such as respect, partialistic forms of love, and universal benevolence as an aggregative form of human concern:

   (i) It is a form of 'coming close'.
   (ii) It is particular.
   (iii) It is universal.
   (iv) It is impartial.
   (v) It is unconditional.

I discuss each of these features in turn.

In Chapter 2, I understood love as a bond-centred mode of moral response. As such, it characteristically involves a coming close, and differs from respect, which need not involve a bond. It is this feature which distinguishes love on my account from love as understood by Velleman as 'an arresting awareness of the value inherent in its object' and as 'similar to wonder or amazement or awe'.[45] His rejection of 'coming close' analyses, discussed above, misses the essential feature of love as a bond, and makes it difficult to distinguish love from a separate mode of moral response—appreciation—which is necessary but not sufficient for virtuous love. The coming close account of love is also to be distinguished from an account such as that of Neera K. Badhwar, on which love essentially or centrally involves pleasure or enjoyment.[46] On my view what is characteristic (Kant says 'in general')is the coming close of a bond, but the bond may involve more pain then pleasure. However, if we accept

[44] *The World as Will and Representation*, trans. E. F. J. Payne (New York: Dover, 1969), i. 375.

[45] 'Love as a Moral Emotion', 360.

[46] See her 'Love', in Hugh Lafollette (ed.), *The Oxford Handbook of Practical Ethics* (New York: Oxford University Press, 2002), 42–69.

Aristotle's view that the exercise of virtue is (characteristically) pleasurable to the virtuous agent, then inasmuch as love is part of the profile of a virtue, and therefore excellent or good, it will be characteristically pleasurable in a good way.

It may be thought that the coming close of universal love essentially involves promotion of the beloveds' well-being and satisfaction of their needs. For universal love to be manifested it is not, however, *necessary* that it involve satisfying another's needs, any more than a love of nature (which also involves a coming close) necessarily involves a sense of the *neediness* of nature. Yet we can distinguish the *impartial* 'coming close' love of nature (e.g. a sense of awe or wonder at, and a powerful desire to come close to or even touch, a previously unencountered kauri tree, from the partial love for a kauri tree that one's grandparents have planted on the family property).[47]

Augustine, too, makes it clear that universal love is not reducible to a readiness to meet the needs of another; nor is it reducible to the emotional components of compassion:

Take away the needy and all the works of mercy become superfluous. The fact that the works of mercy will no longer be needed does not at all mean that the fire of your love will be extinguished. Your love will be more genuine if it is directed towards a happy person to whom you have nothing to give. Such love will be purer and much more sincere.[48]

This passage suggests that universal love requires emotional intensity in particular acts of coming close. One potent reason for scepticism that universal love has a place in ethical theory is that the Christian model (at least) of such love is thought to be too demanding, both at the level of emotion and action. On the threshold conception of virtue, however, universal love need not be understood in this demanding way. Indeed, psychologists such as Peck think of such love in a dynamic way: as a 'work', and a work of courage. It is to some extent relativized to the strength of the agent, and constructive action is demanded, rather than a

---

[47] People may say that 'awe' is not synonymous with 'love'. Indeed this is true. I want to distinguish love awe from fear or respect awe. The phenomenology of awe for the giant kauris of New Zealand (for example) that I know American visitors to have experienced involves a powerful desire to come close, even to hug. That is why the Department of Conservation has had to build protective barriers, since kauris are surface rooting. Yet visitors to New Zealand cannot (on the whole) be said to display a partialistic love for kauri.

[48] In *Epistolian Ionnis* 8, 5 (ML 35, 2038), cited in Raymond Canning, *The Unity of Love for God and Neighbour in St. Augustine* (Hevelee Leuven: Augustinian Historical Institute, 1993), 76.

special feeling. Indeed, at the level of emotion, according to Peck, even dislike and repugnance may be felt. No doubt, however, in the 'work' of love, these emotions too must be worked on, and replaced by something more benign, even if not 'a fire' of love.

We turn now to universal love as particular. The above discussion shows how universal love can have this feature. Constrained by the 'fitnesses' of time, place, and circumstance, one is to come close to another as an individual, an individual who is not fungible with others. Universal love is not aggregative universal benevolence, nor is it love of humanity. A person may have a philanthropic love of humanity, and yet fail dismally in his or her ability to come close to individuals in love. It may even be possible to possess universal love for individual human beings without having a love for humanity as such, thinking that the species is seriously maladapted or flawed.

Frequently, though, hatred of or hostility towards individuals is due to class hostility. But just as hostility to *individuals* qua members of a hated class can be dissolved as one *relates* to members of that class as individuals, so the demands of universal love take that dissolution one further step. One does not slip back into a class-property mentality once there is no longer exposure to those individuals, or even when that exposure is taking place.

The view that universal love is a particularized bond-based mode of moral acknowledgement resolves a putative difficulty with Erich Fromm's view of humanitarian love. For Fromm, even (healthy) erotic love of persons is based on humanitarian love of all persons, an idea found problematic by Mike W. Martin.[49] According to Martin, erotic love is characterized by particularity, and like self-love, is not 'an instantiation of a general love for humanity'. And since a 'general love for humanity' is not a particularized love, erotic love cannot be based on humanitarian love of all persons. However, Fromm may be right if 'humanitarian love' is understood in a particularized way in the manner described by Augustine. Universal love is not love of humanity as such, but a bond (of a certain non-erotic kind) between individual persons. The point made by Fromm is that 'love of humanity' is based on self-love, for only if one does not externalize self-contempt in hostility, defensiveness, fear of closeness, or lack of confidence in one's usefulness or lovability is one

---

[49] E. Fromm, *The Art of Loving* (London: Unwin, 1975); M. W. Martin, *Love's Virtues* (Lawrence, Kan.: University Press of Kansas, 1996), 98–9.

capable of the bond of universal love. Indeed, this capacity is a matter of characterological orientation, as Fromm states, but it is an orientation which permits certain attitudes and expressive behaviour towards *individuals* and not just an abstract love of humanity.[50] Unfortunately Fromm himself muddies the waters by using such language as 'love of one person implies love of man as such'.[51]

Let us turn now to the impartiality and universality of universal love. There are three possible views about the nature of these features. View (1) is the view that human beings have *equal* inherent worth as persons independently of our responses to them, and that the *impartiality* of our love for them is a response to this equality. Furthermore, we love them universally and impartially in virtue of our recognition of this equal worth, which makes our love rational. We need to clarify the sense in which universal love is meant to be a response to the equal worth of all human beings. As James Kellenberger notes,[52] agape or impartial love is not based on what Irving Singer calls 'appraisal'.[53] Singer believes that values found by appraisal are always relative to the appraiser's interests or needs, and that such values as intelligence or skill are standardly called 'merits'. As such, what Singer calls 'appraisal value' is not thought suitable as a basis for impartial love. However, Kellenberger distinguishes an appraisal from both a bestowal and a finding of value. He claims that the sense in which we relate to inherent worth is through a finding or discovery, rather than an appraisal or act of creation or bestowal.[54] View (1) then, can be understood as follows. We love human beings (in the sense of universal love) in virtue of our discovering or finding, and then appreciating and responding to, their equal inherent worth as persons or human beings.

View (2) states that impartial love is creative, in the sense that it creates worth.[55] It creates the worth persons have as persons, and that worth is not pre-existing. Such an idea of love is analogous to the theological view

---

[50] Indeed, if that is what grounds one's benevolence, it may be pathological (see further Chapter 8).

[51] *The Art of Loving*, 50.

[52] *Relationship Morality* (University Park, Pa.: Penn State University Press, 1995), 24.

[53] Irving Singer, *The Modern World*, vol. iii of *The Nature of Love* (Chicago: University of Chicago Press, 1987), ch. 10, esp. pp. 389–92.

[54] See also Martin *Love's Virtues*, 40.

[55] This view is advocated by Irving Singer, who suggests that we bestow value when we love (*The Modern World*, ch. 10).

that divine agape creates the inherent worth of human beings.[56] View (3), which I endorse, claims that impartial love is neither a specific kind of recognition of equal value or worth, nor a creation of such value or worth. Rather, universal love is a bond of a certain kind, a bond which can appropriately be called impartial.

View (3), which I call the expressivist view, will be further elaborated in the next chapter where we will discuss the idea of expression as an aspect of virtue, and its role in universal and self-love. The basic idea is that universal love (as well as self-love) are not resultant properties: one does not love in these ways for reasons, and a fortiori one does not love in virtue of properties of the beloved which then provide justifying grounds or reasons for the love. Such a view avoids the embarrassing requirement to find a universal property common to all human beings (and other objects of universal love) which can ground universal impartial love. Such properties fall into three classes which have prima face difficulties for their bearing the weight of their justificatory role. The first set of properties are merits or other appraised characteristics, but these are not universally shared, or are possessed minimally by some. The second set of properties are both universally shared and relatively unmysterious, such as individuality, but these are arguably insufficiently significant to fulfil adequately their role of underpinning the impartiality and universality of universal love. The third set are universally shared and putatively significant, but are arguably metaphysically mysterious, such as Kantian worth or dignity (as opposed to merits) or (in Christian ethics) the capacity for 'divine gift-love'. I do not intend to discuss these difficulties—I merely note them in order to motivate an account which does not require a search for a grounding property.

Insofar as love is not resultant on beliefs about value or merit, it possesses one of the characteristics attributed by Anders Nygren to God's agape. According to Nygren, God's love is spontaneous and unmotivated. It is 'groundless' in that it is not grounded in a characteristic of the beloved: 'all thought of worthiness of the object is abandoned'.[57] This is not to say that such love is 'arbitrary and fortuitous'. Nygren

---

56 This view I think should be distinguished from that of Anders Nygren, 'Agape and Eros', in Alan Sobel (ed.), *Eros, Agape, and Philia: Readings in the Philosophy of Love* (New York: Paragon House, 1989), 85–95, who claims that divine love refuses 'to be controlled by the value of its object' and is 'determined only by [Christ's] own intrinsic nature' (86). Nonetheless, he does say that agape is a 'value creating principle' (87).

57 Ibid. 87.

concludes: 'When it is said that God loves man, this is not a judgement on what man is like, but on what God is like'.[58] Similarly, when I claim that human universal love is similarly 'groundless' (though not arbitrary), this is a judgement about what humans capable of such love are like, rather than primarily a claim about what the beloved is like. In the case of humans, the capacity for such groundless love lies in their capacity to form bonds. I do not mean to imply that a mother cannot say to her child 'I love you for your courage' or a lover to his beloved 'I love you for your warmth'. This really means 'I admire or appreciate your warmth'. But it is odd to claim that a mother loves her child in virtue of, or because of, the child's courage, or the lover loves her beloved in virtue of her warmth. Furthermore, historical features of a relationship or idiosyncrasies may help cause or strengthen loving bonds, but again, one would not claim to love a person because of or in virtue of even a large collection of historical features or idiosyncrasies.[59]

The absence of a grounding property makes it appropriate that universal love is analogized in certain respects to the sun's light. In the New Testament book of Matthew it is claimed that the sun shines on both the evil and the good. The suggestion is that unconditional love is an *expression* of the nature of the lover and is not grounded in reasons. (The goodness of the love does need a ground, however.) Furthermore, the sun's light is impartial and universal: it does not discriminate on the basis of any property of the irradiated object, and its light extends to all things. However, this very analogy highlights two problems for the expressivist view. First, if there is no grounding of universal love in properties of the objects of such love, how do we determine its scope? Second, if there is no such grounding, how can we love in ways suitable to the object of love?

It may be argued that an expressivist view of universal love does not have the resources to provide an account of its scope. But as I have already argued (in Chapter 2), it is a mistake to look for one highly general criterion of scope, such as a criterion of 'moral considerability'. What we have instead is a range of virtues having different fields, in which uni-

[58] Ibid. 85.

[59] In his *About Love: Reinventing Romance for our Times* (New York, London: Simon & Schuster, 1988), Robert C. Solomon claims that 'love is for reasons' (154), but his view is not necessarily opposed to mine. He claims that 'there are good kinds of reasons for love, and there are bad reasons' (154), suggesting not necessarily that one loves for reasons, but rather that love can be justified as good or bad, for reasons.

versal love (as an aspect of the profiles of the virtues) is contoured in the kinds of ways discussed in section i. Scope issues then should be filtered through accounts of various kinds of virtues having different fields. The nature of love for highly valuable inanimate natural objects will be discussed via an account of various types of environmental virtue; accounts which will determine the goodness of such love. Even the issue of whether we should love machines will be filtered through a discussion of those virtues associated with aesthetic issues and conservation of heritage. Only when the issues are grounded in discussions of this type will we be able to answer whether, for example, each grain of sand, each machine, is part of the scope of universal love as it is manifested in various relevant virtues. It may well be thought, however, that virtue-based reasons for claiming that X lies within the scope of a virtue mandating love of X, are also reasons for loving X. However, this does not follow. What Jonathan Dancy calls an 'enabling condition' for a feature, is not ipso facto a reason for that feature.[60]

Nor does exploration of a scope condition in itself impact on an account of behaviours consistent with appropriately displayed universal love, as expressed in the various virtues. For example, it may be that a virtue of self-protection would permit the death penalty for certain kinds of terrorists in certain kinds of circumstances, even if they are loved somewhat as Sister Prejean loved Sonnier. Even if harmful bacteria are brought within the ambit of universal love through environmental or aesthetic virtue, it does not follow that we should protect their life. It may merely be required that we love them somewhat as a scientist who studies them might. Indeed, it may not be *required* by virtue that we all love such things: such love may merely be desirable or a mark of admirability.

The answer to the second problem—how can we love in ways suitable to the object of love?—is contained in the answer to the first. Though we do not love universally for reasons (any more than we have self-love for reasons), the goodness of that love is grounded inter alia in properties of the object, such as the nature of its good or value, its status, its relation to the agent. As we saw in section i, the nature of both love and respect will be appropriately contoured in the virtues.

Even if universal love is not a resultant property, the goodness and reasonableness of such love may be. However, I shall propose an unorthodox view about the properties on which the reasonableness of love is resultant. I shall claim that its reasonableness and goodness lie as

60 See esp. his *Moral Reasons* (Oxford: Blackwell, 1993), ch. 5.

much in characterological properties of the agent, as in properties of the beloved. These features are explored in the next chapter, but here I note the following.

The goodness of universal love consists in an agent's being receptive to or open to bonds of an impartial nature in a healthy way: a receptivity which is often blocked through the domination of inappropriately exclusivist, partialistic bonds, materialistic concerns, low self-esteem creating fear of closeness or intimacy, pathological dependency, fears, hatreds, envy, anger borne of prejudice, or sense of personal inferiority or vulnerability. Universal love in a form more substantial than humane concern is a capacity difficult to acquire, and is thus particularly admirable. According to M. Scott Peck, it is possible for limitations in our capacity to love to be overcome 'but great self-discipline is required in the extension of oneself in order to avoid spreading oneself too thin'.[61] A requirement of universal love, then, is not a demand for an extension of oneself, beyond one's capacities, in intense and demanding forms of love. (See further Chapter 9.)

The idea that universal love is not a resultant property does not impugn its status as impartial (even though I would be happy to see the term 'impartial' disappear from the ethics lexicon). As the boundaries of love exhibited by humans extend outwards from the familiar terrain of one's children, parents, lovers, and very close friends, to strangers, criminals, animals, and even to non-sentient natural objects, it merits the label 'impartial', even though there is no feature which grounds the impartiality. Even Peck is wrong on my view when he says 'I have said the object of genuine love must be a person, since only persons have spirits capable of growth',[62] since such a view fails to ground the admirability of 'genuine love' for one with advanced Alzheimer's disease,[63] or the love of St Francis of Assisi for animals. However, agent-centred criteria of goodness of love allow for discriminations between 'genuine love' and neurotic and obsessive love for, say, animals. Somebody who 'loves' cats or dogs to the point that she has hundreds living in her house in insanitary conditions is at fault in her love not because such animals are unworthy objects of love since they lack the capacity for spiritual growth or higher forms of rationality. Rather, her love is defective because it is

---

[61] *The Road Less Travelled: A New Psychology of Love, Traditional Values and Spiritual Growth* (New York: Simon & Schuster, 1978), 159.

[62] Ibid. 82.

[63] See John Bayley, *Iris: A Memoir of Iris Murdoch* (London: Duckworth, 1998).

obsessive. Note, however, that although not being obsessive is a feature which makes for goodness of love of X, it is not of course a reason for loving X.

The most controversial and difficult aspect of universal love is its unconditionality. To say that such love is unconditional is to say that it has neither 'acceptance' nor 'terminating' conditions, in the terminology of Dean Cocking and Justin Oakley.[64] That is, there are no 'conditions' on the love, as there are conditions on accepting someone as a friend or terminating the friendship. On this definition, it is consistent with the idea of (universal) unconditional love that we love in virtue of characteristics which provide reasons for our love, even though we do not select as objects of love only some within the range of those individuals who are the kinds of things that are proper objects of such love. (Contrast friendships, where, within the scope of items who can be friends, we can pick and choose, and withdraw.) On my expressivist view of universal love, we do not, however, love for reasons, but my point is simply that accepting unconditionality does not ipso facto commit one to an expressivist account.

Another clarificatory point needs to be made. It may be thought that if we love someone in a certain manner, a feature which is partially definitive of goodness in the love, that feature makes the love 'conditional' because conditioned on something. It may then be thought that this feature would provide a reason for the love, and such a love could not then be analysed in terms of an expressivist account. However, this thought is based on confusion between reasons for love, and features which make for goodness of love. In virtuous universal love, we love persons as ends in themselves and not merely as means, but this does not entail that we love them for the *reason* that they are ends in themselves.

The notion of unconditional love has been subject to criticism. In his *Carl Rogers and Humanistic Psychology*, Richard I. Evans describes some putatively problematic features of unconditionality. He claims that Carl Rogers's love-based therapy has the following essential features:

First and most important is therapist congruence or genuineness—his ability to be a real person with the client. Second is the therapist's ability to accept the client as a separate person without judging him or evaluating him. It is rather an unconditional acceptance—that I'm able to accept you as you are. The third condition

---

[64] 'Indirect Consequentialism, Friendship and the Problem of Alienation', *Ethics* 106 (1995), 86–111.

is a real empathetic understanding ... to find that there is a real person who really accepts and understands sensitively and accurately perceives just the way the world seems to me—that just seems to pull people forward.[65]

In criticism of these ideas, Jeffrey Masson claims:

We do not 'really accept' everybody we meet, we are constantly judging them, rejecting some, avoiding some (and they us) with good reason ... And the mere fact that someone has come to you in need does not in and of itself mean that you will love that person. 'Unconditional regard' is not something that seems either likely or desirable. Faced with a brutal rapist who murders children, why should any therapist have unconditional regard for him? Or a wife batterer?[66]

There is an ambiguity in phrases such as 'really accept' and 'accept you as you are'. As Augustine claims, we can accept the sinner without accepting the sin. Not accepting the sin, however, *does* presuppose evaluation: unconditional love does not presuppose non-evaluation, but rather the non-diminution of regard as a result of evaluation. Sister Helen Prejean certainly evaluated the criminals to whom she was spiritual adviser—she evaluated them as criminals who had committed atrocious crimes.[67] Yet she was able to claim with sincerity in her last moments with Pat Sonnier, 'I love you'.

There is a second source of ambiguity in the notion of 'really accept' or 'accept you as you are'. Let us grant that accepting a person as she is allows for evaluation, indeed negative evaluation. But having evaluated a person, we could accept her as she is in two possible ways. First, we could totally downgrade the importance of her faults. This Masson rightly thinks is unacceptable. But there is a weaker reading of 'accepting a person as she is'. Evaluation of that person must not be 'judgemental', as it is often put. 'Not being judgemental' is a vague idea, but it involves several things. First, it involves not being too ready to evaluate, particularly negatively. We shouldn't think that the most salient requirement of 'coming into the presence of a person'[68] is to evaluate them, as opposed to being receptive to them, for example. Furthermore, not only must one not be too ready to find fault, one should not treat a person as a 'phenomenon', a person with 'interesting' features, the understanding of

---

[65] New York: E. P. Dutton, 1975, 30. Cited in Jeffrey Masson, *Against Therapy* (London: Fontana, 1993, first published 1988), 230.

[66] Masson, *Against Therapy*, 232–4.

[67] Prejean, *Dead Man Walking*.

[68] James Kellenberger's phrase, *Relationship Ethics*.

which is motivated chiefly by curiosity. Finally, insofar as one is engaged in evaluation, one is animated in large measure by a desire to find some good.

So much for the nuances of a requirement of impartial love not to be judgemental. However, although being non-judgemental in the above kind of sense is an important aspect of the unconditionality of impartial love, that feature does not penetrate to the heart of unconditional love. Unconditional love demands a form of coming close, and how can that be unconditional? In Christian theology, we are meant to love our neighbour and our enemy as part of our love of God. This involves our loving them (as far as we are able) in ways analogous to the way God loves them, and God loves them insofar as they are all his children. Such a view provides a vital clue about how to understand unconditional impartial love as a form of coming close, in secular terms. Impartial love has important similarities with love of one's own children.

Love of one's own children is characteristically a form of unconditional love.[69] That is, characteristically, parents love their children despite their defects (and even criminal behaviour) even at the cost of their personal happiness. As the God of Christian theology does not love his errant children less despite their sins (but may be saddened by them), so parents are frequently grieved by the behaviour of their children, while love remains intact. The unconditionality of such love is made possible by the fact that the love is not premised on a feature of the object of love, which the parent can subsequently see as disappearing (e.g. the child's innocence or good behaviour) or as diminishing in importance (e.g. the child's being one's *own* child). Rather, the love flows from a bond between parent and child, a bond whose lack or ineffectiveness would standardly be seen as a defect in the parent. However, insofar as universal love is an aspect of the profiles of virtues such as justice, benevolence, patience, or helpfulness, the kind of 'coming close' required by such love need not be as emotionally demanding as parental love. And how intense is that demand will depend on our situation, capacities, and strength.

---

[69] I say 'characteristically' because this is not a universally applicable norm. One can imagine contexts where love of an extremely deformed neonate requires something like an 'acceptance condition', and sometimes love for an adult child at least may be legitimately terminated, in cases of e.g. severe violence. But even here, such lack of love *may* be laid at the door of a not necessarily culpable lack of capacity *in the agent*.

6

Expression

(i) The Idea of Expression

Central to the profiles of all the virtues, on a virtue-ethical account, is expression; for all virtue expresses fine inner states. What does it mean to say that virtue *expresses* fine inner states? It means that behaviour which is describable as behaviour *from* or *out of* a (state of) virtue must have a certain quality. It must be behaviour which has an *expressive component* in a psychological sense.

In this chapter I first explicate the idea of expression. I then show how the idea sheds light on two puzzles or difficulties concerning virtue ethics. In sections ii and iii, I put the notion of expression to work, showing what a difference it can make if expression is incorporated into the profiles of the virtues. If the modes of moral acknowledgement—promotion, love, receptivity, and so on—constituting the profiles of such virtues as benevolence, caring, friendship, and loyalty are not to be defective, they must be expressive of fine inner states.

The idea of expressive behaviour is elucidated by the psychologist Abraham Maslow. In his 'The Expressive Component of Behaviour',[1] Maslow distinguishes between expressive (non-instrumental) and coping (instrumental, adaptive, functional, purposive) forms of behaviour. The former is largely determined by the state of the organism, and in particular is much more determined than coping behaviour by 'deep-lying character structure'.[2] Indeed, in its 'purest' form, the state expressed in expressive behaviour is unconscious, according to Maslow. Coping is 'usually designed to cause changes in the environment and often does; expression is not "designed" to do anything'.[3] Expression is often 'an end in itself' while coping 'is characteristically means-behaviour'.[4] As examples of coping behaviour, Maslow gives cases of acting so as to get

---

[1] *Psychological Review* 56 (1949), 261–72.   [2] Ibid. 261.
[3] Ibid. 262.   [4] Ibid.

something done, for example, 'walking to some destination, shopping for food, going to mail a letter, building a set of bookshelves, or doing the work for which we get paid'.[5] Expressive behaviour, by contrast, 'mirrors, reflects, signifies or expresses some state of the organism', and is often part of that state, for example, 'the smile and springy walk of the healthy person, the benevolent mien of the kind and affectionate . . . the slumping posture, lowered tonus, and hopeless expression of the depressed person'.[6] Though expression is *essentially* an epiphenomenon of the nature of the character structure',[7] this is not to say that it does not have important environmental effects. Coldness, superciliousness, hostility, or snobbishness may be *expressed* in conversational interaction, even though the speaker neither intended nor wanted this to be expressed, but it may be noticed with deleterious interpersonal effects.[8]

For Alan Tormey, too, expressive behaviour signifies a state of the organism:

If we hear an outburst of nervous laughter *as* an expression of embarrassment we are aware both that something is occurring 'inside' the person, and that there is some event or situation, real or imagined, by which he is embarrassed. Thus an expression points simultaneously in two directions, back toward the person and outward toward the object.[9]

As this passage indicates, however, there is more to expression than behaviour signifying or reflecting a state of an organism. In human beings, according to Tormey, intentionality is a necessary condition of expression; that is, expressive behaviour must have an object, whether 'immediate', 'virtual', or 'latent'. A virtual object is the object believed to be the object of one's behaviour, and the latent object is the real or 'ultimate' object, even if its status as the object of one's behaviour is revealed only after, say, analysis. To use Tormey's example, the immediate object of one's anger may be one's wife, the virtual object one's dentist, but the latent object one's father.[10] A consequence of Tormey's position, as he acknowledges, is that depression and anxiety expressed, say, must have objects, however inchoate or diffuse.[11] Behaviour expressive of character (e.g. a virtue of friendship) both has an object (e.g. one's friend) and reflects or signifies a state of the organism (a virtuous state of character).

[5] Ibid.   [6] Ibid.
[7] Ibid. 264.   [8] Ibid. 265.
[9] *The Concept of Expression* (Princeton, N.J.: Princeton University Press, 1971), 28.
[10] Ibid. 18–19.   [11] Ibid. 33–5.

Though expression is uncalculated, not end-directed, spontaneous, and an 'epiphenomenon' of underlying character, it is criticizable as successful or unsuccessful, or (to use J. L. Austin's language) 'happy' or 'unhappy', 'felicitous' or 'infelicitous'.[12] There are several broad ways of going wrong in expressing. An expression can be 'false', for example, exaggerated or insincere. It can be inappropriate because inapt in the circumstances. For example, expressing emotions of friendship is infelicitous or unsuccessful if you manifest intimate feelings by hugging your friend while introducing him to a formal lecture packed with dignitaries. Certain normal conventions are violated.

Another important way of going wrong occurs when the responses betray or display emotions, feelings, motives, character, which are in fact disvaluable, because unhealthy or vicious. Nietzsche's importance to ethical theory, in my view, lies not only in his characteristic emphasis on the expressive component of morality, but also in his view that depth-psychological analysis reveals that apparently valuable responses can often *express* disvaluable states. Altruism putatively expressing the value of compassion in the manifestation of feelings of pity for the sufferer, may at a deep motivational level, be expressive of disvaluable psychological states: resentment, self-hatred, or masochism, as Nietzsche also argues. Ignoring someone or being dismissive may not be a mere expression of an innocent lack of interest: it may be expressive of racism, chronic hostility, or misogyny. Expressive responses are unsuccessful then, when they are inapt in the circumstances (though normally apt) or inappropriate generally (even if apparently appropriate on a surface analysis). This latter form of unsuccessful expression reminds us that a virtue ethics, as a character-centred ethics, is concerned not just with actions, nor indeed just with an agent's surface intentions and deliberations.

The nature and importance of expression as an aspect of the profiles of the virtues can be understood by showing how it resolves two interesting problems about the role and nature of rationality in virtue ethics. Here is the first problem. It is a standard thesis of virtue ethics that (except in novel, complex, and hard cases) virtuous behaviour is somehow easy, natural, or habitual. There is a spontaneity about it rather than a self-conscious conformity to rule characterizing the enkratic person. But this does not entail that virtuous behaviour is behaviour from inclin-

---

12 *How to Do Things with Words*, ed. J. O. Urmson (Oxford: Clarendon Press, 1962). See further Tormey, *The Concept of Expression*, 91–3.

ation *rather* than reason. Practical wisdom is compatible with spontaneity (except where novel, complex, and hard cases confront the virtuous agent). We need to explain how practical wisdom is compatible with spontaneity and I shall invoke the idea of expressive behaviour in this explanation.

Virtue ethics is also characterized by the claim that virtuous behaviour is behaviour 'for the sake of' virtue. This idea too, is easily misconstrued. We may have the idea that a virtuous agent's intentional acts (e.g. a friendly act) are done with the further intention of being virtuous herself or promoting virtue in herself, and the acts are done for the sake of these ends. Hence the friendly act, for example, is seen as instrumental rather than non-instrumental. However, as Michael Stocker has argued,[13] this too is wrong. Acting for the sake of virtue should rather be understood as acting out of (the relevant) virtue. But how are we to understand the idea of acting 'out of'? Again, my answer involves an elucidation of the idea of expressive behaviour as a distinctive form of non-instrumental behaviour.

Let us now show how the idea of expression elucidates the idea of acting out of virtue in a way that resolves both the problems noted above. Though acting out of virtue is a form of action that is reasonable or rational, it is in standard cases both spontaneous and non-instrumental. Indeed, Maslow claims that expressive behaviour is not only spontaneous and not readily controllable, but is also in its purest form unconscious. Are we to understand virtuous behaviour as *purely* expressive? Is the highest form of virtue manifested in behaviour which as it were springs from virtuous character and is not designed to secure further ends? As Maslow claims,[14] most acts have both an expressive and a coping component, and as I shall claim, this is also true of virtuous behaviour. Altruism, for example, is (properly) often not just expressive of personal 'overflowing', affection, or concern. It is also standardly intended to further the good of the person helped.

The idea that virtuous behaviour need not be entirely expressive in Maslow's 'pure' sense is important in understanding the nature of virtuous forms of moral acknowledgement. The virtue of parental love, for example, may involve purely expressive responses such as affectionate spontaneous hugs, ruffling the hair of one's small child, and so on. But it also involves less spontaneous and often deliberative actions of

---

[13] *Journal of Philosophy* 78 (1981), 747–65.
[14] 'The Expressive Component of Behaviour', 261 n. 3.

promoting the good of someone, for example in responses of tough love where one gives a 'time-out' to a young child or grounds a teenage son or daughter. Again, as we shall see in section iv, spontaneous 'over-flowing' acts of generosity may in certain contexts be virtuous, but in other contexts, where deliberative practical wisdom is called for, may be misdirected, foolish, and even self-indulgent. The important point is that the claim that displays of virtue are *expressive* of fine inner states should not be confused with false claims about the identification of genuine virtue with a reasonless kind of 'natural' virtue.

Though most virtuous acts are not 'purely' expressive but also have a 'coping' component, the problem arises of the rational status of behaviour qua expressive, and in particular, of what Rosalind Hursthouse has called arational, actions.[15] It would seem that purely expressive behaviour is in Rosalind Hursthouse's sense arational, that is, not done for a reason, but then, it would seem, such behaviour couldn't possibly be virtuous, for isn't virtuous behaviour supposed to be behaviour for good reason? On my view, even purely expressive behaviour can properly be described as rational, but this will require of course the decoupling of the idea of rationality from the idea of action done for the sake of an end. Hursthouse gives a number of examples of what I and Maslow would call purely expressive behaviour, such as throwing recalcitrant tin open-ers out the window, jumping for joy, ruffling the hair of a child. Although none of these actions are motivated by a desire to further an end (to pun-ish the tin opener, to show people around you how happy you are, to promote the good of the child), they are all intentional actions, more or less knowingly performed. There is, however, no desired 'upshot', as Hursthouse puts it—there is no intention 'with which' the actions are done. Are we to say that the actions are therefore not done for a reason? Well, yes, if actions 'done for a reason' necessitate that they are done for the sake of furthering an end. But if that is what 'done for a reason' entails, we need to decouple 'rational' from 'done for a reason'. In that case, virtuous actions may be rational even if not done for a reason.

Expressive actions are rational if the expressiveness is apt in the cir-cumstances, and if they are expressive of rational emotional and motiva-tional states. For example, affectionately rumpling the hair of one's teenage child is rational because reasonable when done in private familial circumstances and because expressive of rational affectionate emotions.

---

15 'Arational Actions', *Journal of Philosophy* 88 (1991), 57–68.

It may be less reasonable, or unreasonable, when done where friends are around in a cultural context where such displays of affection by a mother to her son in his teenage years is embarrassing when his friends are present. The application of terms such as 'reasonable' or 'unreasonable' is clearly appropriate where expressive behaviour can either display or fail to display practical wisdom. Inasmuch as expressive behaviour is revelatory of character, it is revelatory of practical wisdom or lack of wisdom, for this is part of character. It can be for example an ingrained feature of character whether one's expressions of affection tend to be out of kilter with the prevailing culture, whether one's inclinations to help and to give are a kneejerk reaction to perceived distress, whether one's conversational interactions with authority figures express hostility or a wise sensitivity to the difficulties of management, whether one's interactions with recalcitrant objects such as tin openers and computers express petulance and frustration or an appreciation of one's ignorance and the need for patience and calmness. In short, practical wisdom is closely tied to emotional life and to one's character.

Let us now consider the importance of expression in the profiles of the virtues. We begin with expressive analyses of universal and self-love (sections ii and iii) before showing how these accounts resolve problems in the understanding of the altruistic virtues (section iv).

(ii) Expression in Self-Love

In recent times, much has been written about the importance of some form of self-respect or self-love to morality. The importance of self-*respect* for morality has been emphasized by, for example, Jean Hampton:

we must define a new conception of morality which recognizes that any 'altruistic' behaviour is morally wrong when it prevents one from paying moral respect to oneself.[16]

There are two basic ways of analysing the ideas of self-respect and self-love in terms of the categories of modes and bases of moral acknowledgement of items in the field of a virtue. According to the first, the idea is understood within the Kantian tradition and involves *respecting* oneself in virtue of one's *status* as, for example, inviolable, having inherent dignity, having moral worth. The basis of a proper sense of self-respect, on

---

16 'Selflessness and the Loss of Self', *Social Philosophy and Policy* 10 (1993), 135–65, at 146.

Hampton's view is Kantian: namely, 'a sense of your own intrinsic and equal value as a human being'[17] grounded in a recognition of your rationality and autonomy. According to the second way of understanding self-respect and self-love, what is fundamental is self-love as an expressive property, understood as a *bonding* with oneself, rather than a recognition of one's status as rational, human, autonomous, or whatever. Self respect comes with (proper) self-love.

In this section, I shall explicate and defend this second understanding of the general idea of self-love. The proposed account is structurally similar to that of universal love in this respect: though self-love is essentially bond-centred and is thereby not resultant upon a recognition of oneself as having a certain status, such love is criticizable if it is deficient in self-respect, and love and respect for others. The excellence of the love, then, is a resultant property, and is dependent on its being limited by the kind of distance enjoined by respect.

I begin with a Nietzschean account of self-love as bond-centred, where the individual's energy is not inhibited or sapped by debilitating self-contempt. For Nietzsche, self-love is basically a form of expressing one's strength, vitality, and energy—what he sometimes calls, perhaps unfortunately, one's 'will to power'.[18] My understanding of self-love through Nietzsche's ideas has several important features.

(1) The idea of 'will to power', as noted in the introduction, is not essentially an idea of power over or augmenting influence. The need to 'expand' is connected essentially with the nature of humans as active, growing, developing beings, rather than mere receptacles of pleasure or need-fulfilment; aspects of passivity to which Nietzsche was implacably opposed. In a well-known passage, Nietzsche claims 'A living thing desires above all to *vent* its strength—life as such is will to power'.[19]

(2) Inasmuch as self-love as a form of expressing one's strength, vitality, and energy is an aspect of the profiles of the *virtues*, what is of normative significance is not will to power, or power

---

[17] Ibid.

[18] There is not space here to discuss in detail interpretations of Nietzsche's 'will to power', though see the Introduction for further discussion. I use the phrase 'will to power' only as shorthand for Nietzsche's idea of expressing or 'venting' or 'discharging' strength, expressing one's vitality and energy.

[19] *Beyond Good and Evil*, sect. 13, p. 44.

as such, but will to power, or power, manifested *excellently*. Self love does not therefore involve mere power-lust, but excellent expression of 'will to power'.

(3) The notion of excellence should not be understood through characterization of a single positive ideal but in terms of a variety of distortions or failure. This idea gives substantive content to an ideal which (in its general form) appears to have little content. In true Austinian manner, the ideal of 'venting strength' is thus explicated by describing (as Nietzsche does) a variety of distortions of 'will to power'—accounts of which give the notion of 'will to power' considerable normative content and ethical significance. The fact that generalizations about self-love need to be understood through the idea of *absence* of distortions rather than a single positive ideal or norm of flourishing or health makes sense of apparent tensions in Nietzsche's thought between a general valorizing of life affirmation (which is an indeterminate idea) and a denial that there is a *single* norm of health or a *single* ultimate norm of excellence in 'man'.[20]

(4) Even though notions of health and strength in Nietzsche should be understood through notions of absence of distortion rather than positive ideals, we should beware of thinking that even understood thus, health is a universal value for Nietzsche. Where lack of self-love, exhibiting itself in, for example, manic grandiosity, fuels creativity, it can be seen as 'life affirming' and also part of virtue. This is not to say that no generalizations about, say, vices of resentment cannot be made. Indeed, Nietzsche makes them, frequently.

The idea of self-love as a bond-centred phenomenon is essentially psychological. It is not a status-centred, metaphysical notion of Kantian moral worth, but rather is the kind of thing psychologists refer to when asking a depressed patient if they have feelings of 'worthlessness'. On a Nietzschean account, self-love is not resultant on recognizing oneself as *equal* or superior to others in worth, merit, humanity, rationality, or whatever, for it is not derived from comparisons with others. Rather, the activities of a person with self-love are *expressive* of a solid bonding with

[20] See Friedrich Nietzsche, *The Gay Science*, trans. Walter Kaufmann (New York: Random House, 1974), sects. 120, 143.

herself, devoid of self-contempt. Her generosity, creativity, concern, are expressive of her vitality, strength, 'superabundance', as Nietzsche puts it. More specifically, the strength, vitality, energy, 'superabundance' of behaviour expressing self-love is devoid of the resentment of the threatened, vulnerable, hostile and envious. These psychological underpinnings are at bottom subrational, the antithesis of the subrational self-hatred in which self-interest 'wilts away' where a failure to bond adequately with oneself results in the various forms of escape:

One must learn to love oneself—thus I teach—with a wholesome and healthy love, so that one can bear to be with oneself and need not roam.[21]

Let us now discuss the nature and causes of distortions of 'will to power' constituting defects in self-love. First, its nature: as will be explored more fully below, the fundamental distortion is self-contempt, understood by Alfred Adler as the 'inferiority complex'. One major manifestation of this, of particular importance to the discussion of the altruistic virtues, is what Nietzsche describes as resentment, and what Karen Horney was later to describe as 'The Self Effacing Solution'. As Bernard Reginster puts it,[22] the person of resentment becomes inhibited by a feeling of incurable impotence while retaining his 'pride' or 'arrogance' and a desire at some level to lead a life of nobility and strength.[23] Furthermore, the conflict between the sense of weakness and expansionist strivings is not resolved either by a stoical elimination of desire or by a full (self-loving) acceptance of one's objectively based weakness. Reginster claims:

Nietzsche's central insight consists in seeing *ressentiment* revaluation as the eminently paradoxical attempt to provide a resolution for the tension which accommodates *both* the desire which the agent refuses to give up *and* his conviction that he is unable to satisfy it.[24]

Let us describe resentment in more detail. The two states in tension, creating the intrapsychic conflict at the basis of varieties of distorted 'will to power', are:

21 F. Nietzsche, *Thus Spoke Zarathustra*, in *The Portable Nietzsche*, ed. and trans. Walter Kaufmann (New York: Penguin Books, 1976), Third Part, 'On the Spirit of Gravity', sect. 2, p. 305.
22 '*Ressentiment*, Evaluation and Integrity', *International Studies in Philosophy* 27 (1995), 117–24.
23 Ibid. 118.
24 Ibid. 119.

(i) a desire at some level to lead a life of strength, nobility, or achievement;

(ii) a sense of oneself as impotent, insignificant, worthless.

These states are in dynamic conflict, creating a need for resolution. Resentment as a manifestation of this conflict consists in a certain sort of distorted resolution of it: a resolution which has two main features. First, there is a 'revaluation of values'. The values associated with one's deep desires, those of power, strength, or achievement, are transformed into those associated with the alleviation or palliation of weak or suffering states. That is, there is a valorizing of the altruistic virtues of dealing with vulnerabilities. Second, the 'resolution' fails to overcome the sense of oneself as impotent. This sense of oneself results in externalized self-hate. Hence the manner in which the altruistic virtues are expressed is one of repressed hostility and revenge.

Now it is part of my purpose in this section to affirm the conventional understanding of the altruistic virtues of care, compassion, or benevolence as *genuine* virtues whose target is the vulnerabilities of others, rather than the expression of the strength or potency of the agent. The problem with resentment-based altruism does not lie in the valorization of the alleviation of suffering states. It does not even lie in the 'revaluation of values'—a revaluation which gives importance to relief of suffering. It lies rather in the second feature of the resolution of the conflict just described, that is, in the nature of the states that are *expressed* in the resentment-filled person's display of such virtue, and in her consequent *manner* of altruistic display. For the pity, care, and so forth displayed by such individuals is repressed hostility—externalized self-hate manifested in revenge, subtle or otherwise.

The nature of defects in self-love receives sharper understanding if we consider further its causes. In line with Nietzsche's own view, Alfred Adler and later analysts such as Karen Horney consider the root cause of failure of self-love to be a failure adequately to resolve a conflict arising from two features endemic to the human condition: a need to grow and 'vent one's strength', and the fact that this basic need or drive is standardly subject to vicissitudes—whether congenital or environmental—with baleful effects, often unconscious, which lead ultimately to distortions in the way we view the world. These distortions result from conflict in our desires for strength, control, mastery, and so on, and our self-conception as inadequate to satisfy those desires. Note that this claim is compatible with a variety of claims about the aetiology of the distortions, and a variety of views about how to resolve the conflict. For on the above view, the root cause of lack of self-love is not the conflict itself, or even the vicissitudes themselves. The root cause is the failure adequately to resolve the conflict.

In more detail, the nature of the conflict is this. A basic drive to grow, expand, and express one's strength, needs to manifest itself consciously in what Nietzsche calls *Machtgefühl*: the feeling of power. We need, in short, to feel in control, we need to feel that we are successful, that others accept us and are responsive to us. Second, *Machtgefühl* is particularly fragile because the vicissitudes which distort it are so manifold and prevalent. As a result, as we have seen, Nietzsche describes us as an imperilled species. The great variety and prevalence of the vicissitudes is standardly noted and described in psychological writings. Indeed, Karen Horney describes the 'adverse influences' or vicissitudes affecting a child's growth as 'too manifold' to list. But she does describe a list of human vices which can produce 'profound insecurity' and 'basic anxiety'.[25]

In simple words [people in the environment] . . . may be dominating, over-protective, intimidating, irritable, overexacting, overindulgent, erratic, partial to other siblings, hypocritical, indifferent, etc.[26]

Erich Fromm locates the imperilled status of humans at least in part, in an even more basic condition, their fundamental separateness:

The experience of separateness arouses anxiety; it is, indeed, the source of all anxiety. Being separate means being cut off, without any capacity to use my human powers.[27]

In short, the basic status of the infant human as powerless and separate, coupled with the environmental and constitutional vicissitudes are liable to thwart his or her healthy growth.

The 'clash' between 'will to power' and the depressing effects of the vicissitudes can lead to a fundamental distortion: what Alfred Adler calls an 'inferiority complex'. On Adler's view, the complex consists in the following feature. The human makes comparisons between her lowly, even contemptible, condition and the condition of those seen as superior, even ideal. This leads to what Adler describes as a 'fiction': an idealized self or 'ego ideal' constructed from the agent's imagination feeding on

[25] *Neurosis and Human Growth*, 18.   [26] Ibid.

[27] *The Art of Loving*, 15.

debilitating comparisons.[28] The intra-psychic conflict caused by the gap between the sense of oneself as impotent and the ego ideal can sap the agent's vitality and prevent the 'overflowing superabundance' character-izing those with self-love.

It is important to note that though libido theorists adhering to the 'pleasure principle' (that our basic drive is to strive for pleasure and avoid unpleasure) take issue with Adler's theoretical emphasis on Nietzsche's 'will to power', some at least agree that 'Adler's formulations on the mode of action of the inferiority complex and its compensations are correct'.[29] For them, the problem with Adler is not that he is wrong, but that libido theory provides a deeper level of character analysis. According to Wilhelm Reich, 'our problem begins precisely where Adler leaves off'.[30] My account leaves open the question whether Reich is correct in his view that libido theory provides a deeper analysis (as opposed to an incorrect one).

Karen Horney, like Adler, describes the 'two selves' of the neurotic, and the resultant conflict. Here is the basic account:

conflict is bound to arise because the neurotic identifies himself *in toto* with his superior proud self and with his despised self. If he experiences himself as a superior being, he tends to be expansive in his strivings and his belief about what he can achieve, he tends to be more or less openly arrogant, ambitious, aggres-sive and demanding; he feels self-sufficient; he is disdainful of others; he requires admiration or blind obedience. Conversely, if in his mind he is his subdued self he tends to feel helpless, is compliant and appeasing, depends upon others and craves their affection.[31]

In such a neurotic structure, you are not integrated: you experience yourself both as a 'proud superhuman being' and also as a 'subdued, guilty and rather despicable creature'.[32]

We have understood self-love in terms of a Nietzschean ideal of expressing strength; an ideal which in turn was explicated by an account of the aetiology and nature of distortions in self-love. Such an under-standing was contrasted with accounts of self-love which assume that we

---

28 See *The Neurotic Constitution: Outlines of a Comparative Individualistic Psychology and Psycho-therapy*, trans. Bernard Glueck and John E. Lind (London: Kegan Paul, Trench, Trubner & Co. Ltd, 1918), 13.

29 Wilhelm Reich, *Character Analysis*, 3rd edn., trans. Vincent R. Carfango (New York: Noonday Press, 1972), 16 n 1.

30 Ibid.

31 Horney, *Neurosis and Human Growth*, 189.   32 Ibid. 188.

possess something called worth or dignity which is to be recognized, and which provides the basis or ground of self-love (as well as other forms of love and respect). However, this very contrast provides the basis of objections to the account. A Nietzschean, expressive account of self-love is vulnerable to objections precisely because it does not seem to be founded on a rationalistic appraisal of oneself as being *worthy* of respect: a respect which constrains one's actions because all others are equally deserving of such respect. Let us now examine this problem.

A central difficulty with founding an account of self-love on a Nietzschean ideal of expressing strength is that it invites a disregard of those limits imposed by requirements of self-respect and respect for others. At one end of the scale we have the deflationary tendencies suggested by the thought that, since there is no suggestion that self-love is based on *equal* worth, one's own strength, interests, and vital concerns may be trivial and worthless compared with those of others. At the other end of the scale we have the expansionist tendencies suggested by the thought that the imperative to express one's strength is no respecter of self or others. We now consider two objections to a Nietzschean account of self-love on these lines.

Here is the first objection. If self-love is not premised on a recognition of one's *equal* status or worth, how can one avoid being oppressed by a sense of one's inferiority to other beings, by subservient roles, or by a sense of one's general insignificance? Indeed, doesn't Nietzsche's philosophy encourage this very sentiment? For Nietzsche, are not the inferior and the non-splendid to be seen as nonentities, to be seen in fact as 'pieces of scaffolding' instrumental to the cultivation and glorification of 'higher types'? Are they not the 'foundation and scaffolding on which a choice type of being is able to raise itself to its higher task and to a higher *existence*'?[33] Indeed, the outlook for the non-splendid—the 'herd', as he puts it—seems dire when we consider such utterances in Nietzsche as the following: 'self interest is worth as much as the person who has it: it can be worth a great deal, and it can be unworthy and contemptible'.[34] If members of the herd are contemptible, and mere instruments, how can they be anything but self-loathing?

Nietzsche does have a reply to this criticism. He can appeal to his distinction between evaluating types of human beings in rank order, and

[33] *Beyond Good and Evil*, sect. 258, p. 193

[34] *Twilight of the Idols*, in *The Portable Nietzsche*, ed. and trans. Walter Kaufmann, 'Skirmishes of an Untimely Man', sect. 33, p. 533.

individual morality. The term 'contemptible' is a term relating to the language of evaluation of types. However, even if we justifiably object to such language, we should appreciate Nietzsche's view that the so-called 'contemptible' can have a strong life affirming *individual morality*.[35] To be life affirming, the 'herd' should not see itself through the eyes of the 'aristocracy'. They should pursue their own projects—pathetic, trivial, and instrumental though they may be from the point of view of some grand perspective—with passion, energy, and determination. To fail to do this, because demoralized by a putatively superior perspective, is to fail adequately to express one's strength, to exhibit self-love. Nietzsche himself does not advocate that even a relatively higher type such as Zarathustra should adopt the stance of 'highest value' in his 'individual morality'. Zarathustra is a tale of someone who comes unstuck in attempting to live his life from the point of view of bridge to superman or saviour to the world:

Such revenge my fullness plots: such spite wells up out of my loneliness. My happiness in giving died in giving; my virtue tired of itself in its overflow.[36]

It might be retorted that in order for the 'pieces of the scaffolding' to be life affirming, to be strong, to think of themselves and their projects as worthwhile, don't they have to go in for massive self-deception? To think this, however, is already to go wrong—it is to think that some grand objective perspective is *the* perspective from which you should in your practical life and evaluations consider yourself. A manifestation of this disorder is to comfort yourself by saying to yourself that the concepts of mediocrity and insignificance presuppose comparison classes which you can adjust to suit. Choose a small enough pond and you can become a big fish. But if you need to do *this* to bolster yourself, you are already disordered: you have already viewed yourself through the lens of a distorted perspective, that of a superior being in comparison to which you are 'contemptible'. And that perspective constantly pressures you to realize that the choice of the small pond in the interests of bolstering your ego has been entirely self-serving. To adopt such a perspective, from which you then need to shield yourself, is a failure of some kind.

This failure is discussed in psychological terms by Michael Stocker and Elizabeth Hegeman, through the psychological concept of narcissism.

---

[35] See further Lester Hunt, *Nietzsche and the Origin of Virtue* (London: Routledge, 1991).

[36] *Thus Spoke Zarathustra*, Second Part, 'The Night Song', 218.

They claim that narcissism is not to be understood as a vice of excessive self-love. On the contrary, they understand narcissism as 'involving a deep lack, an emptiness, in the self, a profound feeling of unalterably not being good, of not being adequate, and certainly not being lovable'.[37] Since narcissistic people need others to reassure them of their worth, they indulge in inappropriate comparisons. Instead of treating 'self-referential' values (i.e. 'those values which agents see and feel as bearing on themselves')[38] appropriately non-comparatively, narcissistic people find it natural to treat such values comparatively. Indeed, Stocker and Hegeman understand a narcissistic treatment of value as follows: 'it is to treat the wrong values as self-referring and comparative, to treat values this way too often, at the wrong time, in the wrong circumstances, and so on'.[39]

I do not think, however, that the above reply to our first objection to a Nietzschean account of self-love as 'expressing strength' entirely lays to rest that objection. Forms of 'self-love' which involve loss of self or a devaluing of the self do not need to be based on invidious comparisons with others.[40] Indeed one of the most serious objections to Nietzsche's own portrayals of strength and 'will to power' is that there seems at times to be no normatively required limit to the agent's expressions of his creativity or benevolence. In *Zarathustra* we reel under Nietzschean hyperbole:

I love him whose soul squanders itself, who wants no thanks and returns none: for he always gives away and does not want to preserve himself.

I love him whose soul is overfull, so that he forgets himself, and all things are in him: thus all things spell his going under.[41]

Though psychologists as far apart as Freud and Maslow describe a life of self-love as one of productivity and creativity, is a life of artistic passion, or proselytizing zeal in which an artist or reformer subjects herself to severe hardship and even mental torment, a good life, or a life of self-destructive self-exploitation? Does she treat herself with a lack of self-respect? A person's commitment to her (worthwhile) projects is licensed by self-love, but, to an extent dependent on contextual features, her pas-

[37] *Valuing Emotion*, 268.   [38] Ibid. 274.

[39] Ibid. 275.

[40] Though, as we see in Chapter 8, they may be based on (unconscious) comparisons with an ego ideal which may ultimately be derived from comparisons with others.

[41] *Thus Spoke Zarathustra*, First Part, sect. 4, pp. 127–8.

sionate attachment to what is dear to her must be tempered also by some form of distance—a recognition that out of respect for herself as a human being she does not act as if she is totally expendable, even in the service of her own ends. Nor should she see herself as a godlike figure to whom human limitations and frailties simply do not apply.[42]

A further ambivalence in Nietzsche's account of 'expressing strength' concerns not so much respect for self as respect for others. Proper self-love does not just involve expressing one's strength and vitality in a way which is non-invasive of the self. Such expression must also be non-invasive of others. This brings us to the second objection to a Nietzschean account of self-love, namely that it might be thought to carry unpleasant overtones of 'will to power' unshackled by concerns for the flourishing of others.

Nietzsche claims:

We want to make the sight of us painful to another and to awaken in him the feeling of envy and of his own impotence and degradation.[43]

And of course, notoriously, there are passages such as the following in *Daybreak*:

They [the gods] smile because they are amused and put into a good humour by our suffering: for to practice cruelty is to enjoy the highest gratification of the feeling of power.[44]

We have seen in Nietzsche a sample of various excesses of will to power: self-immolation in an excess of the 'overflowing' nature of 'will to power' type generosity; the invasiveness of inflicting on others one's talents in such a way as to make them feel impotent; the destructiveness of

---

[42] Other categories of lack of self-respect are discussed by Tom Hill in 'Servility and Self-Respect' and 'Self-Respect Reconsidered', both in Robin S. Dillon (ed.), *Dignity, Character and Self-Respect* (London: Routledge, 1995), 76–92 and 117–24 respectively. Hill shows how lack of self-respect underlies vices of self-deprecation, servility, and lack of integrity. I shall in section iv show how self-love (tempered by self-respect) is a part of the profile of virtues that are not essentially self-regarding.

[43] Friedrich Nietzsche, *Daybreak*, trans. R. J. Hollingdale (Cambridge: Cambridge University Press, 1982), bk. 1, sect. 18, p. 16.

[44] Ibid. Note that Nietzsche does not in the quoted passage *endorse* cruelty, even on a 'will to power' conception of virtue as strength: indeed, he goes on to make clear that he is speaking of 'eras' in which 'suffering counted as a virtue, cruelty as a virtue, while on the other hand well-being was accounted a danger, desire for knowledge was accounted a danger ... and change was accounted immoral and pregnant with disaster' (p. 17).

cruelty. Granted, as Ivan Soll claims,[45] Nietzsche attempts to show that the deepest motive of human action is the will to power rather than the pursuit of pleasure or avoidance of pain. But even if Nietzsche were correct in this claim, it does not follow that all human *virtue* is to be understood solely in those terms. Virtue may be a *corrective* for untutored natural tendencies.[46]

The short answer to the second of the above difficulties has been already stated: the idea of strength, however understood, must be subject to norms. What is good or virtuous is exercising or manifesting will to power well (e.g. not cruelly, resentfully, self-destructively).[47] Similarly, though Aristotle regards pursuit of pleasure as a fundamental human motivation, that pursuit is not itself good: what is good is pursuit of pleasure well (temperately). To express one's strength or vitality or 'will to power' *well*, then, involves finding an equilibrium between the 'coming close' of (self-) love, and the 'keeping distance' of respect for self and other. Where there is failure or defects in self-love of the kinds noted above, a proper equilibrium is missed. There may be, for example, mastery over others involving loss of respect for others, or clinging dependency or servility involving loss of respect for self.

Despite my reply to the above objections critics may feel that the point has been missed. No matter how healthy is self-love, and no matter how well self-love is constrained by respect, the suspicion may remain that I have regarded self-love as the basis of virtue, indeed the ultimate value. Have I not understood the virtuous life in terms of the 'healthy narcissism' advocated by Heinz Kohut?[48] Kohut's view of the good life is criticized by Richardson, Fowers, and Guignon as follows:

[Kohut's] emphasis on the individual can lead to a glorification of subjectivity and a troubling egocentricity in which others are viewed as mere means to one's own ends. Thus, paradoxically, Kohut's attempts to overcome the feelings of isolation and emptiness that result from deficits in social relationships may actu-

---

[45] 'Nietzsche on Cruelty, Asceticism, and the Failure of Hedonism', in Richard Schacht (ed.), *Nietzsche, Genealogy, Morality: Essays on Nietzsche's Genealogy of Morals* (Berkeley: University of California Press, 1994), 168–92.

[46] See Philippa Foot, 'Virtues and Vices', in her *Virtues and Vices* (Oxford: Blackwell, 1975), 1–18.

[47] I discuss the idea of 'distorted' forms of 'will to power' much more fully in Chapter 8, section iii.

[48] *The Restoration of the Self* (New York: International University Press, 1977).

ally work to efface the social life world that first makes meaningful relations possible.[49]

However, the fact that self-love is an *aspect* of the profiles of the virtues defined as forms of responsiveness to the demands of the *world* (which include but obviously do not exhaust the demands of the self) entails that self-love, even understood as healthy narcissism, is not the only or even primary goal of the good life. The virtues are not exhausted by self-love, and as I show in the next section, self-love is not the *aim* of the altruistic virtues, but forms part of what it is to be well disposed in regard to these virtues. Indeed, as I have understood the role of self-love in virtue, self-love functions rather like practical wisdom. Just as practical wisdom is not the aim of all virtue but is a component of all virtue, at least characteristically, so is self-love. Indeed, I am not averse to thinking of self-love as a (depth-motivational) aspect of practical wisdom itself (see further Chapter 8). This is not to deny that in some contexts we can talk about the virtue of self-love, for example, in a context where an agent is striving to overcome a wide range of deficiencies in this area.

We are now in a position to understand our conception of self-love in terms of the philosophical, Kantian, distinction between coming close and keeping one's distance. In general, self-love is a form of coming close: it is a relation of bonding. In self-love this is a bonding with oneself where one expresses one's strength and vitality. However, this expression, which Nietzsche calls 'will to power', can be distorted. It can be invasive of self and of other, in the various forms of internalized and externalized self-hate. In these states the agent fails to 'keep her distance': either from herself or others. Though in Kant's terms, love and respect are opposing *forces*, and are thereby distinct as modes of moral acknowledgement, they should not be opposed as aspects of the profiles of the *virtues*. In particular, we have seen how self-love as expressing strength— a bond with oneself—should make room for both self-respect and respect for others.

As we shall discuss in section iv, even the altruistic virtues (in their ideal form) must incorporate the form of strength constituting self-love. In short, self-love is not just a feature of one virtue (proper pride) whose field is one's own merits, successes, and achievements.

---

[49] Frank C. Richardson, Blaine J. Fowers, Charles B. Guignon, *Re-envisioning Psychology: Moral Dimensions of Theory and Practice* (San Francisco, Calif.: Jossey-Bass, 1999), 251.

(iii) Expression in Universal Love

The basic features of universal love were explored in the last chapter. In this section, attention is focused on the role of expression in the understanding of universal love, with the aim primarily of showing how an expressive analysis can resolve serious objections to universal love as an ethical ideal and component of virtue.

The major objection concerns the compatibility of universal love and self-love, both of which are central components of the profiles of the virtues. The objection has two main facets. The first concerns the apparent downplaying of personal merits in an ideal of universal love, and a consequent apparent downplaying of individual worth. Even if this problem can be resolved, there remains a fundamental complaint that ideals of universal love valorize various forms of weakness and resentment, demanding problematic forms of egalitarianism and excessive self-sacrifice. We discuss each of these problems in turn, showing how a certain kind of expressive account resolves both.

Here is a statement of the first problem, in the form of an argument.

(1) Universal love is the foundation of, and more basic than, other forms of love, such as the partialistic love of eros, affection, friendship.

(2) Universal love is not based on any lovable appraised qualities, such as merits.

(3) Universal love is not based on any worthy non-appraised qualities such as individuality or dignity. For such qualities are either metaphysically mysterious or are insufficient to confer worth.

(4) Given that universal love is much more basic than eros, friendship, and affection, then even if the latter are based on lovable qualities, those qualities are (relatively) insignificant to the point of insignificance.

(5) Given (2), (3), and (4), there is nothing to make us worthy of love.

(6) We are fundamentally worthless.

(7) A sense of ourselves as worthless is justified, and to be valorized.

(8) If a sense of ourselves as worthless is justified, we have no basis for self-love.

(9) Universal love is incompatible with self-love.

The basic ground of the worry that an ideal of universal love is incompatible with self-love is expressed in the following passage (from C. S. Lewis) which also hints at the expressivist solution to be proposed:

All those expressions of unworthiness which Christian practice puts into the believer's mouth seem to the outside world like the degraded and insincere grovellings of a sycophant before a tyrant . . . In reality, however, they express the continually renewed, because continually necessary, attempt to negate that misconception of ourselves and of our relation to God which nature, even while we pray, is always recommending to us. No sooner do we believe that God loves us then there is an impulse to believe that He does so, not because He is Love, but because we are intrinsically lovable . . .

We want to be loved for our cleverness, beauty, generosity, fairness, usefulness. The first hint that anyone is offering us the highest love of all is a terrible shock. This is so well recognized that spiteful people will pretend to be loving us with Christian Charity precisely because they know it will wound us.[50]

Lewis's solution, which like my own I call 'expressivist', appears to be this. Just as the basis of God's love is not our lovable features for he is capable of loving those of us who have no lovable features, so the basis of our (universal) love should not be located in properties of the recipient. Lewis calls this capacity 'Divine Gift-Love', which is part of normal human capacities on his view: 'But Divine Gift-Love in man enables him to love what is not naturally lovable: lepers, criminals, enemies, morons, the sulky, the superior and the sneering'.[51] A secular account will by contrast treat the capacity for universal love as an admirable psychological property to be cultivated as part of virtue. As I argued in Chapter 5, section iv, and in section ii of this chapter, neither universal love nor self-love need a grounding in a property of the object of love (such as worth), but (in their good forms) are expressions of (respectively) an admirable and a healthy capacity to bond. Certainly it is odd to claim that we have a sense of self-worth when there is *ex hypothesi* no such thing as worth whose recognition gives us that sense. But that does not mean that we should not have self-love.

I have shown how an expressivist account of universal love resolves the problem that such love is apparently incompatible with self-love. However, the second aspect of the problem now gets a grip: what if universal love expresses weakness and thereby lack of self-love?

In I Corinthians 13, love is described as 'strong'. The idea that good love is strong provides a way of overcoming a number of obstacles to understanding universal love as central in the profiles of the virtues.

[50] *The Four Loves* (London: Fount, 1977), 119–20.   [51] Ibid. 117.

These obstacles can be overcome by appealing to the idea of resentment-free self-love elaborated in the previous section. In this way we answer the central Nietzschean objection to an ideal of universal love, and Christian love in particular—namely, that it valorizes weakness.

How is universal love meant to be expressive of, and indeed valorize weakness? It is meant to do so several ways.

(a) It allegedly demands a kind of egalitarianism expressive of envy and resentment.

(b) It allegedly demands a 'forgetfulness' of slights, insults, and harms, requiring that one, in a weak way, 'turn the other cheek'.

(c) It allegedly demands excessive self-sacrifice.

If universal love is to be part of the profiles of the virtues we have to show how the emotional components of universal love are to be distinguished from the emotional components of envy and weak disregard for merit-based fairness; how a sense of weak neediness is to be distinguished from genuine love; how the emotional components of (virtuous) forgetfulness are to be distinguished from weak submission; and how resentment-based self-sacrifice is to be distinguished from self-sacrifice exhibiting strength and self-love.

Consider now the first objection.

(a) Universal love is (unacceptably) egalitarian.

In the parable of the landowner, the landowner seems to ignore desert in his payments. He answers complaints thus:

Friend, I am being fair to you. You agreed to work for one coin. So take your pay and go. I want to give the man who was hired last the same pay as I gave you. I can do what I want with my own money. Are you jealous because I am good to those people?[52]

At first sight it looks as if the egalitarianism of the landowner is unacceptable because he fails to distribute according to merit, work, or effort. This is a failure to reward the most meritorious and as such, it might seem, it is a form of resentment—a desire to bring everyone down to a common level. A deeper reading, however, understands the parable as an attack on narcissistic, self-referential comparisons, a tendency of the resentment-filled. In resenting the good fortune of their fellow workers, the workers in the parable are treating self-referring values inappropriately comparatively instead of non-comparatively. Instead of saying, 'I have done a good day's work and have been appropriately paid', they are focusing on the payments of others.

On a deeper reading, then, the parable can be seen as an attack on resentment rather than an expression of it. It claims, first, that the workers have not been exploited. It claims, second, that if you have been treated well, in a non-exploitative manner, then resenting the good or better fortune of others is a form of moral failure. The message is: get on with your own work and derive satisfaction from that. In short, the parable expresses a very Nietzschean message—don't derive your sense of worth from comparisons with others. The egalitarianism of (good) universal love is non-comparative. Everyone's needs are worthy of being met including their needs for work and creativity.

It is not being said here that justice is not and should never be desert-based. The message is merely that, where universal love is present, the good fortune of others is not resented, emphasis on desert should not be obsessive, and in many contexts, generosity is a more important virtue than (desert-based) justice.

We turn to the second objection:

(b) Universal love exhibits and valorizes weakness.

As we have seen, part of Nietzsche's account of resentment is a claim that it involves a revaluation of values. The 'Christian neurosis' is for him an example of self-effacing resentment. Certainly, at first sight at least, the Beatitudes are vulnerable to this criticism, with messages such as 'Blessed are the poor in spirit, for theirs is the kingdom of heaven'. Philip Yancey cites a British psychologist who, in a talk prepared for the British Society of Medicine, claims that a 'much stronger expression' of masochism than the spirit of self-sacrifice permeating Christianity is that expressed in the Sermon of the Mount, which 'blesses the poor, the meek, and the persecuted'. This suggests, as Yancey puts it, that 'lucky are the unlucky', for they are truly blessed.[53]

However, it would be odd indeed for the message of Christian universal love to consist in a claim that persecution, and material and spiritual poverty, are blessed states in the sense that nothing should be done to ameliorate and minimize them. On the contrary, love is to be manifested in satisfying need and eliminating persecution. So what could be meant?

---

[53] *The Jesus I Never Knew* (Grand Rapids, Mich.: Zondervan, 1995), 109.

An answer, foreshadowed in the discussion of the first objection, is suggested by Monika Hellwig,[54] who claims that the poor have certain advantages in the acquiring or fostering of virtues in which love is salient. They recognize their interdependence, they rest their security on people, not on things, they 'can distinguish between necessities and luxuries', they have 'a kind of dogged patience born of acknowledged dependence', and so on.[55] Of course, this may be an overly sanguine picture of those who are desperately poor as a result of vice—injustice, fecklessness, and improvidence—as opposed to ill fortune. But be that as it may, it is not at all clear that universal love, even in Christian form, valorizes weakness as such.

On the contrary, as we have noted, in 1 Corinthians 13 love is described as strong. On what is this claim of strength based? C. S. Lewis gives us a surprisingly Nietzschean answer. He claims:

We begin at the real beginning with love as the Divine energy. This primal love is gift-love. In God there is no hunger that needs to be filled, only plenteousness that desires to give.[56]

Similarly, our capacity for universal love has this divine feature of a non-needy gift-love. In numerous passages, such as the following, Nietzsche offers us a similar version of truly worthy altruism: an altruism that expresses an 'overflowing' rather than needy, weak resentment:

In the foreground stands the feeling of plenitude, of power which seeks to overflow, the happiness of high tension, the consciousness of a wealth which would like to give away and bestow.[57]

This overflowing love, in its universal form, is not based on a *need* to have more people to love. Such a need would be rather like a need for more and more friends, or more and more intimate relationships. It would be expressive of a weak dependency, craving for affection, and lack of self-sufficiency.[58] Pathological universal love is properly analogized to these pathological forms of affection and friendship, but universal love need not have these pathological features. It is a readiness to

[54] *Jesus, The Compassion of God* (Wilmington, Del.: Michael Glazier Inc., 1983). See Yancey, *The Jesus I Never Knew*, 115.

[55] See Yancey, *The Jesus I Never Knew*, 115.

[56] *The Four Loves*, 116.

[57] *Beyond Good and Evil*, sect. 260, p. 195.

[58] See Michael Slote, *Morals from Motives* (Oxford: Oxford University Press, 2001), for criticism of universal love along these lines.

give, not a neediness to give to as many as possible. What would make (pathological) universal love like these pathological forms of friendship is not its *universality* but its deplorable neediness.

Finally, what makes fine universal love strong is that the required 'plenteousness' is a capacity of the strong, and difficult to cultivate. Nowhere is this clearer than in the following passage:

> You have heard that it was said, 'Eye for eye and tooth for tooth'. But I tell you, do not resist an evil person. If someone strikes you on the right cheek, turn to him the other also. And if someone wants to sue you and take your tunic, let him have your cloak as well. If someone forces you to go one mile, go with him two miles. Give to one who asks you, and do not turn away from the one who wants to borrow from you![59]

Though at first sight this passage appears to laud weakness, the teaching contains a message of strength which is also prominent in Nietzsche. Just as the Christian is told to be strong enough to treat slights, insults, and hurts as of little significance (water off a duck's back), so Nietzsche claims:

> It is not impossible to conceive of a society whose *consciousness of power* would allow it the most refined luxury there is—that of allowing those who do it harm to go *unpunished*. 'Of what concern are these parasites to me' it would be entitled to say.[60]

For Nietzsche, 'forgetting is a strength', indeed 'one may appreciate ... to what extent there could be no happiness, no serenity, no hope, no pride, no *present* without forgetfulness'.[61] Of course, it is important to understand what is involved in 'forgetting', especially when serious harms are involved. Certainly, it cannot involve downgrading the seriousness of such harms. The relation between forgetting and forgiveness is an important issue which needs more discussion than I can offer here. Forgetting does not preclude or replace the work of forgiveness, but prevents one being stuck in bitterness.

The message of strength in the 'turning the other cheek' exhortation was understood by Gandhi, who is portrayed in the film *Gandhi* explaining it to a Reverend Charlie Andrews when they were both menaced by gangsters in a South African city. As told by Philip Yancey, Gandhi is portrayed thus:

[59] Matthew 5: 38.

[60] *On the Genealogy of Morals*, Second Essay, sect. 10, pp. 53–4.

[61] Ibid. Second Essay, sect. 1, p. 39.

The movie *Gandhi* contains a fine scene in which Gandhi tries to explain his philosophy to the Presbyterian missionary Charlie Andrews. Walking together in a South African city, the two suddenly find their way blocked by young thugs. The Reverend Andrews takes one look at the menacing gangsters and decides to run for it. Gandhi stops him. 'Doesn't the New Testament say if an enemy strikes you on the right cheek you should offer him the left?' Andrews mumbles that he thought the phrase was used metaphorically. 'I'm not so sure,' Gandhi replies. 'I suspect he meant you must show courage—be willing to take a blow, several blows, to show you will not strike back nor will you be turned aside. And when you do that it calls on something in human nature, something that makes his hatred decrease and his respect increase. I think Christ grasped that and I have seen it work.'[62]

There may, however, be an intermediate stage of standing up for oneself which is a stepping-stone to greater strength in the agent. Rather than allowing oneself to be wounded, cowed, and turned into a victim by insults and harms, retaliation may be in order. The ideal of universal love does not advocate being wounded and cowed: rather the ideal, like that of Aristotle's *megalopsychos*, is to treat as unimportant and superficial the relatively minor harms another can do you. If the harm is significant, then a strong person has to accept that which cannot be changed, rather than engage in futile revenge.

Now to the third objection:

(c) Universal love is excessively self-sacrificing

On my view, the most serious criticism of universal love as an ethical ideal is its apparent requirement for extreme self-sacrifice. Some of the exhortations of the Sermon on the Mount and elsewhere make Peter Singer's approach to the demandingness of ethics seem tame by comparison.

A virtue-ethical approach to universal love may adopt one (or both) of two strategies in overcoming this objection. According to the first, the ethical ideal of universal love should be clearly separated from the ideals of Christian love. This strategy points out that it is not part and parcel of universal love as an ideal that it require extreme self-sacrifice. On the contrary, it is an ideal focused first and foremost on quotidian ethics. It involves firstly, the cultivation of attitudes and emotions which enhance self-love and reduce the externalization of self-contempt. Such externalization results in various resentments and jealousies. Once these are eliminated, one can open up to and come close to estranged relatives, and become friendly to colleagues against whom one once harboured grudges, and towards whom one indulged in petty, competitive hostilities. Hostilities towards other racial, ethnic, and religious groups are reduced, allowing for the breaking down of barriers and the opportunity for kindness and helpfulness towards them.

The second strategy allows for extreme self-sacrifice (free of resentment) to exhibit the greatest love and strength, and to thereby remain as an ethical ideal of perfection. However, it does not follow from this view that *all* should strive to attain this ideal. How can this be?

It is common in virtue ethics to distinguish 'heroic' virtue from ordinary virtue. In Aristotle, the virtues of magnificence and *megalopsychia* are not available to all. In Nietzsche, not only are the 'virtues' of the herd to be contrasted with those of the *Übermenschen*, but we are even exhorted not to be virtuous beyond our strength. Hume explicitly distinguishes heroic virtue[63] from the virtues of goodness and benevolence, which are contrasted with things we call 'great in human affections'.[64] Finally, in Christian ethics, though it is clear that love is either to be seen as the supreme virtue, or is embedded in virtues such as patience, humility, kindness, and compassion, it is unclear (at least to me) how heroic this virtue (virtues) are meant to be. Tolstoy apparently tortured himself and made his life (and the lives of those near him) miserable trying to live according to the edicts of the Sermon on the Mount.

Though (as we saw in my reply to objection b) universal love involves a capacity for 'overflowing', a sense of 'plenteousness' the question arises: what about those who lack the full measure of this form of strength, and thereby 'heroic' virtue? This question is explored more fully in Chapter 9, but virtue ethics is not committed to a conception of highly demanding universal love.

(iv) Virtues of 'Strength' and 'Gentleness'

I have shown how an expressivist account of universal and self-love renders them not only compatible but synergistic. The remaining task is to show how this synergy is manifested in the profiles of the virtues.

---

63 *Treatise of Human Nature*, ed. L. A. Selby-Bigge, 2nd edn. revised P. H. Nidditch (Oxford: Oxford University Press, 1968), 599.

64 Ibid. 602.

More specifically, I offer an account of the role played by universal and self-love which resolves a major problem in the understanding of the altruistic virtues. The problem is: how can self-love feature in such virtues without it being the case that they lose their altruistic point and become self-centred? How can it be that we are not forced to make a choice between an ethics of 'strength' or self-love, and an ethics of 'gentleness', caring, or universal love?

My account of the role of expression in the altruistic virtues will show that there is no stark choice to make. A suitably reconstructed Nietzsche may yet be a not altogether uneasy bedfellow of Nel Noddings, given a proper understanding of, inter alia, virtuous caring.[65] In short, I wish to soften considerably the blunt message given by Nel Noddings in this passage:

A female ethic built along Nietzschean lines might be instructive, but the notion is too outrageous for most of us even to consider, and at bottom it would be self contradictory.[66]

I shall claim by contrast that a tradition emphasizing expressing strength has much to offer an ethics of care, benevolence, or love, arguing that the apparent opposition between what might be called 'strength' and 'gentleness' traditions of the virtues is greatly reduced on a correct understanding of 'virtues of strength' and 'virtues of gentleness'. Indeed, as Rosemarie Tong notes, Mary Wollstonecraft claimed that 'when strong women practise gentleness, it is a grand, even godly, virtue; but when weak women practise it, it is a demeaning, even subhuman, vice'.[67] In other words, the 'gentle' virtues require the expression of strength (self-love), or so I shall argue. Not only must gentleness be suffused by strength, strength must be tempered by gentleness. Self-sufficiency, for example, is a virtue of strength which focuses on the independence and non-neediness aspects of flourishing. But as a virtue, it must recognize our legitimate dependencies and need for the affection of others. Otherwise, it is a vice—a vice epitomized by the well-known Simon and Garfunkle lyric, 'I am a rock, I am an island', or by the Icelandic sheep farmer Bjartur, hero of the novel *Independent People,* who advises his son 'It's a useful habit never to believe more than half of what people tell you,

[65] Noddings, *Caring.*

[66] 'Ethics from the Standpoint of Women', in Marilyn Pearsall (ed.), *Women and Values: Readings in Recent Feminist Philosophy* (Belmont, Calif.: Wadsworth, 1993), 379–90.

[67] Cited by Tong in *Feminine and Feminist Ethics* (Belmont, Calif.: Wadsworth, 1993), 33.

and not to concern yourself with the rest. Rather keep your mind free and your path your own', and whose independence was extremely hard on his family.[68] On the other hand, if a gentle virtue of receptivity is not suffused by strength, it too becomes a vice of excess: a vice of being too open to the demands and needs of others.

I am not denying that it is sometimes appropriate to be undirectedly 'overflowing', for example, where someone is thrilled at having won the lottery and regardless of the personal circumstances of the beneficiaries, stands everyone a round of drinks in a bar.[69] Further, although much heroic generosity and courage is focused, one can imagine situations where heroism is manifested in the heat of battle, for example, in an undirected way.[70]

The key to understanding the role of universal and self-love in the profiles of the virtues is to distinguish between the target of a virtue and a full account of the excellences comprising a virtue. This is what Martha Nussbaum calls the 'thick account' of a virtue.[71] We can define a virtue as a virtue of 'strength' or of 'gentleness' according to its targets, but this is not to deny that both universal and self-love are common features.

For example, the targets of some virtues, such as self-protection, determination, and self-sufficiency, concern aspects of an agent's strength, whereas the targets of others such as compassion, friendship, and generosity, concern others, particularly their welfare. However, the target or aim of a virtue is not all there is to the virtue. Though we may say that self-sufficiency is a virtue of strength because it emphasizes the appropriate independence of the agent, self-sufficiency as a *virtue* cannot be understood in terms of its target or aim (independence) *simpliciter*— the notion of 'appropriateness' suggests the possibility of excessive independence, as displayed by Bjartur in the novel. The delineation of the virtue of self-sufficiency in the thick account of the virtue tells us what it is to be well disposed in regard to the field of self-sufficiency, and that involves giving an account of appropriate independence. *Appropriate*

68 Halldòr Laxness, *Independent People* (New York: Vintage, 1946), 354.

69 See Michael Slote, 'Virtue Ethics and Democratic Values', *Journal of Social Philosophy* 24 (1993), 5–37.

70 See Robert C. Solomon for an account of Nietzsche's overflowing virtues, including generosity and courage: 'Nietzsche's Virtues: A Personal Inquiry', in Richard Schacht (ed.), *Nietzsche's Postmoralism: Essays on Nietzsche's Prelude to Philosophy's Future* (Cambridge: Cambridge University Press 2001), 123–48.

71 See her 'Non-Relative Virtues: An Aristotelian Approach', in Peter A. French, Theodore E. Uehling, Jr., Howard K. Wettstein (eds.), *Midwest Studies in Philosophy* 13 (1988), 32–53.

independence leaves room for receptivity to the affection of others and sensitivity to their needs. By contrast, the target or aim of the virtue of friendship is responsiveness to friends through receptivity, promotion of their good, appreciation, and (appropriate) love. However, the thick account of that virtue must spell out what it is to be well disposed in regard to the field of friendship, and that involves ideas of strength. We would not say that a person's disposition of friendship is a *virtue* in that person if she were so receptive to others that it is impossible for her to have a life of her own. In such a case, she would not be expressing strength. *Full* excellence in responsiveness to friends involves self-love, but self-love is not the aim or target of the virtue of friendship.

A focus on the meanings of the terms referring to the virtues as explicated by their targets can mislead about their nature as virtues, as revealed by their thick accounts. 'Self-sufficiency', 'pity', and 'caring' can be names of both vices and virtues, depending on how these accounts are fleshed out. Caring that involves excessive self-denial, and encouraging the cared-for into parasitism and dependency, would be vices on the present view. For example, consider the following criticism by Sarah Lucia Hoagland of Noddings's notion of caring as an ethical ideal: 'One danger of caring is what Alcoholics Anonymous calls enablement: those close to alcoholics often enable an alcoholic's dependency'.[72] The point is that the carer needs to be needed by the alcoholic, thereby encouraging dependency. Hoagland's concern, however, should not be seen as a criticism of caring as a virtue, but should rather alert us to the fact that caring as a virtue incorporates strength aspects. If we focus only on an account of its target—specifying that caring is a gentle virtue of receptivity and vulnerability—then there will be a temptation to think that this is the end of the story. Caring as a virtue would be seen as *just* involving receptivity to others, and being concerned about their vulnerabilities.

The distinction between the target of a virtue and the thick account of a virtue resolves a debate about the nature of compassion as a virtue.[73] Taking her cue from Aristotle's conception of pity as an emotion caused by the sight of an evil of a certain sort 'which we might expect to befall

---

[72] 'Some Concerns about Nel Noddings' *Caring* (Review Symposium), *Hypatia* 5 (1990), 108–13, at 111.

[73] See Brian Carr's critique of Martha Nussbaum, 'Compassion: The Basic Social Emotion', *Social Philosophy and Policy* 13 (1996), 27–58, in 'Pity and Compassion as Social Virtues', *Philosophy* 74 (1999), 411–29.

ourselves or some friend of ours, and moreover to befall us soon'.[74] Nussbaum claims that the one feeling compassion 'acknowledges that she has possibilities and vulnerabilities similar to those of the sufferer'.[75] Brian Carr takes issue with this claim, arguing that it makes compassion as a virtue too self-centred, when it clearly is an altruistic virtue. However the point, recognized by Nietzsche, is just *how* the self features in the (thick) account of the virtue. It is one thing to be aware in some way of one's personal vulnerabilities; it is quite another for that awareness to feature in the deplorable depth motivations highlighted by Nietzsche's discussion of pity:

An accident which happens to another offends us: it would make us aware of our impotence, and perhaps of our cowardice, if we did not go to assist him. Or it brings with it in itself a diminution of our honour in the eyes of others or in our own eyes. Or an accident and suffering incurred by another constitutes a signpost to some danger to us; and it can have a painful effect upon us simply as a token of human vulnerability and fragility in general. We repel this kind of pain and offence and requite it through an act of pity; it may contain a subtle self-defence or even a piece of revenge. That at bottom we are thinking very strongly of ourselves can be divined from the decision we arrive at in every case in which we *can* avoid the sight of the person suffering, perishing or complaining: we decide *not* to do so if we can present ourselves as the more powerful and as a helper, if we are certain of applause, if we want to feel how fortunate we are in contrast, or hope that the sight will relieve our boredom.[76]

Rather than self-referential comparisons which mask externalized hostility being an integral, though maybe unrecognized, part of compassion, the self features in virtuous compassion in a quite different way, highlighted by Blum:

compassion involves a sense of shared humanity ... the other person's suffering is seen as the kind of thing that could happen to anyone, including oneself insofar as one is a human being.[77]

In short, the thick account of compassion as a virtue requires an account of universal love as it features in the profile of the virtue, and its relation to self-love. It may be that in its highest forms compassion does not

[74] *Rhetoric*, 1385b12–16, cited in Carr, 'Pity and Compassion as Social Virtues', 414.

[75] Cited in Carr, 'Pity and Compassion as Social Virtues', 424.

[76] Nietzsche, *Daybreak*, sect. 133, p. 84.

[77] Lawrence Blum, 'Compassion', in Amélie O. Rorty (ed.), *Explaining Emotions* (Berkeley: University of California Press, 1980), 507–518, at 511.

involve the cognitive 'self-regarding' dimension highlighted by Nussbaum. But that dimension is relatively innocent by comparison with the distorted self-centredness of self-contempt. The proper featuring of self-love in the thick account of compassion is quite compatible with the other-regarding nature of its target.

Several caveats to the account of altruistic virtue should be noted. First, it should not be assumed that all controversy lies in the explication of the thick account of an altruistic virtue's profile. Controversy can occur even at the level of accounts of the target of a virtue—between those in which the target of the altruistic virtues is the promotion of well-being, understood in terms of pleasure and the absence of pain, and those who deny that the good promoted is primarily the relief of suffering, as opposed to the relief of meaningless suffering.[78] Again, one could debate whether the primary target or aim of friendship is promoting the good of one's friend or expressing the bonds of one's friendship (in e.g. behaviour which displays affection or intimacy).

Second, the view outlined should be contrasted with the strong claim that failure to express self-love *always* disqualifies the promotion of good, for example, from being virtuous. It may be that the generosity shown by a person exhibits a slightly weak lack of confidence in the worth of her own personal projects, indicative of lack of self-love, but where this weakness is marginal and the generosity positively saintly, we may welll admire it and consider it virtuous. As I claimed above, virtue should be seen as a threshold concept.

It should, finally, be noted that there is room for debate about the relative contributions made by strength aspects and gentleness aspects in the delineation of a virtue. Take, for example, Aristotle's view that friendship as a virtue has a large component of self-sufficiency—something that is not generally emphasized in the current concern with the importance of relationships and relatedness. For Aristotle, a good friend does not burden her friend with her troubles:

It is painful to observe that he is pained at one's own misfortunes, since everyone tries to avoid causing his friends pain. For this reason a man of a resolute nature takes care not to involve his friends in his own troubles, and unless he is exceptionally insensitive cannot stand the thought of causing them pain; and in

---

[78] See Nietzsche: 'The meaninglessness of suffering, and *not* suffering as such, has been the curse which has hung over mankind up to now'. *On the Genealogy of Morals*, Third Essay, sect. 28, p. 136.

general does not give them a chance to lament with him, because he himself does not indulge in lamention either. But womenfolk and men who are like them, enjoy having others to share their moanings, and love them as friends and sympathizers. However, it is clearly right in all circumstances to follow the better example.[79]

However, such a view is controversial, and arguably pays insufficient regard to friendship as a virtue of vulnerability and receptivity. In these aspects of friendship, a friend recognizes the vulnerability of her friend by not ignoring her problems and sadnesses, and recognizes, too, that one of the points of friendship is to reveal her own vulnerabilities and pains to her friend. The view of Aristotle needs to be modified by a recognition of the importance of the aspects of vulnerability and receptivity—a good friend is one who will judiciously, and occasionally passionately, open up with her troubles, and thereby allow the development and demonstration of further intimacy and affection or love, and sensitivity and knowledge. But this behaviour may not be appropriate at all with an acquaintance or colleague who may use one's confidences as subjects of gossip. Exactly when it is appropriate to share troubles or keep them to oneself is determined by good judgement exercised in particular contexts, and the exercise of such judgement is often very difficult.

I have shown that virtues of strength and gentleness are not properly virtues unless they are understood in their thick accounts as suitably infused with aspects of gentleness and strength, respectively. This view has the advantage not only of reconciling 'strength' and 'gentleness' traditions in ethics, but also of flexibility. It allows considerable room for manoeuvre about the salience to be accorded different aspects of the profile of, say, benevolence in worlds which fall far short of perfection. The salience will depend of course on context. Where, for example, there is enormous and urgent need, adequately expressing self-love will be a less salient aspect of the profile of benevolence than promoting others' good. On the other hand, where there is a concern about the tendencies of certain groups such as women to sacrifice themselves for the sake of need rather limited in nature, expressing self-love will be more salient as a component of altruistic virtues.[80] The precise configuration of the profiles of the altruistic virtues will, in short, vary according to the

---

[79] *Nicomachean Ethics*, 1171a25–b16.

[80] As it rightly is in the case of the self-sacrificing woman of Jean Hampton's example, 'Selflessness and the Loss of Self'.

salience and nature of various types of social problem. For Nietzsche, mediocrity was of paramount concern, and consequently he downgraded to a point unacceptable to most of us the promotional component of the altruistic virtues, seeing them almost exclusively as expressive. They, in short, express an agent's strength, vitality, and creativity in the 'overflowing' exercise of the 'gift-giving' virtues.

7

Creativity

(i) Introduction

In his *Toward a Psychology of Being*,[1] Abraham Maslow claims that his studies of creativity in subjects rid him of an important preconception about the nature of creativity. He had confined creativity to certain conventional categories occupied by professionals, such as artists, composers, novelists, and experimentalists, but he realized that creativity pervades life in general. That is the basis of my claim that creativity is an aspect of the profile of all or virtually all the virtues. Maslow cites, for example, a poor woman who was a marvellous cook, mother, wife, and homemaker. She was 'in all these areas original, novel, ingenious, unexpected, inventive'.[2] It should hardly need emphasizing that this is the stuff of ethics, for the domestic, familial, parental virtues are of obvious centrality in raising happy, healthy children of good character. Again, Maslow speaks of a psychiatrist whose 'great success even with very difficult cases validated his "creative" (rather than stereotyped or orthodox) way of doing things'.[3]

One might wish to claim that creativity is a separate virtue, but I prefer to think of it as a mode of moral acknowledgement which informs a wide range of virtues, just as does love and respect. For example, one can be creative in one's benevolence. Maslow speaks of a person being creative in social service in the broadest sense. A person is creative as a parent, as a homemaker, and as a gardener. Another is creative as a teacher, and another as a business manager. In other words, creativity pervades the good life, and informs goodness in all our roles.

---

[1] *Toward a Psychology of Being*, 2nd edn. (New York: Van Nostrand Reinhold Co., 1968).
[2] Ibid. 136.
[3] Ibid.

(ii) Creativity: Its Nature

In speaking of creativity as an aspect of the profiles of the virtues I do not intend to suggest that it is a phenomenon which is not itself multifaceted. Indeed, it has been said that 'creativity represents a highly complex and diffuse construct'.[4] In my elucidation of the nature of creativity, I shall concentrate on the following question. Is creativity to be evaluated in terms of its products, or in terms of expression?

I shall ultimately argue that exclusive focus on either of these aspects leads to distortion. Let us first, however, briefly explicate each of these aspects. Take, first, expression. In his book, Maslow focuses on creativity as an *expression* of the healthy, self-actualized type. The products of such people can be evaluated as expressive of their creative spirit, and indeed of their health. Creative people are often spontaneous and uninhibited:

All my subjects were relatively more spontaneous and expressive than average people. They were more 'natural' and less controlled and inhibited in their behavior, which seemed to flow out more easily and freely and with less blocking and self-criticism.[5]

However, Maslow is the first to admit that this is not all there is to creativity. First, as we explore more fully in section iii, some of the best creativity is not linked to health. Though his 'self-actualized' subjects were 'healthy and creative', they were not possessed of great talent, and he allows that some of the greatest creative talents (e.g. Wagner, Van Gogh, Byron) were not psychologically healthy. Second, for the *products* of creativity to be great, one needs (at least often or characteristically) 'hard work, long training, unrelenting criticism, perfectionistic standards'.[6] And perfectionistic drivenness does not necessarily or even characteristically make for psychic health.[7]

Jack Glickman defends the view that one determines whether something is creative by evaluating the products of a putatively creative activity: 'it is the product that determines whether we call the activity creating,

[4] M. D. Mumford and S. B. Gustafson, 'Creativity Syndrome: Integration, Application and Innovation', *Psychological Bulletin* 103 (1988), 27–43, at 27, cited in Hans J. Eysenck, 'The Measurement of Creativity', in Margaret A. Boden (ed.), *Dimensions of Creativity* (Cambridge, Mass.: MIT Press, 1994), 199–242, at 207.

[5] *Toward a Psychology of Being*, 137.

[6] Ibid. 143.

[7] For a psychological discussion of perfectionism as an 'expansionist' neurotic strategy, see Horney, *Neurosis and Human Growth*, and Chapter 9.

and also whether we call the agent and the work creative.'[8] In opposition to expressive-process theories, he claims that 'an examination of the process is irrelevant to an evaluation of the product'.[9]

I shall agree with Glickman that creativity is an 'achievement word', but that does not entail that creativity is not to be determined, at least in part, in terms of internal processes and features expressed in the creative act. These features may make the act meet the standards of creativity. To say that *x* is an achievement word may however be thought to *entail* that the criteria of application of the word concern solely the evaluation of outcomes or products. That would be unfortunate. Processes can be successful or not regardless of outcome, and processes may not even be for the sake of producing an outcome. On my view, creativity is what might be described as a 'mixed' form of moral acknowledgement: that is, the evaluation of something as 'creative' contains both externalist and internalist elements. More specifically, I shall claim, 'creativity' as a success or achievement word involves evaluating the product *as* an expression of a state of the agent, but involves, too, something more: namely, the evaluation of the product or outcome with reference to criteria independent of that expression but dependent on standards internal to what Alasdair MacIntyre calls practices.[10] In brief, creativity is a form of expression, but goes beyond that expression. Let us now defend the idea that creativity has an expressive component, before turning to the externalist aspects.

If creativity has an expressive component, creativity is an epiphenomenon of underlying dispositions. That general feature would explain our reluctance to regard 'works' of chimpanzees, young children, machines, or accidental but pleasing results as exhibiting creativity, no matter what the external features of the products. An expressivist view can handle this intuition by claiming that 'creativity', as a success word, makes essential reference to inner states. A work exhibits creativity, on such a view, if it expresses the creator's originality in some sense, intelligence, imagination, skill, inventiveness, or talent. Less central are other features such as excitement, spontaneity, feelings of discovery, delight, joy, and other emotions. Even if these latter less central features are

---

[8] 'Creativity in the Arts', in Lars Aargaard-Morgensen (ed.), *Culture and Art* (Atlantic Highlands, N.J.: Humanities Press, 1976), 131–46, at 152.

[9] Ibid.

[10] See MacIntyre's discussion of goods *internal* to practices in his *After Virtue: A Study in Moral Theory* (London: Duckworth, 1981).

characteristic of the creativity of Maslow's healthy 'self-actualized' types, he admits (as we have seen) that not all creativity is expressive of (psychic) health.

Notice that creativity may express something in the agent without it being the case that creativity involves a prior *act* of expressing. As Maslow makes clear,[11] the expressive component of behaviour should not be understood as an *act* of expressing. Indeed, Maslow argues that as a psychological phenomenon, acts of 'expressing' are motivated acts undertaken by those who are not genuinely expressing something, but are merely *trying* to be expressive of something. A cold person may *try* to express warmth in her demeanour, and may even succeed in projecting warmth, but she does not express warmth in the true sense. This is 'coping' rather than truly expressive behaviour. Similarly, if an artist is trying to express in a self-conscious way originality or inventiveness in her works, that is not expressive behaviour proper. As Maslow would put it, the originality should be an 'epiphenomenon'. Similarly, (in standard cases) a friend lacks full virtue as a friend if she has to motivate herself to display warm or affectionate or giving behaviour, by for example following certain rules. ('Oh yes, a good friend would ring up by now—I had better ring. Or maybe I should even call round. Oh no, ringing will do.')

To say that creativity may express something in the agent without it being the case that creativity involves a prior *act* of expressing, is not to say that creativity is unmotivated. The expressivity of creativity is relatively motivated by comparison with Maslow's 'pure' expressive behaviour. A pleasing effect caused by the disposition of splashes of the paint thrown at the canvas in a fit of rage is the result of a piece of pure expressive behaviour in Maslow's sense, but it is not the result of a creative act. The act is not creative for two reasons. First it is insufficiently motivated, and in particular not motivated by the characteristic aims of creative work, such as to *paint* a picture, and to shape materials (as well as one can) in accordance with one's conception of the work to be produced. Second, it does not express novelty, originality, inventiveness, or ingeniousness,[12] which warrant application of the success word 'creative'.

It is time now to consider the externalist aspects of creativity. I agree with Glickman that creativity necessitates evaluation of the product, if it

[11] 'The Expressive Component of Behaviour'.

[12] Notice that though novelty and originality are criteria of creativity, these notions should not be interpreted in an overly demanding way, since creativity as an aspect of the profiles of the virtues should not be rare. For quotidian creativity, inventiveness is more important.

is to be regarded as creativity. This marks the fact that 'creativity', unlike 'love' and 'respect', can be understood as a 'task' word in the sense that creative acts have products or outcomes. In being a task word, 'creativity' resembles promotion, another mode of moral acknowledgement. To avoid confusion we need to separate two questions. First, given that creativity is a success word, we need to ask what features the product or outcome must exhibit if it is properly to be described as *created* or *creatively* made or produced, as opposed to merely produced or promoted. Second, we need to ask what features must be exhibited if the product or outcome is to be described as *virtuously* created or creative. We need, in short, to know what constitutes creativity as an aspect of the profile of the virtues. We discuss the first of these questions now.

Candidate features of creativity as exhibited in the product or outcome fall into three main categories:

(i) Novelty
(ii) Surprise
(iii) Value

According to Margaret Boden, an act is not genuinely psychologically creative (as opposed to historically creative) unless it is novel in the following sense. It must transform a 'conceptual space'.[13] Given a work W, and a conceptual space C, then if a worker who has produced W could have produced W working within C, then W has not satisfied the novelty condition relative to C. In his 'Creativity and Constraint',[14] David Novitz rejects Boden's novelty condition arguing that genuinely creative 'recombination' of available ideas can occur.[15] He favours instead a surprise condition which is a different relational property of the product of the putatively creative act, namely, the innovation of the product and its unpredictability from 'the point of view of a given population whose members were acquainted with some of the ideas or objects prior to their recombination'.[16]

---

[13] See *The Creative Mind: Myths and Mechanisms* (Reading: Cardinal, 1992), and 'What is Creativity?', in Margaret A. Boden (ed.), *Dimensions of Creativity* (Cambridge, Mass.: MIT Press, 1994).

[14] *Australasian Journal of Philosophy* 77 (1999), 67–82.

[15] S. Bailin, *Achieving Extraordinary Ends: An Essay on Creativity* (Dordrecht: Kluwer Academic Publishers, 1988), is another who rejects the ideas that creativity is necessarily novel, original, and must 'display a radical discontinuity with previous products' (4).

[16] Novitz, 'Creativity and Constraint', 78.

More interesting for my purposes is Novitz's inclusion of a value component for genuine creativity. He claims that to be creative a product must have 'real value to some people', in other words, it must possess 'properties that are of actual or potential benefit to sentient beings'.[17] I think this condition is mistaken, but as we shall presently see it has interesting implications for the idea of creativity as an aspect of the profiles of the *virtues*. Novitz's condition may be thought essential to creativity as an *achievement* word, but what could be essential to this is the product's having quality relative to the standards internal to relevant practices, such as literature, art, or science. Although such practices *as a whole* have (one assumes) high value, for example, beneficial consequences for sentient beings, it may be the case that a given product satisfies standards of quality internal to practices, without that product possessing 'real value' in Novitz's sense. The product may be a new type of highly destructive bomb, or a highly offensive and unlovely 'art work' (e.g. *Madonna in a Condom* exhibited at Te Papa Museum, Wellington, New Zealand, May 1998). Even assuming, for the sake of argument, that such objects have themselves no 'real value', they may have artistic merit, scientific value, or whatever, as assessed by standards internal to these practices. Those standards are criteria for high quality, which is not the same as high value. As R. J. Sternberg notes, where creativity is defined in terms of products, the products must be 'statistically unusual' and of 'high quality'.[18] Margaret Boden may even be wrong in saying that a creative product cannot be uninteresting. A parent may be creative in constructing a meal out of extremely meagre resources, but it may be uninteresting.

To qualify as part of the profile of a *virtue* however, it may be that creativity has to satisfy more stringent standards. Novitz claims that to be creative an act must *intend* to produce 'real value'. Though I reject this condition as essential for creativity, it is much more plausible as a condition for virtuous creativity. The intentionality of creativity as such has characteristically to do with the shaping of materials or the solving of problems more generally, in ways that conform to or modify relevant standards, rather than producing value, such as benefiting sentient beings. I sympathize with Novitz's view to this extent, however: if a per-

---

17 Ibid.

18 'Three-Facet Model of Creativity', in Robert J. Sternberg (ed.), *The Nature of Creativity: Contemporary Psychological Perspectives* (Cambridge: Cambridge University Press, 1988), 125–47, at 126.

son's creativity is designed actively to harm for no good reason, it can hardly be described as virtuous creativity.

In this section, I have discussed the nature of creativity as a mode of moral acknowledgement. Creativity contains both internalist and externalist features. In its internalist aspect, creativity is a form of expression. For putatively creative activity to be 'happy', 'felicitous', or 'successful' qua creativity it must *express* the agent's originality, talent, inventiveness, and so on. As we have seen, this does not entail that the artist, for example, *aims* at being inventive, original, and so forth. Compare:

> But why my productions take from my hand that particular form and style that makes them *Mozartish*, and different from the works of other composers, is probably owing to the same cause which renders my nose so large or so aquiline, or in short, makes it Mozart's, and different from those of other people. For I really do not study or aim at any originality.[19]

Second, in its externalist aspect, creativity is not assessed via the standards for *promotion* as a mode of moral acknowledgement. Promotion is assessed through consequentialist criteria. I promote successfully if I promote sufficient (or maximal) value. However, a work or output is assessable as creative according to the standards of quality in relevant practices.

The two ideas that creativity is both an expression of such factors as originality, inventiveness, and ingeniousness, and that the creative product satisfies requirements internal to practices, are important for my view that creativity is a distinctive mode of moral response. For they ensure that creativity is not reducible to mere promotion of states, or production of things having value or significance. Successful criticism of views such as Boden's does not entail that (a) creativity is a function *merely* of characteristics of the created product or outcome and (b) those characteristics have to do with value or significance. For creativity is a characteristic of processes even if views which exaggerate the specialness or extraordinariness of those processes are flawed.

(iii) Creativity and Virtue

The previous section explored the nature of creativity as a mode of moral acknowledgement. To understand creativity as an aspect of the

---

19 'Wolfgang Amadeus Mozart: A Letter', in Brewster Ghiselin (ed.), *The Creative Process* (New York: Mentor, 1952), 44–5, at 45.

profiles of the virtues we need to go deeper. We need to explore what is the point or rationale of creativity as a mode of moral acknowledgement. In much of Nietzsche's writings, it seems that the point or rationale of creativity is the promotion of a value—the avoidance of the abyss of mediocrity which Nietzsche saw as the greatest ugliness. Creativity's function is to serve that value and thereby to promote the value of the highest cultural and aesthetic ideals. From the writings of psychologists, one gains, or appears to gain, a different understanding of the basis and point of creativity. Creativity is expressive of a bond, a bond with self. It is a foremost expression of self-love, and as such it is expressive of psychic health. Are these understandings in tension? That is the issue to be explored in this section.

For Abraham Maslow, creativity is a pivotal feature of healthy (what he calls 'self-actualizing') people. The capacity to grow in a healthy direction is not a prerogative of the specially talented—those for whom the term 'creative' is traditionally reserved. For Maslow, creativity is 'an aspect of practically any behaviour at all, whether perceptual or attitudinal or emotional, conative, cognitive, or expressive'.[20] In many ways this idea is not opposed to Nietzsche's thought. Nietzsche identified two forms of psychic ill health leading to mediocrity: the danger of the resentment sickness of the 'slave' type which externalizes self-hate, and the danger of 'will-lessness'—the lure of comfort and loss of striving characterizing the 'herd' type. Both are enemies of creativity: the first destroys the creativity of others (as well as inhibiting one's own) and the second constitutes the life of adjustment, conformity, and ease which stifles one's own creativity. Maslow himself is an enemy of the psychology of 'adjustment' because it inhibits what he calls primary creativity.

However, Maslow is more interested in the creativity of the average person than is Nietzsche. Qua psychologist, he is interested in the health of all. Indeed, when he speaks of the intimate connection between creativity and health, he specifically excludes the products of the greatly talented. His interest in health leads him to claim 'we must become more interested in the creative process, the creative attitude, the creative person, rather than in the creative product alone'.[21] Nietzsche, however, does not identify excellence with health, and in his quest for excellence and avoidance of mediocrity, he is particularly concerned with the

[20] *The Farther Reaches of Human Nature* (Harmondsworth: Penguin, 1971), 74.
[21] Ibid. 95.

creativity of especially talented people. Furthermore, he seems particularly tolerant of, indeed praises, the grandiose narcissism that may be expressed by such people. Though such grandiosity is an 'expansionist' form of psychic ill health (to be discussed in connection with objectivity in the next chapter), Nietzsche does not find it deplorable. It is not deplorable, presumably, because it serves the goals of cultural and aesthetic excellence, unlike other 'life denying' forms of psychic sickness.

What implications does this complex picture of the relation between creativity and human psychic health have for a conception of creativity as an aspect of the profiles of the virtues? Here is the problem: creativity seems to serve or be based on two rationales—an expression of the flourishing individual, and societal and cultural goals. It may be overly sanguine to think that these two rationales for creativity—psychic health in a productive life, and societal benefit (whether or not seen primarily in terms of the avoidance of mediocrity), are not seriously in tension, and do not cause problems for a conception of creativity as an aspect of the profiles of the virtues. Although, as Maslow and others point out, creativity is positively correlated with aspects of psychic health, and 'positive' personality traits, it is also correlated with 'negative' personality features. Hans J. Eysenck cites the findings of Welsh suggesting that 'creative as opposed to noncreative students are unstable, irresponsible, disorderly, rebellious, uncontrolled, self-seeking, tactless, intemperate, rejecting of rules, unco-operative, impulsive, and careless'. However, they are also original, adventurous, liberal, refined, tolerant, candid, subtle, spontaneous, interesting, flexible and artistic.[22] Eysenck also cites Dellas and Gaier's findings that creative people are independent (in attitude and behaviour), are dominant (a positive psychological trait distinct from domineering, indicating authoritativeness and 'surgency' rather than authoritarianism), are open to stimuli, have wide interests, are self-accepting, and have social presence and poise.

As Eysenck reminds us, 'the presence of psychopathology does not make the appearance of positive personality characteristics impossible',[23] and the list of negative traits cited above are 'positively indicative of psychopathology'. Even worse, perhaps, Eysenck finds that 'creativity is related to, or is a function of psychoticism as a personality variable.' Psychoticism is not, however, identified by Eysenck as an illness; it is a

---

22 'The Measurement of Creativity', 212–13.
23 Ibid.

predisposition. Having claimed that psychiatric abnormality is dimensional rather than categorical, Eysenck claims that psychoticism is in general a genetic predisposition to develop psychosis (of various forms) under stress. Studies of schizophrenics, he claims, have revealed two types of formal thought disorder (which are not limited to them). These are a tendency to function more at a concrete than an abstract level, and a 'loosening of the concept span', sometimes called overinclusive and allusive thinking. Eysenck claims that 'looseness' is fundamental to creativity, whereas concrete thinking 'has no link with creativity, but rather precludes it'.[24] But notice that in an ordinary language sense of 'concrete thinking' this is an epistemic virtue. The imaginative deliberation required in problem solving (see Chapter 12) requires a very high degree of concreteness in thought, and an ability to grasp the concrete particular is by now relatively routinely argued to be necessary for good and creative moral thinking. And surely this ability is important in creativity. Even in the so-called abstract areas of science, it is interesting how the visualization of, and attendance to, the concrete has resulted in creative thought. Have we not heard of Archimedes' bath, Newton's apple, and I might add, Kekulé's discovery of the benzine ring as a result of the visualization of an object which he described as a snake biting its own tail?[25]

If creativity (in certain forms) is closely related to psychoticism and actual psychopathy, what becomes of the idea that virtue is constrained by psychic health? Or alternatively, how can creativity be an aspect of the profiles of the virtues? Isn't the linkage I have made in Chapter 3 between virtue and psychic health through the 'Constraint on Virtue' seriously undermined? The following replies at least partially solve the problem. First, creativity as I understand it is not necessarily extraordinary; it is quite standardly quotidian. Second, close attendance to what is involved in creativity being an aspect of the profiles of the *virtues* will show a frequent lack of tension between creativity and virtue. Consider creativity as an aspect of the profile of benevolence. A benevolent agent works for an aid organization whose funds have dried up because of the combination of economic recession, the removal of a tax incentive to make charitable donations, and the tendency of door to door collectors

[24] Ibid. 229. Compare also Henry Moore's study of pebbles, 'Henry Moore: Notes on Sculpture', in Ghiselin (ed.), *The Creative Process*, 73–8, at 74–5.

[25] Described in Boden, 'What is Creativity?', 82.

to be attacked by dogs or left on the doorstep by fearful residents. Creative solutions to the problem are desperately needed. However, the organization would benefit most from a creative person who was not uncooperative, tactless, irresponsible, or rebellious. As mentioned above, creativity is one thing, virtuous creativity is another. Though traits positively associated with psychopathy are also apparently associated with creativity, creativity as an aspect of the profiles of the virtues must be shaped, in ways appropriate to context, so that it is part of virtue. Again, consider a creative scientist working with dangerous materials in the presence of many colleagues who cannot always keep an eye on her. Maybe such a scientist is disorderly, careless, irresponsible, and uncontrolled. But she had better work on those traits if her creativity is to be embedded in virtue and she is not to poison her colleagues.

The above reply to the problem of linking creativity with virtue relies on the tried and tested glue of phronesis or practical wisdom. Creative *virtue*, it would seem, is wise creativity, and wise creativity is creativity that is also responsible, temperate, cooperative, and so forth.

However, this reply to the problem of embedding creativity in *virtue* may not fully satisfy, and does not do justice to Nietzsche's understanding of the importance of creativity. What Nietzsche calls 'the philosopher of the future' 'lives a life of creativity and experimentation, is a "free spirit" who lives "unphilosophically" and "unwisely", above all *imprudently*, and bears the burden and duty of a hundred attempts and temptations of life—he risks *himself* constantly'.[26] The notion that there is a linkage between creativity and imprudence is not a thought idiosyncratic to Nietzsche; it is a notion in the common consciousness as well. A study to determine how closely people believed creativity, intelligence, and wisdom to be related found that they believed creativity and wisdom to be the least correlated.[27] Indeed, a subgroup (the business group) found them to be negatively correlated.[28] The lack of tight connection between wisdom and creativity does not, however, invalidate my point (above) about the role of creativity in virtue. Wisdom, creativity, and virtue *are* linked in the quotidian creativity displayed in the 'warp and woof' of life.

[26] *Beyond Good and Evil*, sect. 205, p. 132.

[27] This should not suggest that artistic creativity for example does not involve thought. Though Henry Moore claims that it dissipates creative energy to think or write much *about* one's job, the creative process requires thinking about 'form in its full spatial completeness' (in Ghiselin (ed.), *The Creative Process*, 74).

[28] Sternberg, 'Three-Facet Model of Creativity', 127.

In what might be called 'heroic' creativity, however, the connection is loosened. There is an age-old distinction in the virtues, a distinction explicit in both Aristotle and Hume, which will serve our purposes. This is a distinction between ordinary and heroic virtue. That distinction has traditionally suffered from an unfortunate masculinist tinge, but it can be employed to deal with residual tensions in the two underlying rationales for creativity. Heroic virtue is not for everyone. The excesses of the Nietzschean creative hero would not be a pretty sight in the relatively talentless. For such a hero maybe, marriage may indeed be a calamity,[29] but it is deplorable for a relatively talentless family man to neglect his children while obsessively indulging a passion to change the world with his futile scratchings.

Of course, the boundary between the numerous expressive aspects of creativity described by Maslow and grandiose self-indulgence are not necessarily easy to draw. Maslow cites the courage of creativity, the courage of one who is prepared to drop his mask, drop his efforts 'to influence, to impress, to please, to be lovable, to win applause'.[30] In creativity, one lives intensely in the moment, forgetting the past and the future, one has a loss of ego, one is receptive and open, one has an attitude of trust and acceptance, one loses fear and anxiety.[31] Certainly, the excellent creative product is a product of what Maslow calls 'secondary creativity', where the receptive, open phase submits to critical appraisal. However, the question arises: when does the courage, openness, and self-sufficiency of creativity become an arrogant disregard of peers, a grandiose piece of egocentricity? My general answer is to distinguish heroic from ordinary creative virtue. All (virtuous) creativity has the properties described by Maslow, but where one places the 'mean' is determined by several features: the individual's roles, the nature of her environment, and her calibre in various relevant respects.

Although I have discussed separately a variety of modes of moral acknowledgement in Part II, some common themes emerge with respect to their role in virtue. First, though we can think of love, creativity, and so forth as modes of moral acknowledgement whose existence does not entail the expression of the wide range of fine inner states required for virtue, the expression of those states is required if they are to be excel-

---

[29] *On the Genealogy of Morals*, Third Essay, sect. 7, p. 86.
[30] *The Farther Reaches of Human Nature*, 63.
[31] Ibid. 63–5.

lent, and feature as aspects of *virtue*. Just what fine states are required may not be the same for each mode as it features in various virtues. Second, insofar as love, respect, and creativity feature in the profiles of the virtues, they have to be (to an extent) integrated with each other. Respect as a form of keeping distance has to be integrated with love as a form of coming close; creativity as a form of constructive, ingenious, and inventive solution to problems, or as manifested in original products, has to be integrated with other aspects of the profiles of the virtues such as the promotion of good or value, love, respect, appreciation, or receptivity. The integration may not be total, nor need it be the same for each virtue. Some focus more on creativity, others more on love or respect, for example. Furthermore, the integration required for virtue involves the expression of wisdom and self-love. But, again, this integration may not be total or perfect: creativity or love in virtue may not always express self-love or wisdom in ideal form. Finally, ideally, all or at least most virtues exhibit the full range of modes of moral acknowledgement, including receptivity, love, respect, appreciation, promotion of good, and creativity. But different modes will have salience in different contexts, including those where people have different capacities.

A full account of the profiles of the virtues requires an account of all the modes of moral acknowledgement and how they are integrated in virtue. But a full account of the nature of virtue is not provided just by an account of their profiles. We also need an account of a virtue's shape, constituted by the various aspects of what has sometimes been called 'the limits of morality'. These are the topics of Part III, which begins with an account of objectivity in virtue.

Part III

SHAPE OF
THE VIRTUES

8

Objectivity

(i) Introduction

A neglected, but very important issue in virtue ethics is the moral standing of the agent as she meets the demands of the world. In virtue ethics this general issue takes the form of what I have called the shape of the virtues, and it has three aspects. These are the nature of objectivity in the virtues, the demandingness (or stringency) of virtue, and the place in virtue of what has been called constraints or agent-centred restrictions. Each of these issues occupies a separate chapter in Part III. We begin with objectivity .

On a surface level, an agent is objective if the 'subjective' does not loom too large: if she is not biased or tunnel-visioned, if her dealings with others do not give too much weight to her own interests and desires, if she is not excessively absorbed in her own projects and her own narrow circles. But what counts as bias, self-indulgence, selfishness, self-centredness, or narrowness of concern is not on my view something that can be determined without looking deeply into the agent. We need to know in a deep sense, what the agent's behaviour expresses, and as Alan Tormey claims, 'an expression points simultaneously in two directions, back toward the person and outwards towards the object'.[1] An important tradition in the understanding of objectivity in ethics has been dominated by a focus 'outwards towards the object'. This chapter, unsurprisingly in a virtue ethics, redresses the balance by focusing on what the agent's behaviour expresses. But what are the 'inner components' of bias, self-indulgence, or selfishness is not something *just* under the skin, as Nietzsche recognizes:

among us immoralists at least the suspicion has arisen that the decisive value of an action resides in precisely that which is *not intentional* in it, and that all that in it which is intentional, all of it that can be seen, known, 'conscious', still belongs to

---

[1] *The Concept of Expression.*

its surface and skin—which, like every skin, betrays something but *conceals* even more.[2]

Though Nietzsche here neglects the external components of 'decisive value' in an action, the passage is salutary in reminding us of the depth-psychological features of objectivity in virtue, and those are explicated in this chapter.

I first need to motivate my own virtue-ethical perspective on objectivity by outlining difficulties in the predominant, opposing perspective: that dominated by the 'outer'. The idea of objectivity as impartial 'detachment' in which all features of the agent have been abstracted away has reduced the demands of objectivity to the 'demands of the world' alone. No looking back to what is going on in the agent is forthcoming. However, this general conception of objectivity has run into difficulties highlighted by Thomas Nagel, difficulties which my virtue-ethical conception of objectivity attempts to resolve.

For Nagel, the central problem of moral and political theory is the problem of reconciling two standpoints. These are what he variously calls the subjective and the objective, or the personal and the impersonal. The challenge is to reconcile these standpoints so that two requirements are met. First, an ethics must propose requirements of objectivity on agents where a place is given to the 'subjective', without incurring the charge of being a 'yuppie' ethics.[3] Second, the ethics must not propose requirements of objectivity on agents which are excessively transcendent. Such an ethics Nagel calls 'excessively' objective. For Nagel, excessively objective conceptions of normative ethics fail to make room for the 'subjective', not only because they look only in one direction—'outwards towards the object'—but because they look to the world as a whole. I resolve the problem by providing a conception of objectivity as an aspect of virtue, namely, objectivity is constituted by a disposition to meet the demands of the world in a way which expresses self-love. The idea of expressing self-love is intended to give normative content to Nagel's requirement of making room for the 'subjective' in 'meeting the demands of the world'.

In my virtue-ethical account of objectivity, it is an *agent* who is primar-

---

[2] *Beyond Good and Evil*, 32.

[3] As far as I know, the term 'yuppie ethics' first appears as a philosophical term of art in Marcia Baron's 'Kantian Ethics and Supererogation' (*Journal of Philosophy* 84 (1987), 237–62): '"yuppie ethics" . . . introduces a division, a fence around what "I may choose, as I please", separating it from what I "have to" do' (249).

ily said to be objective. Objectivity is a virtue (or component of virtue) of a special kind, structurally similar to Aristotle's practical wisdom. For Aristotle, practical wisdom is describable as a separate virtue—an 'intellectual' virtue—and I shall sometimes speak of the virtue of objectivity. Yet objectivity (like practical wisdom) on my view is an inseparable part of all the virtues of character, such virtues as temperance, justice, liberality, and friendship. It is arguably better, then, to talk of practical wisdom in virtue, and accordingly I shall also speak of objectivity in virtue. Indeed, I am happy if objectivity in virtue is seen as an aspect of practical wisdom itself, provided the latter notion is understood in a sufficiently broad sense. As we shall see, objectivity will be understood primarily in motivational terms, but the relevant motivations will feed into an agent's emotions, perceptions, and reasonings. One could in fact argue that the description of practical wisdom as an 'intellectual' virtue is misleading, for practical wisdom in its fullest sense involves right ways of seeing the world affectively and motivationally.[4]

A virtue-ethical conception of objectivity must suppose a basic core concept of objectivity which is recognizable by a number of rival theories as a conception of objectivity. Conceptions of objectivity, including virtue-ethical ones, are rival interpretations of the core concept.[5] According to the core concept, the requirement of objectivity is a requirement to meet the 'demands of the world' in a way that appropriately transcends 'subjective' or 'personal' inclinations, attachments, emotions, feelings, and preferences. Following Thomas Nagel,[6] let us call the basic core concept *objectivity as (appropriate) self-transcendence*. Providing a *conception* of objectivity in ethics is a two-pronged affair: giving an account of the demands of the world in relation to *human* agents, and giving an account of meeting those demands in ways which *appropriately* transcend the personal and subjective. The first of these tasks was

---

[4] I concur with Aristotle's view that practical wisdom is inextricably connected with right emotion: no one can be (fully) practically wise without possessing 'natural' virtue, since emotion informs judgement and 'perception' of the particular. See e.g. Nancy Sherman, *The Fabric of Character: Aristotle's Theory of Virtue* (Oxford: Oxford University Press, 1989), and Marcia L. Homiak, 'Aristotle on the Soul's Conflicts: Toward an Understanding of Virtue Ethics', in Andrew Reith, Barbara Herman, and Christine M. Korsgaard (eds.), *Reclaiming the History of Ethics: Essays for John Rawls* (Cambridge: Cambridge University Press 1997), 7–35.

[5] See John Rawls, *A Theory of Justice* (Cambridge, Mass.: Harvard University Press, 1971), 5, for the distinction between a concept of X and rival conceptions of X. The former is the 'common element' in the latter, which are rival interpretations of the former.

[6] In *The View from Nowhere*.

undertaken in Parts I and II, where I discussed modes of moral acknowledgement. This chapter addresses the second of these tasks, providing an interpretation of appropriate transcendence from the 'subjective' or 'personal'.

In the interpretation of *appropriate* self-transcendence, it is common ground that the transcendence must be undistorted. The idea of distortion presupposes a norm relative to which something is distorted. The central point of this chapter is that the norm determines objectivity as an aspect of virtue, and is to be provided by a background theory of healthy human functioning. It is not to be provided by a theory which looks simply to the 'demands of the world' seen in abstraction from such a norm. On the latter kind of view, absence of distortion is interpreted too often as presence of detachment. On such a view, the norm of undistorted transcendence may be provided by an impartial spectator who demands that we be responsive to 'universal good' or 'good generally' rather than to a part of such good.[7]

The idea of undistorted self-transcendence as (forms of) detached self-transcendence has been dominant. It is important, therefore, at least briefly to consider this tradition to help understand and motivate the virtue-ethical account of objectivity to be provided in section iii.

(ii) Objectivity as Detachment

A dominant conception of objectivity, which I shall reject, is detachment from the personal. Where favouring a conception of objectivity as detachment from the personal is common ground, there is room for debate about the characterization of the detached perspective. On Sidgwick's view, the objective point of view is the point of view of the universe:

we have formed the notion of Universal Good by comparison and integration of the goods of all individual human—or sentient—existences. . . . [B]y considering the relation of the integrant parts to the whole and to each other, I obtain the self-evident principle that the good of any one individual is of no more importance, from the point of view (if I may say so) of the Universe, than the good of any other . . . and it is evident to me that as a rational being I am bound to aim at good generally—so far as it is attainable by my efforts—not merely at a particular part of it.[8]

---

[7] See next note.
[8] Henry Sidgwick, *The Methods of Ethics*, 7th edn. (London: Macmillan, 1907; reissued 1962),

For Sidgwick, then, a rational agent with the virtue of objectivity has the perspective of a suitably detached agent. Such an agent is detached from bonds to particular aspects of the good. She must aim (directly or indirectly) 'at good generally'.

An even greater level of 'detachment' is required by Nagel's conception of 'the most objective' point of view. Here, one not only takes on 'the point of view of the Universe', but one takes on the point of view of the universe having stripped oneself of distinctively human characteristics:

a view or form of thought is more objective than another if it relies less on the specifics of the individual's make up and position in the world, or on the character of the particular type of creature he is.[9]

Descriptions of the objective perspective as the detached perspective invites unlimited progression towards greater and greater detachment, with consequent disregard of humanity. An agent obtaining greater objectivity progressively eliminates feelings and emotions in favour of 'reason', disregards the demands of bonds in favour of those of value, the demands of partial bonds in favour of those of impartial bonds, and finally, in its most extreme version, the requirement of 'detachment' removes the human point of view altogether in favour of the 'cosmic' point of view. Here, even significant human suffering will be portrayed as insignificant or absurd.

Consider, for example, Colin McGinn's understanding of objectivity in his review of Thomas Nagel's *The View from Nowhere*. Having identified the objective standpoint with the cosmic standpoint, McGinn says: 'It is consoling to reflect that from a cosmic standpoint none of it really *matters* all that much. . . . It is something of a relief to recall that all those too-human problems don't objectively count for much'.[10] I find this extraordinary. It wouldn't be so bad if the cosmic viewpoint were separated from the objective, so that the huge amount of cruelty and suffering in the world mattered considerably from the objective point of view even if it did not from the cosmic (whatever that is). Objectivity should not 'make us aware of the absurdity of our moral plight', a perception which is 'consoling'. On the contrary, if it does not alert us to its importance and

382. See discussion by Bernard Williams, 'The Point of View of the Universe: Sidgwick and the Ambitions of Ethics', in his *Making Sense of Humanity and other Philosophical Papers 1982–1993* (Cambridge: Cambridge University Press, 1995), 153–71.

9 *The View from Nowhere*, 5.
10 *Mind* 96 (1987), 263–72, at 272.

seriousness, it is distorting. It is therefore not objective, but is rather what I shall later call hyperobjective. That conception of objectivity looks only outwards towards the world, and not back towards the nature of the agent. On an understanding of objectivity where the norms relative to which self-transcendence is distorted are rooted in human nature, the demand for objectivity involves a demand for recognition of the realities of the human condition. These include the realities of our emotions, modes of bonding, commitment, locatedness in culture, gender, and roles. It is a demand of non-abstraction from those features, just as objectivity in colour perception is a recognition of the richness of colour accessible to distinctively human modes of sense perception, and not a hankering for dazzling whiteness or brightness or mistiness, in which that richness has been hidden or washed away.

Nagel's conception of an objectivity suitable for ethics does not appear to suffer from this kind of criticism. Although Nagel's *'most* objective point of view' is one I would call hyperobjective, for Nagel the moral point of view is not the 'most objective'. This, however, seems on the face of it counterintuitive. For shouldn't the most objective point of view be the best, at least characteristically? On my view, this is indeed so. Let me show how my taxonomy differs from Nagel's, and why it is to be preferred.

As I have said, it is common ground that an objective point of view is one in which transcendence from the 'subjective' or 'personal' is undistorted. The conception of 'most objective' that Nagel employs is a conception of 'distortion free' as 'detached', and a conception of 'detached' as 'perspective free'. On that conception, the more detached, the less influenced by perspectives generated by specifics of human character and individual locatedness; the less influenced by perspective, the less distorted. The most objective viewpoint is thus abstract and idealized. But this conception produces tension. Despite the plausibility in the idea that the more objective a point of view the better, because a point of view which is undistorted is better than one which is distorted, Nagel has to make room for the idea of *excess* objectivity in ethics. Excess objectivity in ethics is bad objectivity: that is, objectivity which doesn't make room for the subjective point of view. Thus Nagel has built for himself what he regards as the central problem in normative ethical theory, the 'two perspectives' problem, that is, the problem of combining the subjective and objective viewpoints.

I shall claim that there is but one perspective suitable for constructing an ethics—the objective perspective, the undistorted perspective. That is the perspective of one who possesses the virtue of objectivity. That virtue can only be elaborated through a study of human excellences and failures in regard to one's attitude to the world at large and to oneself in that world. My view avoids the structural tensions inherent in Nagel's view, since characteristically, the more objective a view the better.

Objectivity as a virtue is contrasted with two vices, the vice of hyperobjectivity and the vice of hypersubjectivity. The vice of hyperobjectivity is not a state of greater objectivity—a state involving a greater degree of *virtue*; rather, it is a state of vice, which involves adopting a totally wrong (distorted) perspective. It is a state which is not a properly *human* objective standpoint. Specifically, it is not true on my view that the *more* detached one is from one's personal position in the world, one's human character, and so on, the more (virtuously) *objective* one is.

(iii) Hyperobjectivity and Hypersubjectivity

An account of objectivity as more or less unlimited detachment fails to resolve Nagel's 'two perspectives' problem. In this section, I aim to show that understanding objectivity as an aspect of virtue which avoids both 'hyperobjective' and 'hypersubjective' vice resolves the problem. A psychology which makes sense of such an understanding is one based on the Nietzschean account of self-love developed in Chapter 6. It provides an account of what an agent's attempts to meet the demands of the world express, and hence provides the needed account of what is going on in the *agent* when she is said to be objective (or otherwise) in those attempts. Since psychology is a complex and controversial discipline, I cannot claim for the account completeness or definitiveness. My purpose is to indicate the profit to be gained from a cooperation between philosophical virtue ethics and psychology, resulting in a richer, more humanly relevant conception of objectivity in ethics than can be gained from the resources of analytical philosophy alone.

An understanding of objectivity as an aspect of virtue is best gained by describing the corresponding aspects of vice. In hyperobjective vice, there is excessive self-transcendence: perceived demands of the world are excessive in relation to the demands of the self. In hypersubjective vice, there is deficient self-transcendence: the (perceived) demands of the self are excessive in relation to the demands of the world. The central claim is that distorted self-transcendence, whether hyperobjective or hypersubjective, are both forms of *failure* in self-love: that is, in such vice, one's meeting of the demands of the world is distorted in ways which are *expressive* of such failure. Hyperobjective and hypersubjective vice are two sides of the same coin. Deficient self-transcendence or hypersubjectivity must not therefore be confused with excessive self-love. On the contrary, the narcissistic personality is deficient in self-love, and this results in the self-absorption and focus on the self characteristic of that personality.[11] By the same token, the hyperobjective stance should not be understood as excessive love of the world (as *opposed* to love of the self). Such 'love' should be seen as counterfeit: as forms of resentment, self-effacement, escape.

Before we describe in more detail the nature of hyperobjective and hypersubjective vice, we should note that at least one philosopher appears to have understood the ethical in these terms. Kierkegaard's philosophical writings can fruitfully be seen as a struggle to delineate the ethical as properly objective, in a mean between the hypersubjective and the hyperobjective. In *Either/Or*, Kierkegaard contrasts the ethical with the hypersubjective stance of the 'aesthetic'—a stance described by Patrick Gardiner in the following terms:

the man who lives aesthetically is not really in control, either of himself or his situation. He typically exists *ins Blaue hinein*; he tends to live 'for the moment', for whatever the passing instant will bring in the way of entertainment, excitement, interest. Committed to nothing permanent or definite, dispersed in sensuous 'immediacy', he may do or think one thing at a given time, the exact opposite at some other; his life is therefore without 'continuity', lacks stability or focus, changes course according to mood or circumstance.[12]

In *Concluding Scientific Postscript*, by contrast, Kierkegaard portrays the ethical in contrast to the hyperobjective, and in particular to the Hegelian brand of hyperobjectivity according to which human beings have the rather grandiose perspective of 'living in the world-historical', when they should be firmly engaged in the concerns of their localized context. As Patrick Gardiner puts it:

People were all too disposed to 'lose themselves in the totality of things, in world-history', sinking their identities in collective notions like those of the spirit of the age or the progress of mankind.[13]

---

[11] See further, Stocker and Hegeman, *Valuing Emotions*.

[12] *Kierkegaard* (Oxford: Oxford University Press, 1988), 44.

[13] Ibid. 85.

Accordingly, there is a unity to Kierkegaard's works not apparent on the surface: indeed, as Patrick Gardiner emphasizes, *Either/Or* and *Concluding Scientific Postscript* appear to be in severe tension. In *Either/Or*, the ethical is portrayed as a stance in which the agent acknowledges rules governing his membership of a society and is a participator in organized practices. In *Concluding Scientific Postscript*, it is the 'subjective' aspect of ethics that is emphasized. It is concerned with the self and its personal commitments. The unity in Kierkegaard's thought is discerned if it is appreciated that failure to achieve proper objectivity can take both hyperobjective and hypersubjective forms. In both cases there are forms of escape. In hyperobjective forms of benevolence, there is a grandiose unpleasant need to bolster one's ego in one's efforts to do good. To avoid this kind of hyperobjectivity it is not necessary to cast aside moral precepts and dissolve one's links to society. The importance of abiding by such precepts and maintaining such links is a feature of the ethical emphasized in *Either/Or*, and as Kierkegaard claims in *Concluding Scientific Postscript,* one participates in the 'warp and woof' of life if one is to be ethical.

Let us now discuss in more detail how it is that hyperobjective and hypersubjective vice are both to be understood in terms of various kinds of failure of self-love. It will be recalled that the root cause of failure in self-love is a failure adequately to deal with a clash between two features endemic to the human condition: a need to grow and '*vent* [one's] strength',[14] and the fact that this basic need or drive is standardly subject to vicissitudes with harmful effects, often unconscious, which leads to a distorted sense of self as both idealized and despised.[15]

---

[14] Nietzsche, *Beyond Good and Evil*, sect. 13, p. 44

[15] A claim about the importance of the vicissitudes does not entail that dysfunctional interpersonal behaviour does not cause negative reactions from others which are powerful reinforcers of those very dysfunctionalities. Such reinforcers are environmental vicissitudes, which may thus build on the effects of other vicissitudes. The importance of such interpersonal reinforcement is noted by Richardson, Fowers, and Guignon, *Re-envisioning Psychology*, 103–4, and also by both Adler, *The Neurotic Constitution* and *Understanding Human Nature*, and Horney, *Neurosis and Human Growth*. Furthermore, and in line with the above possibilities, a claim about the importance of the vicissitudes is compatible with all sorts of claims about the best ways of resolving the dysfunctionalities, including right living to improve one's own self-love and the esteem of others, behavioural reinforcements, and therapeutic catharsis and insight. I say nothing to prejudice these issues. It is interesting that Richardson, Fowers, and Guignon claim that the best research on therapy outcomes 'suggests that most approaches work comparably well for most clients'. They claim: 'Clearly there is disorder in the house of theory' (239). I suggest

Nietzsche identifies several forms of distortions in self-love relevant to our discussion—distortions which are more fully described in later psychological writings. These are the 'expansionist' distortions of insatiability, vindictiveness, and cruelty, the 'self-effacing' distortions, and the distortions of 'will-lessness'. These form the basis of both hyperobjective and hypersubjective vice.

Let us begin with the various faces of hyperobjective vice. Karen Horney distinguishes three 'neurotic solutions' to the inner conflict described above; solutions which are remarkably similar to those identified by Nietzsche. These are the 'expansive', 'self-effacing', and 'resignatory' solutions. Consider first the 'expansive' solution. In this solution, the despised self is suppressed, and that is no doubt why Nietzsche fails to emphasize the self-contempt of the expansive type, even where that self-contempt is externalized in cruelty. Here is Horney:

When looking superficially at the expansive types we get a picture of people who, in a streamlined way, are bent on self-glorification, on ambitious pursuits, on vindictive triumphs, with the mastery of life through intelligence and will power as the means to actualize their idealized self. And barring all differences in premises, individual concepts and terminology, this is the way Freud and Adler have seen these people (as driven by the need for narcissistic self-aggrandizement or for being on top).[16]

Though the triumphant solution is preferred by Nietzsche to the solution of self-effacement and compliance, he does recognize it as a distortion of will to power, since it is insatiable as opposed to disciplined. He prefers it because it involves less of an abasement of self than the self-effacing solution in which the self 'wilts away'.

Consider now the compliance solution of self-effacement deplored by Nietzsche. Like the expansive solution, the solution of compliance or self-effacement also involves an excessively transcendent perspective, but it is one in which goodness or saintliness dominates as opposed to the need to triumph over others. Horney describes the following case of neurotic altruism; a description which of course is a summary of a diagnosis resultant on detailed observations, and which can only be seen as a description of neurotic altruism when considered as part of a pattern manifesting itself over time:

that the disorder lies in the classic theorists' tendency to stake territory by exaggerating difference.

[16] Horney, *Neurosis and Human Growth*, 192.

In one girl . . . compliant trends had become predominant. They showed in a blind adoration of certain authority figures, in tendencies to please and appease, in a timidity about expressing her own wishes, and in sporadic attempts to sacrifice. At the age of eight she placed some of her toys in the street for some poorer child to find, without telling anybody about it.[17]

Horney describes further features of this person—features which display a lack of integration. Perspectives such as hers are excessively transcendent because, first, the transcendence involved in living up to the ideals of self-sacrifice, love, generosity, and so forth is distorted, for it is expressive of self-contempt rather than of genuine love or compassion for the other. And, second, the transcendence is 'excessive', since the agent (in distorted ways) overplays the demands of the world in her apparently generous behaviour. The term 'excessive' here is not meant to connote a crude quantitative conception of an Aristotelian mean. Rather, the conception is qualitative, based on background theories of psychic health. The problem is not that the sacrifice or generosity would necessarily be too much or too great in the hands of a strong, healthy person. Rather, it is sourced in characterological states, albeit 'depth' states, that are deplorable and unhealthy.[18]

The self-effacing, compliant solution is unhealthy because it, too, is a specific neurotic solution to the conflict between the idealized self and the self that is deplored. It involves the suppression of the 'superior self' and the bringing to the fore one's conception of oneself as weak, and contemptible. Instead of trying to *be* a master, as in the solution of the 'appeal of mastery', one abases oneself before a 'Master', by comparison to whom one is contemptible, but by whose dictates one still needs to live. This is the type attacked by Nietzsche in his inveighings against Christianity. Interestingly, Horney describes the 'Self-Effacing Solution' as the least satisfactory, since it involves greater feelings of unhappiness. Nietzsche finds it particularly deplorable not for this reason, but because the vindictiveness involved in it is more secretive (as Horney herself

17 Ibid. 20.

18 In their preface to Horney's *Neurosis and Human Growth*, Jeffrey Rubin and Stephanie Steinfeld describe Horney's most radical and yet simplest concept as one where the distinction between what is 'healthy and what is unhealthy [is] in terms of qualitative differences, differences explicable in terms of encrusted characterological defences and structures, rather than in terms primarily of the topographic or economic models'. For a discussion of those models as used by Freud, see Patricia Kitcher, *Freud's Dream: A Complete Interdisciplinary Science of Mind* (Cambridge, Mass.: MIT Press, 1995), esp. ch. 3.

describes, and which Nietzsche describes in *The Genealogy of Morals*) and it involves greater self-abnegation, which Horney describes as a 'shrinking process'.[19] Nonetheless, the idealized self of the self-effacing type is apparently laudable. Horney describes it thus:

His idealized image of himself primarily is a composite of 'lovable' qualities, such as unselfishness, goodness, generosity, humility, saintliness, nobility, sympathy. Helplessness, suffering, and martyrdom are also secondarily glorified.[20]

In the self-effacing type, another face of hyperobjective vice is displayed—the tendency to think of oneself as insignificant, absurd, or contemptible by comparison to a superior perspective which defines the way one perceives one's position in the world. This may be the perspective of the saint. It may be the perspective of Gaia, by reference to which 'pollution' is seen as an anthropocentric and therefore invalid concept, and by reference to which something like the depletion of the ozone layer, leading to escalating rates of skin cancer in certain parts of the world, is downgraded in significance, despite the enormous amount of suffering caused and the ameliorability of the problem. It may be a certain perspective of God, by reference to which one sees oneself as a miserable sinner,[21] or it may be McGinn's 'cosmic' perspective.

There is a third form of hyperobjective vice, identified by Nietzsche, and discussed by Horney under the category of the 'Resignation Solution'. This is the category I identified above as Nietzsche's third form of distortion of will to power, 'will-lessness'. For Nietzsche, this form directly affects cognition and our conceptions of rationality and objectivity:

From now on, my dear philosophers, let us beware of the dangerous old conceptual fable which posited a 'pure, will-less, painless, timeless knowing subject', let us beware of the tentacles of such contradictory concepts as 'pure reason', 'absolute spirituality', 'knowledge in itself'.[22]

Here again the 'search for glory', the impact of the idealized self with its superior perspective, affects cognition and affectivity. But there is no desire for mastery (as in the expansionist solution). Nor is there a desire

---

[19] *Neurosis and Human Growth*, 223.

[20] Ibid. 222.

[21] See, for example, *The Life of Saint Teresa of Avila by Herself*, trans. J. M. Cohen (Harmondsworth: Penguin, 1957).

[22] *On the Genealogy of Morals*, Third Essay, sect. 12.

to abase oneself before a master or superior viewpoint (as in the self-effacing or compliant solution). Rather, the tendencies to excessive transcendence are sourced in a withdrawal or distancing from the particularities and messiness of the world. On Nietzsche's view, it seems, this is the classic philosopher's form of hyperobjective vice. The refusal to face complexity, discord, detail, particularity; the drive for codifiability, absolute certainty, unique and definite solutions to moral issues; consequent tendencies to excessive abstraction, may indeed be symptoms of unhealthy withdrawal from the world. Quoting from passages of Soren Kierkegaard's *Sickness unto Death*,[23] Horney describes some of the cognitive features of this form of hyperobjectivity:

This soaring into the unlimited is determined by the power of the needs behind the drive for glory. The needs for the *absolute* and the *ultimate* are so stringent that they override the checks which usually prevent our imagination from detaching itself from actuality . . . He is no longer capable of submitting to the necessities in himself, 'to what may be called one's limit' . . . His thinking may become too abstract. His knowledge may become a kind of inhuman knowing for the production of which man's self is squandered . . . His feelings for others may evaporate into 'an abstract sentimentality for humanity'.[24]

As we have seen, the distinctions between healthy ambition and vindictive triumphalism, healthy and unhealthy altruism, unhealthy dependency and genuine love, are hard to draw. Likewise, it is not easy to distinguish between unhealthy resignation, which is a 'shrinking process', from healthy asceticism and withdrawal, which may be part of a search for higher ideals of living. This is admitted by Horney herself.[25]

Let us turn now to hypersubjective vice. I said above that hyperobjective and hypersubjective vice are two sides of the same coin. It is not that hypersubjectivity expresses excessive love of self and hyperobjectivity insufficient love: rather, both are manifestations of a deficiency of self-love.

Hypersubjective vice points to a second major form of distorted affective and cognitive dispositions: egocentricity. Adler sums up the phenomenon:

[23] *Sickness unto Death* (1844) (Princeton, N.J.: Princeton University Press, 1941).
[24] Horney, *Neurosis and Human Growth*, 35. It is arguable that Bertrand Russell had the distorted form of benevolence described by Kierkegaard and Horney. See also the discussion of Dostoevsky's views of nineteenth-century Russian utopian socialist reformers in Charles Guignon (ed.), *Dostoevsky: The Grand Inquisitor* (Indianapolis: Hackett, 1999)), esp. pp. xiv–xvi.
[25] See *Neurosis and Human Growth*, 259–60.

The obstacles a child meets within the development of his soul usually result in the stunting or distortion of his social feeling . . . [Such children] have a peculiarly sharp sense of life's hostility, and they unconsciously exaggerate it. Their interest in the bitterness of life is much greater than in its brighter side. For the most part, they overrate both, so that theirs is a lifelong attitude of belligerency. They demand that an extraordinary amount of attention be paid to them, and of course they think far more of themselves than of others. They conceive of the necessary obligations of life more as difficulties than as stimuli.[26]

Karen Horney describes the egocentricity of the neurotic in detail in her chapter entitled 'Neurotic Claims'.[27] These claims in general concern the neurotic's felt need 'to special attention, consideration and deference on the part of others'.[28] The desires, wishes, and preferences of such a person manifest hypersubjective vice insofar as they are insufficiently transcendent. That is, they remain in a juvenile or immature phase and are reminiscent of those of a spoilt child. A central feature of such egocentricity is that '*a wish or need*, in itself quite understandable, turns into a claim. Its nonfulfilment then is felt as an unfair frustration, as an offence about what we have a right to feel indignant'.[29] A mere wish, such that the weather be fine, becomes a strong desire or need, the non-satisfaction of which causes greater than normal frustration. A strong desire or need becomes a claim whose non-fulfilment is a source of resentment. Such claims often take the form of being indignant when regulations, whose general observance benefits one, operate to one's disadvantage. The resentment felt could only be justified if one had a genuine claim to exception. Resentment then is due to an excessively strong sense of entitlement. Benefits not owed or even merited may be thought owed or merited. The desire to escape a self seen as defective or contemptible and the identification with an idealized self cause difficulty in the acknowledgement of necessities, restrictions, losses, or deprivations.

It should be noted that the various forms of distortion constituting failures of objectivity are not hard and fast categories, and may well combine in a single personality, as Horney herself notes. For Nietzsche, too, various forms of distorted will to power can be combined: self-contempt combines with resentment-based compassion, vindictiveness, secrecy, externalized disgust, and will-lessness.

We have described a view explaining how both hyperobjective and

---

[26] *Understanding Human Nature*, 36–7.
[27] *Neurosis and Human Growth*, ch. 2.
[28] Ibid. 41.
[29] Ibid. 42.

hypersubjective vice constitute distorted forms of meeting the demands of the world. On this view, the distortions lie in the fact that they are in various kinds of ways expressive of failures in self-love. Hyperobjective vice can be understood as excessive self-transcendence because the claims of the 'idealized self' predominate in various distorted ways. Hypersubjective vice can be understood as insufficient self-transcendence because 'neurotic claims' are expressive of excessive narcissistic focus on self. Either way, there is a failure of objectivity.

(iv) Some Objections

Let us consider now objections to the above account of objectivity as a component of virtue.

The most interesting and apparently damaging objection to the view outlined above derives from recent findings in social psychology. The findings show that 'violent criminals often describe themselves as being superior to others—as special, elite persons who deserve preferential treatment'.[30] Findings such as these have lead some social psychologists to conclude that the low self-esteem theory (of the cause of aggression) is false. If the low self-esteem theory is false, then it would seem that the view outlined—namely, lack of self-love is the root of both hyperobjective and hypersubjective vice—is false. Before I question this implication, let me first distinguish the conclusion that low self-esteem theory is false from another conclusion. The other conclusion concerns the methods used to generate higher self-esteem in schools and elsewhere. These methods are also criticized by Baumeister and others. Indeed, scepticism about the worth of these practices can be based on the writings of Adler himself, who noted over-protectiveness, spoiling, and failures to set limits as 'vicissitudes' fostering dependency. For him, they are a prime cause of what I have called hypersubjective vice—an inflated sense of oneself, and one's importance—expressed in a low tolerance of frustration when reality checks impinge on the individual in a harsh competitive world.

I want to show now that even if Baumeister's view that the low self-esteem theory is false is correct, there is no implication for the falsity of the view that lack of self-love underpins the forms of hyperobjective and hypersubjective vice. This is so for the basic reason that the term

---

[30] Roy F. Baumeister, 'Violent Pride', *Scientific American* (April 2001), 82–7

'self-esteem' as used by Baumeister is a behavioural notion not identical to the depth-motivational notion of self-love.

On Baumeister's conception, 'high self-esteem' is measured by high self-evaluation as revealed by interview and questionnaires. But, it turns out, the 'high self-esteem' associated with aggression on their view is 'inflated', 'brittle', 'tenuous', 'grandiose'. In short, it is distorted; it is not healthy self-esteem. On Horney's way of describing the matter, this 'high' self-esteem is part of the expansionist solution, a solution manifesting two sides of the same coin: one face of hyperobjective vice (the expansionist solution) and corresponding hypersubjective vice. Indeed, on Baumeister's view, 'Adolf Hitler's exaltation of the 'master race' was hardly a slogan of low self-esteem'.[31] If low self-esteem is definitionally equivalent to features of the self-effacing solution, and the expansionist solution cannot by definition be understood in terms of low self-esteem, then the ideas of high self-esteem and self-love are not synonymous. The fact, then, that the low self-esteem theory is false (where degree of self-esteem is measured by self-evaluation) does not entail the falsehood of the view that lack of self-love (in my depth-motivational understanding) is the root of both hyperobjective and hypersubjective vice.

However, Baumeister appears to express scepticism about such a depth-motivational view. Unfortunately, the target of the scepticism is not that view, but a view in which the violent person with high self-esteem (in his behavioural sense) is 'putting on an act' and just concealing his low evaluation of himself. This he (rightly) questions. On a depth motivational account, however, the neurotic individual has a false sense of reality; there isn't play-acting in the normal sense. Bad educational practices, for example, have caused the false sense of reality. It is this which explains the finding that Baumeister highlights—aggressive people with 'high self-esteem' suffer from 'threatened egotism', where abnormal angry sensitivity to insult, offence, or frustration occurs. These findings are noted by Adler and Horney. It should also be noted that high self-esteem as understood by Baumeister is not part of virtue, for (apart from anything else) it is not part of wisdom. What is wrong with the methods used to generate 'high self-esteem' is the misrepresentation of the good that should be sought—a *genuine* self-love, not (an unmerited, unrealistic) high opinion of oneself.

A second objection claims that the psychological understanding of

---

31 Ibid. 84.

objectivity—its inward focus—trivializes gross immorality such as Hitler's by confusing its cause with its ground. The danger is expressed in the following satirical headlines:

Ravaging of Europe a 'Desperate Cry for Help', Say Therapists ... According to Beaumont, 'This is classic attention-seeking behaviour'.[32]

I would be exposed to this danger if, on my view, the *target* of all virtue is self-love and the promotion of self-love, and what makes something a vice is lack of self-love. However, as I explained in Chapter 6, that is not my view. The ground of Hitler's immorality was maleficence on a very large scale, not lack of self-love. However, a full account of maleficence as a vice and benevolence as a virtue requires an account of practical wisdom enriched by a conception of objectivity (contrasted with hyperobjectivity and hypersubjectivity). For not all harming is vicious nor all benefiting virtuous.

The third objection concerns the role played by psychological theory in the determination of whether or not a particular action manifests hyperobjective or hypersubjective vice. Are we to subject agents to depth-motivational scrutiny on *every* occasion of action for the purpose of determining whether or not an action manifests such vice? The answer is in general, or at least often, we do not subject agents to such scrutiny, and for the same sorts of reasons that John Stuart Mill abhorred the general case by case application of the principle of utility. Mill speaks of the problems of ignorance and self-servingness in the direct application of the principle of utility. Similarly, the assessment of hyperobjective and hypersubjective vice in actual cases will be quite standardly bedevilled by vagueness of theory, ignorance of facts, and overinterpretation. The role of background theory is to provide a crucial plank in the wide reflective equilibrium which yields our virtue-ethical conception of morality. Though not an everyday deliberative tool, it can where appropriate provide an overall critical perspective in individual, institutional, and societal deliberation.[33]

The application of background theory by the relatively ignorant is further complicated by the presence of evil in the world. Jean

---

[32] Scott Dikker (ed.), *The Onion: Our Dumb Century* (New York: Three Rivers Press, 1999), 65.

[33] An excellent example of society-wide assessment in the present kind of terms is Christopher Lasch, *The Culture of Narcissism: American Life in an Age of Diminishing Expectations* (New York: Norton, 1978).

Hampton begins her defence of the moral importance of self-respect with an example of a self-sacrificing mother married to a neglectful and unperceptive husband.[34] It is difficult, however, to describe a mother's sacrifice as exhibiting hyperobjective vice through a failure of self-love when she is surrounded by evil; and the greater the evil, the greater the difficulty. A case much more serious than the (real) case described by Hampton occurred in New Zealand, where a mother of quintuplets was murdered by their stepfather.[35] After years of coping with appalling abuse, serious threats to her children, failure to receive police protection, and failure to have her husband properly diagnosed, she arranged to be separated from her children, who were at that time not letting her out of their sight, knowing that the stepfather was after her with a gun. He shot her before killing himself. There was reason to believe that he could have killed the children as well, and that her actions were aimed at forestalling this. The children described her as a loving and excellent mother whose constant interest was to protect them, even at the cost of her own safety. Was her final act a noble act of sacrifice for the sake of the children, as it appeared to be, or was it the culmination of a series of self-destructive behaviours and option-taking?

The above discussion reminds us that the application of relevant virtue and vice terms is not only difficult; those terms are themselves inherently vague. In this respect, my view differs from that of Samuel Scheffler, whose analysis of the importance of the personal in an adequate moral conception has certain structural similarities to my own. On my view, the demands of self and the demands of the world have to be in some sort of balance[36] if morality is to be objective rather than hypersubjective or hyperobjective. Similarly, for Scheffler, agent-centred prerogatives are integral to a proper conception of morality and do not just circumscribe a territory which can be fenced off from the demands of morality. Scheffler differs from myself, however, in proposing a formula which theoretically removes the inherent vagueness in the idea of 'balancing':

---

[34] 'Selflessness and the Loss of Self'.

[35] Documentary (*Communicado*), TVNZ, 30 August 1998.

[36] The notion of 'balance' is, however, misleading. My view, like Abraham Maslow's, claims that dichotomies such as 'selfish' versus 'selfless', if psychologically uninformed, can be misleading, and can break down when applied to psychologically healthy persons. Both apparently selfish and selfless people can fail to express self-love, while some who may be called selfish are healthily assertive. See further Fromm, *The Art of Loving*.

Suppose ... that each agent were allowed to give M times more weight to his own interests than to the interests of anyone else. This would mean that an agent was permitted to perform his preferred act (call it P), provided that there was no alternative A open to him, such that (1) A would produce a better overall outcome than P, as judged from an impersonal standpoint which gives equal weight to everyone's interests, and (2) the total net loss to others of his doing (P) rather than A was more than M times as great as the net loss to him of doing A rather than P.[37]

In an objection to this proposal, Tim Mulgan postulates a 'Superefficient' Oxfam and an 'Inefficient' Oxfam such that, for any possible degree of sacrifice by an agent, there will be a version of Superefficient Oxfam in which the sacrifices demanded may be greater than we could accept, and a version of Inefficient Oxfam in which the sacrifice may be less than would be expected of a generous person.[38] On my view, the use of virtue and vice terms allows for an abandonment of an algorithmic approach to sacrifice and altruism generally, and thereby avoids the above difficulty. A person may be permitted to stop giving to a Superefficient Oxfam at a point where the donation is generous, and may be censured for miserly or niggardly donations to Inefficient Oxfam (where all aid organizations are similarly inefficient). There is no such value as M. The absence of hyperobjective and hypersubjective vice is not inherently a matter of adhering to some kind of quantitative proportionality between demands of self, near and dear, and distant others, or even more crudely, demands of self versus demands of others. Whether or not meeting the demands of the world is distorted by hyperobjective or hypersubjective vice has to be assessed on complex characterological grounds. Those grounds are qualitative, not quantitative, and judgements of rightness and admirability have to be based on deep and particularistic knowledge of surrounding context. The postulation of M and similar devices may provide clean lines and an illusion of precision, but these merely disguise the messiness within. Let us dispense with clean lines, and employ vocabulary which does not disguise that messiness.

The fourth objection to my account of objectivity questions whether virtue should always be constrained by a requirement of objectivity. Mightn't a dose of hyperobjective vice, at times, be a good thing? Indeed,

---

[37] Samuel Scheffler, 'Prerogatives without Restrictions', *Philosophical Perspectives* 6 (1992), 377–97, at 378.

[38] 'A Non-Proportional Hybrid Moral Theory', *Utilitas* 9 (1997), 291–306.

in imperfect worlds we may on occasion admire and be glad of hyper-objective vice in altruism, and we may admire and be glad of it in creativity.

My reply to this objection is to agree that there are values other than objectivity which demand other forms of virtue, and which may override the value of objectivity itself. One such value may be the avoidance of mediocrity, and if such avoidance is best served by certain forms of hyperobjectivity displayed by certain kinds of people in certain sorts of situations, then so be it. It does not follow, however, that such hyper-objectivity is characteristically part of the fabric of altruistic and creative virtue. In the case of the grandiose artist described by Nietzsche, hyper-objectivity may in the circumstances be part of *creative* virtue *in him*, but that does not make it objective, or part of creative virtue *in all*. Hyperobjective, grandiose creativity is not a virtue in the relatively talent-less. The same point applies to some cases of altruistic behaviour. Some such behaviour may display hyperobjective vice, such as that of the self-effacing solution described above. But again there are values other than self-love and objectivity. One such value is the relief of suffering. As claimed above, virtue is a threshold concept, and in certain contexts, the threshold may be reached where hyperobjective vice is present.

A final problem is this. Isn't the perspective of objectivity proposed here itself excessively transcendent? If it is the case that (more or less) neurotic perspectives on the world are widespread, and if complete free-dom from those perspectives is very difficult to attain, then surely (full) objectivity is on my account as transcendent and unattainable as those criticized. Two replies can be made to this objection. The proposed objective ideal is at least fully human, embedded as it is in a conception of distinctively *human* growth and development. In this respect, it differs from the highly abstract conceptions criticized. Secondly, we may talk of an objectivity that is 'normal', that is, displayed by a person who is 'healthy enough'.

In this chapter, I hope to have presented a conception of objectivity which resolves Nagel's two perspectives problem. We are indeed required to meet the demands of the world without lapsing into yuppie ethics. But we are also required to meet the demands of the world in a way which appropriately respects the subjective. On my conception of objectivity as meeting the demands of the world in ways which express self-love, these requirements are both met. On the one hand, an agent pursuing her own projects may (but need not) display various forms of hypersubjective vice. She may have an excessively strong sense of entitlement, she may feel deprivation too strongly, she may be self-centred in a narcissistic way. On the other hand, an agent may display hyperobjective vice in following an ethics of self-sacrifice, such as (arguably) the mother in Jean Hampton's case. She may display the 'Self-Effacing Solution' such that, to use Nietzsche's phrase, the self 'wilts away.' Another stronger person, performing similar actions, may not, however, display such vice. Note also that I have allowed that we may at times tolerate in altruism the hyperobjective vice of the self-effacing or expansionist sort if such altruism promotes sufficient good. It may be however, that such forms of aid cause subtle harms, because for example, it is unloving or is insensitive to the real needs of people, promotes dependency, humiliates, subtly serves the interests of harmful elites, and so on. That is why it is such a difficult task to determine the nature of virtue in an imperfect world.

9

Demandingness

(i) The Problem of Demandingness

Chapter 8 elaborated the view that objectivity is achieved when one exhibits self-love in meeting the demands of the world. This view may be thought to have the immediate consequence that morality is moderate as opposed to highly demanding or stringent. For if one thinks of morality as highly stringent, if one thinks that the demands of virtue are extremely difficult or uncomfortable or costly, then, surely, morality so conceived would demand hyperobjective vice. One would be excessively transcendent in meeting the demands of the world. However, this conclusion does not immediately follow. It may be the case that due to our imperilled status, having and exhibiting self-love is very difficult. The position on objectivity elaborated in Chapter 8, then, does not have obvious implications for the claims that morality is moderate or stringent. I shall argue, however, for the view that morality is moderate.

Like much else, the issue of demandingness has been driven by agendas embedded in moral-theoretic positions other than virtue ethics. So I shall begin by clarifying the problem of demandingness in ethics, and by arguing against certain prevailing conceptions of that problem. I then propose an understanding of the problem of demandingness more suited to virtue ethics, and conclude that morality is moderate in the sense that agents should not be 'virtuous beyond their strength' on a certain reading of that precept.

We need first to sort out several problems in understanding the claim that morality is 'moderate'. First, there are two notions of ease and difficulty applicable to the issue of the demandingness of morality. The first sense, which appears standard, is that insofar as morality is demanding, it is demanding because the *normal* agent would find it difficult to live up to its demands. Call this sense of demandingness, sense (1). It is then assumed that an adequate morality is more or less demanding in sense (1), and that all (13-year-olds? the old and infirm? the deeply neurotic? those with heavy responsibilities?) are expected to live up to its demands. But virtue ethicists who take seriously at least the spirit of Aristotle's remark, 'The mean is relative to the individual',[1] will find such a conception of demandingness deeply unhelpful if not pernicious. Given that the idea of objectivity as appropriate self-transcendence is understood in terms of expressing self-love, the following possibility arises. One individual who follows a very demanding morality in sense (1) may fail to express self-love, whereas another much stronger individual may follow that same morality and yet express self-love. Accordingly I shall advocate a sense of demandingness that is more agent-relative. Call this, sense (2). The precise way in which that sense is agent-relative will be explored in the remainder of this chapter.

Before we discuss the agent-relativity of demandingness, we need to conceptualize in more detail the issue of demandingness itself. I criticize prevailing modes of conceptualizing the problem before presenting my positive views in sections ii and iii.

A difficulty in speaking of demandingness within a virtue-ethical framework is the pervasive embedding of the problem within a consequentialist framework. Indeed, Shelley Kagan actually defines 'extremism' in these terms:

Extremism is the view that the agent at any time has a moral requirement to perform that act which can reasonably be expected to lead to the best consequences.[2]

However, there could be an extreme (very demanding) kind of virtue ethics, ethics of care, ethics of love, or ethics of creativity. The consequentialist notion of extremism seems natural however, for it seems to flow naturally from consequentialism-friendly notions of objectivity, via the notions of 'impersonality' and 'agent-neutrality'. Here is Kagan:

From this [personal] point of view persons access the world, weighing the relative benefits and disadvantages of various actual or potential changes. The evaluation is relative to the particular person, for it is relative to his particular personal perspective; it is a judgement of what is good from his point of view. Typically it will differ from the agent-neutral evaluation of the impersonal perspective, i.e. an evaluation of what is good objectively.[3]

The moral standpoint is identified with the objective standpoint,

---

[1] *Nicomachean Ethics*, 1106a20–b9.
[2] *The Limits of Morality* (Oxford: Clarendon Press, 1989), 1.   [3] Ibid. 258.

whereas the personal (subjective) standpoint is one 'in which an agent is inclined to give greater weight to his own interests than those interests might merit from the objective point of view'.[4] The view that morality is moderate is then seen as the view that morality permits agents to give greater weight to their own interests than they merit from the objective point of view.

Much mayhem is caused by this conceptualization of the issue. In this section we need to reorient the problem of demandingness by reconceptualizing it. Let me illustrate by employing a useful example of Michael Slote's:

Consider a doctor who wants to help mankind but is for personal reasons particularly affected by the plight of people in India—perhaps he is attracted to Indian art or religion or is very knowledgeable about the history of India.[5]

Imagine that this doctor could save more lives in Africa, and knows this; yet he goes to India. Here is the standard way of conceptualizing the problem of demandingness in relation to this example. Pursuing my project of satisfying my interest in Indian art is a personal project. Saving lives is demanded from the impersonal perspective. Saving the extra lives has more value than pursuing my project, yet (intuitively) personal projects should be integrated with impersonal requirements in the moral point of view. If we reject this intuitively attractive view, morality becomes too demanding. Yet that intuitively attractive view is surely flawed, for it requires that we give disproportionate weight to our personal project (of pursuing a taste in Indian art) given that it has less value than fulfilling the impersonal requirement of saving (the extra) lives.

There are several problems with this conceptualization of the problem of demandingness. First, it assumes a value-centred approach to ethics. As a result, the moderate view is seen as requiring that we give disproportionate weight to a less valuable course of action. That seems irrational, and something in urgent need of explanation and defence. However, if we allow as fundamental bases of moral acknowledgement bonds and status as well as value, pursuing one's passion for art rather than saving the extra lives may well lose its paradoxical air from a moral perspective. The assignment of weight to pursuing one's passion for Indian art will not be based entirely on a value assignment. So the weight

    [4] Ibid. 333.
    [5] 'Satisficing Consequentialism', *Proceedings of the Aristotelian Society*, supp. vol. 58 (1984), 139–63.

given to one's own project in one's practical deliberations may not be the result of egocentric or irrational value assignments, or the result of inventing an arguably problematic category of agent-relative value. Rather, the assignment of weight will be based on considerations of bond rather than value, namely one's bond with oneself (self-love). One manifestation of this bond is one's bonding with one's (worthwhile) projects and interests.

Again, going the extra mile for one's friend or one's colleague when one could promote more value by going the extra mile for lots of strangers will be based on the fact that your friend or colleague has special status as a friend or colleague, and at least in the former case, there is in addition a special kind of bond. Understood thus, the weight given to one's passion for Indian art, or to the interests of one's friend or colleague in one's practical deliberations, will not be seen as 'disproportionate' or 'greater than is merited'. Rather, the weight given will be the result of integrating the demands of value with those of bonds and status. There is no assignment of disproportionate value.

Second, in the orthodox conceptualization of the issue of demandingness, we are invited to contrast the personal point of view with the impersonal view, where, given value-centredness, we tend to assign disproportionate weight to the former. This way of understanding the personal versus the impersonal would not be so objectionable were it not for the slide from 'personal point of view' to 'personal' to 'self-interested'. But imagine the following situation. A mother devotes herself to the care and nurturing of her children in difficult conditions for raising children, thereby neglecting the interests of many strangers' children who are in even worse straits. Assume that she could promote most value if she attended more to the interests of strangers' children. She is then said to give 'disproportionate' weight to the personal point of view. But of course it is objectionable to claim that her point of view is the point of view of the personal understood as the point of view of self-interest. As the 'feminine' ethics of care reminds us, the case is not like the personal project of climbing Kilimanjaro (to use Nagel's example).

As a result of the slide from 'the personal point of view' to 'the personal' to 'the point of view of self-interest', we derive a misconstrual of the problem of demandingness. And this brings us to our third problem. The view that morality is moderate rather than extremely stringent may look unattractive because of the standard linkage between moderateness and a (perhaps) overly large place for self-interest. But the personal point of view, understood in the above way, need have nothing to do with self-interest. It would be absurd to claim that the point of view of the mother of the previous example is the point of view of self-interest, as that idea is commonly understood—with its associations with egoism. Now if self-interest includes the interests of those in whom you have a stake,[6] then the claim is no longer absurd, but it is seriously misleading. Furthermore, such a woman's bond-centred conception of morality may be extremely stringent. Perhaps she puts all projects dear to her heart, such as becoming an opera singer, completely on hold while she both makes herself available emotionally for her children and works extremely hard to feed them or to help them through medical school or law school. In short, the problem of demandingness should not be presented in terms of a false dichotomy between promoting (overall) good and furthering one's own interests. First, requirements of (partialistic) caring can be highly stringent, and second, a morality of care does not have the possibly unattractive flavour of a morality which allows a large place for self-interested pursuits such as climbing mountains, jet skiing, or perfecting the drag flick in field hockey.

How, in more detail, should we conceptualize the issue of demandingness? As I showed in Part I, moral demands come in a great variety of forms. In varying contexts, various virtues focus on value, benefit, status, and bonds; promoting, respecting, honouring, loving, appreciating, creating. However, the world out there is one of limitless possibility of creation and appreciation, there are limitless needs to be fulfilled, and there is limitless opportunity for loving and indeed for respecting. What attitudes should a single individual take towards these varying 'demands of the world'? At the limit, she could see herself as striving to emulate the mystic who appreciates in enormous depth and scope, she could follow Jesus in his capacity to love, she could strive to be a Nietzschean hero in the field of creativity, or a 'moral saint' in the field of helping others or promoting good.

The elucidation of a satisfactory conception of demandingness requires first that we distinguish various aspects of demandingness. Nelson Mandela may have found it harder to eschew the duties of a freedom fighter than to impose sacrifices on his family. But it does not follow from this that the costs of being a freedom fighter for Mandela were less great than the costs that would have befallen him had he been a good

---

[6] In that sense, Nelson Mandela's self-interest includes the interests of all 'his people', namely, black South Africans.

family man and practising lawyer and never joined the ANC. Nor does it
follow that the difficulty of bearing the actual costs of being a freedom
fighter were for him less great than the difficulties he would have borne
had he not been a freedom fighter. The issues of motivational difficulty
in performing an action, costs of performing an action, and difficulty of
bearing the costs of performing an action must all be distinguished. And
it should be recognized that none of those notions is congruent with the
self-interest/altruism distinction. Certain self-interested actions may be
motivationally difficult while altruistic ones may be motivationally easy.
Furthermore, costs to the agent are not just those which bear on her own
interests (narrowly conceived) or even those which bear on near and
dear. They may also be costs borne by those distant others in whose interests the agent has a stake. For example, seeing his people suffer was a
great cost to Mandela.

Given what has been said so far, I prefer to couch the issue of
demandingness in terms different from the 'personal' and the 'impersonal', or self-interest and altruism. I shall claim that a morality is
demanding if it is demanding on the strength of the agent in three
respects: she needs to be very strong to fully cultivate the virtues required
in such a morality; she needs to be very strong to bear well the costs to her
in exercising these virtues; and, given that she herself has not yet cultivated the virtues appropriate to the morality, she needs to be very strong
to motivate herself to perform those acts that the virtues require.

(ii) A Virtue-Ethical Conception of Demandingness

In worlds marred by serious imperfection, what kinds of approach could
a virtue ethicist take to the problem of demandingness? There are three
possible basic approaches.

(1) The standards required for a character trait to be a virtue are
very demanding in the three ways identified at the end of the
last section. Accordingly, generosity is positively saintly,
courage heroic, perseverance tireless, and so on.

(2) The standards required for a trait to be a virtue are such that
their shape is less demanding than in (1). However, the agent is
obligated to rise fairly regularly above her virtue. Obligatory
action is fairly regularly action beyond the call of virtue. Just as
a sorrowing philanthropist has to rise above her virtuously
conducted and felt grief to perform philanthropic acts, so on

the present view, obligatory action is *standardly* demanding even though the standards for *virtue* as character trait are not so demanding. This view denies the standard virtue-ethical claim, derived from Aristotle, that obligatory action is standardly easy or pleasant for the virtuous agent. On the contrary, on this view, it is all too often difficult and unpleasant in an evil world.

(3) The third view, which is my own, is that morality is characteristically moderate, both at the level of virtue and at the level of action.

How might the third view be cashed out? How are we to understand the shape of the virtues in a moderate kind of virtue ethics? In general, as Nietzsche puts it, we should not be virtuous beyond our strength.[7] But what does this mean? This question divides into two. What is the content of the injunction, and what is its formal nature? Consider now the content of the injunction. It does not mean that we should necessarily give a large place to self-interest. For a person in whom self-interest has 'wilted away', it may take strength to be self-protective in a virtuous way, and at a certain point we may say that certain further efforts to think of herself first, in constructive ways, may be overtaxing of her strength. On the other hand, virtuously strong altruism may not give a large place to 'self-interest' at all.

The injunction basically claims that virtue is tailored in some way to one's *strength* (rather than self-interest). This has both a self-regarding and an other-regarding aspect, and a dynamic and a non-dynamic aspect. Both these aspects are intertwined. Take the second aspect. When we say that virtue is tailored in some way to one's strength, we do not mean that there is or should be no progression towards greater strength, a progression which would, in the longer term, make for a greater level of, for example, temperance, benevolence, or perseverance in the pursuit of worthwhile goals. Perfectionistic tendencies in weak agents may be expressive of vice. But they may also be expressive of desirable efforts in the agent, which help her to greater strength and greater levels of virtue in the long haul. So the claim that virtue is tailored in some way to one's strength is not meant to entail that an agent should not strive for greater strength. However, such efforts should not have sufficiently bad other-regarding harmful effects. Efforts to be courageous and so on 'beyond one's strength' may backfire in various ways. For example, assume

---

[7] *Thus Spoke Zarathustra*, 4, 'On the Higher Man', 13.

(counterfactually) that Mandela was a poor negotiator and persuader. He should not be virtuous beyond his strength in taking on (as he in fact did) the underground running of the military arm of the ANC. Tailoring virtue to one's strength, provided that is compatible with making room for (gradually) improving one's strength, is basically a requirement that one's virtue be constrained by one's effectiveness, the desideratum of expressing self-love, and the availability of other agents who will do a job for which one is not very adequate. The Nietzschean injunction not to be virtuous beyond your strength is intended, then, to convey two things: first, one should not overreach oneself in ways which express and display self-contempt, and second, in emulating the virtuousness of the strong, one may cause more harm than good.

We should not confuse the Nietzschean injunction not to be virtuous beyond one's strength with an injunction not to be virtuous beyond what is compatible with one's health and flourishing. Indeed, as Richard Schacht points out, Nietzsche was far from holding that health is the highest value.[8] We saw in Chapter 4 that it is possible for a trait of character to be a virtue in an agent, even where there is no guarantee that possession and exercise of the trait will conduce to the flourishing of the agent, and indeed there may be a high probability that it will not. Tenacity, perseverance, indefatigability are virtues in a freedom fighter fighting for justice, but may significantly reduce the prospects of personal flourishing of that fighter. And such a reduction is not just a matter of ill luck (unless one thinks it a matter of ill luck that we do not live in a perfect world unmarred by evil and conflict). Note also that this claim, as I showed above, is quite consistent with the claim that these virtues may give the life of a freedom fighter meaning. The injunction not to be virtuous beyond your strength, then, can apply to virtues inimical to personal flourishing.

(iii) Perfectionism as a Virtue

The view that one should not be virtuous beyond your strength suggests that there is (paradoxically) a virtue associated with self-improvement.[9]

8 *The Gay Science*, 120. See Richard Schacht, *Making Sense of Nietzsche* (Urbana, Ill.: University of Illinois Press, 1995), p. 219.

9 I discuss this virtue in 'Satisficing and Perfectionism in Virtue Ethics', in Michael Byron (ed.), *Satisficing and Maximizing: Moral Theoretic Perspectives on Practical Reasoning* (Cambridge: Cambridge University Press, forthcoming).

To gain greater understanding of the content of the injunction 'Do not be virtuous beyond your strength', we need to investigate further the nature of this virtue, which I call (the virtue of) perfectionism. Let us first gain a schematic understanding.

Employing the useful distinction between the thin and thick conception of a virtue[10] alluded to in Chapter 6 (where the thin conception simply states a virtue's field and understands the virtue as being well disposed in regard to that field, whereas the thick conception gives an account of what it is to be well disposed in regard to that field), I understand perfectionism as a virtue as follows. The virtue of perfectionism on the thin account is simply understood as the disposition of being well disposed with respect to striving for excellence. Rival conceptions of perfectionism as a virtue differ on what is the correct thick account.

Given a virtue-theoretic framework, a natural understanding of perfectionism as a virtue is that it is a disposition to strive to emulate the acts of supremely virtuous agents. But as a thick account of a *virtue* of perfectionism, this account is questionable. If perfectionism in this sense were a virtue, it would be natural to understand obligatory acts as ones performed by supremely virtuous agents, and it would not be permitted knowingly to fail to perform such acts when these were in one's power and known to be so. In this case, virtue ethics would be a very demanding moral theory.

I shall argue that this natural virtue-theoretic understanding of perfectionism is not a correct thick account of perfectionism as a virtue. Being well disposed with respect to striving for excellence need not involve emulating the acts of supremely virtuous agents, for two broad sorts of reason. First, one may be in various ways imperfect, and the striving by imperfect agents for excellence may be a dynamic process, where direct imitation of the supremely virtuous may be a flawed way of improving oneself, for one overreaches one's strength. Second, one may be 'ordinary' in another kind of way—leading a kind of life that is not the kind of life of the supremely virtuous. I shall argue that the features which make for *virtuous* perfectionism show such perfectionism not to be excessively demanding.

Like many similar terms referring to dispositions—'being trusting', 'loyal', 'honest', 'being laid back', 'being positive', 'being assertive'—'perfectionism' is not straightforwardly a name of a virtue or a vice.

---

10 See Nussbaum, 'Non-Relative Virtues: An Aristotelian Approach'.

'Perfectionism' as such normally just means a disposition to strive for perfection or excellence, but this notion should be distinguished from the thin account of perfectionism *as a virtue*, which is *being well disposed* with respect to striving for perfection or excellence. So it is perfectionism that has certain features which is the virtue. Similarly, 'improper' perfectionism is a vice, trust that has certain features is the virtue, 'proper' loyalty is the virtue, being positive in a way that does not involve suppression of the critical faculties is the virtue, a tendency to tell the truth appropriately, non-readiness to lie or mislead, is the virtue. What is required is a thick account of perfectionism as a virtue.

In questioning whether an act of doing good for someone manifests perfectionistic virtue, we need to ask, for example: does a putative exercise of benevolence constitute a sub-par effort manifesting (anti-perfectionistic) vice? Does a putative exercise of benevolence in which an agent strives to be as good as she can be manifest 'improper perfectionism' as a vice, or perfectionistic virtue? The virtue-ethical task, then, is to give a substantive account of such virtue and vice. One needs to ask: under what conditions should we praise a person for her virtue in her setting of, striving for, and adhering to, high standards, and when should we regard such strivings as in some way problematic? Under what conditions should we condemn a person's action as shoddy, lazy, self-indulgent, selfish; and under what conditions should we praise it as strong or self-protective?

In determining whether a striving for perfection is a mark of virtue, it is not enough simply to look at what is done, what is achieved, or what are the outcomes. In virtue ethics, virtue is also a matter of what is going on inside the individual, and once this is understood, we can see why psychologists do not necessarily regard perfectionism as a virtue. According to Karen Horney, perfectionism, as a trait, can be a vice, being a mark of the 'expansionist' type:

Such a person identifies himself with his standards. This type feels superior because of his high standards, moral and intellectual, and on this basis looks down on others. His arrogant contempt for others, though, is hidden—from himself as well—behind polished friendliness, because his standards prohibit such irregular feelings.[11]

In such a type, according to Horney, perfectionist drives are expressive of 'self-condemnation', which can be externalized in the demand that

---

[11] *Neurosis and Human Growth*, 196

others live up to his standards. The failure to meet this demand provokes his hostility. The problem, of course (which is of a type that Horney recognizes generally in her work), is distinguishing the facts of perfectionistic vice from those of perfectionistic virtue, whose exercise is occasioned by states of the world which merit condemnation rather than by the neurotic needs of the individual. A person with high standards, which she trumpets and attempts to live by, may be living in an anti-intellectual, philistine society where mediocrity flourishes. Or she may be living in a society full of corruption where virtues of integrity and decency are in abeyance. Or she may think that efforts to promote the interests of the worse off are compromising valued standards within the academic and other fields. Determining whether perfectionistic strivings are a mark of virtue or vice requires a sophisticated understanding of the relationships between the individual's own psyche, the facts of her behaviour in a specific context, the social milieu in which she operates, and her attitudes towards that milieu.

To illustrate this point, consider an example of Horney's. Having claimed that the demands for perfection of a self-effacing type may be just as high as those of the expansive types, she describes typical behaviours of the former type. 'Even after a good performance (perhaps in giving a party or delivering a lecture) they still will emphasise the fact that they forgot this or that, that they did not emphasise clearly what they meant to say, that they were too subdued or too offensive, etc.'[12] Whether or not such pieces of behaviour are manifestations of perfectionistic (self-effacing) vice depends on such facts as whether these behaviours are part of a pattern of self-berating behaviour where the objects of displeasure are non existent or trivial, whether the failures in presentation are perceived to be important (because the material conveyed is perceived to be important), whether those perceptions are themselves well founded, and so on.

Even if it is clear that some perfectionistic strivings are expressive of a weak compensatory need to assert superiority, however, it may also be the case that hostility at, say, decline in standards and mediocratization is well warranted. It may be a matter of fine judgement whether such expression should be seen overall as a mark of integrity, courage, and respect for the value of excellence, or whether it bears too much the hallmark of weakness. It should also be noted that self-love is not the whole of virtue, and whether or not perfectionistic strivings are seen as a mark

<hr />

12 Ibid. 317.

of virtue in, for example, generosity, industriousness, integrity, courage, or justice depends in part on what is promoted by such strivings. If the manner of such striving is excessively hostile, for example, efforts at being a role model of excellence may backfire; on the other hand, a more judiciously displayed respect for excellence may shake complacency or compliant acceptance of prevailing norms. Given the complexities outlined, it is clear that perfectionistic strivings to emulate the acts of supremely virtuous agents are not necessarily expressive of virtue.

Given these complexities, too, it is not easy to determine what it is to be virtuously perfectionistic. Consider the following cases:

(1) An artist, highly talented, pursuing the highest values in his art, deserts his wife and family.

(2) An artist, highly talented, unencumbered by dependents, has grandiose, highly narcissistic motivations and thoughts.

(3) A hobby artist, of meagre talent, nonetheless strives to do the best she can in her art, neglecting her children rather seriously.

(4) A career philosopher, talented, but whose work will not be widely read for a long period of time, works very hard at her research, neglects her family somewhat, but none are 'scarred for life'.

(5) A career philosopher, highly talented, publishes very little, on the grounds that she is never satisfied with work in progress.

Hundreds of these kinds of cases could be given—I will spare the reader. At least some agents in the examples exhibit, at least on the surface, various perfectionistically oriented virtues—artistic passion, devotion (to worthwhile ideals and tasks), perseverance, determination, industriousness, (proper) humility, and possibly courage. None of these virtues should be belittled as 'non-moral', given that they are directed at worthwhile ends. Whether the perfectionist strivings should be seen as marks of virtuous perfectionism depends on hosts of factors, including depth motivations, intentions, degree of wisdom, including self-knowledge such as knowledge of one's strength and talents, seriousness of effects on others and the extent to which one has responsibilities to those others, the worthwhileness of the ends to which one is devoted, and the likelihood of one's success in achieving them, even with effort.

I have shown how a proper understanding of perfectionism as a virtue, which gives content to Nietzsche's warning 'Do not be virtuous beyond your strength', is compatible with the idea that a virtue ethics can be moderate. To avoid confusion concerning the commitments of my view on demandingness, we need now to consider the formal nature of the injunction 'Do not be virtuous beyond your strength'. The injunction is not a universal prescription: it is more in the nature of a warning, and a depiction of morality as a whole. It is not absolute, and certainly not so in imperfect worlds. A claim that morality is moderate is a claim about morality as a whole. It does not entail that the exercise of virtue beyond one's strength is never admirable, and never required in certain contexts. To infer, from the claim that morality as a whole is moderate, that morality never requires or finds admirable 'supererogatory' acts, is to commit the fallacy of division. This point takes care of Wolf's criticism of Scheffler's claim that morality is moderate:

If such an ideal [that morality is moderate] is to be understood to lie at the heart of morality, however, it is hard to see what sense is to be made of supererogation . . . whatever is admirable about a more selflessly altruistic life would on this view not be morally admirable. Indeed it might be morally inferior to a life in which mere personal interests are given greater weight.[13]

I agree with Wolf that it would be odd indeed to deny that highly altruistic acts that are very demanding on the agent are never morally admirable. The point is that a claim that 'morality' as a whole is moderate can allow for very demanding acts to be sometimes morally admirable and indeed required. There are two kinds of case. First, though the agent is 'virtuous beyond her strength' and has to act enkratically, her action is admirable because in various ways effective, or showing motivational excellence even if not excellence of character. In the second kind of case, the act of virtue beyond her strength may be effective, indeed highly so, but betrays the kinds of resentments and weakness displayed by Zarathustra when he decides to retreat into his cave. But unlike Zarathustra's ineffective attempts to discharge his gifts, we assume the act is effective. Indeed, we might find such an act admirable in an imperfect world, even if it betrays weakness. The assumption that such acts may be effective rejects the extreme pessimism apparently expressed by Wittgenstein: 'Just improve yourself, that is the only thing you can do to better the world'.[14] Such acts may be admirable in another way. They may be expressive of attempts in the agent to gain greater strength.

[13] Susan Wolf, 'Moral Judges and Human Ideals: A Discussion of *Human Morality*', *Philosophy and Phenomenological Research* 55 (1995), 957–62, at 960.

[14] Ray Monk, *Ludwig Wittgenstein: The Duty of Genius* (London: Cape, 1990), 213 (see also 211, 228).

There are problems then with the idea that each action should be tailored to or be expressive of the current strength of the individual. Certainly, one's altruism is flawed if it exhibits the ills and weaknesses to which philosophers as apparently far apart as feminists and Nietzsche have drawn our attention, and for this reason morality as a whole should encapsulate the dictum 'Do not be virtuous beyond your strength'. As I have suggested, however, the general dictum does not translate into a universal requirement. We must make room for the appropriateness of supererogatory acts which may be effective, not damaging (or excessively so), and may be stepping stones to greater strength in the agent.

10

Virtue and Constraints

(i) Introduction

In the previous chapter, I gave a virtue-ethical understanding of demandingness; in this chapter I propose a virtue-ethical understanding of constraints. Again, the virtue-ethical understanding is premised on the account of objectivity presented in Chapter 8. Central to this understanding is the expression of self-love in meeting the demands of the world. As far as demandingness is concerned, that idea was translated into a characteristic (though not universal) requirement not to be perfectionistic in being virtuous beyond one's strength. As far as constraints are concerned, expressing self-love (one's bonding with oneself) rationalizes the injunction not to dirty one's hands. However, a full defence of constraints is not limited to a defence of this injunction. A correct and full understanding of the basis of constraints requires not only that we understand the role played by expressing self-love in rationalizing constraints, but also that we understand the complex nature of meeting the demands of the world. In particular, we need to appreciate that virtuous acknowledgement of those demands requires not only that we promote good, but that we acknowledge bonds to others and respect others' status. It will be argued that those forms of acknowledgement, too, will directly underpin constraints.

Let us first formulate the problem of constraints. Samuel Scheffler expresses the problem of the rationality of constraints in the following terms. He claims that constraints strike at the heart of a powerful conception of rationality, namely,

if one accepts the desirability of a certain goal being achieved, and if one has a choice between two options, one of which is certain to accomplish the goal better than the other, then it is, *ceteris paribus*, rational to choose the former over the latter.[1]

---

[1] 'Restrictions, Rationality, and the Virtues', in S. Scheffler (ed.), *Consequentialism and Its Critics* (Oxford: Oxford University Press, 1988), 241–60, at 252.

Constraints violate this idea of rationality,

for they appear to identify certain kinds of actions as morally objectionable or undesirable, in the sense that it is morally preferable that no such actions should occur than that any should, but then tell us that there are situations in which we must act in such a way that a greater rather than a lesser number of these actions are actually performed.[2]

Such requirements are 'constraints'. I shall accept Scheffler's way of putting the problem. Constraints do indeed violate Scheffler's 'powerful' conception of rationality.

However, in Chapter 2, I undermined the apparent truisms which support this 'powerful' conception. In particular, I rejected the apparent truism that we are beholden to a moral standard requiring us to see to it that more desirable goals are achieved rather than less. That standard presupposes the 'Hegemony of Promotion Thesis', which itself relies on a failure to appreciate the plurality of modes of moral acknowledgement proper to the human species. Though one such mode is the promotion of desirable goals, others are not tied to a task-oriented conception of morality (such as appreciation, receptivity, and respect). Yet others, though vehicles of change, possess standards of excellence which are not tied exclusively to the *promotion* of valuable ends (whatever these may be). These include creativity and love.

Fundamentally, I argue that constraints are inherent in virtuous behaviour insofar as they are inherent in many of the modes of moral acknowledgement constituting the profiles of the virtues.

The account to be provided accepts the legitimacy of a claim that it is preferable that fewer rather than more morally objectionable actions occur. I shall deny, however, that accepting this claim commits one to the further claim that one is *never* subject to prohibitions (whether absolute or non-absolute) against ensuring that fewer rather than more morally objectionable actions occur. The seeds of my defence of constraints were sown in Part 1. There I defended the view that ethics should not be seen as solely value-centred, but as centred also on bonds, status, and good. Specifically, I shall claim that constraints are sourced in the expression of bonds (whether a bond with oneself or others) and the respect of status (of various sorts). The thought that morality is based exclusively in value makes it easy to think that it is morally imperative to bring about more of what is valuable (such as the reduction of morally objectionable

---

2 Ibid.

acts) than less of what is valuable. This is the root idea behind the putatively paradoxical nature of constraints. The admission of bonds and
status as fundamental bases of moral acknowledgement, however,
allows one to recognize love and respect as fundamental aspects of the
profiles of the virtues, and with that recognition comes the realization
that producing more of what is valuable rather than less is only one moral
desideratum amongst many. The failure to recognize expression, creativity, love, and respect as fundamental aspects of the profiles of the virtues,
and bonds and status as fundamental bases of moral acknowledgement
recognized in the virtues, leads to a failure to see constraints as rational.

A tendentious connection between objectivity and a certain problematic conception of agent-neutrality is part of the explanation for this failure. This problematic conception both is value-centred and assumes the
hegemony of promotion as a mode of moral acknowledgement. If
agent-neutrality is tied to the claim that all agents similarly have reason to
promote value, then it is hardly surprising that the conception of rationality
identified by Scheffler is thought to be powerful and plausible.

According to F. M. Kamm, for example, 'an agent-neutral value is a
value that all agents similarly have reason to promote'.[3] But right here is
the fateful move—the subtle according of primacy to promotion. Now
Nagel's original definition of agent-neutrality does not tie agent-
neutrality to promotion of value: 'If a reason can be given a general form
which does not include an essential reference to the person who has it, it
is an *agent-neutral* reason'.[4] Nagel then provides an *example* of an agent-
neutral reason which is concerned with promoting value: 'For example, if
it is a reason for anyone to do or want something that it would reduce the
amount of wretchedness in the world, then that is a neutral reason'.[5]

However, if agent-neutrality is concerned with the idea of universality of reason, as Nagel's definition suggests, we could claim that an agent-
neutral value is one that all agents similarly have reason to honour, or one
that all agents similarly have reason to express, or one that all agents similarly have reason to love, and so forth. Similarly, we might talk of agent-
neutral bonds as ones that all agents similarly have reason to have. One
may wish to argue, for example, that a bond of love with God or a bond

---

[3] 'Non-Consequentialism, the Person as an End-in-Itself, and the Significance of Status',
Philosophy and Public Affairs 21 (1992), 354–89, at 382.

[4] *The View from Nowhere*, 152.

[5] Ibid. 152–3.

of agape or respect with each and every human being are agent-neutral in this sense, whereas bonds of friendship or eros with given individuals are not. Alternatively, instead of agent-neutral values or bonds, we may talk of agent-neutral reasons to have bonds of given types or respond in given types of way to given values. So one could say (not without controversy) that everyone similarly has reason to have friends or to love with passion some individual(s) or other. If a requirement of morality is that (some) of its reasons apply to all, then we should recognize that not all such reasons pertain to the promotion of value.

I do not want to commit myself, however, to the claim that agent-neutrality (or agent-relativity) should be tied to the idea of agent-neutral or agent-relative reason.[6] A virtue ethics may align itself with David McNaughton's and Piers Rawling's view that constraints should be understood in terms of agent-relative rules (as opposed to agent-relative value or agent-relative reasons). These can admit the existence of agent-relative virtue rules such as 'Be just oneself' (which need not be universal in form).

A pluralistic virtue ethics would accept what McNaughton and Rawling call threshold constraints, where an agent 'is permitted to breach the constraint where the detrimental effects of sticking to it would be too severe'.[7] Furthermore, as I claim in Chapter 11, these constraints may function in a holistic way: they may not always have positive valence in the assessment of actions as right. Such virtue rules, according to McNaughton and Rawling, allow for individuals to share the aim of promoting justice, but in doing so each must ensure (characteristically) that she is just herself.[8] The profile of the virtue of justice allows for this, since a requirement to be just oneself can be based on respect for others in virtue of status, and self-love (see below).

Some virtue rules are fleshed out in ways that are relative to roles, and to culture (all similarly have reason to respect all others by being polite in normal circumstances, but culture will appropriately vary on what politeness demands). Again, some reasons and virtues are relative to age or to psychic strength. It is not the case that all adult agents have reason to

---

6 For criticism of Nagel's notion of agent-neutrality/relativity, see David McNaughton and Piers Rawling, 'Agent-Relativity and the Doing–Happening Distinction', *Philosophical Studies* 63 (1991), 167–85.

7 Ibid. 168.

8 'Value and Agent-Relative Reasons', *Utilitas* 7 (1995), 31–47, at 47.

manifest the motive of child-like trust towards human beings, but that is an excellence (if not a full-blown virtue) in children.[9] (The precise delineation of that virtue will vary according to the conditions of a society, notably the evils contained with it. In many societies now the attitude of child-like trust towards at least strangers is being discouraged in children.)

Finally, some reasons of virtue, not capturable in rules necessarily, are relative to historical, temperamental, and other particularities of an individual's life. For example, although all agents have reason to express or exhibit self-love, the way those reasons figure in the particularities of individuals' lives is relative to the individual. For example, my expressing self-love—a demand of bonding with myself—gives me a moral permission to spend twenty dollars watching New Zealand lose yet again at cricket when I could be spending the same amount of money to reduce the amount of wretchedness in the world. But this reason need not be shared by the average American visitor to New Zealand, or those New Zealand cricket lovers who can no longer bear to see New Zealand lose. Similarly (a Green might want to say), all similarly have reason to appreciate nature. But (unless she is really hard line) she will not wish to say that (regardless of tastes, interests, culture) all similarly have reason to appreciate this virus, this spider, rats, or even roses.

In this chapter, I do not wish to penetrate deeply the thickets of agent-neutrality and agent-relativity—thickets which have not yet been invaded by virtue-ethical species. My task in the following sections is to develop bond- and status-centred defences of constraints.

(ii) Constraints: Value versus Bond, Self versus Other

Constraints or agent-centred restrictions 'place limits on what each of us may do in the pursuit of any goal, including the maximization of the good'.[10] In this section, I defend those constraints which are based on the demands of bonding. These demands place limits on what we may do in the pursuit of goals. The way these demands rationalize constraints is complex. It is common to distinguish agent-focused from patient- or victim-focused rationales for constraints, but this dichotomy distorts the

---

[9] See further Slote, *Goods and Virtues.*

[10] McNaughton and Rawling, 'Agent-Relativity and the Doing–Happening Distinction', 168.

discussion. The rationale of many types of restriction is *relationship-*focused: the pursuit of goals may violate in an egregious way a *bond* with another. Not all constraints based on bonds are like this, however: some are grounded in an agent's bond with herself, and these restrictions can indeed be said to have an agent-focused rationale. I shall claim, then, that constraints based on bonds are grounded in two forms of asymmetry:

(A) A general asymmetry between the demands of bonding with others, and the demands of value.

(B) A general asymmetry between self and others.[11]

The former ground of constraints is relationship focused; the latter agent-focused.

As we shall see, the first kind of asymmetry needs to be supplemented by the second kind if constraints based on bonds are to be completely grounded. Let us now discuss the first kind of asymmetry. Many kinds of constraint are rationalized by bonds of love or concern between individuals. As we saw in Chapter 2, reasons of bonding are of a different order from reasons of value, and the former are not necessarily proportionate to reasons of value. This lack of proportionality rationalizes relationship-centred constraints. Assume that I am a kidney surgeon, and that two of my children can be saved only if I take both kidneys from my third. Assume that a state of affairs in which the former two children are alive and the latter dead is less disvaluable than a state of affairs in which both the former are dead (after protracted illness) and the latter alive. To kill one of my children painlessly in his sleep in order to be used as a 'resource' is an extraordinarily serious violation of a love bond between parent and child. Requirements of bonding demand that one not do this, but that one grieve in great sorrow for the children who die as a result of inability to treat. Demands of bonding, then, do not track demands of value.

It might be replied that it is an even higher value that one not violate bonds in killing an innocent to save more innocents, but that one is permitted to kill in such circumstances to prevent more similar killings. If this reply is accepted, constraints may be defended along different lines (see below).

The way bonds of love and concern feature in constraints depends on

11 See further Michael Stocker, 'Agent and Other: Against Ethical Universalism', *Australasian Journal of Philosophy* 54 (1976), 206–20.

the way they feature in the profiles of the various virtues. Bonds of love for one's child are stronger and carry more moral weight than weaker bonds of concern for colleagues. Virtues associated with eros and commitment in marriage will provide more severe constraints on what one can do in the service of overall good than virtues of friendship which involve concern and appreciation rather than a stronger form of love. Consider: Juliette and Julian love each other, and are planning to marry and have children. Neither Juliette nor Julian are expected to make much of a mark on the world. Now the fact that a rival suitor, an important medical researcher, is likely to become seriously depressed and be unable to work effectively should the marriage take place, will not undermine constraints inherent in a virtue whose profile is centrally constituted by love.[12] On the other hand, say Julian merely cares for Juliette (or indeed, only respects and appreciates her without even caring for her), and wishes to marry her primarily for her money, we might well reverse our view about the wrongness of the marriage, not primarily because of considerations of consequences promoted, but because of the differing nature of the responses manifested.

I have grounded the possibility of constraints on asymmetries between value and bonding. The question arises: how does one integrate competing demands of value and bonding?

The demands of bonding and the demands of value are integrated by the application of virtue and vice concepts to given situations. For example, assume that an agent appreciates that certain policies conducive to growth of an organization maximally promote value, or that certain actions are maximally creative of value. However, she eschews these policies on grounds that they disrupt bonds, whether collegial, familial, or more generally. In one context, the agent may be (justifiably) accused of conservatism, pessimism, and negative thinking, or narrowness of focus and vision, which cause her to over-emphasize the costs of stress-inducing 'growth' of an organization. In another context, her opponents may have the epistemic and attitudinal vices of closed-mindedness and insensitivity to the well-being of families, or the more deep-seated power-related vices of the 'desire for mastery'. The question of the correct application of these and other vice and virtue concepts is usually a

---

[12] For an excellent discussion of virtues of love, particularly as applied to marriage, see Martin, *Love's Virtues*.

matter of controversy requiring great sensitivity to facts and outcomes, and chances of agreement are not always high.

The asymmetry between bonds and value does not completely rationalize constraints. It is certainly bad for me to violate my bonds, but it is also bad that others violate theirs. A constraint may require me not to violate my bonds, but perhaps at the cost of lots of others violating equally strong bonds. A question presses: what is so special about *my* bonds as opposed to others' bonds? The answer to this question involves a recognition not only of an asymmetry between value and bonds, but between self and other. The latter asymmetry is based on expressing self-love—expressing a bond *with oneself*—as a distinctive form of moral acknowledgement. The importance of expressing a bond with oneself underlies the intuition that one is not a (mere) instrument for the promotion of value, even where that value is the minimization of morally objectionable behaviour, including the violation of bonds.

There is no assumption that, in refraining from violating one's own bonds, one is claiming that there is something special about one's own bonds, as if, somehow, they had greater value or merit. Rather, in not violating one's own bonds, or more generally, in not dirtying one's own hands, one is expressing self-love. Notice that not all forms of not dirtying one's hands are (successful or genuine) expressions of self-love. Some such actions, as we have seen, may be expressive of a range of vices—neurotic pride, narcissism, grandiosity, cowardice, squeamishness, or (unhealthy) selfishness or egocentricity.

The importance of one's own agency, grounded as it is in the idea of the importance of bonding with oneself, is not tantamount to the idea that 'each of us is especially responsible for what he does rather than for what other people do'.[13] The idea of bonding with oneself is understood in terms of expressing self-love, which in my account has similarities with the idea of self-respect. How the notion connects with the idea of personal responsibility is another issue. Some forms of taking responsibility for what others do is a manifestation of virtue (e.g. parental virtue, or friendship, or compassion). Other forms manifest vice such as domination, (vicious) paternalism, hostility-based resentment, inability to trust, and parental vice such as lack of respect for one's children's independence.

13 Bernard Williams, in J. J. C. Smart and B. Williams, *Utilitarianism For and Against* (New York: Cambridge University Press, 1973), 117.

(iii) Honouring

It has been thought that a value-based conception of ethics could accommodate constraints by allowing for honouring as a mode of moral acknowledgement. The term 'honouring' has been explicated by Philip Pettit. Here, Pettit introduces the concept of honouring thus:

Suppose I decide, in a moment of intellectualist enthusiasm, that what matters above all in human life is that people understand the history of their species and their universe. How ought I to respond to this perceived value? Is my primary responsibility to honour it in my own life, bearing witness to the importance of such understanding by devoting myself to it? Or is my primary responsibility rather to promote such understanding generally, say by spending most of my time on proselytizing and politics, giving only the hours I cannot better spend to the development of my own understanding? Is the proper response to the value one of promoting its general realization, honouring it in my own actions only when there is nothing better I can do to promote it?[14]

In this passage, it looks as if it is the case that to honour a value X is to be X, or bear witness to X in one's own life, as opposed to promoting these responses generally. If this is so, David McNaughton's and Piers Rawling's understanding of the notion of honouring X as:

To honor X is to strive to be as X as possible oneself[15]

seems the correct reading. As McNaughton and Rawling point out however, it is not clear what it is to honour some values such as happiness and freedom in this sense. Is to honour freedom to be free oneself, as opposed to not violating the freedom of others? Is to honour happiness to be happy oneself, as opposed to not rendering others unhappy? Pettit's writings suggest a second way of understanding the idea of honouring when he claims that the important thing (for a deontologist) is not to produce the goods but to keep your hands clean.[16] Such an understanding of honouring value fits better with the idea of a constraint. If the motivation for the idea of *honouring* value is that of a constraint, we should understand honouring value not in terms of instantiating it in one's own life, but rather in terms of the idea of not dirtying one's own hands in regard to that value. In the case of justice that means one should not be unjust oneself. In the case of health and freedom, to *dirty* one's hands in

---

14 'Consequentialism', 230–1.
15 'Honoring and Promoting Values', *Ethics* 102 (1992), 835–43.
16 'Consequentialism', 233.

regard to those values is not to fail to be healthy or free oneself. It is rather to destroy the health and freedom of others (and perhaps oneself). Perhaps all values can be honoured in this sense.

If the rationale of honouring is, however, that we should instantiate the value honoured in our own lives, then to honour a value V is to be V oneself or to instantiate V. On this account, though, it seems not all values can be honoured by all agents and some, such as sublimity, may not be able to be honoured by any agents. I cannot honour beauty if I cannot myself be or become beautiful, I cannot honour intelligence if I cannot be intelligent myself, and maybe no human agent can be herself sublime.

However, even if I can't honour beauty or intelligence in this sense, I can honour those values in the sense of not dirtying one's hands in respect of a value. I can honour beauty by not destroying, marring, or rendering ugly beautiful things. I can honour intelligence in not harming intelligent people by constant displays of resentment. It seems then that we should understand honouring not in terms of instantiating a value in one's own life, but as follows:

To honour a value V is to not dirty one's hands in respect of V.

Not only is it the case that one cannot instantiate all values in one's own life, but it is not the case that requirements to instantiate values in oneself always have something to do with constraints. Admittedly the requirement to be just oneself undercuts requirements to promote justice by being unjust. But a requirement to be beautiful or healthy oneself has nothing to do with undercutting requirements to be ugly or unhealthy oneself in order to promote beauty or health.

I have suggested a sense of 'honouring' as a form of moral acknowledgement, which links it to the idea of a constraint. However, the appeal to honouring as such does nothing to further our understanding of the force or rationale of constraints. To understand that rationale, we need to know why it is rational to not dirty one's hands. It is rational to not dirty one's hands if such behaviour is appropriately expressive of a bond with oneself or others. This is not to say that all expressions of bonds are virtuous: as I have claimed, some manifest narcissism, callousness, neurotic pride, cowardice, (vicious) favouritism of various sorts, and so forth. The application of terms referring to these states is neither easy nor free of controversy and indeterminacy. Not only are details of context and situation often unknown and complex, but the nature of virtue and vice itself is a deep matter, not assessable simply by the methods of conceptual analysis.

(iv) Constraints and Status

Bonds, whether to self or others, are not the only grounding for constraints. Frances M. Kamm has grounded constraints in the status of humans as inviolable,[17] and insofar as bonds involve a 'coming close' and inviolability involves respect as 'keeping one's distance', it would appear that bonds cannot ground all constraints. However, inviolability is not the sole basis for status-centred constraints. On Kamm's view, a type of entity is more or less inviolable, and its inviolability seems to depend on the degree to which it possesses the property or properties on which the inviolability is resultant, namely rationality.[18] This suggests that a type of entity that was more rational (for example) would be more inviolable, hence would have higher moral status, and hence be less vulnerable to being used as resources for the sake of greater good. Michael Otsuka thinks that despite the fact that degree of inviolability is supposed to track the degree to which properties forming the resultance base of inviolability are possessed, the moral principles that apply to human beings would also apply to superhuman beings who were more rational.[19] However, this is not necessarily the case. If we think of constraints in terms of the application of bond- and status-centred virtues, and if we think of status-centred virtues as not necessarily concerned with inviolability alone, the application of these virtues cannot be determined in the absence of considerable knowledge about the nature of those beings and their relationship to us.

Another objection of Otsuka's is this. According to this objection, Kamm's justification of constraints in terms of status as inviolable does not generalize to all constraints. He gives the example of not letting a cheating student go unpunished in order to catch five further cheating students. The justification for this constraint does not appeal to status as inviolable. However, appeal to status does not entail appeal to status as inviolable. There are all kinds of status characteristics which license constraints. One such characteristic is status as person deserving of punishment. To respect that status is to treat a person in a way that befits that status, and to respect a person having that status is to keep a distance in a way that befits that status. (Hence punishment should not be cruel or excessive.)

---

[17] See her *Morality, Mortality*, vol. ii (New York: Oxford University Press, 1996).

[18] Ibid. 273–7.

[19] 'Kamm on the Morality of Killing', *Ethics* 108 (1997), 197–207.

We have not yet explained why various forms of respect for status (whether or not based on inviolability) give rise to constraints. The reason is that respect, like love, is a mode of moral acknowledgement that is particularized. Just as you cannot *love* an individual if you are prepared to sacrifice that individual whenever greater good is known to occur, so you cannot *respect* an individual having a certain status (as e.g. one deserving of punishment) if you are prepared to forgo what befits that status whenever you know that forgoing this would promote a great number of acts similarly befitting of status. Respect and love, as distinctive modes of moral acknowledgement, are focused on individuals rather than the aggregate. Hence, if the dominant aspect of the profile of benevolence is love (of individuals), it cannot be an aggregative virtue; if the dominant aspect of the profile of justice is respect of individuals in ways which befit their status (as e.g. inviolable, a friend, a client, one's child, one deserving of punishment), then justice is not an aggregative virtue. And if this is so, benevolence and justice are virtues which can allow for constraints.

Part IV

VIRTUE AND ACTION

11

A Virtue-Ethical Account
of Right Action

(i) Introduction

Part III concerns the relation between virtue and action. Two major
issues have been thought to be a problem for virtue ethics: the account of
right action, and the application to applied ethics and practice generally.
This chapter is concerned with the former issue; Chapters 12 and 13 with
the latter.

There are two types of explicit, developed, virtue-ethical accounts of
right action in modern virtue ethics. One I call a 'qualified agent'[1]
account of rightness, the other is motive-centred.

In 'Virtue Theory and Abortion', Rosalind Hursthouse proposed the
following 'qualified agent' account, which has received widespread attention, and which has often been thought canonical for a virtue-ethical
account of rightness:

An act is right if and only if it is what a virtuous agent would do in the circumstances.[2]

In a later article, Hursthouse modified the above as follows:

---

[1] I thank Linda Zagzebski for this terminological suggestion.

[2] *Philosophy and Public Affairs* 20 (1991), 223–46, at 225. An earlier 'qualified judge' account
of rightness was offered by Yves R. Simon in *The Definition of Moral Virtue*, ed. Vukan Kuic (New
York: Fordham University Press, 1986): 'We say that an action will be the right action under the
circumstances if the judgment about what to do is determined, is rendered, by a person of virtuous disposition' (112). Cf. also the qualified agent account of rightness proposed by Linda
Zagzebski: 'A *right act* is what a person who is virtuously motivated, and who has the understanding of the particular situation that a virtuous person would have, might do in like circumstances . . . A moral duty is what a person who is virtuously motivated, and who has the
understanding of the particular situation that a virtuous person would have, would do in like circumstances' (*Virtues of Mind*, 135).

An act is right if and only if it is what a virtuous agent would characteristically (i.e. acting in character) do in the circumstances.[3]

A second kind of virtue-ethical account of rightness is proposed in Michael Slote's 'agent-based virtue ethics', according to which an action is right if and only if it exhibits or expresses a virtuous (admirable) motive, or at least does not exhibit or express a vicious (deplorable) motive.[4]

In this chapter I propose a third account, whose central theses are:

(1) An action is virtuous in respect V (e.g. benevolent, generous) if and only if it hits the target of (realizes the end of) virtue V (e.g. benevolence, generosity).

(2) An action is right if and only if it is overall virtuous.

In section ii, I consider difficulties in Hursthouse's and Slote's accounts. In section iii, I explain what it is for an act to be virtuous, by explaining what it is to hit the target of (realize the end of) the relevant virtue. In section iv, I offer an account of what it is for an action to be overall virtuous, and thereby right.

(ii) Rival Accounts

The following problem arises in Hursthouse's notion of rightness. The rightness of an act is criterially determined by a qualified agent, but how qualified is a virtuous agent? If 'virtue' is a threshold concept, then it is possible that you, I, and our friends are virtuous, but it is also possible (indeed likely) that others are yet more virtuous. The problem has both a vertical and a horizontal dimension. On the latter dimension, a standardly temperate, courageous, just, generous, individual does not have expertise in all areas of endeavour. She may be inexperienced in medicine, or in law, or in child-rearing. She may therefore lack practical wisdom in those areas. Even though we may call her virtuous *tout court*, she is not a qualified agent in the areas where she lacks practical wisdom. On the vertical dimension, our virtuous agents (you, I, and our friends) are surpassed in temperance, courage, generosity, justice, by greater moral

---

[3] 'Normative Virtue Ethics', in Roger Crisp (ed.), *How Should One Live? Essays on the Virtues* (Oxford: Clarendon Press, 1996), 19–36.

[4] 'Agent-Based Virtue Ethics', in Peter A. French, Theodore E. Uehling, Jr., and Howard K. Wettstein (eds.), *Moral Concepts. Midwest Studies in Philosophy* 20 (1996), 83–101.

paragons. So even though on a threshold concept of 'virtue', you, I, and our friends are virtuous, we are not as virtuous as we might be, let alone ideally so, and maybe we should defer to our betters in moral decision-making.

Hursthouse could resolve the above problem in the following ways. She may assume that 'virtue' is a threshold notion, but where the threshold is set depends on context. For example, in the field of medical ethics not *any* virtuous agent will be a qualified agent. A medical ethicist, for example, needs to be not merely benevolent, kind, and a respecter of autonomy, but also knowledgeable about medicine, or at the very least, in excellent communication with those who are. She needs to possess the full array of dialogical virtues. Another resolution is to drop the threshold concept of virtue in the definition of rightness. Perhaps 'virtue' is an idealized notion. However, it seems clear that Hursthouse wants *actual* human agents to be qualified agents. In her later account of rightness, Hursthouse realizes the danger that actual virtuous agents may at times judge and act out of character, so she inserts into the definition a qualification to rule out this possibility.

However, the above resolutions do not completely resolve the problem of whether a virtuous agent is a qualified agent. Actual human agents, no matter how virtuous and wise, are not omniscient. As a result, an important end of a virtue may be something about which there is large-scale ignorance, and for which no blame can be attached to individuals or even cultures. To illustrate the point I am making, consider the relatively newly discovered virtue, that of environmental friendliness. As the debates in journals like *Scientific American* show, controversy rages about whether or not environmental friendliness requires various drastic measures to reduce a perceived threat such as global warming. The Aristotelian virtuous agent possesses phronesis, but phronesis, with its connotations of fine sensibilities and discriminatory powers, is impotent in the face of massive ignorance of the entire human species. No matter how well motivated and practically wise the virtuous policy maker, if her policies prove environmentally disastrous, one would think, they cannot be understood as environmentally friendly, and cannot be regarded as right. Here is another example. Wise, suitably cautious, and benevolent policy makers may decide to severely restrict genetically modified food on the grounds that large-scale ignorance about genetic modification still persists. But it may be that, though the caution expresses practical wisdom, it does not exhibit knowledge. For though the possible dangers of genetically modified products of various kinds may not in fact be realized, reasonable people in the face of ignorance should guard against such possible dangers. The caution, even if wise, may have the result that important ends of the virtue of benevolence, such as the production of cheaper and more plentiful food, may be missed.

The above problem has a more general manifestation, to be explored more thoroughly in Chapter 12. Any virtuous agent is necessarily limited, and in a variety of ways. Janna Thomson puts the problem this way:

> The belief that the right answer to an ethical problem is what the virtuous person judges is right is not compatible with the recognition that ethical judgments of individuals are limited and personal. It would be irrational for us to place our trust in what a single individual, however virtuous, thinks is right.[5]

The problems facing Slote's account are quite different from those facing Hursthouse's. Slote does not aspire to a 'qualified agent' account of rightness, and so avoids the above difficulties. Rightness is tied firmly to quality of motive, but this arguably leads to counterintuitive results. Since Slote explicitly does not require practical wisdom as a feature of admirable *motive*, he (unlike Hursthouse) is vulnerable to a version of the 'bungling do-gooder' criticism of virtue ethics. Slote, however, does deal with the problem of the foolish or ignorant well-motivated agent in the following way. The well-motivated agent is concerned to determine facts: an agent genuinely desirous of being helpful is concerned that her help reaches its target, in a suitable way.[6] To a reply that such an agent may not be aware of her ignorance, Slote would claim that a motive to help contaminated with intellectual arrogance is not an admirable motive. However, not all ignorance about one's expertise need be so contaminated.[7]

In general, it could be argued that Slote has failed to take account of a distinction between rightness and goodness of action. For W. D. Ross, quality of motive has nothing to do with rightness (although, as will be seen, my own view will not be so stark). Ross claims:

> Suppose, for instance, that a man pays a particular debt simply from fear of the legal consequences of not doing so, some people would say he had done what was right, and others would deny this: they would say that no moral value attach-

---

[5] *Discourse and Knowledge: A Defence of Collectivist Ethics* (London: Routledge, 1998), 73.

[6] 'Agent-Based Virtue Ethics'. See also his 'The Justice of Caring'.

[7] For further criticism of Slote's failure to incorporate notions of *successful* relation to the external world in his criterion of rightness, see Julia Driver, 'Monkeying with Motives: Agent-Basing Virtue Ethics', *Utilitas* 7 (1995), 281–8.

es to such an act, and that since 'right' is meant to imply moral value, the act cannot be right. They might generalize and say that no act is right unless it is done from a sense of duty, or if they shrank from so rigorous a doctrine, they might at least say that no act is right unless done from *some* good motive, such as either sense of duty or benevolence.[8]

Ross distinguishes between a right act and a morally good act understood as one which is well motivated. Virtue ethicists are inclined to sidestep or belittle this distinction by speaking of acting *well*, but this idea does not obliterate, or even downgrade the importance of, the distinction Ross is trying to draw. Unsurprisingly, however, on my view a virtue-ethical employment of the distinction between right act and good act is not going to be quite the same as Ross's. First, on my view, quality of motive *can* sometimes make a difference to rightness,[9] and second, as Aristotle believes, goodness of motive is not the only inner state of the agent relevant to acting well. Since this chapter is about rightness and not about acting well generally, I shall not elaborate further on the latter point.

(iii) A Target-Centred Virtue-Ethical Conception of Rightness

The first stage in the presentation of my virtue-ethical account of rightness is the provision of an account of a virtuous act (or more precisely, an act which is virtuous in respect V).[10] The basis of my account of such an act is Aristotle's distinction between virtuous act, and action from (a state of) virtue. On my account, rightness (as opposed to full excellence) of action is tied not to action from virtue but to virtuous act.

Let me first present Aristotle's distinction, before elaborating further on the notion of virtuous act. Aristotle introduces the distinction thus:

A difficulty, however, may be raised as to how we can say that people must perform just actions if they are to become just, and temperate ones if they are to become temperate; because if they do what is just and temperate, they are just and temperate already, in the same way that if they use words or play music correctly they are already literate or musical. But surely this is not true even of the

---

[8] *The Right and the Good* (Oxford: Oxford University Press, 1930), 2.

[9] Indeed, I agree with Stephen Sverdlik's view that *sometimes* the quality of a motive can change the deontic status of an action from right to wrong. See his 'Motive and Rightness', *Ethics* 106 (1996), 327–49.

[10] Henceforth 'virtuous act'.

arts. It is possible to put a few words together correctly by accident, or at the prompting of another person; so the agent will only be literate if he does a literate act in a literate way, viz. in virtue of his own literacy. Nor, again, is there an analogy between the arts and the virtues. Works of art have their merit in themselves; so it is enough for them to be turned out with a certain quality of their own. But virtuous acts are not done in a just or temperate way merely because *they* have a certain quality, but only if the agent also acts in a certain state, viz. (1) if he knows what he is doing, (2) if he chooses it, and chooses it for its own sake, and (3) if he does it from a fixed and permanent disposition.[11]

How can an action be just or temperate if it does not exhibit a just or temperate state? The answer I shall propose is this. An action can be just or temperate if it hits the target of the virtues of justice or temperance, and an action may hit those targets without exhibiting a just or temperate state. According to Robert Audi, one 'dimension' of virtue is 'the characteristic targets it aims at'.[12] This idea requires explication if it is to be employed in the service of an account of rightness. The task of the remainder of this chapter is precisely to offer what may be termed a 'target-centred' virtue-ethical account of rightness.

It will first be noticed that a target-centred view will tolerate moral luck in the attainment of rightness, for rightness may depend in part on results not entirely within the control of the agent. This understanding sits well with Aristotle, one of whose strengths on my view is his distinction between character (virtue) which is concerned with *choice* (rather than the results of choice), and the target of a virtue which may be missed. He allows for the possibility that the target of choice (virtue) may be missed through no fault of the agent. For example, the aim of magnificence is a *result*: 'the result must be worthy of the expense, and the expense worthy of the result, or even in excess of it'.[13] Though of course the magnificent person has wisdom, are all results of largesse predictable by the wise? Aristotle seems to allow for the possibility that a choice from the virtue of magnificence may not be a magnificent act. And, indeed, that will be my position.

Let me now explicate the idea of hitting the target of a virtue. To understand the idea of hitting the target of a virtue, recall our basic definition of a virtue.

[11] *Nicomachean Ethics*, 1105a9–b2.
[12] *Moral Knowledge and Ethical Character*, 180.
[13] *Nicomachean Ethics*, 1122b1–21.

(V₁) A virtue is a good quality or excellence of character. It is a disposition of acknowledging or responding to items in the field of a virtue in an excellent (or good enough) way.

We can now present schematic definitions of an *act from virtue* and a *virtuous act* in the light of (V₁). First, a definition of action from virtue:

(V₂) An action from virtue is an action which displays, expresses, or exhibits all (or a sufficient number of) the excellences comprising virtue in sense (V₁) to a sufficient degree.

In the light of (V₁) also, we can understand what it is to hit the target of a virtue.

(V₃) Hitting the target of a virtue is a form (or forms) of success in the moral acknowledgement of or responsiveness to items in its field or fields, appropriate to the aim of the virtue in a given context.

A *virtuous act* can now be defined.

(V₄) An act is virtuous (in respect V) if and only if it hits the target of V.

In the remainder of this section, I first elucidate the idea of hitting the target of a virtue, before showing how a virtuous act differs from an action from virtue.

Recall that to hit the target of a virtue is to respond successfully to items in its field according to the aim of a virtue. We need now to discuss this idea further in order to clarify the distinction between virtuous act and action from virtue. What counts as hitting the target of a virtue is relatively easy to grasp when the aim of a virtue is simply to promote the good of individuals, and *hitting* that target is *successfully* promoting that good.[14] However, this relatively simple paradigm is complicated by several features. I shall discuss five. These are:

(1) There are several modes of moral response or acknowledgement appropriate to one kind of item in a virtue's field, so

---

14 But 'relatively easy' does not entail 'easy'. There is still complexity. Does one hit the target of benevolence if one benefits people, but not those whose benefit one aimed at? There are circumstances where that could count as success: the target of the virtue (though not one's own target). Thanks to Michael Slote for pointing out this difficulty (personal communication).

hitting the target of a virtue may involve several modes of moral response.

(2) The target of a virtue may be internal to the agent.

(3) The target of a virtue may be plural.

(4) What counts as the target of a virtue may depend on context.

(5) The target of a virtue may be to avoid things.

I discuss these features in turn.

(1) *Hitting the Targets of Virtue May Involve Several Modes of Moral Response*

Even with respect to one field, hitting the target of a virtue may be complex, since it may involve successful response in several modes, and what counts as success with respect to modes such as promotion, creativity, respect, and love will differ. One may argue that the target of benevolence, or friendship, generally involves success in responding to people in their fields (people at large, friends) through a variety of different modes of moral responsiveness. In a justly famous example, cited earlier, Iris Murdoch highlights the importance of attention or proper receptivity in the friendly or benevolent treatment of a daughter-in-law.[15] This requires first seeing her in the right way, through a loving rather than a hostile gaze, by thinking of her via honorific rather than pejorative concepts. Then, in one's treatments, respect should be displayed in any promotion of good: a person should not be lied to, manipulated, or coerced, unless circumstances are quite exceptional. Finally, the expression of appropriate forms of closeness tempers the distance required by respect if the latter is not to appear cold and unfeeling.

What counts as success in exhibiting modes of moral responsiveness appropriate to the aim of a virtue is a complex matter, requiring discussion of each mode. How each is to be integrated in virtuous behaviour is also a complex issue. For example, if Kant is correct in his understanding of love as a form of coming close, and respect as a form of keeping one's distance, there remains the issue of how these modes come into equilibrium in virtuous behaviour.

(2) *The Targets of Some Virtues are Internal*

It is granted that the target of many virtues is external, for example, the target of beneficence, efficiency, or justice. A just act is one that, for example, conforms to legitimate rules of procedure, an efficient act is

---

[15] 'The Idea of Perfection'.

timely and poses little cost for a worthwhile gain, a beneficent act successfully promotes human welfare. We sometimes speak, too, of a generous act of giving without any knowledge of, or even interest in, the motivation of the donor. The same point applies to wrongness. Consider the action of ex-Prime Minister Keating of Australia, who ushered the Queen to her place by putting his arm round her waist. Many considered this action wrong—even egregious, even outrageous—because it was disrespectful or impolite. He did not suitably keep his distance (as Kant puts it), and his action was therefore deemed wrong by many because disrespectful, regardless of his motivations. He may have been innocently operating within Australian mores of informality and egalitarianism, or he may have been striking another blow for turning Australia into a republic by subtly undermining the Queen's prestige or mystique.

However, the supposition that the target of all virtue is external to the agent, or is only external to the agent, is false. Though the target of some virtues is external or is external in many contexts, the target of others seems to be entirely internal, such as determination or (mental) strength. The target of the former virtue is trying hard in a sustained way, and that target may be reached even if the agent fails rather consistently in her endeavours. More commonly, the targets of virtues such as caring are a mixture of features within the agent's mind, features of an agent's behaviour (her manner), and features external to the agent. Similarly, the target of the virtue of (racial) toleration is not merely external: the pro forma respecting of the rights of people in certain racial groups. We may call an act *wrong* because racist if the agent, in respecting a right, possessed racist motivation, even if that motivation was not displayed.[16] Notice, however, that the application of terms such as 'racist' to acts is controversial, and what is required for an act to not be racist may be more or less demanding depending on context. Though the full virtue of racial toleration may demand that we morally acknowledge those of other races through a variety of different modes (e.g. respect, promotion of good, appreciation, even a form of love), the conditions under which we call an act racist and thereby wrong may be more or less stringent.

(3) *Some Targets of Virtue are Plural*

According to Robert Audi, the target of courage is the control of fear.[17] However, one may have thought that hitting the target of courage is to

---

[16] See Sverdlik, 'Motive and Rightness'.
[17] *Moral Knowledge and Ethical Character*, 180.

handle dangerous or threatening situations successfully. Perhaps then, the target of courage is plural, embracing both regulating certain inner states and handling certain sorts of external situations. On my view, regardless of what one wants to say about courage, there is no requirement for a virtue to have only one target, for a virtue may have more than one field. Even with respect to inner states, Aristotle thought that courage involved the regulation of both fear and confidence.

(4) *Contextual Variability of Targets*

One might wonder how the target of a virtue is to be determined if the profile of a virtue is complex. Part of the answer to this question lies in the contextual variability of the target of a virtue. What counts as a virtuous act is more heavily contextual than what counts as an action from virtue. In some contexts, for example, where there is considerable need, one may be said to have performed a generous act if one donates a large amount of money, say, even if that donation is made with bad grace. However, in other contexts, we may deny that an act of giving is generous on the grounds that it was not made in a generous spirit. Here the target of generosity is to alleviate need, *in the right way*, where 'in the right way' makes reference to manner of giving, and even motivation. Perhaps the context is a more personal one, and the hostility or ill grace noticed by the recipients. We may at other times mark the fact that the target of a virtue is reached, but only in a minimalist sense, by claiming of an action that it is all right, but not right *tout court*. At yet other times we may mark the fact that the target of a virtue has been reached in its richest sense, by claiming of an action not merely that it was right, but that it was splendid or admirable because lavish, nobly performed, or performed in the face of great difficulty or cost.

Here is another example, illustrating the contextual nature of the target of a virtue, and thereby of a virtuous act. I am an aid worker, working ceaselessly saving lives. Are my actions benevolent because successful in saving lives, or not benevolent since they do not manifest caring or loving attitudes? People at this point may not worry about whether my actions manifest love for others. The target of benevolence here is simply to alleviate need. My actions are deemed benevolent and right—indeed admirable. However, after several years of tireless activity in famine-stricken areas, I come home in a state of deep depression. I feel burdened by an inability to love or be creative. I am filled with resentment and rush to an analyst. She is worried about my tendencies to promote good. She tries to teach me that *truly* benevolent actions flow from love of humanity (in a *particularized* form) and inner strength. My continued knee-jerk 'beneficent' actions are wrong. In this context. the aim or target of benevolence is richer. It is no longer mere promotion of others' good.

Contextual variation and disagreement about salience occurs also with the attribution of vice terms to acts. A term such as 'cruel' may, when applied to acts, sometimes make reference to inner states of agents, and sometimes not. Sometimes one will say of an act of poisoning opossums of Australian origin with cyanide bait in New Zealand forests overrun with these pests: 'That's cruel'. The action is said to be cruel simply because of its effects on the opossums. Another person, knowing the mental anguish suffered by the poisoner (who is nonetheless determined to save coastline pohutukawa trees), says 'Sure, the act hurts the opossums but it's not a *cruel* act'.

(5) *Some Targets of Virtue are to Avoid Things*

Talk of 'hitting the target' of a virtue suggests that the aim of a virtue is always positive, as opposed to the avoiding of certain things. However, some virtues seem to be targeted at the avoidance of certain states, and to illustrate this, let me briefly discuss the controversial virtue of modesty. There is disagreement about the targets aimed at by the virtue of modesty, and such disagreement may be explained by differing views about what makes a trait a virtue. On a consequentialist view, such as Julia Driver's,[18] a trait is a virtue if and only if its exercise tends to bring about valuable states of affairs. According to Driver, what makes modesty a virtue is that it 'stops problems from arising in social situations',[19] such problems as jealousy. It does not follow that this is the *aim* of the virtue, but a consequentialist view of what makes a trait of virtue may drive the account of its aim, and this is the case with Driver's account of modesty.

On Driver's view, the modest agent avoids spending time ranking herself, and avoids seeking information to enable her to have a correct estimation of her worth. But so far, modesty as a virtue has not been distinguished from laziness as a vice. Driver goes further. The target of modesty is not just to avoid these things, it is to attain something positive: the ignorance of underestimation. The agent need not directly aim at this, but must achieve it if the target of the virtue of modesty is to be

---

[18] See 'The Virtues and Human Nature'.
[19] 'Modesty and Ignorance', 828.

reached. And it is the hitting of this target which leads to the valuable social consequences of absence of jealousy and so forth.

On my view, by contrast, the target of modesty is simply to avoid certain things. The modest agent avoids certain behaviours, including those mentioned by Driver, but it is also the case (if modesty is to be distinguished from laziness) that the modest agent avoids drawing attention to herself, talking about herself excessively, boasting, and so forth. One might accept all this without buying into the consequentialist justification of modesty as a virtue, and without buying into an account of its target as something positive: the ignorance of underestimation. One may reject that account because one may believe (as I do) that what makes modesty a virtue is not its tendency to promote valuable states of affairs (absence of jealousy, etc.), but its being the expression of a valuable or flourishing state of the agent—namely, an agent who has self-love, and who does not therefore need to get a sense of self-worth from comparisons with others. Though this is what makes modesty a virtue on my view, that is not its target, however. Its target is simply to avoid certain things—the kinds of behaviour mentioned above.

We are now in a position to give an account of the distinction between an action from (a state of) virtue and a virtuous act. The requirements for hitting the target of a virtue and for action from virtue are demanding in different kinds of ways. We have seen already that an act from virtue may fail to hit the target of a virtue if the virtuous agent's practical wisdom does not amount to complete knowledge. So an agent with virtues of benevolence or environmental friendliness may act *out of* those virtues and miss the targets of those virtues.

Second, for an action to be from a state of virtue, in an ideal case, all modes of acknowledgement of items in a virtue's field, constituting the profile of the relevant virtue, must be displayed. However, this is not always, or even standardly, a requirement for virtuous action, even in an ideal case. Furthermore, for an act to be from a state of virtue (in an ideal case), not only must all modes of moral acknowledgement comprising the virtuous disposition be displayed, they must be displayed in an excellent way, in a way which expresses fine inner states. For Aristotle, this involves fine motivation (including having fine ends), fine emotions, practical wisdom, and the possession of a stable *disposition* of fine emotions, feelings, and other affective states. But even though the targets of some virtues are (at least in part) internal, it is not generally the case that they involve the expression of *all* those fine inner states required for action from virtue. For example, we might say that obedience (to legitimate authority) as a virtue requires the existence of fine depth states: not only the practical wisdom which distinguishes obedience as a virtue from related vices such as blind obedience, but also the absence of deep-seated hostile resentment of all authority figures, whether legitimate or not. However, the end or target of that virtue is compliance with legitimate rules and instructions, not the elimination of such deep-seated feelings.

Let us now summarize the key differences between action from virtue and virtuous act.

(1) An action from a state of virtue may not be a virtuous act because it misses the target of (the relevant) virtue.

(2) A virtuous act may fail to be an action from virtue because it fails to manifest aspects of the profile of the relevant virtue at all.

(3) A virtuous act may fail to be an action from virtue because it fails to manifest the profile of a virtue in a good enough way; namely, it fails to express sufficiently fine inner states (such as practical wisdom, fine motivation, or dispositions of fine emotion).

(4) What counts as a virtuous act is more heavily contextual than what counts as an act from virtue.

We have seen how it is possible to draw a distinction between virtuous act and action from virtue. We have also seen that the drawing of this distinction in particular cases is by no means easy, for there is a constellation of modes of moral acknowledgement constituting the profiles of the virtues, and it is often a matter of context which aspects of the profile of a virtue are salient in determining the target of a virtue.

It is time now to discuss rightness as the *overall* virtuousness of an act.

(iv) Overall Virtuousness

According to my account, an act is right if and only if it is overall virtuous. There is much ambiguity about the idea of rightness. In particular, a target-centred virtue-ethical view is compatible with three possible accounts which are now discussed. I illustrate with the virtue of generosity.

(1) An act is right if and only if it is overall virtuous, and that entails that it is the, or a, best action possible in the

circumstances. *Assuming that no other virtues or vices are involved*, we could say that a given act is right insofar as it is the most generous possible. The target of generosity on this view is very stringent: there is no large penumbra such that any act which falls within it is deemed right.

(2) An act is right if and only if it is overall virtuous, and that entails that it is good enough even if not the (or a) best action. Here it is assumed that there is much latitude in hitting the target of virtues such as generosity. Right acts range from the truly splendid and admirable to acts which are 'all right'.

(3) An act is right if and only if it is not overall vicious. Here it is assumed that not being overall vicious does not entail being overall virtuous. An act may avoid the vices of meanness or stinginess, for example, without hitting the target of generosity, which demands more than mere avoidance of stingy, mean acts. This may be true even if the target of generosity is interpreted as in (2), rather than (1).

My own target-centred view rules out (3), since rightness is understood in terms of overall virtuousness rather than the avoidance of overall viciousness. This leaves open a choice between (1) and (2). I prefer (1). Provided a distinction is made between rightness and praiseworthiness, and between wrongness and blameworthiness, it seems natural to think of the targets of a virtue as best acts (relative to the virtue), though it does not follow that a rational agent should always *aim* at such a target directly, or should necessarily deliberate about reaching that target.

It should also be noted that a belief in (1) is compatible with considerable indeterminacy about what is best. 'What is best' may not be a single action, but any of a number of actions, none of which are ruled out by reasons that could be defeated. (See further, Chapter 13.)

Finally, the distinction between (1), (2), and (3) raises the issue of what should be called wrong. Should wrong actions include or exclude actions which fall short of rightness in sense (1), but are 'all right' in the sense of 'good enough'? My own preference is to employ three categories: right actions (conforming to (1)), 'all right' actions (which exclude actions which are overall vicious), and wrong actions (actions which are overall vicious).

The question arises: how does my conception of right action tie with the notions of obligation and prohibition? Three difficult kinds of case need addressing.

Case 1. Cases where a right act seems excessively demanding and thus not obligatory (e.g. an act of extreme generosity).

Case 2. Cases where a right act is undemanding and seems not to be an obligation.

Case 3. Cases where an act is wrong on my view because contrary to virtue, but seems not 'swallowed up by the category of the forbidden'.[20]

My virtue-ethical reply to all these kinds of case is relatively straightforward. Where one draws the line between wrong and undesirable, and wrong and not only undesirable but also forbidden, will depend on the theorist. For example, depending on how demanding is one's ethics, an act contrary to virtue (such as relatively minor rudeness or inconsiderateness, e.g. lingering too long at a table at a restaurant when others are waiting)[21] will be undesirable only, or prohibited (see Case 3). Again, depending on how demanding is one's virtue ethics, an act of returning a minor favour will be morally desirable but not obligatory, or obligatory (see Case 2). Furthermore, supererogatory acts may be seen as highly desirable, or admirable, but not obligatory, or, if one's ethics is very demanding, obligatory (see Case 1). Virtue ethics as such is neutral on this issue.

That an action may be right without being obligatory (but, rather, desirable or admirable), and that an agent may fail to perform such an act without being blameworthy, is particularly important given my conception of the demandingness of ethics. Although I have admitted context-dependence of what counts as the target of a virtue, it may well be the case on occasion that the *overall* virtuous act lies not merely outside the scope of an agent's wisdom, but also beyond her strength. Admittedly, notwithstanding the incorporation of (virtuous) anti-perfectionism, self-protection, and virtues of self-improvement into the assessment of the overall virtuousness of acts, it may the case that it is right for the doctor of the example in Chapter 9 to go to Africa, where he will save more lives, or it may be the case that it is right for someone to become a freedom fighter. But it is not necessarily obligatory. Nor is it necessarily the case that failure to do these things is blameworthy. For the targets of relevant virtues may reach beyond the strength of particular agents.

We turn now to the account of rightness as overall virtuousness. Assume that it is determined whether an act is properly describable as hitting the target of an individual virtue, such as justice, generosity, friendship, and so forth. Disagreement about *overall* virtuousness centres on the resolution of conflict when an action is said to be virtuous in respect V and non-virtuous or even vicious in respect W. Given that an act can be virtuous in respect V if merely certain aspects of the profile of V are displayed, it is not necessary that such an act is in all ways excellent. It is possible for vice terms to also apply. Actions are, for example, both just and weak, or just and malicious, or friendly and unjust, or self-protective and non-beneficent, or independent and unkind, or cruel and environmentally sound, or assertive and hurtful, or efficient and uncaring.

How is overall virtuousness determined? Like Jonathan Dancy, I wish to highlight the holism of right-making features of action.[22] The point is this. We cannot claim that certain features *always* contribute positively (or negatively) to the overall virtuousness of an act, even if those kinds of feature characteristically contribute positively (or negatively).

A strong version of particularism should be distinguished from a weaker version. According to the strong version, there are no moral principles at all. According to the weaker version, though there may be a very few moral principles, characteristically reasons relevant to rightness or wrongness function holistically. I do not want to commit myself to the strong version, but merely wish to emphasize that even virtue-based reasons can function holistically.

Though it is beyond the scope of this chapter to write at length about the moral view labelled 'particularism', it is important to clear away one misunderstanding. Particularism, even in its strong version, does not deny the existence of moral 'principles' in a weak sense described by Tom Sorrell: 'By a "principle" I mean a reason for doing or committing something, a reason that is, in the first place, general. It must apply in a wide range of situations'[23] Indeed, what Hursthouse calls virtue-rules are principles in exactly this sense. What is denied in the strong version of particularism is the existence of any *universal* moral principles in the sense that reasons (which may constitute principles in the above sense) always have negative or positive valence (as opposed to operating holistically).[24] Dancy makes it clear that principles of the form 'Characteristically thus and so' or 'Normally thus and so' are perfectly acceptable to the particularist.[25] This fact undermines the objection that moral life under particularism would be unpredictable.

Let us now see how virtue-based reasons function holistically in the assessment of actions as overall virtuous. Say that we have a bunch of virtues, such as kindness, generosity, frankness, tactfulness, assertiveness, justice. Remember that for an *action* to be described as virtuous (insofar as it is kind, generous, frank, tactful, just, and so forth), it has to hit the target of the relevant virtue, but it does not characteristically have to display all the excellences which would make it an act *from* the relevant virtuous state. Indeed, the agent who performs a tactful action on an occasion may not possess the virtue of tact at all. It is possible even for such terms as 'tactful' and 'kind', which *normally* contribute positively to the rightness of actions, to contribute neutrally or even negatively on occasion. I want now to show how this can be possible, using two illustrations.

Consider an act which hits the target of the virtue of kindness. We are at a conference where a stranger looks lonely. It turns out he is a person from overseas with a poor command of English, and cannot participate in the scintillating and sophisticated discussion on moral theory. Our agent Tim performs a kind act, namely, going to talk to the stranger. However, let us look at further features of this situation. Tim is exceptionally keen to participate in the discussion, but leaves in order to talk to the stranger who could have made more effort to amuse himself in other ways and whose hangdog expression is expressive of a rather weak, spoilt approach to life. The conversation with the stranger is difficult, and Tim

---

[24] Walter Sinnott-Armstrong thinks that such principles can be turned into universal form provided they are formulated thus: do (or don't do) thus and so provided there are no underminers, reversers, exclusions, and overriders. See 'Some Varieties of Particularism', *Metaphilosophy* 30 (1999), 1–12, at 6. For Dancy, however, an 'underminer' is the absence of a background ('enabling') condition and not a reason (a fact accepted by Sinnott-Armstrong). Since moral *principles* state reasons and not all enabling conditions, the above cannot be a principle (even if a defender of universalizability can appeal to it, as Sinnott-Armstrong claims). This is made clear in Jonathan Dancy, 'Defending Particularism', *Metaphilosophy* 30 (1999), 25–32, at 26.

[25] *Moral Reasons*, 60. For a defence of the view that particularism is compatible with the existence of presumptive generalizations, see Margaret Olivia Little, 'Moral Generalities Revisited', in Brad Hooker and Margaret Little (eds.), *Moral Particularism* (Oxford: Clarendon Press, 2000), 276–304.

does not enjoy it. Furthermore, Tim is always doing this kind of thing, sacrificing his interests in the performance of such kind acts. He has resolved to be more self-protective and strong, and encourage others to do their share of burdensome tasks. But he consistently fails to abide by the resolution. In this context, the kindness of the act contributes negatively to the overall virtuousness of the act.

The second example concerns intrafamilial justice. I have been training my children not to be obsessive about justice or fairness, particularly in an intrafamily context and where the stakes are not high. I want them to be more caring, magnanimous, and generous. Despite my personal tendencies to be overly concerned with justice, I resolve to drive the lesson home at the next opportunity. An opportunity soon arises. A family tradition of 'fair shares' requires that the person making the division has last choice. There is a cake to be cut. I allow my older son to cut the cake. I notice that he has cut carelessly, but in a state of unawareness takes the biggest piece. The target of (procedural) justice has not been reached. My younger son, apparently unnoticing and uncaring, looks delightedly at the smaller piece that he has been left with. Instead of praising my younger son, I make my older son swap pieces, telling him that the division, and his action in going first, having cut, is unjust. My intervention is just, but in the circumstances that is a wrong-making feature of the situation. The justice of the intervention is in this context expressive of the obsessive, weak quality of my behaviour.

My point in the above examples is that the virtuousness of an act in a given respect (e.g. its friendliness, justice, or kindness) can be wrong-making (i.e. can contribute negatively to the rightness of an act). My point is not that the virtuousness of an act is not *characteristically* right-making. Indeed, if the virtuousness of acts were not characteristically right-making, we could not subsume features under *virtue* concepts.

(v) Objections

A number of objections to my target-centred virtue-ethical notion of rightness might be raised. The first objection is that virtuousness (or viciousness) may not feature at all in the list of right-making properties. In the claim 'It's wrong because it is distasteful' it may be thought that 'distasteful' is not a vice term.[26] In reply one should note the following. It

---

[26] An example suggested to me in conversation by Jonathan Dancy.

should first be determined how properties such as being distasteful are to be understood as relevant to rightness. The notion of distastefulness, for example, needs to be unpacked. One would need to say, for example, 'It is distasteful because indecent'. Ideally, the vice term 'indecent' needs itself to be further unpacked into such notions as 'manipulative', 'dishonest', 'disrespectful', and so forth.

Another example is 'It's right to stop considering this problem because there isn't enough time'. It may be supposed that 'because there is not enough time' is a right-making property not involving virtue. However, to know the impact of 'lack of time' on rightness, we need to see how it impacts on virtues and vices. The sense that there is no time may reflect laziness. Or it may involve self-indulgence or lack of temperance. Perhaps we are wanting to rush off to a party. On the other hand, the reason may implicate the virtues of courage, self-protection, or parental virtue. Virtues such as these need to operate in the face of a pressuring administration which thinks that we have limitless capacities to cope with stress, or no families to go back to.

Secondly, it may be objected that my account of rightness is too agent-centred. Rightness, it may be claimed, has nothing to do with an agent's motives or reasons, but has entirely to do with success in the external realm. However, my target-centred virtue-ethical view (by comparison with some virtue-ethical and Kantian views) does accommodate this conscquentialist intuition about rightness. My problem with consequentialism is that it has too narrow a conception of modes of moral acknowledgement or response that are relevant to rightness. Once the plurality of modes of moral response is accepted, it can be appreciated that the target of some virtues, such as caring, can include the internal.

Indeed, the fact that my account allows for some agent-centredness overcomes an objection that can be levelled at some versions of qualified agent accounts. The objection is this. An action which is one that a virtuous agent would perform could be one that merely mimics an action of a virtuous agent. It seems possible, therefore, that a non-virtuous agent could perform an act describable as, say, uncaring, even though it is an act which a virtuous agent would perform, and which would therefore be right on a qualified agent account of rightness. The act is uncaring because, though mimicking a virtuous agent's act, it nonetheless fails to exhibit the internal qualities that would be exhibited by a virtuous agent's caring act. We may wish to say, therefore, that such an act was unvirtuous, even though mimicking the act of a virtuous agent. Indeed, on my view, an act which mimics the action of a virtuous agent may be wrong, because *in the hands of the actor* it is unvirtuous. It is, for example, uncaring, or racist because expressive of racist attitudes.

The following reply could be made to this possible difficulty in a qualified agent formula of rightness. As Justin Oakley points out,[27] the formula that an action is right if and only if it is what an agent with a virtuous character would do in the circumstances is ambiguous between two interpretations. The formula could furnish what Oakley calls an 'external criterion' of right action, or the idea of 'doing what the virtuous person would do' is to be understood as requiring more than 'merely the performance of certain acts'. Acting rightly also 'requires our acting out of the appropriate dispositions and motives'.[28] However, the strong interpretation would tie rightness not to the virtuousness of action but to action out of virtue, and that is implausibly strong as a criterion of *rightness*. The point of connecting rightness to the former idea is to recognize a virtue-ethical variant of a distinction between good and right act, and to recognize that the latter notion is less agent-centred than the former.

Another objection to my account of rightness is this. If the claim that an act is virtuous in respect V is the claim that the act falls under a virtue term 'V', then, it may be argued, the idea of rightness does not track the truth, but merely culturally dependent beliefs. For virtue *terms* reflect our culturally determined and possibly false beliefs about virtue.

Notice, however, that to say that an act is virtuous in respect V if and only if it hits the target of V is not quite the same as saying that an act is virtuous in respect V if and only if it falls under a virtue term 'V'. This is so for two reasons. First, some virtue terms refer to states which only approximate to virtue. Take, for example, 'honest'. We are happy to say that 'honest' is a virtue term, but 'honesty' is arguably not an accurate description of a virtue. Honesty is a disposition to tell the truth, or at least a disposition to not lie. We do not describe an act of evasiveness or an act of telling a lie as honest acts. Yet such acts may hit the target of a virtue— namely, a virtue of a correct disposition with respect to the field of divulging information. Certainly, this disposition involves being a respecter of truth, and is normally manifested in honest acts, but arguably practical wisdom in this area does not always mandate honest

---

[27] *Ratio* 9 (1996), 128–52.

[28] Ibid. 136. In her *On Virtue Ethics*, 125, Hursthouse suggests that acting rightly does include the agent's reasons (her point being that reasons often enter into the appropriate description of the action), but virtuous feelings and attitudes belong to the realm of acting well (as opposed to acting rightly).

acts. Furthermore, some of our virtue terms may not refer even to states which approximate virtues, and a correct theory of virtue may demonstrate this. Nietzsche's 'revaluation of values', for example, called into question pity as a virtue and justice as a virtue, on the assumption that 'justice' refers to egalitarian propensities expressive of resentment. Secondly, as Aristotle remarks, not all virtues have names. The fact that our language is insufficiently rich to capture all forms of virtue does not tell against (V_4).

A slightly different accusation of relativism is this. According to Soran Reader,

we are not told [by the particularist] what makes *this* consideration the right one to act on here . . . we are told that rationality is a matter of judgement anchored in a way of life (anthropology), and that we are all competent to recognize it even if we can never make it explicit (intuition).[29]

A particularism embedded within a virtue ethics need not be wedded to these claims. An epistemology suitable for a virtue-ethical particularism is a completely open question. Particularism is a theory emphasizing the holism of reasons; it is not a theory about the basis of those reasons, nor is it an epistemological theory.

Finally, it is sometimes claimed that since virtue-ethical accounts of rightness are not rule-based, they lack resources for resolving moral dilemmas. In fact, virtue ethics has more resources for determining overall rightness of acts in dilemmatic situations than may be appreciated.

The question is whether it is possible that an agent cannot do something which is virtuous overall and therefore right, when faced with alternatives all of which are extremely repugnant. The richness of virtue and vice vocabulary allows us to admit the possibility of right action even in such cases. For virtue-based act evaluations allow us to think of 'actions' as embracing demeanour, motivation, processes of deliberation and thought, reactions, and attitudes. We can describe demeanour, motivation, thought processes, and reactions as callous, arrogant, or lightminded, or as anguished. We can describe them as strong, or decisive, or courageous; or as cowardly, feeble, pathetic, vacillating. We can describe them as dignified or weak. In short, the choice of a repugnant option can be understood as right (virtuous overall) when we take account of the full nature of the action, including the way it was done. In *Sophie's Choice*,[30] for

---

29 'Principle Ethics, Particularism and Another Possibility', 275.
30 William Styron, *Sophie's Choice* (New York: Random House, 1979).

example, it is possible that Sophie acted virtuously overall.[31] One might argue that she acted virtuously because she acted as a good mother in that situation. Or (someone may argue), in such a tragic situation, Sophie had to rise above the normal traits of goodness in mothers, and virtuous action required a certain coolness and deliberateness. One might in that case say her choice was not overall virtuous because it failed to display virtuous calmness and strength in the process of choice. This kind of question (of how a good mother would react) cannot be answered from within the resources of the philosopher. For a start, research on the behaviour of mothers required to make life and death decisions for their children, in different kinds of contexts of scarcity and evil, would be required.

Finally, the idea that virtue ethics is not rule-based should not be misunderstood. On my account, the determination of rightness is partly a matter of publicly accessible rules, rather than the essentially private deliberations and intuitions of a virtuous agent. (What more is required is the topic of the next chapter.) For rightness depends on the applicability of terms like 'caring', 'efficient',[32] 'kind', 'friendly'; and their applicability is rule-governed.[33] But I do want to express an important caveat here. The correct applicability of virtue concepts in any sophisticated context is not a matter of the application of relatively perspicuous rules. When, for example, I praise an act as right because strong, or right because caring, or wrong because weak or uncaring, ensuing controversy may precipitate entire accounts of the concepts of strength, weakness, and caring. And good accounts will extend into terrain well beyond the expertise of the analytic philosopher.

---

[31] Such a view would be at odds with Hursthouse's view of (resolvable) tragic dilemmas, whose resolutions (she believes) are too terrible to be called 'right'; see *On Virtue Ethics*, 79.

[32] If we can think of a dithering, muddling, vacillating, pusillanimous person as having those features as part of character, we can surely think of efficiency as a virtue. For example, see a claim concerning the notoriously inefficient Tallis in Iris Murdoch's *A Fairly Honourable Defeat* (London: Chatto & Windus, 1970), 13: 'I do think a reasonable account of efficiency is an aspect of morals. There's a sort of ordered completeness of life and an intelligent use of one's talents which is the mark of a man.'

[33] For more on the rule-based aspect of virtue ethics, see Hursthouse, 'Normative Virtue Ethics'.

12

Virtues of Practice

(i) The Practical Task of Ethics

More work needs to be done in providing an adequate epistemology for virtue ethics. This and the next chapter address that need. It is well known by now that virtue ethics has been criticized for its supposed epistemological inadequacy. Such criticism can be understood as making three general claims:

(1) Though the (or a) virtuous agent is meant to be the (a) rule and the measure of the right, such an agent is necessarily limited and (as we saw in the last chapter) possibly wrong.

(2) The epistemic resources available to a non-virtuous agent are thin: in the absence of robust determinate rules, she is supposed to find, and then imitate, virtuous agents. Such an epistemological requirement is problematic.[1]

(3) Virtue ethics yields an insufficient guide to action (even for the virtuous), for specific virtues are vague and indeterminate, and can conflict. Hence virtue ethics is impotent in the field of applied ethics.

The first two of these problems are addressed in the present chapter. The problems are solved by revising the traditional conception (or misconception) of virtue-ethical epistemology as 'the virtuous agent as oracle'. In its place, I propose a virtue-ethical species of dialogic ethics. The third problem, addressed in Chapter 13, is solved by a revision of traditional modes of moral reasoning based on a model of mind as 'logic machine'.[2] Rather than virtues being seen as constellations of rules, they should be understood on the model of prototypes whose indeterminacy is not

---

[1] But defended by Harold Alderman, 'By Virtue of a Virtue', in Daniel Statman (ed.), *Virtue Ethics: A Critical Reader* (Edinburgh: Edinburgh University Press, 1997), 145–64.

[2] See Clark, *Being There*.

resolved at a fine-grained level by rules, or even necessarily by sentential processes.

A resolution of the first two problems—the concern of this chapter—begins with a certain conception of ethics conceived practically. It shares Christine Korsgaard's view that, conceived practically, ethics 'takes its start from a plight'.[3] What is the 'plight' that drives our conception of the problem of ethics? It is that expressed by Nietzsche: in addressing the demands of the world, each of us, even the most virtuous of us, is limited in his or her perspective. Nietzsche puts the point this way:

Perspectival seeing is the *only* kind of seeing there is, perspectival 'knowing' the *only* kind of 'knowing'; and the *more* feelings about a matter which we allow to come to expression, the *more* eyes, different eyes through which we are able to view this same matter, the more complete our 'conception' of it, our 'objectivity', will be.[4]

The task, in response to the plight, is to integrate these perspectives, constrained as they are by ignorance, cultural embeddedness, and role demands. Such integration is the attainment of what Nietzsche calls objectivity: a less limited response to the world.

It may be thought that the plight is simply that each of us is epistemically limited. But in claiming that morality is 'deeply' practical,[5] Korsgaard is claiming more than this. The plight is not just that we have limited perspectives and expertise—epistemic deficiencies. The need to integrate perspectives is not just an epistemic need, it is a social need. We have to solve problems of relating to the world in ways that we can live with. The fact that some of us believe that there are inalienable rights, not subject to negotiation, and that others believe that the salvation of our souls is the most important thing, not subject to negotiation, are not facts that are beyond the reach of dialogue because (let us suppose) it is simply *true* that there are inalienable rights or the salvation of our souls is of supreme importance. In claiming that morality does not start from a premise but from a plight, Korsgaard is claiming that the central practical task of ethics is not *simply* the search for truth. That search is constrained

---

[3] Christine M. Korsgaard, 'Rawls and Kant: On the Primacy of the Practical', *Proceedings of the Eighth International Kant Congress*, Memphis, Tenn., 1995, vol. i (Milwaukee, Wis.: Marquette University Press, 1995), 1165–73, at 1168.

[4] *On the Genealogy of Morals*, Third Essay, sect. 12, p. 98.

[5] 'Rawls and Kant', 1167.

by an even more fundamental problem: of our needing to live together, solving our problems in ways consistent with this end. Dialogue does not *just* serve an epistemic truth-seeking goal, it serves also the social goal of solving problems. This chapter elaborates a dialogical conception of virtues of practice designed to serve this goal.[6]

Before outlining our conception of virtues of practice, we need to address a problem. Virtues of practice are dialogical, but how does this fit into a *virtue* ethics? According to a traditional view of virtue ethics, the arbiter of rightness is a virtuous agent, namely he or she who has fine sensibilities, 'situational appreciation', practical wisdom (which involves fine emotions), good character. Not only is the say-so or choice of a virtuous agent criterially determinative of rightness, on this view, but that say-so or choice provides also an epistemology. If you are not virtuous yourself, just imitate the virtuous. In short, virtue ethics is thought to possess a monological epistemology incompatible with dialogic ethics.

The criticism that virtue ethics has a monological epistemology has two aspects. First, there is the charge that virtue ethics has an intuitionistic epistemology: a virtuous agent is rather like the experienced cook who just 'sees' when the cake is ready. The 'situational appreciation' of a virtuous agent is just a kind of perception.[7] However, in response to this criticism, a virtue ethicist could maintain that a virtuous agent is a rule and measure of rightness, while eschewing a problematic perceptual model of moral epistemology. In particular, she could claim, a virtuous agent is a rule and measure of rightness having exercised dialogical virtues. In other words, she doesn't just *see*, she consults virtuously.

The second aspect of the criticism that virtue ethics has a monological approach to ethics is more radical. Ethics is not a matter of *individual* judgement, as virtue ethics (allegedly) supposes. Janna Thompson expresses this more radical criticism as follows: 'virtues as they are usually treated are personal characteristics, and therefore, to the extent to

6 The remainder of this chapter is partly based on an unpublished paper co-written with Viviane Robinson, 'Virtues of Practice'. Some of the material is derived from her *Problem-Based Methodology: Research for the Improvement of Practice* (Oxford: Pergamon Press, 1993). Some of the examples are derived from her work as an educational practitioner and theorist.

7 David Bakhurst, 'Ethical Particularism in Context', in B. Hooker and M. Little (eds.), *Moral Particularism* (Oxford: Clarendon Press, 2000), accuses both Jonathan Dancy and John MacDowell of believing that moral competence 'should be understood as a kind of perceptual capacity to respond to the specific configurations of morally relevant properties each case presents' (165). I reject this view as an account of moral competence.

which judgement is informed by the virtues, ethics is a matter for individual judgement'.[8] This conclusion does not, however, follow from the idea that virtues are personal characteristics. A virtue ethicist can accept that 'there is no such thing as the virtuous man or woman who can authentically make judgements which others ought to accept',[9] and can therefore accept that ethics is not characteristically a matter for individual judgement. For judgement informed by the virtues is informed by wisdom, which in turn feeds into virtues of self-knowledge; and these tell us that we are not only limited in perspectives, experience, and expertise, but that the constellation of virtues possessed by us will not exactly match that possessed by others. Hence a virtue ethicist could and should accept that ethical decision-making in social contexts is and ought to be collective. This does not entail that the procedures for doing this necessitate agreement. What kind of agreement (if any) is necessary for construction of solutions to problems is itself a problem, and the problem has different manifestations in different contexts, whether these contexts concern families or large organizations.

I conclude that virtue ethics is not wedded to monological epistemology. It can and should meet the challenge of Nietzsche. It is met by developing a virtue-ethical dialogical ethics, in which I describe what I call virtues of practice.

Let me now give a summary of the account of virtues of practice and their aim, to be developed in subsequent sections. The *aim* in exercising virtues of practice is to get things right (act virtuously overall) in solving problems ranging from the relatively mundane, such as how do I get my kids to rugby football training, to a life and death medical problem. All such problems implicate the virtues. I could get my kids to training, for example, by failing to act virtuously—by forcing them to walk a great distance in dangerous areas when other options are available. That would be callous and uncaring.

Any problem has constraints on its solution. Not only are there constraints of time or cost and energy on such activities as gathering information and consulting, constraints involve virtues whose targets may come into conflict. For example, the virtue of efficiency may conflict with those of caring and openness. Acting in an overall virtuous way involves integrating the various constraints on the solution of the rele-

8 *Discourse and Knowledge*, 135.
9 Ibid. 137.

vant problem. In summary, the aim is to get things right by acting in an overall virtuous way in integrating constraints on solutions to problems.

Two further caveats need to be noted. First, the general requirement of hitting the targets of virtues need not mandate a specific solution to the problem of acting rightly. The process of accommodating the various constraints on the solution of a specific moral problem may allow for indeterminacy. The problem of indeterminacy is the topic of the next chapter.

Second, it is not the case that whatever solution emerges from exercise of the virtues of practice is right. Procedural constraints are not the only constraints on solution adequacy. On my target-centred virtue-ethical view of rightness, what is reasonable may not be right, precisely because real agents are not idealized, and 'right' is not equivalent to 'done for good reason'.[10] Though practitioners may make mistakes while acting reasonably, they nonetheless need to be committed to virtues which allow for improvement,[11] virtues such as readiness to learn and executive virtues which facilitate improvement in the collective environment.

The remainder of this chapter elucidates the two key components of my conception of the practical task of ethics. These are the aims of the agent in constructing a solution to a problem, and the virtues of practice. In section ii, I give an account of the aims of an agent facing a problem, namely the resolution of a problem by integrating constraints. In section iii, I offer an account of virtues of practice which emphasizes a dialogical (as opposed to monological) method for constructing solutions. These virtues fall into three main categories. First, practitioners need virtues of focus, so problems can be identified and addressed. Second, given the understanding of problem resolution in terms of the integration of constraints, practitioners need a variety of moral or epistemic virtues, including creative virtues and others associated with what John Dewey has called 'imaginative deliberation'. Third, given the need to integrate constraints having due regard to a variety of 'voices', or perspectives, we need virtues of dialogue.

---

[10] Contrast certain Kantian views according to which a maxim of action contains its reason, and a right action is one where the maxim so understood satisfies a test for maxims, so it would appear that a distinction between moral rightness and reasonableness cannot be drawn.

[11] See further on this feature and its importance, Robinson, *Problem-Based Methodology*. I am much indebted to Viviane Robinson for my understanding and use of the constraint integration account.

(ii) The Constraint Integration Account

The aim of an agent in attempting to solve a problem is to integrate the various constraints on its solution. This section explicates this aim. The next section elaborates the virtues needed by agents in prosecuting this aim.

In his article 'What is a Problem that We Might Solve It?', Thomas Nickles defines a problem as a 'demand that a certain goal be achieved, plus constraints on the manner in which the goal is achieved, i.e. conditions of adequacy on the problem solution'.[12] Constraints could include relevant values, material conditions such as resource levels, time, energy, and existing practices which any proposed solution must accommodate. If the only constraint on the solution were the goal itself, any procedure for realizing the goal would be acceptable.

Problem-solving requires constraint integration. The process of integration is not a process of choosing to ignore certain constraints while focusing on others; of choosing one horn of a supposed dilemma over another. Rather, the process is one of transformation of a problem—a process admirably described by Dewey:

> The aim in deliberation should be to devise an action in which all [competing tendencies] are fulfilled, not indeed in their original form but in a 'sublimated' fashion, that is, in a way which modifies the original direction of each by reducing it to a component along with others in an action of transformed quality.[13]

For example, a school principal determined to provide elite programmes for the children of a politically powerful parent group achieves an incomplete resolution of its curriculum provision problems if that constraint is not set alongside other constraints, like the need to maintain the financial viability of the school and to meet equity goals. The process of 'transforming' a problem so that 'competing tendencies' can be fulfilled, then, is the process of integrating constraints rather than choosing between them.[14]

---

[12] *Synthese* 47 (1981), 85–118, at 111.

[13] John Dewey, *Human Nature and Conduct: An Introduction to Social Psychology* (New York: Henry Holt & Co., 1922), 194.

[14] The model of integrating norms by the progressive specification of a constraint structure has some affinities with Henry S. Richardson's 'specifying norms': 'Specifying Norms as a Way to Resolve Concrete Ethical Problems', *Philosophy and Public Affairs* (1990), 279–310. The model shares his view that the point of values needs to be grasped if there is to be a successful attempt to integrate, i.e. cohere across, norms. However, it is not committed to his view that a specification must end with a more concrete specification of a norm which is itself a norm—

How do we integrate constraints? Constraints are integrated through a process of progressively specifying and respecifying the constraint structure of a problem. In this progression we move from a problem that appears intractable or even dilemmatic to one which is transformed so that newly specified constraints take on a more tractable air. Constraints become more tractable because the transformed specifications open up a richer range of possibilities for their satisfaction—the fulfilment of what Dewey terms 'competing tendencies'.

Let us illustrate the method of integrating constraints by discussing an example of R. M. Hare's:

> I have promised to take my children to the river at Oxford, and then a lifelong friend turns up from Australia and is in Oxford for the afternoon and wants to be shown round the college with his wife.[15]

At first sight, Hare's problem looks like a classic hard-edged moral dilemma, with a clash between two big principles: the duty of keeping one's promise and the duty of hospitality to friends.[16] Hare himself describes the 'moral conflict' in this kind of way. However, while the constraints are expressed in such terms, the possibilities for integration seem poor. Flexibility can be gained, however, by modifying the constraints in ways that preserve their basic point. To assess the point of a constraint, one must go beyond abstract discussion of principle, and try to understand what that constraint seeks to preserve in the particular context in which it is held to be relevant.

First, we can see the problem as one which implicates two virtues, hospitality and fidelity. The target of hospitality is (in this kind of case) providing entertainment and perhaps food and shelter to friends, the target of fidelity (in this kind of case) is keeping promises. Now, integrating the constraints constituted by these targets is made possible by the appreciation that virtues are complex, are closely connected to other virtues, and that this interconnection allows for their interpretation in the light of situation, role, and so on. For example, fidelity implicates trust,

---

albeit one which admittedly need hold sway only for the most part. Rather, the final point is a decision relating to this case.

[15] R. M. Hare, 'Moral Conflict', in Sterling M. McMurrin (ed.), *Tanner Lectures on Human Values*, vol. i (1980), 169–93, at 171.

[16] Although the process of modifying constraints is, as we shall see, very commonsensical, the kind of activity any parent does more or less well—Hare's own discussion does not progress beyond the *initial* formulation of constraints as the duty not to break promises and the duty of hospitality.

sincerity, and in this case, parental virtue. Hospitality implicates friendship (in this case) as well as trust and sincerity. Just which virtues are implicated and how, depends on the case. That fidelity in this case implicates parental virtue and not, say, virtue as a lawyer or business person suggests avenues for constraint integration not available in a legal context. That hospitality implicates (in this case) the virtue of friendship may similarly suggest specific types of avenues for integration.

Second, then, we can see the point of constraints by interpreting the targets of the two virtues (fidelity and hospitality) in the light of other contextually implicated virtues. This allows us to reformulate the constraints by understanding the point of a constraint in its context, leading to greater flexibility in attempts to transform the problem into one which achieves greater integration of constraints. Just as cognitive research comparing expert and novice solvers of physics problems has shown that the advantage of the latter lies in their flexible understanding of the principles of physics,[17] so those who understand the point of constraints in specific contexts will be freed from an inflexible rule-bound approach which will stymie their imaginative deliberation.

Having assessed the point of the constraints and hence discovered what needs to be preserved, we can now postulate a richer set of modified constraints which permit greater possibilities for resolution than would have been the case if we had stayed with the initial set. So we have:

I. *Initial Constraints*	II. *Modified Constraints*
(a) Keep promise to children.	(a) Be sincere. Show respect to the children and consult with them. Maintain trust, enjoyment.
(b) Be hospitable to friends by acceding to their wishes.	(b) Respect friends and consult. Be sincere about meeting their wishes as far as is possible within negotiable constraints.

The transformation of initial into modified constraints does not occur magically. It occurs after exercising virtues of practice (see section iii). It may be that the promise is a severe constraint since it is both solemn and reiterated; furthermore the danger of lessening trust is severe. Room for manoeuvre may be limited or even nonexistent as far as initial constraint (a) is concerned.

---

[17] See M. T. Chi, P. J. Feltovich, and R. Glaser, 'Categorization and Representation of Physics Problems by Experts and Novices', *Cognitive Science* 5 (1981), 121–52.

Even where movement from I to II has occurred, we still have not resolved the problem, however. We need, thirdly, to construct hypotheses which deal with the concrete specificities of the case. Action hypotheses throw up more specific constraints which allow hypotheses to be rejected or accepted. Thus, for example, the constraint of it being a child's birthday may disqualify the option of putting off the children's entertainment till next week. On the other hand, the constraint of being unable to eat a leisurely home-cooked meal may not be sufficiently serious to disqualify the option of seeing both the river and some of the college's facilities, perhaps at least the college gardens, which happen to be the best at Oxford, and which the friend's landscape gardener wife is very keen to see.

We now have *specific* constraints tagged to *specific* hypotheses which allow for rejection or pro tem acceptance of a hypothesis. Thus we have:

III. *Specific Constraints*

(a) The promise was solemn.
(b) It's a child's birthday today.
(c) The weather report is very bad for next week.
(d) The lake in the college grounds has no ducks.
(e) The visitors cannot stay overnight.
(f) We have to eat junk food

And so on.

Fourthly, and finally, we approach the bottom line of the transformation process in the reaching of a decision. The eating of junk food may not be regarded as a sufficiently serious constraint to disqualify the option of seeing both the college and going to the river; the lack of ducks may disqualify the option of substituting for the river the lake in the college grounds; the bad weather report for next week disqualifies the option of putting off the children's entertainment until next week.

Integrating constraints needs to satisfy normative standards if it is to be done in an excellent manner. In a virtue ethics, these standards derive from the virtues in the following way. Full excellence in constraint integration requires excellence in two respects:

(i) The decision reached must be overall virtuous in the sense specified in Chapter 11. That is, it must be right.
(ii) The process of integration must be done from a state of relevant virtue. That is, virtues of practice (elaborated in the next section) must be exercised.

The above conditions of excellence may be thought too harsh in two respects. First, a decision may be reached where participants have exercised virtues of practice (e.g. good dialogue), yet that decision not meet the targets of relevant virtues. Second, participants may lack the character traits required for virtue in their practical deliberations and decision-making. Their character may be authoritarian or vacillating as opposed to decisive, tactless as opposed to frank, soft as opposed to appropriately caring. Yet the participants strive to overcome these weaknesses and indeed meet the targets of relevant virtues in the process of constraint integration.

Where the first of these limitations exist, we may call the decision reasonable as opposed to right. Where the second limitation occurs (but not the first), we may call the decision both right and reasonable, but not fully excellent from a virtue-ethical point of view.

As stated above, excellence in constraint integration requires the exercise of virtues of practice. These are described in the next section.

(iii) Virtues of Practice

Our account of virtues of practice is both virtue-centred and dialogue-centred. It is virtue- rather than rule-centred because 'real life' problems are what we shall call (following Herb Simon) 'ill-structured'.[18] It is dialogue-centred both because the reasoning of a single agent, no matter how virtuous, is limited, and because of the social context of problems. We discuss each of these issues in turn.

Most 'real life' problems are ill-structured. A problem is defined as ill-structured when (i) it lacks obvious criteria for solution adequacy, (ii) the means for reaching a solution are unclear, and (iii) there is uncertainty about the nature of the information required for solution.[19] Well-structured problems. by contrast, such as those specified by an algebraic problem, have clear solution criteria, definable procedures for reaching the solution, and specifiable information requirements.

Resolving ill-structured problems requires wisdom, experience, and localized expertise that is not necessarily generalizable to other practices in which the agent is inexperienced or not proficient. When problem

---

[18] For an account of ill-structured and well-structured problems, see H. Simon, 'The Structure of Ill-structured Problems', *Artificial Intelligence* 4 (1973), 181–201.

[19] Ibid.

solvers are practised in solving particular types of problems, the process of specifying constraints and finding ways of integrating them becomes virtually automatic.[20] As new practices become routine, they become disconnected from the problem-solving processes that give rise to them, so people forget that there are alternative ways of formulating and resolving the problem. While the cost of such automaticity can be a loss of critical acumen, its benefit is the freeing of cognitive resources to engage in more deliberative problem-solving in other contexts. When experts encounter a novel problem, they spend more time than non-experts checking the accuracy of their problem representation, whereas non-experts are more immediately solution-oriented. Similarly, experts are more likely to recognize when automatic processing needs to be interrupted to incorporate new constraints on solution adequacy. Simon summarizes the balance between automatic and deliberative processing as follows:

Of course, thinking is more analytic sometimes and more intuitive at other times. In particular, the thinking of experts dealing with ordinary situations is highly intuitive. It becomes analytic only when the going gets tough, when novelty enters into it, when new problems have to be solved.[21]

A person needs the dialogical virtues, both to overcome her own limitations, and to participate adequately in a social context. These virtues (and corresponding vices) form a rich array. In any largish group engaged in dialogue, we are lucky not to find a range of vices which block constructive and productive dialogue, and which are exemplified in persons such as the following. There is the person who talks too much, failing to appreciate that there are ten others in the room, there are also the bad listener, the person insensitive to local context who keeps talking about how things are done elsewhere, the combative type, the prejudiced or culturally insensitive or 'unsafe' one, the arrogant one who fails to recognize superior expertise in others, arguing the toss (on the basis of ignorance) at every available opportunity, the bully, the non-participator with good ideas who hides her light under a bushel, the non-participator who is hostile and withdrawn, the non-serious individual who makes light of

[20] R. G. Lord and K. J. Maher, 'Cognitive Theory in Industrial and Organizational Psychology', in M. D. Dinnette and L. M. Hough (eds.), *Handbook of Industrial and Organizational Psychology*, 2nd edn. (Palo Alto, Calif.: Consulting Psychology Press, 1991), 1–62.

[21] 'Decision-Making: Rational, Nonrational, and Unirational', *Educational Administration Quarterly* 29 (1993), 392–411, at 405.

anything or turns everything into a joke, the contemptuous one who is derisive of others' intelligence or acumen, the one who can't focus on the topic, the oversensitive one who takes everything personally, the unimaginative or rigid one, the one who is overly pessimistic, or overly optimistic. The dialogic virtues and vices are legion. I cannot hope to focus on them all. I here concentrate on those I regard as central.

Let us now discuss in more detail the three categories of virtues of practice, mentioned above. First, the need for 'virtues of focus'. An attempt to solve a problem requires that participants have the disposition and ability to establish and maintain a shared focus. A shared focus suggests the nature of the information likely to be relevant, motivates the involvement of the parties, and provides a context for the operation of dialogical virtues involved in disclosure, testing and facilitation. While such a focus is frequently established (and maintained) implicitly, more explicit moves may be required when the topic is difficult or embarrassing. Where this is required, the virtues of focus require not just acumen, discipline, sensitivity, and wisdom, but also may require courage and persistence. There is a need, then, for virtues designed to overcome the numerous obstacles to an adequate and shared understanding of the focus. Research suggests, for example, that informal employee appraisals frequently occur without a shared understanding of the focus of the conversation. Post-appraisal interviews have revealed that the employee is frequently unaware that the conversation was an appraisal, designed to convey a warning about his or her performance. The supervisors, on the other hand, are convinced that they have fulfilled their obligation to convey their concerns to their subordinates.[22]

Apparently opposed to our conception of dialogue in which conversational focus is central, is N. Burbules's[23] conception of dialogue and its point. For Burbules, dialogue is expressive of a relationship, and more indirectly, expressive of the value of relationship. He claims: 'In its purest forms dialogue becomes intrinsic; we are carried forward in the dynamic of the to-and-fro movement without regard to any particular goal or end

---

[22] For empirical evidence on the 'vanishing appraisal' phenomenon, see M. Beer, 'Performance Appraisal', in J. Lorsch (ed.), *Handbook of Organisational Behaviour* (New York: Prentice-Hall, 1987), 286–300, and E. M. Bridges, *The Incompetent Teacher*, Stanford Series on Education and Public Policy (Lewes: Falmer Press, 1986).

[23] Nicholas C. Burbules, *Dialogue in Teaching: Theory and Practice* (New York: Teachers College Press, 1993), and V. M. J. Robinson's review of the above, 'Dialogue Needs a Point and Purpose', *Educational Theory* 45 (1995), 235–49.

point'.[24] For him, dialogue resembles a game: in a game, 'we can very easily lose track of time and place; we forget the score, forget winning or losing, forget the last game or the next game, and simply *play*'.[25]

Although an important aspect of dialogic virtue is the aspect of expressiveness, and in particular the expressiveness of play in a relationship, even this feature can be problematized. A husband who greets his wife's enthusiastic descriptions of the juxtaposition of setting sun and surf with the occasional bored or irritated grunt is behaving in a problematic manner. The most apparently pointless dialogue, then, may have features which should be problematized, and then focus is essential. Nor is losing track of time and place always ethically acceptable. In meetings where participants have work or family to get back to, or necessary leisure to enjoy, little is more irritating than colleagues who 'lose track of time and place' (and agenda), and treat dialogue as a to-ing and fro-ing kind of play.

We turn now to a discussion of the second broad group of virtues of practice, namely the imaginative and analytic virtues required to facilitate constraint integration. The account of constraint integration presented in section ii suggests a variety of virtues needed for success. Central are insight and depth of understanding, creativity, and commitment to valid information. Insight and depth of understanding are required to understand the point and rationale of constraints, so that they can be re-specified in ways which both preserve their point (as far as is possible) and render the problem more tractable. In ill-structured problems, creativity is essential for the imaginative deliberation required to form hypotheses which will allow the specific constraints to be integrated. Given the centrality of creativity for constraint integration, I am opposed to the common idea that creativity and originality are epistemically 'supererogatory'[26] and to the common definition of creativity as essentially a rare phenomenon.[27] As we saw in Chapter 7, creativity is a quotidian virtue (or aspect of virtue) exemplified in all walks of life.

---

[24] *Dialogue in Teaching*, 50.

[25] Ibid. 51.

[26] See Zagzebski, *Virtues of the Mind*.

[27] For example, Colin Martindale claims that 'A creative idea is generally defined as one that is novel and, in some sense, useful or appropriate for the situation in which it occurs' Given this definition, creativity is rare if not impossible in most lines of endeavour. 'How Can We Measure a Society's Creativity?', in Margaret A. Boden (ed.), *Dimensions of Creativity* (Cambridge, Mass.: MIT Press, 1994), 159–97, at 159.

Another important constellation of virtues is associated with a commitment to correct information, an important requirement for the integration of constraints. Such virtues are dispositions to disclose one's own perspective, interests and beliefs, to gather data and acknowledge facts, to publicly test claims made during the process of problem resolution, to acknowledge expertise and to trust that expertise, to recognize when trust is misplaced, and to change one's beliefs on the strength of evidence and publicly acknowledge mistakes. Many of these virtues are strengthened by the presence of other virtues, such as courage to disclose and admit errors; humility in the face of superior knowledge, expertise, or conceptual skills; or a disposition not to be threatened by superior knowledge or expertise.

The point of disclosure is not only to reveal one's perspective, but also to facilitate its testing. While private examination of one's own views can result in the detection and correction of error, it is no substitute for public testing, for the same reasoning processes that lead us to believe as we do are likely to inform our examination of our beliefs. In many cases, especially when dealing with matters with which we are closely involved, errors can only be detected and corrected through exposing them to the scrutiny of others. For example, if we state why we believe the chairperson behaved dictatorially, rather than making a bald assertion, others can begin to understand the basis of our inference and to evaluate its validity. Public testing is particularly important where relevant information is based on attributions about others' mental states and reactions. If such attributions are based on private monitoring strategies such as mind-reading and second-guessing, they have a higher likelihood of error than if publicly tested. This does not of course mean that others' claims about themselves are automatically accepted.

Apart from creativity and the ability and willingness to test assumptions, beliefs, and understandings, possibly the most important cognitive moral virtue is that of contextualized, concrete, and non-dichotomized thinking. An abstract formulation of the constraint structure robs it of the richness that makes it possible for a problem to be resolved. Constraint structures must be developed and resolved in concrete contexts, so that the accuracy of their formulation and hypotheses about their implications and compatibility can be tested through feedback from the empirical situation in which they apply. The tendency to abstraction is also seen in the depersonalization of ethical problems so that only idealized or decontextualized individuals actually operate upon them. The failure to take into account the additional constraints, such as limits of time, energy, and skill that real problem-solvers bring to the situation, has laid various communicative ethics open to the charge that they are utopian. Habermas's discourse ethics, for example, has been frequently criticized as requiring conditions for ethical judgement that are simply impossible to meet. In his defence, writers like S. Benhabib[28] and R. Young[29] point out that Habermas is putting forward an ideal which enables us to evaluate critically the institutional and interpersonal conditions under which what is right is currently determined, not a specification of how such judgements should be reached in concrete circumstances. As Benhabib puts it, 'the discourse theory does not develop a positive model of the functioning of institutions, which after all will always be subject to space/time constraints, as well as to those of scarce resources and personnel'.

We have pointed out how abstract formulation of constraints can rob one of the detail needed to fashion an integration between them. Integration can also be blocked, not so much by an impoverishment of description, as by the tendency to set up stark oppositions and to assume the incompatibility of various concepts. The implications of this mode of thinking for ethical problem-solving are shown in the following example. The head of a university department is concerned that his staff do not implement agreed procedures for completion of certain administrative tasks. As a result, the administration of the department is inefficient and more work falls on his shoulders than is appropriate, given staff's espousal of a democratic, collegial form of self-governance. He attempts to resolve the problem by specifying the following constraints on the solution. First, he believes it is crucial to treat his staff as professional colleagues rather than as subordinates; second, he believes that any solution should be consistent with a principle of collegial accountability; and third, the solution should, if possible, improve departmental efficiency. Despite the frustration he feels, the head can find no suitable course of action and the problem continues. This impasse is difficult to explain without probing more deeply into why the head sees professional treatment as incompatible with direct questioning of his colleagues about their failure to complete a task. He argues it would be like him

[28] S.Benhabib, 'In the Shadow of Aristotle and Hegel: Communicative Ethics and Current Controversies in Practical Philosophy', in M. Kelly (ed.), *Hermeneutics and Critical Theory in Ethics and Politics* (Cambridge, Mass.: MIT Press, 1990), 1–32.

[29] R. Young, *A Critical Theory of Education: Habermas and Our Children's Future* (New York: Harvester Wheatsheaf, 1989).

asking them why they had not included a particular reference in the reading list for their course. It is simply not his business. This notion of professional treatment rules out most forms of accountability except the most indirect of generalized reminders to staff. Given that these have failed, the head feels that he has no further options.

The way out of this impasse is to reformulate the constraints in a way that renders them more mutually compatible, without distorting the integrity of their underlying values. If professional treatment is understood, for example, not as non-interference, but as the basis for shared inquiry and problem-solving, it is perfectly compatible with accountability, understood as being answerable to one's peers. Given this understanding, the constraint structure can be satisfied by a solution which ensures the head discloses his concern to his staff, inquiring with them into why the failures occur and confronting them about the need to make decisions to which they are personally committed, so that they do not waste his and each other's time making decisions which they will not or cannot implement. The resolution is made possible by asking whether a different construal of the constraints could render them compatible while still preserving their point and purpose.

The third broad group of virtues of practice are specifically dialogical, and are required for the resolution of problems in group contexts. An important set of these virtues are those involved in facilitation. Most institutional contexts incorporate various imbalances of power which militate against criticism of taken-for-granted assumptions about what is desirable, and which exclude from participation in dialogue some of those groups who should be considered relevant participants. In addition, many groups which are free from power imbalances sustain their solidarity through a cosy acceptance of a shared belief system. Against such a background, many participants in a dialogue will either not expect their views to be taken seriously, or lack confidence in their articulation and defence.

It is not sufficient, therefore, to articulate one's own views. One must do so in a way that encourages others to do so in return. This is accomplished by expressing one's own views non-dogmatically and inviting others to express theirs, especially when disagreement is sensed. Rather than ignoring opposition, good dialogue requires that it be surfaced through such statements as 'You're frowning; are you sure this suits you?' or 'It's important that we can all live with this, so please tell me of your doubt'. Contrast these requests with the more aggressive strategy captured by the phrase, 'When persuasion fails, persuade harder'. Non-verbal behaviours such as expression, eye-contact, and posture are also involved in facilitation. Congruence between verbal and non-verbal behaviours is also relevant. Claims from the Australian friends in the Hare example that they don't mind the children coming will seem untrustworthy if accompanied by a studious ignoring of their presence.

The operation of virtues of practice is a dynamic process of feedback, learning, and modification, so that more successful integration can take place. As a result, the model of constraint integration is different from a model of problem-solving as simply a choice between alternative solutions. It is not simply that there is a smorgasbord of alternatives to which a decision-maker assigns weights, selecting one and then acting on it. Rather, integrating constraints is an active, developmental process of transformation at an intellectual, emotional, and behavioural level. The understanding is developed first perhaps in a relatively abstract way such as through mission and vision statements, and then progressively deepened through narrowing the constraint structure. In this process of narrowing, much learning and developing needs to take place. The point of constraints has to be understood, they have to be set in context, imaginative deliberation has to be employed to construct solutions which do the least violence to various values, and the behaviour changes needed to develop the solutions have to be made if resistance and distortions are not to feature as further constraints on the possible space of solutions.

To show the dynamic, developmental process of constraint integration, consider the following example. A superannuation expert visits a large company in order to speak to the workers about the company superannuation scheme. He operates with the following constraint structure.

Goal: To perform a fee-paying job, thus helping the company's bottom line.
Constraint: To give value for money to the business client.
Modified Constraint: To present the information to the workers in a way that is both clear and accurate.

The actuary rightly judges that giving value for money in this context demands that he satisfies two constraints: accuracy and clarity. Narrowing the constraint structure has rightly led to this modified constraint set. However, the actuary learns through feedback that many workers have not understood the information. On further reflection, the actuary realizes that he has operated with a third constraint, so that the modified constraint set really includes:

(a) Present with clarity.
(b) Give accurate information.
(c) Project a professional image.

Constraint (c) has effectively operated as a tacit constraint. Furthermore, constraint (c) has not been integrated with constraint (a)—present with clarity. The actuary does not work on analysing the point of constraint (c), and continues to have an uneasy feeling that (a) and (c) are in tension, the workers are congenitally stupid, and nothing much can be done. Eventually the actuary loses the client. This forces a rethink. The actuary then considers constraint (c): Project a professional image. He reflects on the point of (c). After deliberation he formulates the following modified constraint:

> The need to project a professional image, which involves thoroughness, care, and respecting clients.

The actuary re-enters the fray. Alas, his behaviour has not significantly changed. His presentations are still not understood by the workers. The actuary thinks more deeply. He realizes that, though on a surface, intellectual level he has sorted out the constraint structure, he has not integrated them in an excellent way. This is because the integration has lacked virtue in the following respect. He realizes that at a behavioural and emotional level, projecting a professional image for *him* involves projecting a superior image, where displaying expertise is a matter of showing how clever you are through use of lots of jargon and complex sentence constructions. The actuary, with some pain, realizes that he is a snob and has power needs. Over a long period of time he works on these vices, eventually succeeding in integrating the constraints in an excellent way.

(iv) Dialogic Ethics?

Given the role of dialogue in excellent constraint integration, and recent interest in dialogic ethics, the question arises: is my view a version of dialogic ethics? It is unclear what is meant by 'dialogic ethics' as a complete, independent, normative ethical theory, but if the term is understood sufficiently broadly, I would be happy to class my view as a dialogic version of virtue ethics. It is important then to clarify the commitments of this view, and to answer some common objections to dialogic ethics.

According to a strong version of dialogic ethics, whatever decision is reached as result of excellent dialogue is right. This is a dialogic version of the 'qualified agent' conception of rightness in virtue ethics, and it will be clear by now that I reject that view along with the 'qualified agent' conception of rightness. For it is possible that, through no fault of the dialoguers, the products of even excellent dialogue may miss the target(s) of relevant virtues. In short, a distinction is enforced between reasonableness and rightness.

My view, however, does share two standard commitments of dialogic ethics. The first is that it is a moral requirement that, in standard sorts of situations, decisions are made collectively. This is recognized in a number of role virtues, such as good parent, good business manager, good doctor. As noted above, it does not follow from this fact that, no matter what the context, all participants' opinions carry equal weight, all partners have equal input, or unanimity is required. Given the collective nature of decision-making, and given that conversation is characteristically the medium through which collective decisions are made, excellent dialogue is necessary properly to satisfy the moral requirement that (in standard sorts of situations) decisions are to be made collectively.

The second commitment is epistemological. Dialogic ethics emphasizes the need for dialogue to overcome a lack of virtue, lack of expertise, limited perspectives, or limited resources (of time, energy, or money).

Dialogic ethics has been subject to a number of standard objections.[30] I shall argue that all can be overcome if dialogic ethics is embedded in a constraint-integration account of solving problems. The first objection claims that there is no criterion for a stopping place for dialogue. What is to stop a dialogue from proceeding interminably? The problem is not resolved by the postulation of an abstract 'moral principle' which sets out when dialogue is to be terminated. Rather, the need for termination is a constraint, which has to be understood in a context and set alongside other constraints, including perhaps the need for an accurate decision and the inability to revisit any decision. These constraints are then modified in the process of narrowing the constraint structure; for example, the need for termination constraint may be modified—made more concrete—by a formal procedure, which specifies that the meeting lasts from 4 p.m. to 6 p.m. That constraint in turn is modifiable by further

---

[30] These objections have been made salient in Gillian Brock's review essay of Daryl Koehn, *Rethinking Feminist Ethics: Care, Trust, and Empathy* (London: Routledge, 1998) entitled 'Rethinking Feminist Ethics: Is Dialogical Ethics a Better Approach?', *Social Theory and Practice* 25 (1999), 531–7.

constraints such as the failure to get through the agenda. Integration may be achieved by extending the meeting until 6.30 p.m., or, if people have to leave, by having an extra meeting, by finishing the meeting by e-mail, or by delegating decisions.

Another common objection is that it is unclear with whom we are to dialogue. Is there a moral requirement to dialogue with all affected parties? At the most abstract level, there is a constraint to dialogue with relevant parties. But this constraint remains at a useless level of abstraction until it is set in context, alongside other constraints. A universal moral principle that *all* affected parties have a *right* to dialogue so as to have input into a decision ignores other constraints such as the urgency of the decision, efficiency, and cost. Nor do I accept that privileged groups, such as owners, have a right not to dialogue with stakeholders. Or rather, if they do have some institutional right of this kind, it may generally be wrong for them to exercise that right.[31] Rather, there is a constraint of social responsibility which itself involves a process of determining relevant parties for dialogue, such as environmentalists, or (in New Zealand) Maori as required by the Treaty of Waitangi. The latter constraint may itself be modified in the light of further problems; for example, though Maori are salient as parties of dialogue because of the treaty, other Polynesian groups such as Tongans and Samoans may need to be consulted for multi-cultural reasons, and because they may both be more populous in a given area and importantly affected.

Another objection may also be met by the constraint integration account. Dialogic ethics is sometimes thought to be deficient because it cannot deal with intractable disagreement. But again, we need to remove ourselves from the abstract and the utopian. The process of modifying constraints may result in formal procedures for resolving disagreement, such as majority voting and chairpersons' casting votes, or if time is not a serious constraint, conversation may go on for a very long time with various devices for reducing antagonisms, such as feasting on seafood (in certain cultures) and motivational bonding games, so that (hopefully) obstacles to resolving disagreement can be overcome.

A fourth objection is a sceptical one concerning 'collective unreason' expressed as follows by Philip Pettit:

---

[31] See Jeremy Waldron's claim that one can have a right to do wrong in his 'A Right to Do Wrong', *Ethics* 92 (1981), 21–39.

Is it not enough to know that truth is that property which would cause a proposition to be accepted by anyone, even when the proposition is subjected to radical interrogation? Why does one have to be told how to ensure that the interrogation is radical in the case where a number of people open discussion with one another, rather than each thinking the matter out on his own?[32]

According to Pettit, the problem gets worse when one considers that collective reasoning may result in a 'foreclosure of radical questioning . . . since it is notorious that in collectivities people quickly succumb to pressures of conformity and co-ordination'.[33] Finally, 'if the participants are lazy thinkers no amount of democratization will guarantee that their interrogation is radical'.[34] The problems outlined by Pettit precisely highlight the need for virtues of practice. They do not show that deliberation in applied ethics ought to be private rather than dialogical. Rather, what is needed are virtues which guard against the hazards of collective unreason such as uncritical democratization and equalization of influence, laziness, failure to test, impoverishment of imagination, or conformity pressures through compromise mentality.

A fifth objection concerns the demandingness of the constraint integration model. If virtuous practice triggers people's concerns about their ability to meet its interpersonal and cognitive demands, it could be that those demands are excessive, and that as a result its use by the great majority of ordinary mortals is ruled out. While suggesting that there are minimal analytic and interpersonal competencies required to engage in good dialogue, I do not believe that it requires a utopian degree of wisdom and skill. As Habermas reminds us, the basic competencies of making and redeeming various validity claims are given to us by virtue of our membership of various language communities. In acknowledging this point, however, one must take seriously the considerable evidence that these competencies are, in practice, frequently overshadowed by institutional and interpersonal pressures to act in ways that are contrary to the requirements of virtuous practice. Despite it being grounded in these competencies, therefore, the model will still be utopian if it does not show how such practice can operate despite such pressures. However, evidence from social psychology demonstrates that people can learn to detect and criticize their own and others' taken-for-granted assumptions,

32 In G. H. R. Parkinson (ed.), *Marx and Marxism*, Royal Institute of Philosophy Lecture Series, 14 (suppl. to *Philosophy*), 207–28, at 215.

33 Ibid.   34 Ibid.

to confront the political and unilateral moves of others, and to help others move from unilateral to more bilateral modes of problem-solving.[35] While the evidence shows that even the most skilled exponents of dialogue will revert to strategic forms of communication in the face of high levels of internal or external pressure to achieve particular ends, the objection of utopianism is refuted by the evidence that dialogue builds on skills that are already within us, and that can be further developed by the type of training described by C. Argyris and V. M. J. Robinson.[36]

A final objection is that dialogic ethics is one-sided, for it neglects the external structural conditions required to support the dialogical process. Here is an example of the alleged problem. Ted, the boss, brings Don into his office. Ted claims that Don's work is below acceptable standards, and that colleagues claim he is uninterested because he has a chip on his shoulder. Before dismissing Don from his office, Ted claims that he is not interested in supposed injustices suffered by Don in the past, because they occurred before his time and at any rate are irrelevant in the here and now. Ted's intervention is perceived by Don and others as dictatorial, devoid of testing, monological, and generally incompetent. It might be objected to my account of virtues of practice that the real problem lies not in Ted's lack of virtues of practice, but in the authoritarian structures of the workplace.[37] In general, it may be claimed, virtuous dialogue and virtues of practice generally are impotent in the face of problematic external structures. These are social and institutional practices, whether formal or informal, that require decisions and actions which would not be endorsed by the type of virtuous procedures outlined, and which prohibit the challenge or review of existing (non-virtuous) practices.

In reply to the objection that external structures rather than lack of virtue is the real problem, one may note several points. First it should be noted that the type of institutional arrangement that is more or less conducive to virtuous practice is frequently debatable. While some generalizations about the absence of force and coercion are possible, further specification is extremely difficult because it requires speculation about the lengthy causal chains that link external structures and the agents

---

[35] For more on the educative processes involved, see C. Argyris, *Strategy Change and Defensive Routines* (Marshfield, Mass.: Pitman, 1985), and C. Argyris, R. Putnam, and D. McLain Smith, *Action Science* (San Francisco, Calif.: Jossey-Bass, 1985).

[36] Agyris, *Strategy Change and Defensive Routines*, and Robinson, *Problem-Based Methodology*.

[37] For further discussion of this example, see Robinson, *Problem-Based Methodology*.

involved in a problem.[38] It is not at all clear, for example, that hierarchical or bureaucratic organizational forms are any more or less conducive to the conduct of good dialogue than are collectives or more organic organizational structures. The empirical literature that is available suggests that when the stakes are high, dialogical practices that reflect respect and a search for quality information are as elusive in either form.[39]

Let us imagine that further empirical research did provide us with trustworthy accounts of the external conditions that were more or less conducive to the exercise of virtues of practice. What implications could be drawn from such research for the applicability of the model in those conditions which the research showed to be in general inhibitory? The presence of conditions which are in general inhibitory should not preclude exercise of virtues of practice, but exactly how they are exercised will depend on structural and other inhibitors. The presence of countervailing external constraints is recognized via the constraint-integration account of ethical problems; the more such constraints are evident, the more difficult it will be for actors to counteract them through their practice. Rather than assume the inapplicability of the model in such circumstances, however, actors should use the resources it provides to test the causal force of the alleged external constraints on the conduct of dialogue. The counsel of despair is of no practical use to participants.

A related problem is that a virtue-based approach to problem-solving is unacceptable, not because it omits structural variables altogether, but because the focus on particular agents produces an inappropriately small-scale or microcosm analysis. How can analyses of individual virtues tell us anything about large-scale structural problems? The general problem, of which this is a part, is the relation of virtue *ethics* to political philosophy, and this book is not (directly) a book on political philosophy. Yet scepticism about the application of virtue *ethics* to applied *ethics* can take precisely this form. How can emphasis on the virtues of agents, even when those virtues are not 'individualistic' but involve relationship and dialogue, contribute to issues in applied fields, beset as they are with large-scale structural problems? In reply it could be argued that formulating problems on a small scale has both practical and psychological advantages. Our virtues and information-processing

[38] See P. S. Adler, 'The Learning Bureaucracy: New United Motor Manufacturing Inc.', *Research in Organizational Behavior* 15 (1993), 119–94.

[39] A. Swidler, *Organization Without Authority* (Cambridge, Mass.: Harvard University Press, 1979).

capabilities are better matched to modestly rather than grandly formulated problems. Robinson puts the point this way:

Psychologically, the chances of success are increased when massive social problems are recast into smaller ones, because problem-solvers are more likely to judge the challenge as within their capacities, and as less risky. As Weick puts it, aiming for small wins produces a more functional level of arousal for those involved:

'A small win reduces importance ("this is no big deal"), reduces demands ("that's all that needs to be done"), and raises perceived skill levels ("I can do at least that"). When reappraisals of problems take this form, arousal becomes less of a deterrent to solving them.'[40]

Admittedly, a gap in a theory of structural constraints may lead to exaggeration of the possibilities for virtuous dialogue and practice generally. An imbalance of this sort is preferable, however, to an overly determinist account of the constraints on virtuous dialogue and practice, because the former imbalance can be corrected through feedback from dialogical attempts. The latter imbalance is far less likely to be detected and corrected because its structural determinism is less likely to suggest how its own claims can be tested in the particular context under investigation. There is a practical payoff, in other words, in formulating analyses in ways that encourage agents to confront constraints and thus test their theories about what is and is not possible. Not only is the incremental approach more practical and efficacious, it may also promote the development of virtues appropriate to facing large-scale problems. At the very least it may forestall the development of despair, cynicism, bitterness, and hopelessness. For the agent exercising virtues of practice is more likely to feel productive, creative, and effective. Integration of constraints is not a utopian exercise and the achievements may be somewhat limited. However, even limited achievements may be the fruit of hard, productive labour in the face of great complexity, great conflict, and limited resources of all kinds.

[40] *Problem-Based Methodology*, 52.

13

Indeterminacy

(i) The Problem of Indeterminacy

This chapter discusses the third problem for virtue ethics identified in Chapter 12, and the supposed consequent impotence of virtue ethics in the field of applied ethics. The rejection of the epistemological model of 'virtuous agent as oracle', and its replacement with a virtue-based constraint-integration account of dialogic ethics, may be thought to silence the well-known criticism of Robert B. Louden:

It has often been said that for virtue ethics the central question is not 'What ought I to *do*?' but rather 'What sort of person ought I to *be*?' However, people have always expected ethical theory to tell them something about what they ought to do, and it seems to me that virtue ethics is structurally unable to say much of anything about this issue. If I'm right, one consequence of this is that a virtue-based ethics will be particularly weak in the areas of casuistry and applied ethics.[1]

However, the supposed 'structural' inability of virtue ethics to be useful in applied ethics is thought to reside in the disagreement amongst virtuous agents whose virtues do not appear to mandate the same courses of action. Nor is it clear that such disagreement would be resolved by exercising virtues of practice. The resultant indeterminacy undermines confidence that virtue ethics can meet Louden's objection. Though a standard virtue-ethical reply to the objection is the appeal to the standards of practical wisdom possessed by the virtuous, applied on a case by case basis, R. Jay Wallace draws our attention to the problem of disagreement:

if there were extensive lack of convergence among connoisseurs of wine as to which wines are good and which bad, then it would be correspondingly

---

[1] 'On Some Vices of Virtue Ethics', *American Philosophical Quarterly* 21 (1984), 227–36, at 229.

implausible to suppose that their judgments are rationally well-supported, or that they represented a normative ideal of correct discrimination.[2]

Wallace suggests that the virtuous are precisely in the position of 'extensive lack of convergence'. He continues:

other connoisseurs of the moral life are apt to be moved by case-specific reasons for acting in quite different and incompatible ways, and this will undermine the normative dimension of practical reason: the idea that the exercise of judgment enables its possessor to discern the uniquely *correct* or right thing to do, in particular circumstances of action.[3]

It will be replied that the search for the *uniquely correct* thing to do is misguided: why should uniqueness be required? But the real problem, one may think, is not the need for *uniquely* correct solutions to moral problems, but the fact that there is too much disagreement even between virtuous agents exercising virtues of practice. Even if the sets of reasons available to a virtuous agent for undertaking a given course of action are good reasons, there may exist good reasons for undertaking other courses of action that are available to several other virtuous agents, and they may disagree about which actions are best or right, even where they are not committed to the idea of uniqueness.

Indeterminacy, characterized as follows by Susan Wolf, appears therefore to be the lot of virtue ethics:

There will be cases in which there are good reasons for one position and good reasons for an incompatible position and no further overarching principle and perspective from which these can be put into any further objective balance. In such cases, one might say that both positions are equally right. Or one might say that there is no right answer; no fact of the matter about what is right.[4]

In cases like this, as indicated in Chapter 11, I prefer to talk about each alternative being a best or right 'position' (or action as the case may be), rather than being equally right (for that suggests commensurability) or there being 'no fact of the matter' as to which is right. For the latter locution may suggest that choice of one option is without good, undefeated, reason.

In the light of the notion of indeterminacy defined above, we can offer a general statement of the problem supposedly besetting virtue

2 'Virtue, Reason, and Principle', *Canadian Journal of Philosophy* 21 (1991), 469–95, at 490.
3 Ibid. 491.
4 'Two Levels of Pluralism', *Ethics* 102 (1992), 785–98, at 788.

ethics. In deliberation, or a process in which virtues of practice are being exercised, different virtues may seem, as Hursthouse puts it, to point us in conflicting directions.[5] Self-protection points towards finishing the dialogue now, perseverance points towards continuing; tolerance and openness point towards bringing into the discussion yet more affected or potentially affected parties, efficiency points towards neglecting or ignoring some of them. Caring (towards an incompetent individual) points to giving her further chances, benevolence (towards the larger group) points towards sacking her. Small wonder, then, that different virtuous agents may recommend different courses of action.

Given that virtuous agents are at least characteristically sources of good reason for action, and that the virtues in terms of which reasons are characterized point in different directions, there seems to be no ground within virtue ethics for adjudicating between the different recommendations of virtuous agents. Recourse to the kind of virtuously conducted dialogue described in the last chapter just seems to push the problem further back: such virtuously conducted dialogue can still result in disagreement whose resolution appears groundless.

To determine how serious is the existence of indeterminacy in virtue ethics, we need to discuss what model of practical reason is supported by models of mind, and how virtue ethics integrates with that model. To those issues we now turn.

(ii) Virtues as Prototypes

In order to understand the problem of indeterminacy as it relates to virtue ethics, we need first to gain a clearer understanding of what is meant by 'virtues pointing us in different directions'. This claim can be understood in two ways. According to the first, virtues themselves encapsulate rules which yield precise instructions to perform certain kinds of actions in certain kinds of situations where the virtues 'point in different directions': virtue X tells us to do A in C where virtue Y tells us to not do A in C. Indeterminacy would result when such dilemmas cannot be resolved by the provision of an 'overarching principle' which can put the reasons supporting A and not-A into 'further objective balance'.

According to the second understanding of 'virtues pointing in different directions', virtues are not constituted by sets of rules which lead all

---

5   *On Virtue Ethics*, 43.

too frequently to dilemmas, but are rather prototypes. On this understanding of a virtue, indeterminacy in Wolf's sense is the result of a process of constraint integration where individual virtues, though providing good reason for conflicting actions, may not require those actions. Indeterminacy results, but not as a result of virtues mandating different courses of action.

The notion of a prototype is embedded in a certain model of mind, which has considerably enriched discussion of moral reasoning and moral expertise. I need briefly to outline the model in order to understand the idea of a virtue as a prototype. I then show how the notion can underwrite the second understanding of 'virtues pointing in different directions' and provide a resolution of the so-called problem of indeterminacy.

In moral theorizing there has been debate between two rival conceptions of moral expertise: the moral expert as conscientious follower of relatively transparent and perspicuous moral rules, and the moral expert as endowed with appropriate emotional sensibilities and context-sensitive practical wisdom whose deliverances are uncodifiable. Fortunately, in recent times, this debate has been considerably enriched by developments in cognitive science. These developments, unsurprisingly, have shown that at the extreme ends of the continuum these models are straw models, whose more plausible versions cry out for integration. Andy Clark has shown how such integration can be achieved.[6] Clark espouses a 'connectionist' model of mind while supporting a robust place for sentential reasoning in moral discourse.

According to connectionist models of mind supported by work on the biological basis for the brain, we do not characteristically reason deductively, subsuming particular cases under innumerable, relatively perspicuous, universal principles. If our practical reasoning is not basically deductive, what is it like? According to Clark, we are 'at root associative pattern-recognition devices', which is not to say that though 'good at Frisbee and bad at logic'[7] we cannot 'engage in long-term planning and carry out sequential reasoning'.[8] Pattern recognition, with its ability to detect salience and associate, to render invisible hosts of environmental features, and to learn from repeated sufficiently similar experiences, enables us to cope with a complex and constantly changing

---

[6] Clark, *Being There*.   [7] Ibid. 60
[8] Ibid.

environment. Because of this complexity, real-life biological cognition, according to Clark, is 'opportunistic'. He claims:

faced with the heavy time constraints on real world action, and armed only with a somewhat restrictive, pattern-completing style of on-board computation, the biological brain takes all the help it can get. This help includes the use of external physical structures (both natural and artifactual), the use of language and cultural institutions . . . and the extensive use of other agents. To recognize the opportunistic and spatiotemporally extended nature of real problem solving is, however, to court a potential and methodological nightmare. How are we to study and understand such complex and often non-intuitively constructed extended systems?[9]

Though Clark claims that we are 'at root' pattern-recognition and completion devices, he denies that pattern-completion style reasoning exhaustively explains expertise.[10] He opposes the 'down-playing' and 'marginalisation of summary linguistic formulations and sentential reason' found allegedly in Churchland and Dreyfus and Dreyfus.[11]

It turns out, however, that Churchland and Clark are not in disagreement on much that is fundamental. Here are crucial areas of agreement:

(1) We are 'at root' pattern-completing creatures.

(2) As a result, appropriate dispositions of sensitivity (virtue) are fundamental to moral expertise, and 'stateable rules are not the basis of one's moral character'.[12] Clark objects to Churchland's subsequent claim that '[rules] are merely [character's] pale and partial reflection at the comparatively impotent level of language'. However, it appears the disagreement is a matter of emphasis.

(3) The 'know-how involved in a biological neural network' can no more be reduced to a set of summary moral rules than can the knowledge of an expert chess player.[13]

---

[9] Ibid. 80.

[10] Ibid. 203.

[11] Andy Clark, 'Word and Action: Reconciling Rules and Know-How in Moral Cognition', in Richmond Campbell and Bruce Hunter (eds.), *Moral Epistemology Naturalized: Canadian Journal of Philosophy* 26 (suppl. issue) (2000), 267–89, at 279.

[12] Paul M. Churchland, 'The Neural Representation of the Social World', in L. May, M. Friedman, and A. Clark (eds.), *Mind and Morals* (Cambridge, Mass.: MIT Press, 1996), 92–108, at 107, cited in Clark, 'Word and Action', 270.

[13] Clark, 'Word and Action', 271.

(4) Experience and learning is crucial to the development of the sensitivities mentioned in (2). As Clark puts it: 'the development of moral knowledge and expertise is crucially dependent on rich and varied moral experience'.[14]

(5) Linguistic formulations and sentential reason provide much of the external scaffolding necessary to overcome the inherent limitations of the individual biological brain. Reasoning is built on the products of prior learning and external aids, such as other people and organizational procedures. As Clark puts it:

> We use intelligence to structure our environment so that we can succeed with *less* intelligence ... [I]t is the human brain plus these chunks of external scaffolding that finally constitutes the smart, rational inference engine that we call mind.[15]

A crucial instrument of augmentation is the use of signs, labels and words.[16] As Clark claims:

> it is our exposure to moral labels (labelling such as kind, greedy, selfless, misguided and so on) that enables our pattern-sensitive brains to isolate morally salient patterns that might otherwise remain buried beneath the noise of more superficial similarities and dissimilarities.[17]

Appropriate moral labels provide the lens through which the world is classified from the moral point of view. I might add that if these labels are rich (as is provided and endorsed by a rich virtue ethics), then the job specified under (5) will be better done.

(6) It might be thought, however, that maxims of the above kind are only employed by novices. But as Clark claims, research on expert players of a game suggests that even expert reasoners 'rely not solely on a set of past adaptive responses produced by (as it were) a trained up network but also on a set of high-level concerns or policies, which they use to monitor the outputs of the skilled network'.[18] But how is this done, given time constraints? Clark suggests that the role of maxims and policies in reasoning is probably indirect; their role is to 'alter the focus of

---

[14] Ibid.

[16] Clark, 'Word and Action', 275.

[18] Ibid.

[15] *Being There*, 180.

[17] Ibid. 277.

attention for subsequent inputs'.[19] The key mediator in keeping outputs in line with normative maxims is language, in its communicative, refining, and critical role. Clark warns, however, that our conception of the communicative role of language remains 'impoverished' unless we see it in the context of 'the broadly connectionist models of the biological brain'.[20]

(7) Linguistic formulations and sentential reason are necessary to negotiate one's way in the social world. As Clark puts it, it is necessary to 'communally negotiate a course of action that meets the different constraints of multiple individuals and interest groups'.[21]

Given that 'the larger picture' includes (1)–(7), then, as Churchland himself recognizes, Clark's views on the sentential reasoning aspects of moral cognition provide an augmentation, rather than a criticism, of 'the recent non-discursive neural network models of human cognition'.[22] Properly understood, the findings on the biological basis of expertise (whether moral or otherwise) do not downplay the importance of language, rules, communication, deliberation, and reasoning. Rather, they undermine certain conceptions of virtue, namely their being describable in terms of universal principles. In short, it supports the notion of a virtue as a prototype.[23] Let us now describe that notion of a virtue before showing how it resolves the problem of indeterminacy described in section i.

According to the notion of virtue as prototype, one might think of a virtue as a framework of broad constraints (the prototype) which is then 'contoured' (made more specific) in the various ways described in Chapter 5, section i. These contourings make the prototype applicable to concrete situations, and progressively occur as the constraint structure is narrowed in the process of constraint integration. Contourings of virtue depend on the constraints set by the concept of the virtue as it is interpreted in various contexts, which themselves impose further sets of

---

19 *Being There*, 204.   20 Ibid.

21 'Word and Action', 275.

22 Paul M. Churchland, 'Rules, Know-How and the Future of Moral Cognition', in R. Campbell and B. Hunter (eds.), *Moral Epistemology Naturalized: Canadian Journal of Philosophy* 26 (suppl. issue) (2000), 291–306, at 292.

23 For further discussion of virtue and neural network models, including the idea of prototype, see Paul M. Churchland, 'Toward a Cognitive Neurobiology of the Moral Virtues', *Topoi* 17 (1998), 83–96.

constraints. For example, benevolence and respect are constrained to varying degrees, according to the objective requirements of a culture: requirements which constitute what has been called 'cultural safety'. (This is not a cultural relativist view. Benevolence and justice provide frameworks within which some cultures may not operate.) Within cultural parameters, the manifestation of a virtue is subject to the constraints of role differentiation. These constraints are objective requirements of roles as defined by reference to the rules and procedures of institutions within which the roles are embedded—rules and procedures which in turn are answerable to norms determined or rationalized by the functions of those institutions. Within role parameters, the manifestation of a virtue is further contoured according to what has been called the 'narrative structure' of an individual's life. Within this 'narrative structure' are located specific problems requiring knowledge of our best theories as they impact on those problems. These theories in turn may help us interpret our roles and the virtues defining excellence in these roles. The norms of so-called narrative ethics (a topic beyond the scope of this book) may impose further requirements (and permissions) for the proper contextual interpretation of virtue.

As we saw in the last chapter, the task of ethics in the 'interpretation' of the constraints set by virtue is to integrate those constraints exercising virtues of practice, sensitive to various contexts. But there is no reason to believe that there is a single understanding that is *the* best in a given context, when virtues are interpreted in the light of situation, role, culture, and the narrative of individuals' lives.

The model of mind as pattern completer rather than 'logic machine' supports the view of a virtue as a prototype whose interpretation in practice is standardly immensely complex, involving excellence in pattern completion rather than the application of rules. Furthermore, the model is consistent with our account of the process of constraint integration described in the previous chapter. Rather than virtues supplying rules which may result in dilemmas, their role in excellent pattern completion may yield an indeterminacy without dilemma.

The idea of a virtue as prototype sets the framework for discussion of indeterminacy, but does not, however, resolve the problem posed by Louden. We have replaced the idea of virtues yielding conflicting requirements with the idea of virtues yielding good but often insufficient reasons for the performance of actions. As we have seen, excellence in pattern completion does not preclude the processes of sentential reasoning, justification, and deliberation, but it is unclear how such a model can guide us all the way to action and how it can yield a source of justification for our actions. We need an account of how practical reason can be understood with such a model. To the discussion of this issue we now turn.

A virtue ethicist may consider the following two models of practical reason.

(P1) It is always the case that one ought, all things considered, to do whatever one ought to do on the balance of reasons.[24]

(P2) 'One ought always, to act for an undefeated reason for action.'[25]

If the virtue ethicist goes with (P1), disagreement amongst the virtuous is a serious matter, for it seems impossible to meet the demands of (P1). If the virtue ethicist goes with (P2), disagreement is not so serious, for the demands of (P2) can still be met. Certainly, disagreement amongst the virtuous may still occur: there will be disagreement about whether or not to bring more people into the conversation, there will be disagreement about when to stop the conversation, there will be disagreement about whether to go for caring towards an individual, or efficiency or benevolence towards the group. But from the point of view of both decision-making and assessment of action the disagreement is not necessarily serious, or so I shall argue in the remainder of this chapter. Say the conversation stops as the result of a vote properly conducted. Or it just stops, without coercive or otherwise vicious acts being displayed. Perhaps certain parties run out of steam (without being lazy) and the conversation grinds to a halt. A decision to φ is then made. Agents exercising virtues of practice disagree over merits of actions, but reasons for the chosen action φ-ing have been undefeated. It need not be the case, however, that φ-ing is the course of action which the balance of reasons favours.

If (P2) is adopted for virtue ethics, it would seem, the demands on virtue ethics required by Louden, Wallace, and others are unnecessary. For if (P2) is adopted, it is not required that the good reasons in favour of an action must outweigh countervailing reasons. So even if it is true that virtue ethics cannot satisfy the demands of Wallace and Louden—that it yield reasons which uniquely determine a course of action as the one to

[24] Joseph Raz, *Practical Reason and Norms* (London: Hutchinson, 1975), 36.
[25] Ibid. 40.

be undertaken (or which specify a determinate range of permissible options)—this inability may not matter. Good reasons are undefeated, not necessarily outweighing.

We need an account of when it is virtuous and reasonable to rest with an undefeated reason when it does not outweigh. The framework of this account is given by Joseph Raz's theory of exclusionary reasons, which are reasons for agents to rest with an indefeated reason.

An exclusionary reason is a second-order reason: specifically any reason to act for a reason or to refrain from acting for a reason.[26] Exclusionary reasons do not outweigh or override first-order reasons, but rather exclude them for consideration by the agent (unless certain 'escape clauses' operate). The concept of exclusion from consideration will receive further elucidation, but let us gain some insight by using the example of decisions, whose status as providing reasons is particularly important in a defence of (P2). Raz classes decisions to close—decisions to cease the search for defeating conditions—as a species of exclusionary reason, and argues that the existence of such reasons shows (P1) to be false. A decision is an exclusionary reason for Raz because 'it is logically true that if x has decided to A then x believes that his decision is a reason for him to disregard further reasons for or against doing A'.[27] 'Once a decision is made, it is a reason to avoid further consideration.'[28] Raz elaborates thus: usually a decision 'is accompanied by some unspecified rider provided no new information becomes available, or more strongly, provided no major change occurs etc. Not all decisions are of the same strength, not all of them are subject to the same escape clauses.'[29] According to Raz, the existence of exclusionary reasons entails that there are reasons which exclude the reasons brought under the principle (P1), but which are not weighed with those reasons.

We need to be clearer about the concept of 'exclude'. There are two broad types of exclusionary reason corresponding to two senses of 'exclude'. First, the exclusionary reason enjoins disregarding other reasons in the sense of not considering them. Such a reason is simply a reason for terminating deliberation (or conversation) and remaining with one's pro tem weighing reasons. Call these type A exclusionary reasons.

Second, the exclusionary reason acts as a kind of side constraint

[26] Ibid. 39.   [27] Ibid. 68.
[28] Ibid. 69.   [29] Ibid. 67.

which excludes reasons in a stronger sense. Call these type B exclusionary reasons.[30]

Functional explanations can be given for the rational desirability of the institution of type A and type B exclusionary reasons. Consider first those of type A. The most important case, for my purposes, concerns the exercise of virtues of practice. The demands of collectivist, socially grounded dialogic ethics, which recognize the plight of ethics (the need to integrate a variety of perspectives, roles, and interests), appear to conflict with a desideratum of efficiency in decision-making. On the model of (P1) rationality, we need to search for outweighing reasons, but that search will seem endless. The result is a sense of irrationality unless we revert to the idea that ethics is just a matter of direct route to truth, via the pronouncements of an 'expert' (the virtuous agent as oracle) or homogeneous group of experts. On a model of (P2) rationality, the dilemma is less intractable. Decisions to close can be understood as exclusionary reasons provided they are the result of the exercise of virtues of practice which involve a commitment to learning and improvability. This commitment in turn demands a sensitivity to 'escape clauses' (such as when new information appears).

Consider now type B exclusionary reasons. These allow closure on undefeated reasons for somewhat different reasons. Raz's functional argument for legal norms and other norms of authority operating as exclusionary reasons is well known and discussed.[31] I shall sketch analogous arguments in other cases.

Moral rights can also function as type B exclusionary reasons. If P has a right that I not touch him and exercises that right (i.e. does not waive it), I have no moral authority to touch him even if I judge (in my wisdom) that there is an excellent reason for me to do so (his hang-ups will disappear, and we will all live happily ever after, and these powerful benefits outweigh the force of the right).[32] There is a functional argument for rights as exclusionary reasons which is analogous to that pertaining to

---

[30] The difference between types A and B of exclusionary reason is noted and described as an 'ambiguity' by Michael S. Moore, 'Authority, Law, and Razian Reasons', *Southern California Law Review* 62 (1989), 829–95.

[31] See, for example, Roger A. Shiner, *Norm and Nature: The Movements of Legal Thought* (Oxford: Clarendon Press, 1992).

[32] The idea that an appeal to a moral right is not an appeal to the merits of an action is elaborated in Waldron, 'A Right to Do Wrong'. Waldron goes so far as to say that, consequently, rights do not function as reasons. I do not share that view.

legal norms. The institution or practice of moral rights prohibits people from always acting on *their* judgements of the merits of actions. The underlying value of this practice is the value of non-interference in the autonomy and integrity of individual agents, even if putative interference is not misguided, ill-informed, or badly motivated.

Let us now consider appeals to virtues as type B exclusionary reasons. Can 'I will not report him because he is my friend' appeal to an exclusionary reason? Let us get out of the way a possible confusion between an appeal to exclusionary reasons and a simple denial of consequentialist reasoning. The two issues are distinct. A denial of consequentialism is consistent with a belief in (P1) as the correct model of rationality: one simply denies that acting on the balance of reasons is always performing that action which has the best *results*. We are asking not whether appeals to virtues block consequentialist reasoning: we are asking further whether it can block reasoning in accordance with (P1).

Until an escape clause operates, 'being my friend' is a good undefeated reason for acting as a friend acts. One does not ensure that this reason is outweighed by all other reasons before acting as a friend acts. Being a friend is a reason which, to use Raz's phrase, 'is taken out of the competition' of conflicting reasons for acting. For example, I have reason for reporting on my friend. But he's my *friend*. Though this is not a reason which outweighs my reasons for reporting, it operates as an exclusionary reason, a kind of side constraint. It is taken out of the competition of competing reasons. So I don't report him. My reason for not reporting has the force of 'my not reporting is expressive of a worthy character trait which relates to a worthy relationship'. Such an expressive reason has authority over reasons pertaining to the merits of actions in a particular case, in the sense that the former is not weighed with the latter except where escape clauses operate.

A functional explanation for the operation of virtue-based reasons as exclusionary reasons can be constructed. Just as human beings need social codes to keep them in line, to prevent them from always carrying out and acting on full weighing of reasons, as Conrad Johnson recognizes,[33] so they need character to provide a backdrop of habit and authority. Living well involves having good character, because only if one has good character does it become effortless and natural to act rightly. But this effortlessness and naturalness comes from being happy to con-

---

[33] See his 'The Authority of the Moral Agent'.

form one's behaviour to the patterns laid down by one's character. Now, these habits cannot be rigid or inflexible—there must be creative adjustment to novel situations. This creative adjustment is not tantamount, however, to ignoring the dictates of character whenever a novel situation arises. Just as a judge cannot exercise total discretion in hard cases, pretending that legislation does not exist or has no authority at all, so the agent will feel the pull of her character in her claims that she feels very uncomfortable doing something, even though that reason does not outweigh.

I shall finally consider whether a certain understanding of (P1), namely, Stephen R. Perry's,[34] might remove the apparent need for exclusionary reasons. According to Perry, the operation of exclusionary reasons is that of reweighting reasons. A soldier who believes that ϕ-ing is the thing to do, but then receives an order to not ϕ will then reweight his reasons, assigning a value of zero to ϕ-ing. In more detail, Perry describes reweighting thus:

A subjective second-order reason is a reason to treat a reason as having greater or lesser weight than the agent would otherwise judge it to possess in his or her subjective determination of what the objective balance of reasons requires. (An exclusionary reason is then just the special case of a reason to treat a reason as having zero weight).[35]

This understanding of practical rationality is counterintutive. Consider a soldier who receives an order to kill civilians in reprisal for resistance activities. The soldier believes he should obey the order even though, on his evaluation, the balance of reasons favours not killing. Does he really now assign no disvalue to the pain, the suffering, the loss of lives? To suggest this would be to downplay the extreme compunction the soldier feels in the carrying out of the order. In obeying, the soldier does not reweight reasons: rather, he recognizes his lack of authority to act on his own weightings.

(iii) Too Much Indeterminacy?

A defence of (P2), and of the idea that exclusionary reasons can provide good reason for acting on an undefeated (but not outweighing) reason,

---

[34] 'Second Order Reasons, Uncertainty and Legal Theory', *Southern California Law Review* 62 (1989), 913–94.
[35] Ibid. 932.

goes part of the way towards defending virtue ethics from the charge of rampant indeterminacy. Nonetheless, although indeterminacy as such is no bar to rationality, it may be thought that there is too much slack in a virtue-ethical system of the type described. Since there may be many individuals suitably placed to resolve problems, and since there are many possible conversations and termini of conversations, there could be many—too many—incompatible resolutions to moral problems.

A second problem is this. It may be thought that decisions *as such* do not provide any sort of reason.[36] I agree. What provides an exclusionary *reason* is a decision having normative features, namely a decision made where virtues of practice have been exercised.

I discuss each problem in turn. The extent to which there is a problem of excess indeterminacy depends in part on one's views about the unity of the virtues. How true is it that the virtues point in different directions? On a weak reading of the unity of the virtues thesis, it is the case that 'to have any particular virtue, you must at least be alive to the moral considerations that pertain to the other virtues'.[37] They could still point in different directions. On the strongest reading of the unity thesis, no action can both manifest a virtue and a vice. Such a reading is favoured by John McDowell in the following passage:

So we cannot disentangle genuine possession of kindness from the sensitivity which constitutes fairness. And since there are obviously no limits on the possibilities for compresence, in the same situation, of circumstances of the sorts proper sensitivities to which constitute all the virtues, the argument can be generalized: no one virtue can be fully possessed except by a possessor of all of them, that is, a possessor of virtue in general.[38]

If McDowell is correct, there could be no serious disagreement amongst the virtuous: any disagreement would simply amount to differing choices amongst a range of permissible options. However, McDowell's view has been criticized by A. D. M. Walker, who adopts what he calls the 'Intermediate View'.[39] His position poses a threat to the view that disagreement amongst the virtuous (or those exercising virtues of practice)

[36] See, for example, Tim Dare, 'Raz, Exclusionary Reasons, and Legal Positivism', *Eidos* 8 (1989), 11–33: 'We want an account of why the facts of the case at hand are such that "I've decided" is a good reason' (21).

[37] Gary Watson, 'Virtues in Excess', *Philosophical Studies* 46 (1984), 57–74, at 60.

[38] 'Virtue and Reason', *Monist* 62 (1979), 332–3, cited in Watson, 'Virtues in Excess', 59.

[39] 'Virtue and Character', *Philosophy* 64 (1989), 349–62.

is not serious. For according to Walker, it is not possible to possess all the virtues to a high degree: there will be pervasive serious disagreement amongst people specializing in certain virtues.

On my view, it is possible to possess all the virtues to a high degree. The realization of this possibility will still, however, leave room for disagreement and moral conflict. But, I shall argue, the nature of this disagreement allows for a non-serious indeterminacy rather than a serious pervasive incompatibility of judgement.

Before arguing this, let us outline and criticize Walker's position. Walker's 'intermediate' position contains three theses:

(1) No set of characteristics counts as a virtue if it leads to violation of the minimal requirements of any other virtue.[40]

(2) Provided (1) is satisfied, the stronger the disposition the greater the virtue.[41]

(3) Certain character traits, e.g. kindness and justice, are incompatible with each other in the sense that justice and kindness for example 'are beyond a certain point incompatible as traits because they presuppose personal qualities which do not cohere well in a single personality'.[42]

For example, kindness presupposes warmth, justice cool detachment, and impartiality.

The thesis of incompatibility is true in the case of justice and kindness only if detached impartiality—the mark of a just person—*requires* that a person be 'cold in temperament and indifferent to the suffering of others'.[43] The standard Aristotelian picture of virtue does not, however, presuppose such a requirement. Admittedly, cold indifference may make it easier to be just when to be so appears to be unkind to your friend. But why should the exercise of virtue in hard cases be painless, or even easy, for the virtuous individual? The especially kind person can, when justice requires, appear unkind to his friend. So he will agree with the just individual, though it may cost him pain.

Walker's reply would be that possession of a virtue involves possession of a firm and unshakeable disposition. This feature, combined with the hypothesis about the nature of the personality traits possessed by just and kind individuals, precludes the following hypothesis: the especially just person and the especially kind person will form the same judgements

---

[40] Ibid. 357.   [41] Ibid.
[42] Ibid. 356.   [43] Ibid. 353.

in hard cases. Rather, for Walker, provided the minimal requirements of justice and kindness are met, given thesis (2), the kind and the just person will disagree, for their dispositions are unshakeable if they are genuinely virtuous.

My reply is that the Aristotelian 'firm and unshakeable' thesis has been misinterpreted. Firmness and unshakeability are features of the virtuous only at the general, rather undifferentiated level of prototypical virtue. Take generosity. One must have a firm natural tendency to give of oneself as opposed to being stingy and mean with one's resources. But at the level of the particular, flexibility is necessary. For the exercise of phronesis demands that one judge when it is appropriate to manifest this tendency. The firm, unshakeable tendency to give of one's resources is not the firm, unshakeable tendency to give of one's resources whenever one detects need, or whenever one is asked.

I think therefore that thesis (3) is false. Walker seems to believe it because he believes in (2) plus the unshakeability thesis. So for Walker, the genuinely just individual cannot be also genuinely kind, because to be just you cannot be warm, a disposition required for kindness. If you are warm, you cannot resist the blandishments of the demands of preventing suffering. On my view, however, the virtuous are in a relevant sense flexible. A just person can be warm, but his exercise of phronesis may be painful for him on occasion.

My conclusion is that disagreement amongst the virtuous is not necessarily as serious as is painted by Walker's picture of the virtues. However, because of specialization in the virtues, the virtuous will not necessarily converge on a *unique* resolution to a problem. I shall now investigate whether this possibility poses a serious problem of indeterminacy.

As in wine connoisseurship, there is room for taste in the development of the virtues. A wine connoisseur may enjoy all kinds of chardonnay with most dishes, another may not like chardonnay at all except for a few robust, buttery, New Zealand ones; another only French chardonnay. Similarly, the emphasis of some virtues over others is a matter of taste, not arbitrarily, but as a result of inclinations shaped by personal and social factors such as personality, career choice, friendships made, and so forth. This phenomenon is well noted by Stuart Hampshire in his claim that different lives will have different legitimate foci of concern and such foci will go with different emphases on the various virtues.[44] He argues

---

[44] In *Two Theories of Morality* (Oxford: Oxford University Press, 1977).

that all choiceworthy lives will have a place for all the central virtues, but some will be more or less limited or emphasized. A famous example of Sartre's discussed by Hampshire is the choice between joining the resistance or staying behind to support the dependent family. A less dramatic example is provided by Watson:

> Suppose A asks B and C for an opinion of his book. B is characteristically more frank, more straightforward and open than C; C is more sensitive to other's feelings than B. B expresses her low opinion of the work, without brutality or aggression. Tactfully, C shifts the discussion, without deception. We may suppose that neither response is wrong. Each may be admirable in its own way, expressing a virtue. B's response did not express kindness, but nor was it unkind. C's response did not express honesty, but it was not dishonest either. Each life and character has a different focus and emphasis, but both may be said to have due concern for the relevant considerations. In another context, C would see that evading such a question would be wrong, and would respond frankly despite the other's wounded self-esteem. In other circumstances, B would refrain from speaking her mind to the other to avoid this hurt. It is in the indeterminate cases that B and C reveal their moral individuality.[45]

How serious for our account is disagreement among the virtuous? I shall deal with the problem by way of several replies. First, richer understanding of the particulars of the case will reduce disagreement. The difficulty with philosophers' examples is that there is never enough detail supplied. Even Watson's example falls into this category.

Second, we must be clear about the nature of the differences. Are the virtuous disagreeing about *the* thing to do? It need not be the case that each is saying that the other is wrong. The understanding of a virtue as a protoype shows why this is so: a virtue is not a constellation of rules mandating actions in complex or hard cases. More likely, they permit different actions. May it not merely be the case that they act differently, while each action is permissible? This could be what Watson means by his claim of indeterminacy. 'It is in the indeterminate cases that B and C reveal their moral individuality.'[46]

Finally, and most importantly, we should appreciate that virtuous agents having different roles, perspectives, forms of life, and expertise need to exercise the virtues of practice. The analogy between wine connoisseurs and virtuous agents is inapt. For wine connoisseurs in wine

---

[45] Watson, 'Virtues in Excess', 65.
[46] Ibid.

tastings taste wine operating with their own powers of discrimination and without consulting the views of others. In morally charged practices, virtuous agents are not like wine connoisseurs operating in isolation in wine-tastings, disagreeing in their rankings and descriptions. They have to exercise the virtues of practice in solving problems. Model (P2) requires supplementation by a non-monological theory of virtue in decision-making; a theory of the kind offered in the last chapter. In acting for an undefeated reason, an agent may have been lazy, lacked perseverance, or lacked integrity or courage in the face of opposing views or potentially opposing views.

This point brings us to the resolution of the second problem of the normativity of exclusionary reasons. Consider a situation where the participants in a dialogue working on a problem decide to terminate the conversation. There is a decision in favour of closure. Let us hypothesize that, from the point of view of (P1), there is a 'problem' of indeterminacy. Though several courses of action have reasons in their favour which are not defeated by further reasons, there is a decision to close on one of these possibilities. According to Raz, the 'problem' is solved insofar as the participants believe that there is a reason to disregard further reasons for or against adopting the proposed course of action. The reasons for closure may include the difficulty of reaching agreement on overriding reasons, a belief that a further search for such reasons will yield little that is new or nothing that is decisive, perceived lack of time or energy, a belief that the complexity of the problem is beyond the expertise of all available experts, a feeling that one is impotent when dealing with higher authorities, and so on.

However, such 'reasons' may not be good reasons. The discussion of the previous chapter shows what counts as *good* reasons to close. The reasons to close in the face of putative indeterminacy are *good* if the decision to close is taken by participants who have exercised, to adequate degree, the virtues of practice. This, of course, may not occur. The difficulty of reaching agreement may be due to bad temper with colleagues, closed-mindedness, and a host of other vices. The belief that further search for reasons will be fruitless may be due to lack of imaginative deliberation, laziness, sloppiness, lack of perseverance in the search for relevant facts, or lack of analytical skills or insight.[47] The supposition of lack of time or energy may be due to lack of surgency, lack of resilience

---

[47] These skills are part of *virtue* insofar as practical wisdom is part of virtue.

to stress, or self-indulgence (e.g. giving in to an urgent desire to get to the golf course). The belief that the problem is too complex even for experts may be due to a deep-seated fear of being exposed as inadequate by experts (so appropriate experts are not consulted). A sense of impotence may be due to excessive pessimism, inferiority complex, or paranoia about authority figures. A virtue-ethical employment of the notion of exclusionary reasons will resolve the problem of when it is right or reasonable to rest with undefeated reasons.

A virtue-based constraint integration version of dialogic ethics does result in indeterminacy. But the indeterminacy is not incompatible with the requirement that such an ethics yield good reason for one's choice of actions. Virtue ethics can indeed resolve all three epistemological problems described in Chapter 12, section i.

Conclusion

Consider the basic definition of virtue given in Chapter 1, p. 19. With respect to this basic definition, types of virtue ethics vary on several dimensions, since they vary in their responses to many different questions. Important questions include the following.

1. What are the modes of moral response or acknowledgement comprising the profiles of the virtues?
2. What are the modes of moral response determinative of rightness?
3. What are the bases of moral responsiveness?
4. What is it to act from a state of virtue?
5. What characteristics make traits of character virtues?
6. What are the targets of virtues?
7. How does virtue enter into an account of rightness?
8. What are the limits of morality understood in a virtue-ethical way—that is, what is the shape of the virtues, and how is that determined?
9. What epistemology should a virtue ethics possess?

1. Controversy centres on the issue of the complexity of modes of moral responsiveness comprising the profiles of virtues such as benevolence, justice, friendship, courage, perseverence, and loyalty. On my view, the profiles of all or virtually all virtues contain at least receptivity, appreciation, love (in various forms), respect (in various forms), creativity, honouring, and promotion (of good or value). Receptivity is essential for the 'attention' of which Iris Murdoch speaks, so that the world and its demands can be properly registered. The world can thus be perceived with a 'loving gaze' rather than through the distortions of egocentricity, resentment, and hostility. Appreciation is necessary for wisdom, involving as it does fine discrimination so that the merits and qualities of things can be properly understood. As such, it is essential for the environmen-

tal virtues, for without appreciation, it is difficult to gain respect for, let alone love, the natural order. Appreciation is obviously involved in virtues of connoisseurship, but is a part of the profile of all the virtues. Respect is essential for appropriate distance, and love for appropriate closeness, whether the virtue exercised is benevolence, friendship, or justice. Creativity is necessary not just for the perpetuation of culture and art, but for the exercise of imaginative deliberation in the virtues of practice as they apply in quotidian ethics. Subject to the constraints of other modes of moral acknowledgement, we should both promote good and promote and honour value. The fact that the virtues have a complex profile is compatible with the view that aspects of that profile are more salient than others in various different virtues.

2. On my view, all the modes of moral response enter in context-dependent ways into a virtue-ethical account of rightness. Of course, these modes may come into tension with each other, providing need for constraint integration through the exercise of virtues of practice. Notice that even though a plurality of modes comprises the profiles of the virtues, it is possible that only one mode is criterially determinative of rightness. I argued in Chapter 2 against the consequentialist version of this view.

3. In Chapter 2, I argued against monistic views of the bases of moral acknowledgement, in particular value-centredness. Though value-centredness is most clearly associated with monistic (consequentialist) views about modes of moral acknowledgement, it need not be. However, the admission of bonds and status (respectively) as fundamental bases of moral acknowledgement makes good sense of the moral importance of love and respect as modes of moral acknowledgement. A pluralistic virtue ethics is in a good position to accommodate the insights of many types of moral theory (be they value-centred, good-centred, status-centred, or bond-centred) by recognizing that the virtues have a complex profile. This pluralism allows for tensions within the virtues. Chapters 11 and 12 in particular addressed this issue in its discussion of virtues of practice, including the dialogic virtues, and indeterminacy.

4. In order to act *from a state of* virtue one needs to *express* a variety of fine inner states, such as fine motivation, practical wisdom, and fine emotional states. Controversy exists about what fine inner states are required for different virtues, even within virtue ethics. Within virtue ethics, how-

ever, there is general agreement that practical wisdom is not a narrow intellectualist notion: fine emotions and right reason are mutually informing and dependent.

5. My account (T) (p. 93) of what makes a trait of character a virtue is pluralistic. It contrasts with eudaimonism and Hursthouse's naturalism in two respects. The features which make traits virtues can be expressive as well as promotional (that is they do not need to *serve further* ends), and ends served by virtues need not be confined to agent (or even human) flourishing. Furthermore (contrary to eudaimonism), certain virtues may characteristically be inimical to agent-flourishing.

6. One 'dimension' of virtue is the target(s) at which a virtue aims. Such a target may be internal or external, one or many, and will vary according to context. Hitting the target of a virtue is not the same as acting from a state of virtue. One may act from a state of virtue without hitting the target of a virtue (because one lacks complete knowledge, though one possesses practical wisdom). One may hit the target of a virtue without acting from a state of virtue, because one lacks all the fine inner states constitutive of virtue. The target of a virtue need not be the same as a feature which makes a trait of character a virtue. One may have a consequentialist view about the latter (what makes a trait of character a virtue is its tendency to promote certain ends or values such as human flourishing) without having a consequentialist view of the former.

7. Virtue ethics may adopt a variety of virtue-centred conceptions of rightness. My own target-centred view differs from both 'qualified agent' accounts, and motive-centred accounts. The aspect of excellence in responsiveness to items in the fields of the virtues, constituting rightness of action, is not identical with the possession of right reasons, or excellence in motivation. But as I argued in Chapter 11, this is not to say that the target of many virtues does not include states internal to the agent. The standards of success required for hitting the targets of the virtues constituting rightness are multiple, since success may involve success in many different modes of moral acknowledgement. Nor (as we saw in Chapter 6) is the target of a virtue to be confused with what it is to be well disposed in regard to the field of a virtue. The target of a 'gentle' virtue may be the relief of suffering, for example, but to be well disposed in that respect involves aspects of strength (self-love) in the agent.

8. Though my target-centred account of rightness understands by 'right act' a best possible act, this does not entail that my virtue ethics is excessively demanding, for several reasons. Not only is it the case that self-love is an important component of the profiles of obviously self-regarding virtues like self-protection, it is an aspect of all virtue. As a result, the striving for perfection (optimality) is not necessarily a virtue in contexts where it expresses lack of self-love. Second, in determining a right act, self-regarding as well as other-regarding virtues are factored in. Third, in many contexts, various actions may count as 'best possible', since none may be able to be defeated by reasons. Finally, on my account, 'right' is not equivalent to 'praiseworthy'; nor 'not right' or 'wrong' to 'sanctionable' or 'blameworthy'.

A virtue-ethical approach to the problem of the limits of morality offers distinctive conceptualizations of the problem: the demands of the world on the agent are understood through important aspects of virtue. On my view, practical wisdom in this area is an enriched idea: enriched through depth-motivational aspects of self-love. This idea allows us to avoid the twin extremes of 'yuppie' ethics and excessively transcendent ethical demands. The idea of self-love is central to a virtue-ethical elucidation of several notions necessary for the clarification of the limits of morality—objectivity, demandingness, perfectionism, and constraints.

9. As far as virtue-ethical epistemology is concerned, I rejected the perceptual–intuitionistic model of 'virtuous agent as oracle', replacing it with a virtue-ethical form of dialogic ethics. The constraint integration account of resolving moral problems, embedded in good dialogic practice, showed how a virtue as prototype is 'contoured', so that a broad framework of constraints is made more specific and determinate, rendering it more applicable to the concrete situation in which it is to apply.

In this book I have presented a type of moral theory where the notion of virtue (as opposed to, say, consequences, agent-neutral value, or the categorical imperative) is sufficiently central to have resulted in a distinctive form of virtue ethics. True, as Martha Nussbaum claims,[1] moral theories of various stripes offer a place for virtue, but it does not follow from the fact that 'lots of people' are writing about virtue within the Kantian and

---

1 In 'Virtue Ethics: A Misleading Category?', *Journal of Ethics* 3 (1999), 163–201.

utilitarian traditions that there is no 'unitary' approach warranting the name 'virtue ethics', as Nussbaum claims. Of course, if virtue ethics as a category is analogized to consequentialism rather than utilitarianism (as it should be), there will be seen to be many types of virtue ethics. So in that sense, the approach is no more unitary than consequentialism. But a moral theory where the notions of the demands of the world, rightness, demandingness, objectivity, and problem resolution are understood through the notion of human virtue will be distinctive.

BIBLIOGRAPHY

ADAMS, D. *The Hitch Hiker's Guide to the Galaxy: A Trilogy in Four Parts*. London: Pan, 1979.

ADAMS, R. M. 'Saints', *Journal of Philosophy* 81 (1984), 392–401.

ADLER, A. *The Neurotic Constitution: Outlines of a Comparative Individualistic Psychology and Psychotherapy*, trans. B. Glueck and J. E. Lind. London: Kegan Paul, Trench, Trubner & Co. Ltd., 1918.

—— *Understanding Human Nature*, trans. W. B. Wolfe. London: Allen & Unwin, 1932.

ADLER, P. S. 'The Learning Bureaucracy: New United Motor Manufacturing Inc.', *Research in Organizational Behaviour* 15 (1993), 119–94.

ALDERMAN, H. 'By Virtue of a Virtue', in D. Statman (ed.), *Virtue Ethics* (q.v.), 145–64.

ANDERSON, E. *Value in Ethics and Economics*. Cambridge, Mass.: Harvard University Press, 1993.

ANNAS, J. 'Aristotle and Kant on Morality and Practical Reasoning', in S. Engstrom and J. Whiting (eds.), *Aristotle, Kant and the Stoics: Rethinking Happiness and Duty*. Cambridge: Cambridge University Press, 1996, 237–58.

—— *The Morality of Happiness*. New York: Oxford University Press, 1993.

ARGYRIS, C. *Strategy Change and Defensive Routines*. Marshfield, Mass.: Pitman, 1985.

—— PUTNAM, R., and MCLAIN SMITH, D. Action Science. San Francisco, Calif.: Jossey-Bass, 1985.

ARISTOTLE. *Nicomachean Ethics*, trans. J. A. K. Thomson, revised H. Tredennick. Harmondsworth: Penguin, 1976.

AUDI, R. *Moral Knowledge and Ethical Character*. New York: Oxford University Press, 1997.

AUSTIN, J. L. *How to Do Things with Words*, ed. J. O. Urmson. Oxford: Clarendon Press, 1962.

BADHWAR, N. K. 'Altruism versus Self-Interest: Sometimes a False Dichotomy', *Social Philosophy and Psychology* 10 (1993), 90–117.

—— 'Love', in H. Lafollette (ed.), *The Oxford Handbook of Practical Ethics*. New York: Oxford University Press, 2002, 42–69.

BAILIN, S. *Achieving Extraordinary Ends: An Essay on Creativity*. Dordrecht: Kluwer Academic Publishers, 1988.

BAKHURST, D. 'Ethical Particularism in Context', in B. Hooker and M. Little (eds.), *Moral Particularism* (q.v.), 157–77.

298   BIBLIOGRAPHY

BARON, M. 'Kantian Ethics', in M. Baron, P. Pettit, and M. Slote, *Three Methods of Ethics* (q.v.), 3–91.

—— 'Kantian Ethics and Supererogation', *Journal of Philosophy* 84 (1987), 237–62.

—— *Kantian Ethics Almost Without Apology*. Ithaca, N.Y.: Cornell University Press, 1995.

—— 'Love and Respect in the Doctrine of Virtue', *Southern Journal of Philosophy* 36, suppl. (1997), 29–44.

—— 'On Admirable Immorality', *Ethics* 96 (1986), 557–66.

—— P. Pettit, and M. Slote. *Three Methods of Ethics: A Debate*. Oxford: Blackwell (1997).

BAUMEISTER, R. F. 'Violent Pride', *Scientific American* (April 2001), 82–7.

BAYLEY, J. *Iris: A Memoir of Iris Murdoch*. London: Duckworth, 1998.

BEER, M. 'Performance Appraisal', in J. Lorsch (ed.), *Handbook of Organisational Behaviour*. New York: Prentice-Hall, 1987, 286–300.

BENHABIB, S. 'In the Shadow of Aristotle and Hegel: Communicative Ethics and Recent Controversies in Practical Philosophy', in M. Kelley (ed.), *Hermeneutics and Critical Theory in Ethics and Politics*. Cambridge, Mass.: MIT Press, 1990, 1–32.

BLUM, L. 'Compassion', in A. O. Rorty (ed.), *Explaining Emotions*. Berkeley: University of California Press, 1980, 507–18.

BODEN, M. A. *The Creative Mind: Myths and Mechanisms*. Reading: Cardinal, 1992.

—— (ed.) *Dimensions of Creativity*. Cambridge, Mass.: MIT Press, 1994.

—— 'What is Creativity?', in M. A. Boden (ed.), *Dimensions of Creativity* (q.v.) 75–117.

BRIDGES, E. M. *The Incompetent Teacher*, Stanford Series on Education and Public Policy. Lewes: Falmer Press, 1986.

BROCK, G. 'Rethinking Feminist Ethics: Is Dialogical Ethics a Better Approach?', *Social Theory and Practice* 25 (1999), 531–7.

BURBULES, N. *Dialogue in Teaching: Theory and Practice*. New York: Teachers College Press, 1993.

BUSS, S. 'Appearing Respectful: The Moral Significance of Manners', *Ethics* 109 (1999), 795–826.

CAMPBELL, R., and HUNTER, B. (eds.). *Moral Epistemology Naturalized: Canadian Journal of Philosophy* 26 (suppl. issue) (2000).

CANNING, R. *The Unity of Love for God and Neighbour in St. Augustine*. Hevelee Leuven: Augustinian Historical Institute, 1993.

CARR, B. 'Pity and Compassion as Social Virtues', *Philosophy* 74 (1999), 411–29.

CHAPPELL, T. D. C. *Understanding Human Goods: A Theory of Ethics*. Edinburgh: Edinburgh University Press, 1998.

CHI, M. T., FELTOVICH, P. J., and GLASER, R. 'Categorization and Representation of Physics Problems by Experts and Novices', *Cognitive Science* 5 (1981), 121–52.

CHURCHLAND, P. M. 'The Neural Representation of the Social World', in L. May, M. Friedman, and A. Clark (eds.), *Mind and Morals*. Cambridge, Mass.: MIT Press, 1996, 92–108.

—— 'Rules, Know-How and the Future of Moral Cognition', in R. Campbell and B. Hunter (eds.), *Moral Epistemology Naturalized*. (q.v.), 291–306.

—— 'Toward a Cognitive Neurobiology of the Moral Virtues', *Topoi* 17 (1998), 83–96.

CLARK, A. *Being There: Putting Brain, Body and World Together Again*. Cambridge, Mass.: MIT Press, 1997.

—— 'Word and Action: Reconciling Rules and Know-how in Moral Cognition', in R. Campbell and B. Hunter (eds.), *Moral Epistemology Naturalized* (q.v.), 267–89.

COCKING, D., and OAKLEY, J. 'Indirect Consequentialism, Friendship and the Problem of Alienation', *Ethics* 106 (1995), 86–111.

COOPER, J. M. 'The Unity of Virtue', *Social Philosophy and Policy* 15 (1998), 233–74.

COTTINGHAM, J. 'Partiality and the Virtues', in R. Crisp (ed.), *How Should One Live?* (q.v.), 55–76.

CRISP, R. (ed.) *How Should One Live? Essays on the Virtues*. Oxford: Clarendon Press, 1996.

CUPIT, G. 'Justice, Age, and Veneration', *Ethics* 108 (1998), 702–18.

—— *Justice as Fittingness*. New York: Oxford University Press, 1996.

DANCY, J. 'Defending Particularism', *Metaphilosophy* 30 (1999), 25–32.

—— *Moral Reasons*. Oxford: Blackwell, 1993.

DANIELS, N. 'Wide Reflective Equilibrium and Theory Acceptance in Ethics', *Journal of Philosophy* 76 (1979), 256–82.

DARE, T. 'Raz, Exclusionary Reasons, and Legal Positivism', *Eidos* 8 (1989), 11–33.

DARWALL, S. 'Agent-Centred Restrictions from the Inside Out', *Philosophical Studies* 50 (1986), 291–319.

—— 'Rational Agent, Rational Act', *Philosophical Topics* 14 (1986), 35–57.

DEWEY, J. *Human Nature and Conduct: An Introduction to Social Psychology*. New York: Henry Holt & Co., 1922.

DILLON, R. S. (ed.). *Dignity, Character, and Self-Respect*. London: Routledge, 1995.

DORIS, J. M. 'Persons, Situations, and Virtue Ethics', *Nous* 32 (1998), 504–30.

DRIVER, J. 'Introduction', *Character and Consequentialism: Utilitas* 13 (2001), 136–51.

—— 'Modesty and Ignorance', *Ethics* 109 (1999), 827–34.

—— 'Monkeying with Motives: Agent-Basing Virtue Ethics', *Utilitas* 7 (1995), 281–8.

—— *Uneasy Virtue*. Cambridge: Cambridge University Press, 2001.

—— 'The Virtues and Human Nature', in R. Crisp (ed.), *How Should One Live?* (q.v.), 111–29.

—— 'The Virtues of Ignorance', *Journal of Philosophy* 86 (1989), 373–84.

EVANS, R. I. *Carl Rogers and Humanistic Psychology*. New York: E. P. Dutton, 1975.

EYSENCK, H. J. 'The Measurement of Creativity', in M. A. Boden (ed.), *Dimensions of Creativity* (q.v.), 199–242.

FINNIS, J. *Natural Law and Natural Rights*. Oxford: Oxford University Press, 1980.

FOOT, P. *Natural Goodness*. Oxford: Clarendon Press, 2001.

—— 'Utilitarianism and the Virtues', *Mind* 94 (1985), 196–209.

—— *Virtues and Vices*. Oxford: Blackwell, 1978.

—— 'Virtues and Vices', in *Virtues and Vices* (q.v.), 1–18.

FROMM, E. *The Anatomy of Human Destructiveness*. London: Penguin, 1977.

—— *The Art of Loving*. London: Unwin, 1975.

GARCIA, J. L. A. 'Interpersonal Virtues: Whose Interests do they Serve?', *American Catholic Philosophical Quarterly* 71 (1997), 31–60.

GARDINER, P. *Kierkegaard*. Oxford: Oxford University Press, 1988.

GHISELIN, B. (ed.). *The Creative Process*. New York: Mentor, 1952.

GLICKMAN, J. 'Creativity in the Arts', in L. Aargaard-Morgensen (ed.), *Culture and Art*. Atlantic Highlands, N.J.: Humanities Press, 1976, 131–46.

GOLEMAN, D. *Emotional Intelligence: Why it can Matter more than IQ*. London: Bloomsbury, 1996.

GRACYK, T. A. 'Rethinking Hume's Standard of Taste', *Journal of Aesthetics and Art Criticism* 52 (1994), 169–82.

GRIFFIN, J. *Well-Being*. Oxford: Oxford University Press, 1986.

GUIGNON, C. B. (ed.). *Dostoevsky: The Grand Inquisitor*. Indianapolis: Hackett, 1993.

—— (ed.). *The Good Life*. Indianapolis: Hackett, 1999.

HALES, S. D. 'Was Nietzsche a Consequentialist?', *International Studies in Philosophy* 27 (1995), 25–34.

HAMPSHIRE, S. *Two Theories of Morality*. Oxford: Oxford University Press, 1977.

HAMPTON, J. 'Selflessness and the Loss of Self', *Social Philosophy and Policy* 10 (1993), 135–65.

HARE, R.M. 'Moral Conflict', in Sterling M. McMurrin (ed.), *Tanner Lectures on Human Values*, vol. i (1980), 169–93.

HELLWIG, M. *Jesus, the Compassion of God*. Wilmington, Del.: Michael Glazier Inc., 1983.

HILL, R. K. 'MacIntyre's Nietzsche', *International Studies in Philosophy* 24 (1992), 3–12.

HILL, T. Jr. 'Self-Respect Reconsidered' in R. Dillon (ed.), *Dignity, Character, and Self Respect* (q.v.), 117–24.

—— 'Servility and Self-Respect', in R. Dillon (ed.), *Dignity, Character, and Self-Respect* (q.v.), 76–92.

HOAGLAND, S. L. 'Some Concerns about Nel Noddings' *Caring*'. Review Symposium, *Hypatia* 5 (1990), 108–13.

HOGAN, R., CURPHY, G. J., and HOGAN, J. 'What We Know about Leadership', *American Psychologist* 49 (1994), 493–504.

HOMIAK, M. L. 'Aristotle on the Soul's Conflicts: Toward an Understanding of Virtue Ethics', in A. Reith, B. Herman, and C. M. Korsgaard (eds.), *Reclaiming the History of Ethics: Essays for John Rawls.* Cambridge: Cambridge University Press, 1997, 7–35.

HOOKER, B., and LITTLE, M. (eds.). *Moral Particularism.* Oxford: Clarendon Press, 2000.

HORNEY, K. *Neurosis and Human Growth: The Struggle Toward Self Realization.* New York: Norton, 1970.

HUME, D. *Enquiries Concerning Human Understanding*, ed. L. A. Selby-Bigge, 3rd edn. revised P. H. Nidditch. Oxford: Oxford University Press, 1975.

—— *Treatise of Human Nature*, ed. L. A. Selby-Bigge, 2nd edn. revised P. H. Nidditch. Oxford: Oxford University Press, 1968.

HUNT, L. *Nietzsche and the Origin of Virtue.* London: Routledge, 1991.

HURKA, T. 'How Great a Good is Virtue', *Journal of Philosophy* 95 (1998), 181–203.

—— *Perfectionism.* Oxford: Oxford University Press, 1993.

—— 'Virtue as Loving the Good', *Social Philosophy and Policy* 9 (1992), 149–68.

—— *Virtue, Vice, and Value.* Oxford: Oxford University Press, 2001.

HURSTHOUSE, R. 'Applying Virtue Ethics', in R. Hursthouse, G. Lawrence, and W. Quinn (eds.), *Virtues and Reasons* (q.v.), 57–75.

—— 'Arational Actions', *Journal of Philosophy* 88 (1991), 57–68.

—— 'Aristotle, Nicomachean Ethics', in G. Vesey (ed.), *Philosophers Ancient and Modern*, Royal Institute of Philosophy Lecture Series 20 (supp. to *Philosophy*). Cambridge: Cambridge University Press, 1985, 33–53.

—— 'A False Doctrine of the Mean', *Proceedings of the Aristotelian Society* 81 (1980–1), 57–72.

—— 'Normative Virtue Ethics', in R. Crisp (ed.), *How Should One Live?* (q.v.), 19–36.

—— *On Virtue Ethics.* Oxford: Oxford University Press, 1999.

—— 'Virtue Ethics and the Emotions', in D. Statman (ed.), *Virtue Ethics* (q.v.), 99–117.

—— 'Virtue Theory and Abortion', *Philosophy and Public Affairs* 20 (1991), 223–46.

—— LAWRENCE, G., and QUINN, W. (eds.). *Virtues and Reasons.* Oxford: Clarendon Press, 1995.

JAMISON, K. R. *An Unquiet Mind: Memoir of Moods and Madness.* New York: Vintage, 1996.

JENNINGS, P. *The Jenguin Pennings.* Penguin, 1963.

JOHNSON, C. 'The Authority of the Moral Agent', in S. Scheffler (ed.), *Consequentialism and Its Critics.* Oxford: Oxford University Press, 1988, 261–87.

JOHNSON, R. 'Love in Vain', *Southern Journal of Philosophy* 36, suppl. (1997), 45–50.

KAGAN, S. *The Limits of Morality*. Oxford: Clarendon Press, 1989.

KAMM, F. M. *Morality, Mortality*, vol. ii. New York: Oxford University Press, 1996.

—— 'Non-Consequentialism, the Person as an End-in-Itself, and the Significance of Status', *Philosophy and Public Affairs* 21 (1992), 354–89.

KANT, I. *The Doctrine of Virtue: The Metaphysics of Morals*, trans. and ed. M. Gregor. Cambridge: Cambridge University Press, 1996.

KAUFMANN, W. *Nietzsche: Philosopher, Psychologist, Antichrist*, 4th edn. Princeton, N.J.: Princeton University Press, 1974.

KEKES, J. *The Morality of Pluralism*. Princeton, N.J.: Princeton University Press, 1993.

KELLENBERGER, J. *Relationship Ethics*. University Park, Pa.: Penn State University Press, 1995.

KIERKEGAARD, S. *Concluding Unscientific Postscript*, trans. D. F. Swenson and W. Lowrie. Princeton, N.J.: Princeton University Press, 1941.

—— *Either/Or*, trans. D. F. and L. M. Swenson and W. Lowrie, 2 vols. Princeton, N.J.: Princeton University Press, 1959.

—— *Sickness unto Death*. Princeton, N.J.: Princeton University Press, 1941.

KITCHER, P. *Freud's Dream: A Complete Interdisciplinary Science of Mind*. Cambridge, Mass.: The MIT Press, 1995.

KOEHN, D. *Rethinking Feminist Ethics: Care, Trust, and Empathy*. London: Routledge., 1998.

KOHUT, H. *The Restoration of the Self*. New York: International University Press, 1977.

KORSGAARD, C. 'Rawls and Kant: On the Primacy of the Practical', *Proceedings of the Eighth International Kant Congress*, Memphis, Tenn., 1995. Milwaukee, Wis.: Marquette University Press 1995, i. 1165–73.

LASCH, C. *The Culture of Narcissism: American Life in an Age of Diminishing Expectations*. New York: Norton, 1978.

LAXNESS, H. *Independent People*. New York: Vintage, 1946.

LEITER, B. 'Nietzsche and the Morality Critics', *Ethics* 107 (1997), 250–85.

LEWIS, C. S. *The Four Loves*. London: Fount, 1977.

—— *Mere Christianity*. London: Fontana, 1955.

LITTLE, M. O. 'Moral Generalities Revisited', in B. Hooker and M. Little (eds.), *Moral Particularism* (q.v.), 276–304.

LORD, R. G., and Maher, K. J. 'Cognitive Theory in Industrial and Organizational Psychology', in M. D. Dinnette and L. M. Hough (eds.), *Handbook of Industrial and Organizational Psychology*, 2nd edn. Palo Alto, Calif.: Consulting Psychology Press, 1991, 1–62.

LOUDEN, R. B. 'On Some Vices of Virtue Ethics', *American Philosophical Quarterly* 21 (1984), 227–36.

McDOWELL, J. 'The Role of Eudaimonia in Aristotle's Ethics', in A. O. Rorty (ed.), *Essays on Aristotle's Ethics*. Berkeley: University of California Press, 1980, 359–76.

—— 'Virtue and Reason', *Monist* 62 (1979), 331–50.

McGINN, C. Review of T. Nagel, *The View from Nowhere*, *Mind* 96 (1987), 263–72.

MacINTYRE, A. *After Virtue: A Study in Moral Theory*. London: Duckworth, 1981.

McNAUGHTON, D., and RAWLING, P. 'Agent-Relativity and the Doing–Happening Distinction', *Philosophical Studies* 63 (1991), 167–85.

—— —— 'Honoring and Promoting Values', *Ethics* 102 (1992), 835–43.

—— —— 'Value and Agent-Relative Reasons', *Utilitas* 7 (1995), 31–47.

MANDELA, N. *Long Walk to Freedom: The Autobiography of Nelson Mandela*. London: Little, Brown, 1994.

MARTIN, M. W. *Love's Virtues*. Lawrence, Kan.: University Press of Kansas, 1996.

MARTINDALE, C. 'How Can We Measure a Society's Creativity?', in M. A. Boden (ed.), *Dimensions of Creativity* (q.v.), 159–97.

MASLOW, A. H. 'The Expressive Component of Behaviour', *Psychological Review* 56 (1949), 261–72.

—— *The Farther Reaches of Human Nature*. Harmondsworth: Penguin, 1971.

—— *Toward a Psychology of Being*, 2nd edn. New York: Van Nostrand Reinhold Co., 1968.

MASSON, J. *Against Therapy*. London: Fontana, 1990.

MELLEMA, G. 'Offence and Virtue Ethics', *Canadian Journal of Philosophy* 21 (1991), 323–9.

MERRITT, M. 'Virtue Ethics and Situationist Personality Psychology', *Ethical Theory and Moral Practice* 3 (2000), 365–83.

MIDGLEY, M. *Animals and Why They Matter*. Harmondsworth: Penguin, 1983.

MILGRAM, S. 'Behavioural Study of Obedience', *Journal of Abnormal and Social Psychology* 67 (1963), 371–8.

MOLLER-OKIN, S. 'Feminism, Moral Development, and the Virtues', in R. Crisp (ed.), *How Should One Live?* (q.v.), 211–29.

—— *Justice, Gender and the Family*. New York: Basic Books, 1989.

MONK, R. *Ludwig Wittgenstein: The Duty of Genius*. London: Cape, 1990.

MOORE, M. S. 'Authority, Law, and Razian Reasons', *Southern California Law Review* 62 (1989), 829–95.

MULGAN, T. 'A Non-Proportional Hybrid Moral Theory', *Utilitas* 9 (1997), 291–306.

MUMFORD, M. D., and GUSTAFSON, S. B. 'Creativity Syndrome: Integration, Application and Innovation', *Psychological Bulletin* 103 (1988), 27–43.

MURDOCH, I. *A Fairly Honourable Defeat*. London: Chatto & Windus, 1970.

—— 'The Idea of Perfection', in *The Sovereignty of the Good*. London, N.Y.: Routledge, 1970, 1–45.

—— 'The Sovereignty of the Good over Other Concepts', in *The Sovereignty of the Good*. London: Routledge, 1970, 77–104.

NAGEL, T. *The View from Nowhere*. New York: Oxford University Press, 1986.

NICKLES, T. 'What is a Problem that We Might Solve It?', *Synthese* 47 (1981), 85–118.

NIETZSCHE, F. *Beyond Good and Evil*, trans. R. J. Hollingdale. London: Penguin, 1973.

—— *Daybreak*, trans. R. J. Hollingdale. Cambridge: Cambridge University Press, 1982.

—— *The Gay Science*, trans. W. Kaufmann. New York: Random House, 1974.

—— *On the Genealogy of Morals*, trans. D. Smith. Oxford: Oxford University Press, 1996.

—— *Thus Spoke Zarathustra*, in *The Portable Nietzsche*, ed. and trans. W. Kaufmann. New York: Penguin, 1976.

—— *Twilight of the Idols*, in *The Portable Nietzsche*, ed. and trans. W. Kaufmann. New York: Penguin, 1976.

NODDINGS, N. *Caring: A Feminine Approach to Ethics and Moral Education*. Berkeley: University of California Press, 1984.

—— 'Ethics from the Standpoint of Women', in M. Pearsall (ed.), *Women and Values: Readings in Recent Feminist Philosophy*. Belmont, Calif.: Wadsworth, 1993, 379–90.

NOVITZ, D. 'Creativity and Constraint', *Australasian Journal of Philosophy* 77 (1999), 67–82.

NUSSBAUM, M. 'Compassion: The Basic Social Emotion', *Social Philosophy and Policy* 13 (1996), 27–58.

—— *The Fragility of Goodness: Luck and Ethics in Greek Tragedy and Philosophy*. Cambridge: Cambridge University Press, 1986.

—— 'Non-Relative Virtues: An Aristotelian Approach', in P. A. French, T. E. Uekling, Jr., and H. K. Wettstein (eds.), *Midwest Studies in Philosophy* 12 (1988), 32–53.

—— 'Virtue Ethics: A Misleading Category?', *Journal of Ethics* 3 (1999), 163–201.

NYGREN, A. 'Agape and Eros', in A. Sobel (ed.), *Eros, Agape and Philia: Readings in the Philosophy of Love*. New York: Paragon House, 1989, 85–95.

OAKLEY, J. 'Varieties of Virtue Ethics', *Ratio* 9 (1996), 128–52.

O'NEILL, O. *Towards Justice and Virtue*. Cambridge: Cambridge University Press, 1996.

OTSUKA, M. 'Kamm on the Morality of Killing', *Ethics* 108 (1997), 197–207.

PECK, M. S. *The Road Less Travelled: A New Psychology of Love, Traditional Values and Spiritual Growth*. New York: Simon & Schuster, 1978.

PERRY, S. R. 'Second Order Reasons, Uncertainty and Legal Theory', *Southern California Law Review* 62 (1989), 913–94.

PETTIT, P. 'Consequentialism', in P. Singer (ed.), *A Companion to Ethics*. Oxford: Basil Blackwell, 1991, 230–40.

—— 'The Consequentialist Perspective', in M. Baron, P. Pettit, and M. Slote, *Three Methods of Ethics* (q.v.), 92–174.

—— 'Habermas on Truth and Justice', in G. H. R. Parkinson (ed.), *Marx and Marxism*. Royal Institute of Philosophy Lecture Series, 14 (suppl. to *Philosophy*). Cambridge: Cambridge University Press, 1979, 207–28.

PREJEAN, Sister H. *Dead Man Walking*. New York: Vintage, 1993.

RAILTON, P. 'Alienation, Consequentialism and Morality', *Philosophy and Public Affairs* 13 (1984), 134–71.

RAND, A. *Fountainhead*. New York: Signet, 1952.

RAWLS, J. *A Theory of Justice*. Cambridge, Mass.: Harvard University Press, 1971.

RAZ, J. *Practical Reason and Norms*. London: Hutchinson, 1975.

READER, S. 'Principle Ethics, Particularism, and Another Possibility', *Philosophy* 72 (1997), 269–96.

REGINSTER, B. '*Ressentiment*, Evaluation, and Integrity', *International Studies in Philosophy* 27 (1995), 117–24.

REICH, W. *Character Analysis*, 3rd edn., trans. V. R. Carfango. New York: Noonday Press, 1972.

RICHARDSON, F. C., FOWERS, B. J., and GUIGNON, C. B. *Re-envisioning Psychology: Moral Dimensions of Theory and Practice*. San Francisco, Calif.: Jossey-Bass, 1999.

RICHARDSON, H. S. 'Specifying Norms as a Way to Resolve Concrete Ethical Problems', *Philosophy and Public Affairs* (1990), 279–310.

RICHARDSON, J. *Nietzsche's System*. New York: Oxford University Press, 1996.

ROBINSON, V. M. J. 'Dialogue Needs a Point and Purpose', *Educational Theory* 45 (1995), 235–49.

—— *Problem-Based Methodology: Research for the Improvement of Practice*. Oxford: Pergamon Press, 1993.

ROSS, L., and NISBETT, R. E. *The Person and the Situation: Perspectives of Social Psychology*. Philadelphia, Pa.: Temple University Press, 1991.

ROSS, W. D. *The Right and the Good*. Oxford: Oxford University Press, 1930.

SCHACHT, R. *Making Sense of Nietzsche*. Urbana: University of Illinois Press, 1995.

SCHEFFLER, S. 'Prerogatives without Restrictions', *Philosophical Perspectives* 6 (1992), 377–97.

—— 'Restrictions, Rationality, and the Virtues', in S. Scheffler (ed.), *Consequentalism and Its Critics*. Oxford: Oxford University Press, 1988, 241–60.

SCHNEEWIND, J. 'The Misfortunes of Virtue', in R. Crisp and M. Slote (eds.), *Virtue Ethics*. Oxford: Oxford University Press, 1997, 178–200.

SCHOPENHAUER, A. *The World as Will and Representation*, trans. E. F. J. Payne, vol. i. New York: Dover, 1969.

—— *On the Basis of Morality*, trans. E. F. J. Payne. Providence, R.I.: Berghahn Books, 1995.

SCHUELER, G. F. 'Why IS Modesty a Virtue?', *Ethics* 109 (1999), 835–41.

—— 'Why Modesty is a Virtue', *Ethics* 107 (1997), 467–85.

SHERMAN, N. *The Fabric of Character: Aristotle's Theory of Virtue*. Oxford: Oxford University Press, 1989.

—— *Making a Necessity of Virtue: Aristotle and Kant on Virtue*. Cambridge: Cambridge University Press, 1997.

SHINER, R. A. *Norm and Nature: The Movements of Legal Thought*. Oxford: Clarendon Press, 1992.

SIDGWICK, H. *The Methods of Ethics*, 7th edn. London: Macmillan, 1907, reissued 1962.

SIMON, H. 'Decision-Making: Rational, Non-Rational, and Unirational', *Educational Administration Quarterly* 29 (1993), 392–411.

—— 'The Structure of Ill-Structured Problems', *Artificial Intelligence* 4 (1973), 181–201.

SIMON, Y. R. *The Definition of Moral Virtue*, ed. V. Kuic. New York: Fordham University Press, 1986.

SIMPSON, P. 'Contemporary Virtue Ethics and Aristotle', in D. Statman (ed.), *Virtue Ethics* (q.v.), 245–59.

SINGER, I. *The Modern World*, vol. iii of *The Nature of Love*. Chicago: University of Chicago Press, 1987.

SINGER, P. *Practical Ethics*, 2nd edn. Cambridge: Cambridge University Press, 1993.

SINNOTT-ARMSTRONG, W. 'Some Varieties of Particularism', *Metaphilosophy* 30 (1999), 1–12.

SLOTE, M. 'Agent-Based Virtue Ethics', in P. A. French, T. E. Uehling, Jr., and H. K. Wettstein (eds.), *Moral Concepts: Midwest Studies in Philosophy* 20 (1996), 83–101.

—— *From Morality to Virtue*. Oxford: Oxford University Press, 1992.

—— *Goods and Virtues*. Oxford: Clarendon Press, 1983.

—— 'The Justice of Caring', *Philosophy and Social Policy* 15 (1998), 171–94.

—— *Morals from Motives*. Oxford: Oxford University Press, 2001.

—— 'Satisficing Consequentialism', *Proceedings of the Aristotelian Society*, supp. vol. 58 (1984), 139–63.

—— 'Virtue Ethics', in M. Baron, P. Pettit, and M. Slote, *Three Methods of Ethics: A Debate* (q.v.), 176–233.

—— 'Virtue Ethics and Democratic Values', *Journal of Social Philosophy* 24 (1993), 5–37.

—— 'The Virtue in Self Interest', *Social Philosophy and Policy* 14 (1997), 264–85.

SMART, J. J. C., and Williams, B. *Utilitananism For and Against*. New York: Cambridge University Press, 1973.

SOBEL, A. (ed.). *Eros, Agape and Philia: Readings in the Philosophy of Love*. New York: Paragon House, 1989.

SOLL, I. 'Nietzsche on Cruelty, Asceticism, and the Failure of Hedonism', in R. Schacht (ed.), *Nietzsche, Genealogy, Morality: Essays on Nietzsche's Genealogy of Morals*. Berkeley: University of California Press, 1994, 168–92.

SOLOMON, D. 'Internal Objections to Virtue Ethics', in D. Statman (ed.), *Virtue Ethics* (q.v.), 165–79.

SOLOMON, R. C. *About Love: Reinventing Romance for our Times*. New York: Simon & Schuster, 1988.

—— 'Nietzsche's Virtues: A Personal Inquiry', in R. Schacht (ed.), *Nietzsche's Postmoralism: Essays on Nietzsche's Prelude to Philosophy's Future*. Cambridge: Cambridge University Press, 2001, 123–48.

—— 'The Virtues of a Passionate Life: Erotic Love and "The Will to Power"', *Social Philosophy and Policy* 15 (1998), 91–118.

SORRELL, T. *Moral Theory and Capital Punishment.* Oxford: Basil Blackwell, 1987.

STATMAN, D. (ed.). *Virtue Ethics: A Critical Reader.* Edinburgh: Edinburgh University Press, 1997.

STEEL, D. *His Bright Light: The Story of My Son Nick Traina.* London: Corgi, 1999.

STERNBERG, R. J. 'Three-Facet Model of Creativity', in R.J. Sternberg (ed.), *The Nature of Creativity: Contemporary Psychological Perspectives.* Cambridge: Cambridge University Press, 1988, 125–47.

STOCKER, M. 'Agent and Other: Against Ethical Universalism', *Australasian Journal of Philosophy* 54 (1976), 206–20.

—— 'The Schizophrenia of Modern Ethical Theories', *Journal of Philosophy* 14 (1976), 453–66.

—— 'Values and Purposes: The Limits of Teleology and the Ends of Friendship', *Journal of Philosophy* 78 (1981), 747–65.

—— and HEGEMAN, E. *Valuing Emotions.* Cambridge: Cambridge University Press, 1996.

STOHR, K. 'Harmony, Continence, and Virtuous Agency'. Unpublished paper read to the American Philosophical Association, Pacific Division, Albuquerque, N. Mex., April 2000.

STYRON, W. *Sophie's Choice.* New York: Random House, 1979.

SVERDLIK, S. 'Motive and Rightness', *Ethics* 106 (1996), 327–49.

SWANTON, C. *Freedom: A Coherence Theory.* Indianapolis: Hackett, 1992.

—— 'On the Essential Connectedness of Political Concepts', *Ethics* 95 (1985), 811–27.

—— 'Outline of a Nietzschean Virtue Ethics', *International Studies in Philosophy* 30 (1998), 20–8.

—— 'Profiles of the Virtues', *Pacific Philosophical Quarterly* 76 (1995), 47–72.

—— 'Satisficing and Perfectionism in Virtue Ethics', in Michael Byron (ed.), *Satisficing and Maximizing: Moral Theoretic Perspectives on Practical Reasoning.* Cambridge: Cambridge University Press, forthcoming.

—— 'The Supposed Tension Between "Strength" and "Gentleness" Conceptions of the Virtues', *Australasian Journal of Philosophy* 75 (1997), 497–510.

—— 'A Virtue Ethical Account of Right Action', *Ethics* 112 (2001), 32–52.

—— 'Virtue Ethics and Satisficing Rationality', in D. Statman (ed.), *Virtue Ethics* (q.v.), 82–98.

—— 'Virtue Ethics, Value-Centredness, and Consequentialism', *Utilitas* 13 (2001), 212–35.

SWIDLER, A. *Organization without Authority.* Cambridge, Mass.: Harvard University Press, 1979.

TERESA OF AVILA, ST. *The Life of Saint Teresa of Avila by Herself,* trans. J. M. Cohen. London: Penguin, 1957.

THOMSON, J. *Discourse and Knowledge: A Defence of Collectivist Ethics*. London: Routledge, 1998.

THOMSON, M. 'The Representation of Life', in R. Hursthouse, G. Lawrence, and W. Quinn (eds.), *Virtues and Reasons* (q.v.), 247–96.

TONG, R. *Feminine and Feminist Ethics*. Belmont, Calif.: Wadsworth, 1993.

TORMEY, A. *The Concept of Expression*. Princeton, N.J.: Princeton University Press, 1971.

TUDOR, S. *Compassion and Remorse: Acknowledging the Suffering Other*. Leuven: Peeters, 2001.

VELLEMAN, J. D. 'Love as a Moral Emotion', *Ethics* 109 (1999), 338–74.

WALDRON, J. 'A Right to do Wrong', *Ethics* 92 (1981), 21–39.

WALKER, A. D. M. 'Virtue and Character', *Philosophy* 64 (1989), 349–62.

WALLACE, R. J. 'Virtue, Reason, and Principle', *Canadian Journal of Philosophy* 21 (1991), 469–95.

WATSON, G. 'On the Primacy of Character', in D. Flanagan and A. O. Rorty (eds.), *Identity, Character, and Morality*. Cambridge, Mass.: MIT Press, 1990, 449–83.

—— 'Virtues in Excess' *Philosophical Studies* 46 (1984), 57–74.

WELSHON, R. C. 'Nietzsche's Peculiar Virtues and the Health of the Soul', *International Studies in Philosophy* 24 (1992), 73–89.

WILLIAMS, B. *Ethics and the Limits of Philosophy*. London: Fontana, 1985.

—— 'The Point of View of the Universe: Sidgwick and the Ambitions of Ethics', in *Making Sense of Humanity and Other Philosophical Papers 1982–1993*. Cambridge: Cambridge University Press, 1995, 153–71.

WOLF, S. 'Meaning and Morality', *Proceedings of the Aristotelian Society* 97 (1997), 299–315.

—— 'Moral Judges and Human Ideals: A Discussion of *Human Morality*', *Philosophy and Phenomenological Research* 55 (1995), 957–62.

—— 'Moral Saints', *Journal of Philosophy* 79 (1982), 419–39.

—— 'Two Levels of Pluralism', *Ethics* 102 (1992), 785–98.

WONG, D. *Moral Relativity*. Berkeley: University of California Press, 1984.

YANCEY, P. *The Jesus I Never Knew*. Grand Rapids, Mich.: Zondervan, 1995.

YOUNG, J. *Heidegger's Later Philosophy*. Cambridge: Cambridge University Press, 2000.

YOUNG, R. *A Critical Theory of Education: Habermas and Our Children's Future*. New York: Harvester Wheatsheaf, 1989.

ZAGZEBSKI, L. T. *Virtues of the Mind: An Inquiry into the Nature of Virtue and the Ethical Foundations of Knowledge*. Cambridge: Cambridge University Press, 1996.

INDEX